Lake Peipus (1242)

Borodino (1812)

Grunwald/Tannenberg (1410)

Kursk (1943)

Stalingrad (1942/1943)

Tsaritsyn (1919/1920)

57)

866)

z (1805)

rg (1683)

Poltava (1709)

Kalka (1223)

ohács (1526)

BLACK SEA

CASPIAN SEA

Abrittus (251)

Adrianople (378)

Byzantium (626, 718, 1204, 1453)

Pydna
(168 B.C.)

Angora (1402)

Pharsalus
(48 B.C.)

Gaugamela (331 B.C.)

Leuctra (371 B.C.)

Marathon (490 B.C.)

Lechaion (390 B.C.)

Salamis (480 B.C.)

C SEA

A N E A N

Markov/Helmert
Battles of World History

Edited by Walter Markov

Presentation of Illustrations
Henry Schumann

MARKOV/HELMERT

BATTLES OF WORLD HISTORY

HIPPOCRENE
BOOKS, INC.

Contents

Translated from the German by C.S.V. Salt

Copyright © 1979 by Edition Leipzig
Produced by Druckhaus Weimar
Designed by Volker Küster, Leipzig
Designs of the sketches by Heinz Helmert,
Arthur Oeser, Helmut Schnitter
Battle sketches by Rolf Herschel
Maps by Matthias Weis

All rights reserved
Published in the United States 1979 by

Hippocrene Books
171 Madison Avenue
New York, N.Y. 10016

Library of Congress Catalog Card Number 78-78242
ISBN 0 88254 481 0

Printed in the German Democratic Republic

II

III

The presentation of a series of selected battles in word and picture cannot claim to be an exhaustive history of warfare or even a symbolic thread through the labyrinth of the muse Clio. The aim of the authors has been merely to place the mosaic from individual military actions in a wider social context so that the appreciation of their real importance is facilitated. The space available means that certain restrictions have had to be accepted and many justifiable wishes disregarded.

There is no doubt at all that the chronicle of world events lists more battles than can be dealt with in one book. The big problem for the authors was consequently that of choice. This has been done not according to a rigid approach but from the viewpoint of the variety of the significant features. It is not always the case that the "greatest" battle is characteristic of the epoch in which it takes place. Sometimes it is a contest between armies of equivalent strength while on other occasions one side is vastly superior to the other. At times, the importance of the political consequences overshadows that of the military decision or the converse may be the case. Here, attention is centred on the emergence of a new kind of weapon while there it is the magnetism of ideas which heralds a change in the state of the world.

Account has likewise been taken of warlike events which, although they cannot be classed as battles in the strict sense, outstrip in their strategic relevance many a battle of the classic type. The latter is usually defined as the clash of two hostile concentrations of troops when these represent the principal forces of either side or at least when they move into action independently in a separate theatre of war. The term has naturally been subject to modification in the course of history and it is obviously always difficult, by definition, to relate the military operations of the 20th century in their organization, duration, sequence and scale with the battles of Antiquity and the Middle Ages.

Not every eventful military confrontation has found an appropriate echo in the reports and literature on the subject nor can a review covering three millennia ignore the variations in the accuracy of its sources which, in certain cases, have influenced the choice of the battles examined. Information of a more or less reliable character is an exception up to the time of the Thirty Years' War and very many of the more ancient battles are only known from the biased account of the victor. There are even gaps in the records of many of the later battles, too, necessitating reconstructions of a more or less imaginative character. It is then inevitable that the most divergent views of known and less well-known authors should be reflected in such reconstructions. The arguments between the various authorities fill not just volumes but complete libraries. The present work cannot attempt to examine all these and decide between them. Sparing use is therefore made of conjecture in the sketches of battles and the descriptions of them have been presented in good faith and in keeping with the knowledge available.

Frederick Engels, who was nicknamed "General", once said that the entire organization and tactics of armies and thus victory or defeat was dependent on the material and thus the economic conditions: on the men and weapons available, i.e., on the quality and quantity of the population and on their equipment. It is also the opinion of the authors that the best way to convey an understanding of the course of the military events is to start with the initial stages and list or at least indicate the totality of the circumstances which finally decided the outcome. Sometimes the emphasis is on the constellation of the social forces and their political reflections, at other times on the development of weapons and the art of leadership, on strategy and tactics. Coincidences, personalia and anectodes are not excluded but are not allowed to obscure the more profound reasons for success or failure.

No attempt has been made to ascertain the "score" of the states concerned nor has victory been measured against defeat. Above all, it is the development of the art of warfare in the course of centuries which is shown with the aid

8 of outstanding examples. The fact that this is concentrated at turning points in history, such as Classical Antiquity, the time of appearance of firearms, the Napoleonic Wars, the transition to industrialized methods of production and the First and Second World Wars underlines this aim.

Pictures play a dominating part in this book—as source material, as contemporary evidence, as reconstructions or as works of art. Very few military events have been painted by eye-witnesses in accordance with what actually happened and, accordingly, accurate reproductions are rarely available. This does not necessarily mean that the perspicuity of the subject has suffered from this. Chisels, brushes, styli, pencils or cameras have unceasingly recorded all the phenomena of human society, the contradictions of which have necessarily manifested themselves at points of conflict in the form of armed confrontations, both at the present time and in the past. Their works are not a substitute but testimony to the continuity of historical driving forces in the future.

We would like to express our thanks to the following for their friendly support and collaboration in the part of the book dealing with military history:

Gerhard Förster, Peter Haupt, Manfred Kossok, Hermann Rahne, Helmut Schnitter, Sei'ishirô Seno and Yukio Tominaga (†).

BATTLES
OF
ANTIQUITY

ERACLITUS of Ephesus is said to have remarked: *polemos pater panton*. Opinions differ as to the exact interpretation but it may be said to mean that either the dispute or war is the father of everything. We are inclined—with good reason, as it seems to us—to favour the first meaning but consider that the more comprehensive term "dispute" also includes the battle at the culmination of a quarrel.

To be sure, primitive society also experienced violent conflict between hords and clans in the course of their search for food and without doubt these continued between settled and nomadic tribes. However, their feuds can scarcely be regarded as wars nor their raids as battles. The number of people involved was low. Warriors, to be distinguished by military training from the "civil population", did not yet exist. The men, utilizing their hunting experience and the hand-weapons to which they were accustomed, staked their claims to hunting and fishing grounds, watering and grazing rights and later to settlement areas as well. The stealing of livestock, the abduction of womenfolk and vendettas were often the cause of protracted hostilities which subsequently formed the subject of sagas and legends.

In the course of time the art of warfare slowly developed, furthered by the formation of larger units made up of several tribes. Men endeavoured to fight battles according to strict rules, based on the spontaneous insight that war and warfare had their own inherent logic. A military sector was only able to develop after the emergence of well-established social hierarchies within certain civilizations and following the social division of labour on an increasing scale, which, in turn, was due to advances in production and techniques. Ruling groups, whose class-character grew in the course of time, created the state on the territory they controlled as an instrument of power to assert their interests within and without. This necessarily assumed a certain organization of the means of defence which, as a rule, could just as well be employed for purposes of attack and expansion.

The first enduring states—still modest in size—emerged in the Orient. No reliable accounts have survived of the struggles they waged with each other or with the "Barbarians" they tried to subjugate or who attacked them. The magnitudes involved indicate that the theatre of war could not have been so very extensive. By way of substitution, the gods themselves step into the breach as individual combatants in the most ancient literature on the subject, as already in the epic poem of *Gilgamesh* of the Babylonians. We can still find them doing so in Homer's *Iliad* and in the Indian epic poem *Mahabharata*.

At the beginning of the 3rd millennium B.C. two strong concentrations of power of considerable stability appeared in areas where civilization had developed on the basis of irrigation: in the fertile alluvial land of the Nile valley through the union of Upper and Lower Egypt under the legendary King Mena; somewhat later in the Land of the Two Rivers—the Euphrates and the Tigris—through the subjugation of Sumerian city-states under the Semitic Accad. The deeds of the Sumerians are immortalized by the cuneiform characters on the *vulture stele*, the first "war report" still extant. Although disintegration and rebirth under new leadership occurred several times in both areas, they may be termed the two great powers of the Ancient Orient. With Fortune favouring one side and then the other, they fought for supremacy in an intermediate zone stretching from Sinai to the Euphrates—the ancient area of civilization of Syria together with Palestine and the rich maritime trading cities of the Phoenicians.

About the middle of the 2nd millennium B.C., the voice of a third contestant began to be heard, that of the Hittites, advancing southwards from Asia Minor. At this particular time, the Land of the Two Rivers was passing through a period of political powerlessness. Egypt, on the other hand, had shaken off the temporary domination of Asiatic nomadic tribes known as the Hyksos. From that time, the use of the horse as a draught animal pioneered by these tribes led to an increased mobility in warfare. In the 15th and 16th centuries B.C., it was the turn of the Egyptian pharaohs to pursue an active expansion policy which took Thutmose III again as far as the Euphrates. This inevitably led to a serious confrontation with the Hittites which continued for many generations.

The mighty clash at *Kadesh* (after 1300 B.C.) came at the end of this trial of strength and showed the two rivals, who were both beginning to decline in power, the desirability of a lasting peace in the form of a compromise. This is justly famed as the first great battle between the armies of two great states struggling for supremacy. On the Egyptian side, it is evidence of a noteworthy advance in the art of warfare although it demonstrated the military shortcomings of the time, too.

Whilst in the years that followed the realm of the Hittites collapsed in the face of the attacks launched by the tribes from the North and West, and Egypt, wracked by internal struggles, rapidly lost ground in the Near East, the kingdom of the Assyrians on the Tigris spread out. In the 8th century B.C., through expeditions of conquest based on a realistic approach to warfare and the use of a more advanced form of chariot, it became the first oriental "empire" in the sense of the term at that time. It covered not only the whole of the Land of the Two Rivers but also the regions around it, extending to the Iranian Plateau, Armenia, Asia Minor and Arabia. After the subjugation of Syria, the Assyrians were even able to occupy Lower Egypt for a time. Their campaigns were noteworthy for the capture of fortified cities, a formidable task in those days, rather than for pitched battles in the field.

As regards the unsuccessful siege of Jerusalem by King Sennacherib in about 700 B.C., three independent sources of information have survived—a rare stroke of luck. We have the pious version of the prophet Isaiah for whom the wondrous success of the weak defenders came in handy for enforcing a stricter monotheism among the people of Judah; the report of Herodotus, the Greek "father of history", which probably originated from Egyptian informants; and finally a boastful Assyrian account of what was actually a failure on clay tablets from the excavated "library" of King Ashurbanipal. From the fairytale-like narratives of rats and mice said to have intervened in the events, it might be concluded from the essential agreement of the facts that it was a plague which forced the withdrawal of the evidently unclean besiegers. However, it was a military happening of third-rank importance and the short respite which Egypt gained from it proved to be of no long duration.

Despite all its military glory, the inadequately organized conqueror-state of the Assyrians was unable to keep the peoples it had defeated in subjection for an indefinite period of time. It collapsed in the face of a coalition of Egyptians, Lydians, Chaldeans and Medes who destroyed Nineveh in about 612 B.C. The hegemony of a single state gave way temporarily to a balance of power shared by four independent kingdoms, although admittedly this did not last for very long.

At about the middle of the 6th century B.C., the Persians rose up against the supremacy of the Medes, who were a kindred people, and made themselves the overlords of their great realm. Not satisfied with this, King Cyrus also subjugated Lydia and the Second Babylonian Empire of the Chaldeans. He extended the eastern frontier of his state as far as India but was killed in 529 B.C. when fighting against the mounted Scythian warriors of the Massagetae in the northern steppes. It fell to his son Cambyses to complete the "second empire" after his crushing victory at Pelusium in 525 B.C. with the incorporation of Egypt, whose princess he had married by way of precaution.

After the decline of the last Egyptian ruling family, it seemed that the state of the Persians was no longer faced with a rival of any consequence on its borders. The unrest among regional forces in the interior was eased by a reform of the state-structure by Darius I. He established a uniformly organized administrative network of twenty provinces, each headed by a Persian of the highest rank, the satrap, acting as the royal governor and responsible to the central government.

A combination of circumstances, however, brought Darius into conflict with the Greeks in the extreme western border region of his realm. Contrary to all expectations, they held their own during the "Wars of the Persians" (500–449 B.C.) in memorable battles with the armies and fleets of the great Achaemenidian kings. A new people thus came to the fore in the course of world history.

The loose structure of the Oriental empires was ruled by classes which had mainly emerged from clan nobility and the elders of the tribes. These "high-born" aristocrats were usually landowners, dignitaries and slave-owners, all in one person. For the most part, the key political and military posts were reserved for members of the particular "state people" which was often only a small minority within a colourful ethnic mixture. The "god-like" king from its midst exercised power very despotically, the military system reflecting this state of affairs.

In the Greek city-states, the *poleis*, social development in the 5th century B.C. was considerably more advanced. Kingship was a phenomenon of the past almost everywhere, and the hereditary nobility in the prosperous trade centres had lost much of their political influence to merchants, shipowners and trades people. Although it was restricted to free citizens and supported a slave-owning society instead of curtailing it, the first historically acceptable form of democracy was evolved in Athens. The relatively high degree of political freedom fostered a material and cultural civilization of astonishing scope and influence. The citizen of the *polis* took part in the affairs of the state—in politics—and carried weapons for the defence of the community in which he spent his existence. Thus the Greeks, when obliged to measure their strength with the empire of the Persians, were able to mobilize an economic, moral and military potential which made up for the quantitative advantages of their adversary, especially as they were favoured by their far better connections to the hinterland—the Persian homeland being very far indeed from the Aegean theatre of war.

That the new Greek ships manned by oarsmen repeatedly outfought the outdated fleets of the Persian "auxiliaries" from the Mediterranean after the sea battle of *Salamis* (480 B.C.) was perhaps less astonishing than

Achilles in his fight with Hector,
on an Attic hydria of the painter of the Aucharides, *c.* 475 B.C.
Vatican, Museo Etrusco Gregoriano, Rome

the successes of the militia forces on land. After the defeats of *Marathon* (490 B.C.) and Plataea (479 B.C.) at the hands of the Greek phalanxes, no Persian army dared to set foot on European soil again. Safe from any danger from outside, the Golden Age of Ancient Greece flourished around the Acropolis under Pericles until the outbreak of an open struggle for ascendancy between Sparta and Athens interrupted it.

No "classic" battles took place between the land-power on the one hand and the sea-power on the other during the long Peloponnesian War (431–404 B.C.). Neither side was easy to pin down, they laid siege to and relieved important bases, they tried diplomatic approaches and they set up sea and land blockades. It was only when Sparta, after initial failures, succeeded in building a powerful fleet, too—with Persian financial assistance— that the exhausted Athenians were forced to capitulate in 404 B.C. The war produced the first military historian in the person of the great Thucydides. He was followed by Xenophon, a pupil of Socrates and the commander of the "Ten Thousand", the Greek mercenaries who fought in the service of a pretender to the Persian throne.

After the latter's death in the battle of Cunaxa (401 B.C.), they found themselves faced by overwhelming odds in the midst of the Land of the Two Rivers despite their victory and had to fight a rear-guard action all the way to the safety of the Black Sea. After Xenophon, there developed in the 4th century B.C., which was characterized by the spread of Greek mercenary activities, a specific theory of warfare to which even the universal genius of Aristotle was not ashamed to contribute.

The efforts of Athens and Thebes to free themselves from the regimentation of aristocratic Sparta led to new wars among the Greeks in which lightly-armed soldiers began to be more prominent after the battle of *Lechaion* (390 B.C.). With the victories of *Leuctra* (371 B.C.) and Mantinea (362 B.C.), the Theban general Epaminondas, the first exponent of the "oblique line of battle", brought the success desired but the ascendancy of another hegemony was already apparent. King Philip of Macedonia made clever use of the political disunity of the Greek *poleis* to subordinate them to his leadership after his decisive victory over the Thebans at Chaeronea (338 B.C.) and, with united forces, to attack the state of the Achaemenidae who were weakened by a profound crisis. Only sulky Sparta did not take part in this venture.

His son and successor, Alexander, completed the undertaking. Alexander's campaigns, which stimulated artists' imaginations time and again until the age of Renaissance, brought victory after victory. The battle of *Gaugamela* (331 B.C.) destroyed the empire of the Persians and it was only under the scorching sky of India that the tireless conqueror was persuaded by his mutinous troops to turn back for home. When Alexander died at an early age in his new capital of Babylon in 323 B.C., he left his eager heirs a great store of military experience and a "third" world-empire.

It disintegrated even more rapidly, it might be said, than it had been put together. Finally, after the battle of Ipsus (301 B.C.), his successors divided it up among themselves. India and the Parthians in Iran severed all their connections with a world which, since Droysen, has come to be known as "Hellenistic".

Chandragupta forced the Macedonian troops of Seleucus, a former general of Alexander and one of his "heirs", to withdraw from the Punjab. His grandson Ashoka, the most vigorous advocate of Buddhism, extended the state of the Maurya dynasty from Magadha to large areas of India in the 3rd century B.C. This expansion had considerable cultural consequences, with the heart of the state being moved to the East and the South, but practically nothing is known about its military aspects.

Much more detailed are the accounts by court chroniclers such as Sun-dsi or Wu-tsi concerning the military actions between the principalities into which the Old Chinese monarchy along the middle reaches of the Hwang Ho began to disintegrate in the 8th century B.C. Advances of great significance in trade and techniques were linked with the transition from the Bronze Age to the Iron Age and were reflected on the intellectual level in the "Contest of the hundred schools of philosophy" in which the doctrines of Confucius and Lao-tse, in particular, acquired pre-eminence. The political main beneficiaries of the social regrouping which began then and was characterized by feudal traits of a bureaucratic state at an earlier date than in Europe were the lords of the expanding border marches in the "Period of the Quarrelling Realms" (approx. 475–222 B.C.), particularly Ch'in in the West.

The time was ripe for unification under a strong central power. The struggle among the contenders for the imperial throne reached a climax in the 3rd century B.C. Due to the need to move larger bodies of troops over greater distances, their generalship is characterized by great concern with questions of strategy and tactics which is not at all inferior to the thinking of the Greek authors. This is also demonstrated by the battle of *Chang-ping* (280 B.C. or somewhat later) which opened the last act in the confrontation between the "Quarrelling Realms". Victory for Ch'in cleared the way to the "Celestial Throne" and it was he who was the architect of China's development as the empire of the world with the most people.

Hellenistic armies were characterized by the development of siege engines, especially by Demetrius "Poliorketes", and by the use of Indian war-elephants. As a whole, however, the states of the eastern basin of the Mediterranean under Greco-Macedonian rulers did no more, at best, than maintain their political and military standards while in the West the city-state of Rome emerged and dominated a further epoch in the history of warfare.

The beginnings of the city on the Seven Hills by the Tiber still remain a controversial subject in many details. The facts are obscured by legends but there is no doubt that the *gens Romana* was of Italic origin and traced its descent from a union of small tribes (*tribus*). They established a kingdom after freeing themselves from temporary Etruscan overlordship at the turn of the 6th and 5th centuries B.C. The earliest historical evidence shows Rome already as a *res publica*, a republic, in which power was exercised by the patricians, a landowning aristocracy which had developed from the tribal chiefs, through the senate, their representative body. Although no change took place in the leading status of the aristocracy, the *nobiles*, the common free-men known as the plebeians who had achieved a measure of prosperity nevertheless won recognition as *cives*, i.e., full citizens, in the course of protracted struggles between the different estates and, as time went by, even achieved restricted rights to a say in state affairs. One of the two ruling consuls was elected by the plebeians.

The Roman version of antique democracy provided the Republic with a broad social basis and thus with admirable energy. That gained the upper hand over its more immediate neighbours in Latium in the 4th cen-

Darius I, King of Persia, hunting lions.
His punitive expeditions against the Greeks
returned in disgrace.
Impression from the cylindrical seal of Chalcedon.
British Museum, London

Battle of the Greeks and the Persians.
Detail from the south frieze of the temple to Athena Nike
on the Acropolis, *c.* 420 B.C. Staatliche Museen zu Berlin

tury B.C. and then subjugated not only the Italian tribes but also the numerous Etruscan and Greek city-states throughout the entire Appenine Peninsula.

During this, Rome did not escape dramatic defeats which were not forgotten. It was sacked by the Gauls under Brennus and, in the second war against the bellicose Samnite mountain tribes, an entire demoralized Roman army had to submit to the "Caudine yoke". Brilliant victories on the battlefield tended to be rare events. Rome owed its ultimate success to its social organization. Although this was not far removed from a slave-owning society comparable with the Hellenistic model, it was more astute in that it allowed most of the Italic people to gradually acquire allied status, partial citizenship and ultimately full citizenship. This awakened and maintained their interest in the welfare of the Roman Republic.

Up till 280 B.C., it did not come into conflict with non-Italic powers but in that year the Roman legionaries were scattered by the elephants of a minor Hellenistic potentate. Once they had got over the initial shock, however, they spied out the weak side of these cumbering "big guns" and put King Pyrrhus to flight with their third attack at Maleventum—subsequently known as Beneventum (good event).

The rise to its status as an "empire" began with the destruction of its rival, Carthage, in the three Punic Wars. It was the second, in particular, which almost brought Rome to its knees after its defeat at *Cannae* (216 B.C.) by the military genius of Hannibal but, at the same time, it was precisely this which demonstrated the rugged quality of its social and political structure. After gaining control of the western Mediterranean, the Republic

following double page:
Battle of the Romans and Barbarians. Sarcophagus from Luni.
Gallery Borghese, Rome

successively eliminated the Hellenistic powers: the Macedonians (at *Pydna*, 168 B.C.) and the Seleucids of Syria and ultimately the Ptolemies of Egypt as well (31 B.C.). Three decades later, the Roman *orbis terrarum* included all the shores of the Mediterranean and their hinterland. Its frontiers advanced beyond the Euphrates, Danube and Rhine, and even Britain became a Roman province.

In the course of this and after several violent spasms in the form of civil wars (battle of *Pharsalus*, 48 B.C.), Rome ceased to exist as a republic. The crisis-shaken slave-owning state needed the strong hand of a single man —first as princeps ruling within the legal restrictions of the constitution and then as emperor with absolute power. The army of Italic citizens and peasants, the shield of the young Republic, had long since become a highly specialized professional force which was increasingly dominated first by Illyrian and then Germanic contingents. As an instrument for suppressing never-ending uprisings in Judaea (A.D. 67–70, 132–135), Britain, Africa, Iberia and Gaul, as a line of defence along the far-flung frontiers and as the political force of the Pretorian Guard which overthrew and installed emperors one after the other, it became the *ultima ratio* in an age of social turmoil which led to the decline of the Late Roman Empire and ultimately disintegration.

Naturally enough, military science did not remain unaffected by these changes. The Roman foot-soldiers, the legionaries, had become the most advanced fighting-force of Antiquity and warfare reached its highest state of development at the beginning of the Imperial Period. The need for careful training produced a wealth of literature on the subject by such authors as Frontinus, Onosandros or Vegetius. Accuracy of detail was a matter

22 taken seriously not only by certain historians but also by generals such as Caesar who themselves produced excellent written accounts. Since many of their works have survived, we know more about Roman military history and a number of their battles than about any other state of Antiquity.

Even while they were on the way to world supremacy, the Romans suffered defeats in campaigns and actions against the Celtiberians in Spain and the Numidians in Northwest Africa, when these defended their liberty in the face of invasion. The legions were beaten by raiding Cimbri, Teutons and Helvetians of the Zurich area— the *pagus Tigurinus*, by rebel slaves under Spartacus (73–71 B.C.) and by kings of Pontus and the Parthians. They had no need to keep this secret since they won the war in the end and were prepared to learn from their failures. During the Empire, however, defeats in the field began to indicate that the limit had been reached. The defeat in the *Teutoburger Wald* at the hands of the Germans under Arminius (A.D. 9) marked the forced change to the defensive on the Rhine in the same way that the victory of the Scythians at *Abrittus* in 251 was soon followed by the withdrawal across the lower reaches of the Danube.

In the period when the Imperium was fighting for its life against the inroads of the Barbarians in the 4th and 5th centuries, the time of the great migration, a victory such as that of Julian over the Alemanni at *Argentoratum* in 357 was already an exception. An astute diplomacy of "divide and rule" among the Barbarians was often the only course left. The rather expensive Roman troops, whose organization in legions had also broken down by now, were routed by the Visigoths at Adrianople in 378 and were obliged to withdraw from the provinces of Britain and Africa. While the eastern half of the Empire survived until the threshold of modern times, Rome itself was swamped by its adversaries. Even the celebrated victory of the Imperial general Aetius—without a "government" to back him up and on his own initiative, so to speak—together with German auxiliaries scorned over Attila's Huns and their vassals in 451 on the *Catalaunian Plains* in Gaul was nothing more than a dignified exit from the scene. Exactly a quarter of a century later, the mercenary leader Odoacer overthrew the last of the West Roman emperors and in 486, after the victory of Clovis at Soissons, the Franks occupied the last remaining Roman outpost of Lutetia (Paris).

Titus on a quadriga.
Relief (detail) on the Arch of Titus in Rome, A.D. 81

KADESH / 1292/1285 B.C.

The first great battle of the class society of the Orient—or at least the earliest on which fairly exact information exists—took place in the fifth year of the reign of the Egyptian Pharaoh Rameses II Melamoun of the XIXth dynasty. However, since Egyptologists have been unable to agree on this, the date of the battle of Kadesh immortalized in the poem of Pantaur can only be said to be between 1312 and 1285 B.C., possibly around 1290.

What is certain is that Egyptian military prowess in the "New Kingdom" attained quite a high standard after the expulsion of the Hyksos. The economic power of the state and the ruthless exploitation of the compulsory labour of the peasants permitted the accumulation of the resources necessary for the development of military power whilst the successful campaigns in Asia and Africa provided military experience. The army formed a separate and isolated caste, trained to despise the common people and to be unquestioningly obedient to the god-like pharaoh. Depending on their period of service, the warriors were divided into two groups which wore different clothing and carried different arms. From this, it may be concluded that the chiefs of the army attached importance to a permanent cadre of soldiers on active service. The nucleus of the army consisted of foot-soldiers, all of whom were organized according to the particular weapon they carried: archers, slingers, spearmen and swordsmen. Chariots played a major role since they contributed greatly to mobility and protected the foot-soldiers against attacks on their flanks.

In the period of the "New Kingdom" evidently several parts of armament were adopted from the Hyksos: it was not only the draught-horse but also the short and composite bow, edged weapons and bronze arrow tips.

War against the state of the Hittites in Asia Minor became imminent when King Suppiluliumas in the 14th century B.C. put an end to Egyptian influence in Syria and compelled the minor princes there to pay tribute to him and to supply troops.

The backbone of the Hittite forces operating in Syria was the Semitic religious cult centre of Kadesh, situated on the left bank of the River Orontes. The ruins of Tall Nabi Mand may still be seen on this site. This centre had been turned into a stronghold and was enclosed by thick, high walls. The defensive line on the north side was a tributary river flowing into the Orontes there, the two streams being linked on the south side by a canal. The base dominating the north-south route across Syria was thus safe against surprise attack. The combat strength of the Hittite foot-soldiers amounted to 20,000 men, these being provided by twelve tribes. This was a considerable problem in respect of a unified command. The principal offensive weapon of the Hittite king were his 2,500 war-chariots, a noteworthy figure indeed.

Rameses II was determined to eliminate the chief Syrian base of the Hittites and consequently had to defeat their field army before he could think of laying siege to Kadesh. For this purpose and within a short time, he assembled 20,000 infantry and about 2,000 war-chariots in the vicinity of the border stronghold of Jara. In addition to the Egyptian troops forming the nucleus of the forces, his infantry was recruited from Nubian mercenaries and Shardana (Sardinians), who were members of the "Sea Peoples" of the Mediterranean and included prisoners of war. The majority of the foot-soldiers was equipped with shields, spears, curved swords, arrows, bows or clubs. Metal parts consisted of bronze. The Asiatic war-chariot had only slowly won acceptance in Egypt, not becoming an important part of the army before the time of Rameses II. Each of these light vehicles was drawn by two horses and manned by a warrior and a charioteer. On one side there was the sheath for the bow and a quiver, on the other two crossed quivers containing arrows, spears and sometimes even clubs. The equipment of the war-chariot was complete

Charioteer and archer on a Hittite chariot in battle. Orthostate relief from Kargamis. Basalt, height 1.75 m, c. 850–700 B.C. Archaeological Museum, Ankara

enough for the warrior and the charioteer to have enough weapons for attack and defence at their disposal. At the commencement of the attack, it was the warrior's task to protect the charioteer with his shield from enemy arrows. Once battle was joined, this protection could no longer be provided and the charioteer himself had to do his share of the fighting with a spear or with bow and arrow. In Egypt, the war-chariots were incorporated in the army and were not organized in special formations.

War-lions, reared and trained at the court as cubs, ran at the side of Rameses's chariot. These were not merely a royal status symbol but, like his bodyguard, served for the protection of his person. War-lions were never used on a massive scale, however, in the Egyptian or any other army.

Rameses divided his army into a number of independent units named after the gods Amon, Ra, Ptah and Seth, he himself commanding the first of these. At the end of the winter rainy period, the Egyptians set out from Jara and, after 29 days, arrived at their objective on the heights south

Rameses II on his chariot breaks through the Hittite line of battle. Tracing from the bas-relief of the temple of Rameses II at Abydos. From: Mémoires publiés par les Membres de l'Institut Français d'Archéologie orientale du Caire.

of Kadesh. With this successful march, they attained full combat readiness. The establishment of a permanent camp provided the army with the rest and security needed for the preparation of the struggle ahead. With his intention to force a decisive battle, the pharaoh had to consider the nature of the terrain, the arms and equipment of his adversary and the relative numerical strengths of the forces involved.

Even in those early days, stratagems of war and the tricking of the enemy were of no small importance. Thus two Hittites, claiming to be deserters, reported that their field-troops were still almost a hundred miles away. Rameses believed them since what they said confirmed the reports of his own, obviously incompetent scouts. He rashly marched his forces out of their camp in preparation for an attack on the stronghold of Kadesh whose garrison, so he assumed, was now cut off from the other enemy forces. In the early hours, all four units started off in an orderly manner along the right bank of the Orontes. At Shabtun, six miles before Kadesh, they had to cross a ford. Since he believed his adversary to be unaware of his intentions, he neglected to take any military precautions while the crossing was carried out which, with his 20,000 men, chariots and baggage train, must have taken at least six hours. The units became strung out, lost contact with each other and crossed the ford one by one.

Amon unit was the first over the Orontes and, under the command of Rameses with his bodyguard, reached the fortress where, to the northwest of this, they set up a fortified camp commanding the road leading from Kadesh to the North. This camp was carefully laid out and was lined by shields and vehicles, the horses being unharnessed for this. In the meantime, the pharaoh had lost touch with the other units. He assumed that they were likewise not far distant from the vanguard of the army whereas in actual fact they were still in the process of crossing the river and there were even fairly big gaps between them.

Muwatallis, the Hittite king, made good use of the advantage of being able to operate with his army in the shadow of the stronghold and the safety that this implied and was also responsible for the manoeuvre with the so-called deserters. He had taken up a concealed position northwest of Kadesh and, on learning that the Egyptians were marching towards its, crossed to the right bank of the Orontes. His formations advanced southwards with the aim of launching an attack on the flank of the enemy. This tactic ran into difficulties, however, since the Egyptian units no longer formed a single column and were marching at some distance from each other.

The battle started with a flank attack by the Hittites on Ra unit which was moving up south of Kadesh. The Hittite chariots crossed the Orontes without difficulty and launched a fierce attack, breaking the centre of their adversary and killing most of his troops who were simply on the march, had taken no precautions to inform themselves of hostile movements and were completely unprepared for combat. Only a few survivors, including two sons of the pharaoh, succeeded in reaching Amon unit in the fortified camp. At the same time, the Hittites also began with the encirclement of

this latter unit. Rameses still did not realize how serious his position had become. It was only when members of his bodyguard used torture to force a statement from two other "deserters" and learned that the Hittites had concealed troops behind Kadesh that it dawned on him that he had entered a trap. He ordered Amon unit to prepare for battle and sent instructions to Ptah unit to join him as quickly as possible.

With their superior numbers, the Hittites succeeded in penetrating the defences of the camp despite the stubborn resistance of the Egyptians under the command of the pharaoh. At this critical moment, even his lions were turned loose on the enemy. The first attempt of Amon unit to break out in a westerly direction ended in failure but on the east they succeeded in driving the weaker enemy troops into the river, on the opposite bank of which there were 8,000 Hittites who had not yet joined the battle.

The units of the Hittites which had broken into the camp assumed that the fight was over for the time being and began to plunder it with complete disregard for anything else. Rameses recognized the chance offered, collected his troops and with a counter-attack wiped out the surprised marauders. By this, Amon unit gained a brief respite. Muwatallis did indeed call up his reserve of 1,000 warchariots but without success since the Egyptians stood firm and, in turn, launched six counter-attacks.

The battle had already been in full progress for three hours when Ptah unit, in accordance with its instructions, appeared on the scene in a well-ordered combat formation three lines deep and protected on its flanks by chariots. The first line was likewise made up of chariots, the second consisted of the infantry in ten ranks and the third was formed by more chariots. They attacked the Hittites in the rear and almost encircled them. Only some of the chariots succeeded in breaking out of this ring and withdrawing to the stronghold of Kadesh.

With Ptah unit arriving in the nick of time, Rameses II won the day. Nevertheless, his losses were serious: one of the four units of his army had been almost totally destroyed and another decimated. This meant that the Egyptian forces were in no position to be able to storm the stronghold of Kadesh. However, the serious decimation of the Hittite field-forces had removed the peril to the frontiers and Egyptian interests and the pharaoh, together with the troops which he still possessed, could return home with some degree of satisfaction at least.

The campaign of Kadesh began with a disciplined march by the Egyptian army and it culminated in a pitched battle at several points. The total participation of all his units, with the exception of Seth unit wandering around outside the combat area, and his successful tactical manoeuvres enabled Rameses to gain the upper hand in the end. Although the Hittites lost a great part of their army, they were still able to reinforce Kadesh with the units which remained and prevent its capture by the Egyptians. As a consequence, the latter were unable to attain the third of their aims, i.e., the occupation of the fortress.

Rameses had neglected to send out scouts and to protect his troops on the march, he had also allowed himself to be outwitted by his opponent and he had entered the trap set. Through their successful deception, the concealment of their troop movements and the inclusion of the protection at their rear offered by the stronghold, the Hittites had the better starting position and, at the beginning, the battle went their way. The tactical mistake of the Hittite king was that he did not attack with his chariots and infantry at the same time and did not do this with strong enough forces at the critical points. This is why he failed to destroy Amon unit in the fortified camp before the arrival of Ptah unit.

The Egyptian chariots, mostly manned by archers, proved more effective than those of the Hittites which carried spearmen since the former were able, with their arrows, to slay the horses of the Hittite war-chariots. In the action, it was the good co-ordination of infantry and war-chariots under a single command which proved superior in carrying out the disciplined march to the battlefield; nevertheles,s mistakes in the orders given took their toll. Rameses II, at the cost of heavy losses, resisted the attacking army of the Hittites who consequently lost the military advantage of mobility. The stronghold of Kadesh, although it was not taken, was no longer a threat to Egypt. But, naturally, this success was not sufficient to expel the Hittites from Syria.

In a broader context, the match ended as an honourable draw with Hattusilis III nearly seventeen years later when a peace treaty was concluded, the long hostility between the two powers ending in a dynastic alliance. The rediscovered text of this treaty is the first in history of which we have the wording in hieroglyphs and Accadian cuneiform characters for both of the parties concerned. Neither the treaty nor the marriage with Naptera, the daughter of the Hittite king, prevented the old Rameses from having carved the story of the great battle in the prime of his life on one temple wall after another, together with a few flattering "decorations" in keeping with the glory of a pharaoh, of course. In this way, he has saved the battle—and himself—from oblivion. The impressive reliefs and engravings at Karnak, Abu Simbel, and Abydos are no less enduring than the art of Egyptian morticians who preserved the sharp profile of the "first general" for the admiration of later generations.

Egyptian army with chariots and foot-warriors on the march. Bas-relief from the temple of Rameses II in Abydos. From: Mémoires publiés par les Membres de l'Institut Français d'Archéologie orientale du Caire.

MARATHON / 490 B.C.

From the time, in the course of the second millennium B.C., when Achaean and then Dorian tribes invaded Greece and intermarried with the original Mediterranean inhabitants to form the people of the Hellenes, they remained free from foreign attack for many centuries. The Barbarian raids of this period were directed against the civilized regions of the Near East, and Greece was of relatively little interest to their leaders. The lack of pressure from foreign powers, together with the mountainous terrain and the rugged coastline contributed to a situation in which the Greek tribes maintained religious affinities but did not feel the need for political unity. They developed into a group of rural communities and city-states in which the recognized military leadership was exercised from the 7th century B.C. onwards by Sparta in the Dorian district of Lacedaemon on the Peloponnesian Peninsula. When hostilities broke out between individual Greek states, it occasionally acted as a peacemaker or arbitrator.

By and large, the frontiers of the city-states were regarded as unalterable. Feuds between them were consequently not carried on for the sake of gaining more territory. Confrontations of a more serious nature were usually the result of the bitter competitions between the leading maritime trading centres and slave markets such as Corinth, Megara, Aegina, and, from the 6th century B.C., Athens, too, which now ruled the twelve rural communities of Attica as well. The armed forces of the individual *poleis* were thus essentially of a citizens' militia character and their tasks were of a defensive nature. All free men who were fit and of suitable age for military duties served in them. Almost overnight, in the early 5th century B.C., they found themselves face-to-face with the world-power of Persia.

With Lydia, whose ruler Croesus of legendary riches was defeated by the Persians in 546 B.C., the flourishing Greek colonies on the west coast of Asia Minor also fell under the domination of the great kings of the race of the Achaemenidae. In 500 B.C., with the assistance of Athens and Eretria, they rose against Darius (Darayavaush) I in the "Ionian Revolt". After a victory over the united Greek forces in the naval battle of Lade in 495 B.C., and after having crushed the rebellion, he considered it advisable to teach the "foreigners" a lesson as well for interfering. He demanded symbolic submission from them but the Athenians and Spartans slew his emissaries as a sign that they accepted the challenge.

The first Persian punitive expedition under Mardonius, the son-in-law of the king, in 492 B.C. had to turn back in Macedonia after a storm had devastated the fleet accompanying him. Two years later, an expeditionary force under Datis and Artaphernes crossed the Aegean Sea, subjugated Rhodes and Naxos, landed on the island of Euboea, destroyed Eretria, and, from there, crossed to Attica. In 490 B.C., two worlds and their different military concepts met head on at the village of Marathon, as vividly described in the sixth book of Herodotus.

With the battle of Marathon, the tactics of infantry forces in the shape of the "phalanx" left their mark on the history of the world in a situation of critical importance. They ended the epoch of heroic individual combat celebrated by Homer in his immortal epic of the legendary Trojan War.

The structure of the Athenian phalanx had been greatly improved by the reforms of Solon who divided the citizens into four classes on the basis of the wealth they possessed. The most prosperous ones also held the highest posts in the military sphere; the second group—usually drawn from the rural nobility—was a mounted force. The "zeugites", as the third group, were mostly peasants of sufficient means or respected master craftsmen and provided the heavily armed infantry or "hoplites" from which the phalanx was drawn. The lowest-ranking group, the "thetes", consisted of poorer craftsmen, smallholders and free wage-labourers—who also served in the fleet as oarsmen—and were used in the army as lightly-armed skirmishers.

The heavily armed troops were equipped with a two metres long thrusting lance, the short Greek iron sword and

The Greek phalanx of hoplites at the beginning of the battle against the Persian cavalry in the battle of Marathon. Painting by Heinz Zander (1973). Armeemuseum der DDR, Dresden

protective clothing while their more lightly armed comrades had a javelin and a bow and arrow; the Athenians even possessed a respectable number of small special units of master-bowmen. The phalanx was a compact, linear unit of several files of heavily armed infantry. Each man was equipped at his own expense with standard equipment and, on flat terrain, this formation could strike deep into the ranks of the enemy. Its flanks and rear were vulnerable, however, and had to be shielded by lightly armed troops and cavalry. When the phalanx had to fight or march across terrain of an intersected nature, difficulties were encountered which had to be borne in mind by the commander. In particular, he had to be capable of making a realistic assessment of the position before the start of the battle.

The military leadership of Athens was shaken time and again by disputes as to whether priority should be given to the army or to the fleet. It was only just before the battle against the Persians that Miltiades was given supreme command. He advocated the strengthening of the phalanx since he regarded it as the most effective answer to Persian military might and had gained personal experience of Persian military organization in his younger years.

On the Persian side, Darius had reshaped the military system. An excellent road network permitted rapid troop movements and on the principal roads there were garrisons every 20 kilometres for the protection of the area at the rear. The King's Road from Susa to Sardis functioned as the longitudinal axis of the speedy courier and post service in particular. The elite unit of the army, of which the nobility formed the backbone, was the veteran Royal Guard, consisting of the 10,000 foot-soldiers known as the "Immortals", 1,000 halberdiers, 1,000 mounted bodyguards and a number of war-chariots. This force was the king's personal reserve and always remained close to him. All the other units varied in origin, equipment and combat techniques. The mass of the infantry was made up of Persians, Medes and Bactrians, although Greek mercenary formations played a certain role. Their equipment consisted of bow and arrow, the short lance, an iron sword and protective clothing of scale armour plus a woven shield. The army was organized in groups of a thousand, a hundred and ten but was not a coherent whole and there was little co-ordination between the infantry and the cavalry. Both of these were arbitrarily assembled from tribal contingents according to their availability and without regard to any specific considerations. The commander-in-chief had his hands full in keeping control over his irregular cavalry which, as his most manoeuvrable force, was an important factor. The scythed chariots which had been copied from the Assyrians and were much feared did not really fit into the Persian military organization and were thus used only sporadically.

The landing of the Persians on the flat shore of Marathon with the hills encircling it reflected their desire to force a decision with the cavalry on terrain that favoured this tactic. The horses were transported on ships specially equipped for this purpose. It was, so to say, the first great "amphibian operation" in history. Their action shows that they underestimated the driving force of the phalanx and indeed their choice of terrain even played into the hands of their opponents. Greek authors relate that the Persian force consisted of 20,000 men with equal numbers of cavalry and infantry but it would have been impossible for the fleet to have carried such a number. It is more probable that—not counted their sailors—they were approximately as strong as the Greek army which is said to have con-

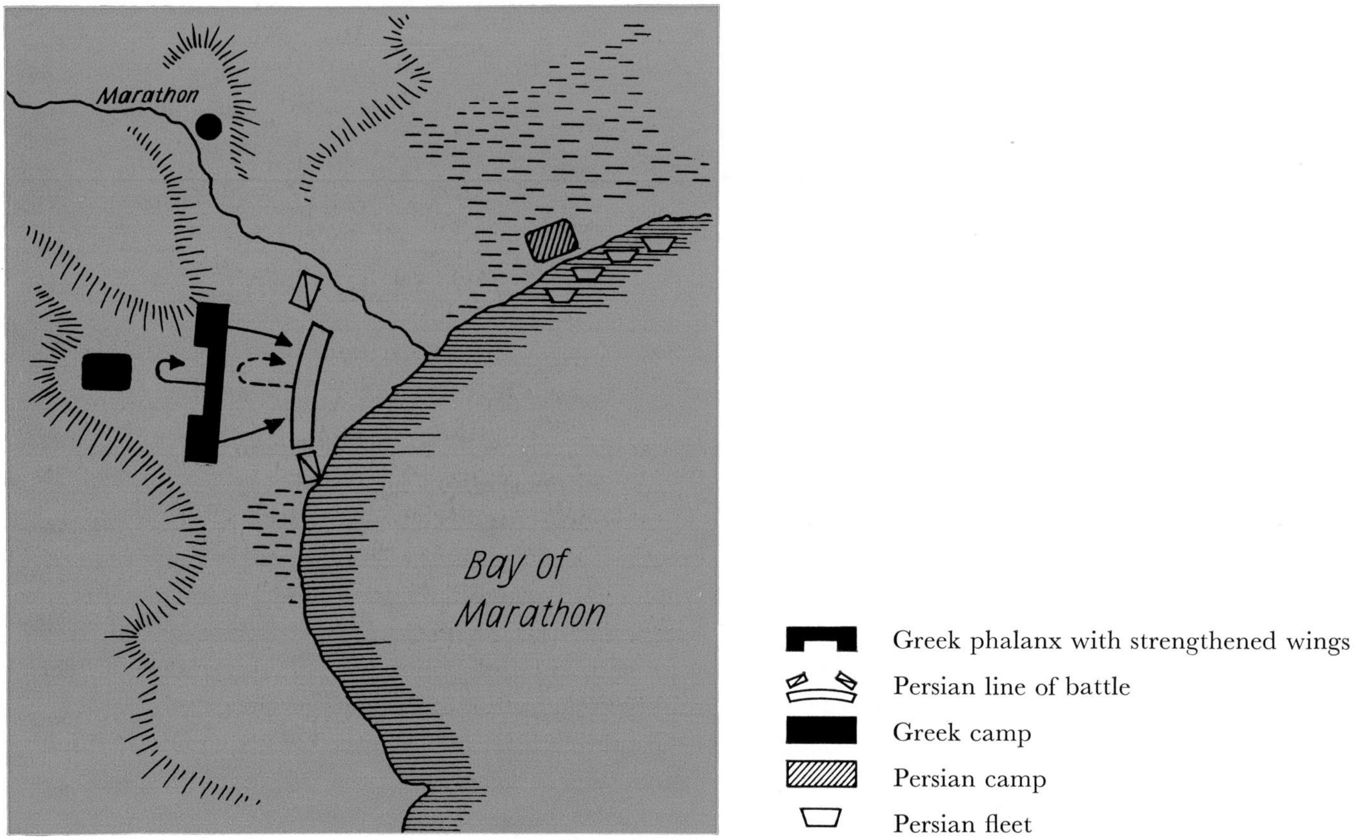
Marathon
Bay of Marathon
Greek phalanx with strengthened wings
Persian line of battle
Greek camp
Persian camp
Persian fleet

Battle-scene at Marathon depicted on the side-panel of a sarcophagus. Civico Museo Romano, Brescia

sisted of 10,000 Athenians and 1,000 Plataeans, but certainly it was only half that number.

The Greeks had established their camp in the hills, blocking the way to Athens. Miltiades was right to move out to meet his adversary with the phalanx instead of waiting for him to come to the Acropolis. His initiative secured the tactical advantage. He drew up his phalanx at the entrance to the valley of Marathon, the best hoplites of Athens on the right wing and the Plataeans on the left. The original intention to attack with the phalanx in a deep formation had to be abandoned since the valley was too wide. To safeguard the flanks, Miltiades increased the number of ranks at the wings and reduced them in the centre. The front of the phalanx was about a thousand metres across.

The Persians used their customary tactics of placing the infantry in the centre with the cavalry on the wings but this had already been countered by the way in which Miltiades had deployed his forces. He opened the attack with a charge by the phalanx along the whole line since there was the danger of encirclement by the enemy cavalry and other ships could arrive with reinforcements. The speed of the attack meant that the arrows of the Persians caused only slight losses to the Greeks whilst on the other hand the irregular units of their opponent were demoralized by the iron wall of the phalanx bearing down upon them. The Persians concentrated the attack of their infantry, mainly consisting of archers, on the weakened Greek centre. They did indeed

34 achieve a breakthrough and then pursued the Greeks as they fell back. In the meantime, the mounted units which had to climb the hills on narrow paths had failed to attain their objective and were driven back. It was here that the strengthening of the wings of the Greek line paid off. Nevertheless, since the position in the centre had first to be stabilized, the pursuit of the Persian horsemen fleeing to their ships was not possible. The withdrawal of the cavalry had exposed the flanks of their own infantry and this enabled Miltiades to use his wings against the Persian units which had now been split. With this concentration of forces, he was able to destroy them, close the gap in the centre and restore the original order of battle. The Greeks then drove the enemy back about one kilometre and a half to the spot where they buried their 192 dead and erected a mound to them.

It was here that Miltiades regrouped his breathless army in preparation for an attack on the camp and the anchored fleet of the Persians. In the meantime, however, their infantry had begun to embark as quickly as possible so that only seven ships fell into the hands of the Greeks. According to reports by the victors the Persians lost about one third of their forces; this, however, is very doubtful. When the battle was already at an end, some 2,000 Spartans arrived behind time, be it deliberate or not, who could do no more than congratulate the victors.

Miltiades ordered one of his soldiers to bring the good news to Athens as quickly as possible. The swift-footed messenger, the first to run this "marathon race" covering a distance of 42 kilometres, collapsed on arrival, crying "We have won!".

The battle of Marathon was of great military importance. It was the first major land battle between the Greeks and the Persians, between two armies of different social upbringing and methods of warfare. It was the crucial test for the phalanx of the hoplites. An important role was played by the initial position, the location of the strategic camp of the Athenians. The actual fighting demonstrated the strength of the tactical formation and its flexibility in use, both on the wings and in the centre. Despite this, the pursuit of the enemy revealed its weak point, the inability of the heavily armed troops, whose armour had the considerable weight of 70 pounds, to move rapidly. Thus the Persians managed to get out of the affair fairly well. After

having sailed round Attica, they even planned a direct surprise attack on Athens, since they assumed the city to be bare of troops. It was only the swiftly undertaken counter-march of the Greek troops after the battle of Marathon that prevented their second landing and caused Datis and Artaphernes to return to Asia.

The disciplined phalanx of the Greek hoplites proved superior to the horsemen and archers of the Orient. It was evident that the heavily armed and physically well-trained civil militia could withstand the onslaught of larger irregular forces and even take up a new battle order if necessary, as illustrated by the wheeling manoeuvre of the Athenians which sealed the defeat of the Persians. A significant factor here, in addition to the better military organization, was the well-thought-out plan of operations and the personal leadership of Miltiades.

Even more significant were the political consequences of the battle. They lent additional weight to the prosperous *polis* of Athens and increased its authority among the Greeks. Obliged to take the initiative in the face of the deadly danger represented by the Persians, it needed the active efforts of all its free citizens for its defence. This gave an exceptional impetus to the democratic forces and principles which were beginning to influence Greek society in an exemplary manner.

The victory at Marathon demonstrated the vulnerability of the Persian land forces and at the same time avenged the catastrophe of the Ionian revolt. It promoted a feeling of All-Greek nationalism and consolidated the alliance of all those who had to assume that sooner or later the Great King would demand revenge. The Greeks regarded this prospect with equanimity. After Marathon, they considered themselves the equal of their adversary in the military sphere and far superior to him in respect of morale in their just defence of an honourable cause.

Archers of the Persian Guard. Frieze (detail) from the palace of Darius I at Susa, *c.* 500 B.C. Louvre, Paris

SALAMIS / 480 B.C.

The death of Darius (486 B.C.) and insurrections in Egypt delayed the carefully planned vengeance of the Persians. It was only in 480 B.C. that King Xerxes (Khshayarsha) crossed the Hellespont, whose waters he had thrashed with chains as retribution for the rough passage, and then marched overland on Athens. Thrace was already part of the Persian sphere of influence and Macedonia and Thessaly bowed before the ominous display of superior force. Although the 1,500,000 warriors told of in the eighth book of Herodotus were purely fictitious, this was the largest army which ever descended on Ancient Greece. Modern researchers estimate it at almost 200,000 men, including the camp-followers and the mariners and oarsmen. Their long march was an astonishing organizational achievement and was only possible because of the great fleet accompanying the expedition. The elements behaved themselves and the fleet always remained in touch with the land forces.

On the advance of the enemy Sparta summoned a congress of the Greek *poleis*, being about thirty in number. They all agreed upon a common defence. Their vanguard evacuated the position in the Tempe valley by Olympus and withdrew to the pass of Thermopylae. This gateway to Central Greece was defended by King Leonidas of Sparta. When the Persians found a way over mountain paths to bypass this obstruction, the little band of 300 Spartans and their 700 allies fought to the last man to delay Xerxes's advance and allow the Greek main army to make an orderly withdrawal to the Isthmus of Corinth. The allied fleet broke off an indecisive encounter off Cape Arthemision at the northern tip of Euboea and rowed back to the island of Salamis.

Xerxes forced some of the central Greek *poleis*, headed by Thebes, to join in on his side. He then occupied Athens, whose inhabitants had sought safety on Salamis, and captured the Acropolis after a brief siege. Understandably, those who had fled the city were in favour of an offensive without delay while the Spartans would have preferred to defend the fortified Isthmus of Corinth since they believed they could resist the Persians indefinitely there. Sparta was in favour of a land battle on a favourable terrain on the assumption that a Persian defeat on land would also force a withdrawal of the ships. The Athenians, for their part, had come to the conclusion that the elimination of the Persian fleet would make the extended positions of the Great King untenable within a short time. It seems that Xerxes, too, considered this to be the weak spot of the whole affair and decided to encircle and destroy the enemy ships, which he believed to be trapped in the Saronic Gulf, with the aim of solving once and for all the key problem of dominating the sea and the routes of communication. This is why he himself sought a confrontation.

The Persians had a powerful fleet of seaworthy vessels manned by oarsmen but they consisted exclusively of contingents from subdued peoples. This meant that the integrated leadership of the Phoenician, Cilician, Carian, Egyptian and Cypriot squadrons was exceptionally difficult. There was no question of an admiral-in-chief invested with supreme powers or of a co-ordinated range of equipment. The warships and auxiliary vessels of the Mediterranean cities owing allegiance to the Persian Empire varied substantially in their construction and armament, which made it almost impossible for them to be used to full effect in combat. Most of the crews regarded war-service as a burdensome necessity arousing no particular enthusiasm, though they were not particularly fond of their Greek rivals in the field of trade.

Most of the citizens of Athens, on the other hand, fully realized that the future of their trading city was linked with the sea. In the experienced squadron commander Themistocles, they had a statesman who, after Marathon, made an emphatic demand for a fleet programme and got what he wanted. Although there were great difficulties in not only increasing the number of ships but also in training the

Warrior with pelta and short spear, on a red-figured eye-dish, *c.* 500 B.C. Antiquities Museum of the Karl Marx University, Leipzig

hoplites, accustomed to the lance and the shield, as sailors and exercising their combat readiness at sea, this problem was solved by 480 B.C. As a sea-power, Athens had outstripped its allies.

When Xerxes gave the signal to attack, the fleet of the Greek allies lay at anchor in the sound between the islands of Salamis and Attica in the bay of Ambelaki and Paluki while the Persians had assembled their units in the roadstead of Phaleron. There is no reason to doubt the number of 358 Greek warships quoted; much more questionable is the figure of 1,207 enemy vessels, although in numbers and especially in tonnage (estimated at 150,000 t) they were certainly far superior. In both respects, the Persian naval forces were hardly ever surpassed in a naval battle up to the 20th century.

Warship manned by oarsmen with ram at the stem, depicted on an Attic vase. Louvre, Paris

A part of the Persian fleet sailed around Salamis in order to hem in the enemy between the west coast of the island, the east coast of Megaris and the two lines of the Persian vessels. Xerxes relied on his superior strength and decided to watch the course of the battle, which promised to be a great triumph for him, from the heights of Aigaleos. Here he had his throne set up and around it he grouped his personal guard in a decorative but useless fashion. Even before the start of the conflict, the disadvantages of the mostly high-sided, deep-draft ships for a battle in the narrow and shallow sound had already become apparent. In addition, by his presence on the scene, the king restricted the freedom of action of his commanders since he did not take a direct part in the fighting but nevertheless issued one instruction after another.

The Greeks had a few older and weaker types of ships such as those manned by fifty oarsmen but the majority consisted of speedy and manoeuvrable triremes. These were 35 to 38 metres in length and had a beam of 5.8 metres. The ship's hardwood planks were cleft with the axe and shaped over a fire. Wooden and iron nails were used. The underwater part of the stem was fitted with an iron shoe and was shaped as a ram so that it could penetrate the planks of enemy ships. Above the ram, there was an ironclad beam designed to break the oars of the hostile ship when a diagonal attack was made. The benches of the 170 rowers were arranged in three decks, one above the other, sails only being used as a secondary means of propulsion. The advantage of the trireme was its shallow draft and extreme manoeuvrability. The ships of the Great King, more suitable for hand-to-hand fighting on board, were rammed by the Greek vessels, whose crews were familiar with the navigable waters and the shallows, knew every reef and fought as free citizens against their enslavement.

Themistocles had indirectly caused the Persian king to decide on the battle, had selected its locations and—like Miltiades at Marathon—had retained the tactical advantage offered by the particular features of the situation. He had to take care that the will of the allies at that time to seek a decisive sea-battle did not change in favour of a land-battle on the Isthmus since the Greek units were not numerically strong enough for the encounter on the open sea which would probably then follow.

For a month and a half, the two fleets had faced each other without taking any action of note and it was now September. The Greeks had refused to be lured out of their excellent defensive position. They did not even react when the Persian fleet, with its right flank moved up, at last entered the sound and took up battle position, facing the south along the coast of Attica, although this meant that the Greek vessels were now encircled at Kamatero. This action by the Persians was even encouraged by Themistocles who was worried that the Greeks might opt for the Spartan alternative of a land campaign and sent out some "deserters" with the information that the Greek fleet was about "to steal away".

The narrow navigable channel, the close formation of the ships and the lack of local knowledge of their crews which were drawn from many different peoples were all handicaps which put the Persian fleet at a disadvantage. Besides, a small island in front of the Greek battle line disturbed their battle order. Themistocles moved up the right wing of his fleet. While the Spartans attacked the right Persian wing, Themistocles launched a vehement attack against the left one, thus causing a general confusion. The Persian battle line was rolled up on two sides and broke apart. The Greeks boarded and sank the big vessels which were hampered in the shallows. Many of the Persian vessels were destroyed by the triremes by ramming. Due to the circumstances of the situation, they were obliged to fight

The Great King Xerxes observes the naval battle of Salamis. Woodcut illustration, *c.* 1880

as individual units without the mutual cover used to tactical advantage by the Greeks.

The situation in the sound did not allow a battle in which duels were fought by individual craft. This meant that the Persians had lost the advantage of quantitative superiority and it was mostly so that each of their ships was attacked from two directions at the same time. About 200 of them were sent to the ground, a number were captured by the Greeks who used them to make up for the rather heavy losses of about 50 vessels they themselves had suffered. Nevertheless, there were notable maritime performances on the Persian side, too. The Carian princess Artemisia with her ships fought her way through the enemy craft surrounding her and escaped from the sound after sinking a Greek vessel. Some captains reached the open sea without regard to the fate of their squadrons. The ships that succeeded in reaching Phaleron subsequently set off for their home-ports unmolested.

Xerxes, an unwilling witness to the defeat of his naval forces, withdrew from Athens and retired to winter-quarters in Thessaly. Uprisings in the east of his realm obliged him, however, together with his guard, to leave the Greek theatre of war, the command over the troops remaining there being given to the veteran Mardonius.

The Greeks did not immediately realize the full extent of the strategic significance of their victory and feared that the Persians would launch further attacks. Themistocles did not find support for his plan to advance to the Hellespont and cut the main Persian line of communications. On the other hand, the *poleis* doubled the numbers of their land-forces in preparation for the coming spring offensive expected from the hostile army which was still very strong.

It is also probable that the Great King sought the battle at Salamis on account of the difficulties in logistics which the winter would bring if he did not succeed in gaining mastery of the sea. On the other hand, if he withdrew without a fight, this could be interpreted as an admission of his weakness. However, lacking experience in maritime questions, he made the fateful mistake of seeking the decisive battle in the worst of all places—the sound. Conversely, Themistocles was astute enough to exploit the specific situation to the utmost and achieve such a memorable victory bef.re the position of the immobilized Greek fleet off Salamis became untenable.

Since the Greeks did not allow themselves to be provoked by their more powerful adversary to an engagement on the open sea, they forced him to meet them on their own terms and attack them in the worst possible circumstances for the Persians. On the Greek side, Salamis was an action within the framework of a combined land and sea operation. Themistocles very skilfully changed over to the offensive from a defensive starting position. His success demonstrated that the fleet and the army had to be co-ordinated if great feats of arms were to be achieved.

This was the first truly outstanding sea-battle of history and was celebrated by Aeshylus—not just an eye-witness but himself a combatant at Marathon and Salamis—in his drama *The Persians*. The battle of Salamis was a turning-point in the Greco-Persian wars since, in the same year, Carthage, Persia's ally in Northwest Africa, suffered an overwhelming defeat at the River Himera in Sicily at the hands of the Greek tyrant Gelon of Akragas. The Greeks now took the initiative and kept it. In 479 B.C., a strong Greek army under Spartan leadership vanquished Mardonius at Plataea in Boeotia and drove the Persians from European soil. The latter even lost their bridgeheads at the Hellespont and the Bosporus. In the same year still, victory in the simultaneous land and sea battle at Cape Mycale in Caria also freed the Ionian Greeks from Persian domination. Although fighting continued for a long time even after the death of Xerxes until 449 B.C., the nightmare of alien rule had long since disappeared from the Greek scene. Athens, the living heart of the resistance and from 477 B.C. the head of the Delian League, became synonymous with the "Hellenic Spring" of a world civilization whose creative achievements outlived its commercial and political heyday by thousands of years.

LECHAION / 390 B.C.

With its victory in the Peloponnesian War (431–404 B.C.), aristocratic Sparta had consolidated its supremacy in Greece. Resistance to the harsh methods with which it maintained its hegemony led to an alliance between Thebes, Athens, Corinth and other city-states, most of which were ruled by democrats. In the Corinthian Wars (395–387 B.C.), they initially received support from the king of the Persians, who had fallen out with Sparta.

Significant changes had taken place in the Greek armies in the course of the 5th century B.C. Whilst in the Persian Wars the warriors still had to provide their own arms and equipment, the custom of paying for their services became established in the Peloponnesian War. The lightly armed infantry forces were found to be useful for an increasing number of tasks and the demand for soldiers steadily grew. It was frequently the case that the *poleis* could not recruit all the military contingents needed from their own male population any longer. The need for mercenary formations consequently emerged. These were drawn from the free peasants and artisans who had been impoverished by the endless wars and simply had to be given money for food and arms.

A similar development had already taken place in the fleet at an earlier date since the number of warships steadily increased until it outstripped the numbers of mariners available to man the ships.

Then there was the fact that rich slave-owners avoided service in the civil militia by buying themselves out or by providing a substitute. In this way, the militia forces gradually became mercenary armies. As a result, since they could now be used in different ways, new tactics and strategies emerged.

After Konon had defeated the Spartan fleet at Knidos in 394 B.C. and had devastated the Peloponnesian coastal settlements, he advanced on the Isthmus of Corinth. Athens received assistance from the Persians for the reconstruction of its harbour fortifications razed in 404 B.C., for the expansion of its fleet and for the recruitment of infantry forces. Despite this, Athens was not able to put any great hoplite phalanxes in the field. For reasons of economy, simplifications were made in the fitting out of the newly formed units. The iron cuirass was replaced by a padded linen buff-coat and a leather shield took the place of the metal shield. There was a reduction in the weight of the armament, the units thus becoming more mobile and manoeuvrable. The heavy, iron-clad phalanx with its thrusting lance, which had even been made longer, was still retained but as a formation it could now develop a higher speed of attack.

The re-equipment of the land army was carried out by the mercenary leader Iphicrates in exemplary manner. He recognized the specific military potential of the peltasts who, as lightly armed infantry, had played a subordinate role hitherto. Their training, arms and equipment were accordingly improved until they learnt to perform every manoeuvre on the move—outflanking, encirclement, ambushing and flank protection. They could open the attack by a frontal movement or by striking at the wings or the rear of the enemy. They also proved extremely useful for the pursuit of the enemy and for covering their own army on the march or during withdrawals. This demonstrated their operational versatility in reconnaissance and for missions behind the lines.

The peltasts were armed with javelins and long swords and equipped with helmet and linen buff-coat with a light harness, which gave protection to the hips and legs, too. Rapid attack was constantly practised, the tactic being to hurl the javelin when ten to twenty metres from the enemy and then to engage him with the short sword. The peltast units thus operated with missiles and close-combat weapons both in defence and in attack.

The battle of Lechaion (390 B.C.), as related by Xenophon in the third book of his *Greek History*, may be regarded as the first great test of the peltasts and the more manoeuvrable Athenian phalanx. The battlefield lay between two fortresses on the Corinthian Gulf.

42

Lechaion sheltered a Spartan garrison whilst fairly large Athenian units were assembled in Corinth. The hoplite phalanx of Athens was commanded by Callias and the peltasts by Iphicrates. The two fortresses acted as concentration points for the two armies and were the bases for the expected battle. The Athenians saw their chance when a 600-strong Spartan hoplite unit marched past Corinth on its way to Lechaion.

Since the Spartans believed that their heavy infantry unit was practically unassailable and had not bothered about protecting the flanks by light units, the Athenian leaders decided to risk an attack. The peltasts were given the task of attacking the Spartan hoplites by hurling their javelins from a distance but of withdrawing in the face of a direct onslaught by the Spartans. The Athenian hoplite

Greek hoplites in combat with javelins and shields, on a Chalcidian vase. End of 6th century B.C. Hermitage, Leningrad

phalanx took up position in front of the fortress of Corinth to cover the attack by the peltasts.

The peltasts attacked the enemy, who suffered many losses. The Spartan commander had the wounded taken to Lechaion and, following the usual combat technique of the phalanx, launched a counter-attack. For the first wave, he drew up the hoplites who had been on active service for ten years. The peltasts met their advance by withdrawing but remaining within javelin range. Under the constant and unaccustomed hail of javelins, the battle-order of the hoplites broke up. The commitment of a second phalanx of warriors with 15 years' service did not change the situ-

Spartan phalanx of hoplites dispersed by Theban peltasts in the battle of Lechaion. Painting by Heinz Zander (1976). Armee-museum der DDR, Dresden

ation either whilst in the meantime the casualties mounted up enormously.

In this phase of the engagement, the Spartan hoplites were reinforced by the approach of a cavalry unit. The phalanx reformed and attempted to launch a counter-attack with the assistance of the mounted force. This failed, too, because of the tactics used by the peltasts. They took advantage of the circumstances that the Spartan cavalry—never the pride of the Lacedaemonian army—did not follow the customary tactics of cavalry units but imitated the combat technique of the phalanx. They attacked in serried ranks and were consequently decimated. They robbed themselves of their advantage of mobility and co-ordinated action by the two formations did not take place.

The remaining Spartans occupied a small elevation about three kilometres from Lechaion and 300 or 400 metres from the sea where they took up a defensive position. The intention to obtain reinforcements from Lechaion to relieve the Spartan detachment did not materialize since in the meantime the Athenian hoplites from Corinth had formed up to attack the elevation. Only a part of the Spartan force succeeded in breaking through to Lechaion.

For the first time, the lightly armed peltasts had gained a victory by concerted action with the phalanx. It proved that lightly armed and manoeuvrable units were capable of wearing down and then defeating heavily armed infantry formations. At the same time, it was clear that the peltasts could not operate as an independent force either but had to be covered by heavily armed infantry or by mounted units since it was only the commitment of the Athenian phalanx, which had been held in reserve, that ensured a total victory.

The defeat of the Spartans underlined the inadequate cooperation between the cavalry and the heavy infantry. In the following period, the Spartans were also obliged to train more of their soldiers as light infantry and to use the peltasts in association with the phalanx.

The peltasts of Athens again demonstrated their tactical usefulness with a second victory at Abydos. From the political point of view, it has to be admitted that these two battles did not exercise a long-term influence on the balance of power in Greece and, despite its loss of prestige, Sparta maintained its supremacy, at least on the mainland. Athens regained complete freedom of action although only as a second-rank power now. It was the Persian Empire, as a complacent onlooker, that derived the greatest advantage from the Corinthian Wars. The weakening of Sparta, which was unable to wage war both in Europe and in Asia at the same time, sealed the fate of Ionia and of the many Greek cities on the west coast of Asia Minor which were again placed under the rule of the Achaemenidae by the Peace of Antalcidas in 386 B.C., the so-called "Royal Peace".

LEUCTRA

371 B.C.

The Spartans utilized the "Peace of Antalcidas" concluded in Susa to consolidate their hegemony in Greece which had been badly shaken by the preceding events. Their policy towards Thebes hardened in consequence and it came to a clash between the two.

A democratic transformation took place in the greatest city-state of Boeotia. The pro-Spartan oligarchy was removed and the mass of the citizens demonstrated that they were prepared to fight for independence with all the means at their disposal. A bold attack by the democratic leader Pelopidas on the town stronghold Cadmea forced the Spartan garrisons to withdraw in 379 B.C. Pelopidas was aided by Epaminondas, the commander of the young élite corps known as the "Sacred Guard" and a strategist of great experience. He soon appreciated the limited economic and military potential of Thebes in the coming campaign and thus endeavoured to compensate for the superiority of his opponent by tactical adroitness.

At this time, an alliance seemed likely with Athens which had founded a second but smaller Attic League in opposition to the interests of Sparta. However, fearing that its neighbour Thebes might become too powerful in the event of victory, Athens assumed a position of benevolent neutrality towards Sparta when the latter organized a strong army to "establish order" in Boeotia. In the summer of 371 B.C., at a peace congress in Sparta attended by most of the Greek city-states, the hosts made clear their intention, with the assistance of Athens and Persia and using force if necessary, of insisting on respect for the status quo. This led to an open break with the Thebans leaving the meeting, trusting to the striking force of their army which had been reorganized by Epaminondas. Thus the Boeotian War broke out, as described in the fourth book of Xenophon's *Greek History*.

There was a speedy reaction by the leaders of Sparta to the situation which had now developed. An army headed by King Cleombrotus set off along a mountain road skirting the coast in the direction of Boeotia with the intention of overwhelming the enemy in a surprise attack.

Apart from the Theban contingent, the only troops that Epaminondas had to oppose him were those from the allied Boeotian cities. He concentrated his forces in a fortified camp at the foot of a hill near Leuctra about 13 kilometres southwest of Thebes and waited for the Spartans to approach. There could be no question any longer of a surprise attack. Cleombrotus was obliged to take note of the opposing forces and likewise established a fortified camp only 2 kilometres from the enemy, a plain separating the two armies. With his 10,000 hoplites and 1,000 horsemen, the king possessed numerical superiority. Epaminondas had only 6,000 infantry but disposed of 1,500 mounted warriors, in keeping with the renown of Boeotia as a centre of Greek horse-breeding. From the relative strengths of the two armies before the battle, it was apparent that the only chance for Thebes of victory was by deviating from the customary hoplite tactics. The traditional phalanx battle-order offered no prospect of success against the greater numbers of the Spartans.

In his dispositions prior to the battle, Epaminondas took account of the advantage in numbers of his cavalry and of the good manoeuvrability of his units. As an experienced general, he paid great attention to the situation report and the reconnaissance of enemy activity. He was able to choose the field of battle since the Spartans had failed to surprise him and he had been able to set up a fortified camp in readiness for them.

While Cleombrotus's troops were still in their camp, Epaminondas formed up his units in an oblique line of battle. On the left wing, he positioned 50 ranks of infantry, the centre was held by the 300 men of the Sacred Guard and the remaining infantry formed the phalanx only eight shields deep on the right. By strengthening the left wing to an unusual degree at the expense of the right, Epaminondas created a spearhead with which to crush the right wing of the enemy phalanx which normally dictated the course of the battle. Cleombrotus followed conventional tactics, arraying his phalanx twelve shields deep on the right wing

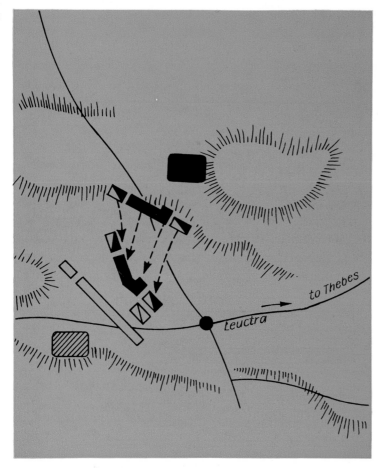

	Theban phalanx with strengthened left wing
	Theban camp
	Theban cavalry
	Spartan phalanx
	Spartan cavalry
	Spartan camp
--→	deployment for the oblique battle-order

with the infantry of the Peloponnesian allies forming the left. The Spartan cavalry —like their Theban counterparts, and presumably to deal with them—were drawn up in front of the phalanx.

As in many other actions, there were certain special details which played a part of Leuctra. Thus the day of the battle happened to fall on a public holiday when the Spartans had little inclination for fighting. Epaminondas used this opportunity for a ruse by instructing some of his troops to return to the camp. The Spartans concluded that there would be no battle and large numbers of them returned to their base, too. Epaminondas took advantage of this situation to re-form his units and ordered his cavalry to attack the weaker force of the enemy, who was overcome and routed in no time at all. The weakness of the Spartan line of battle was now only too apparent. Some of the cavalry had to withdraw to the flanks where they were unable to influence the further course of the battle while the rest

caused confusion in the phalanx positioned behind them. The Theban cavalry, on the other hand, left their original position at the front after launching their successful attack and, as planned, strengthened the left wing which was to decide the outcome of the battle.

At this point, Epaminondas had approximately made up for the initial inequality between the two armies. The Theban infantry exploited the confusion in the ranks of the Spartan phalanx and went over to the attack. Cleombrotus answered this by attempting an encircling manoeuvre with his right wing but the presence of the Sacred Guard in the front line thwarted this. The powerful left wing of the Thebans broke through the enemy ranks at critical points and prevented the Spartans from re-forming. After the right wing had been hopelessly beaten, the units of the Pelopon-

Attack by phalanx. Battle-scene on a Chalcidian vase, 6th century B.C. Cabinet des Médailles, Louvre, Paris

EVPVTION

nesian allies on the left likewise fell back. Cleombrotus was killed and the leaderless army, leaving a thousand of their comrades dead on the field of battle, fled back to their camp, where they asked the Thebans for a truce.

With this victory in open battle, Epaminondas had attained his immediate objective in full. However, the battle had so exhausted his own units that he did not consider that he was strong enough to storm the fortified camp of the Spartans and complete the destruction of their forces. Such an end to the action would have taken a heavy toll of human life. This he had to avoid since he believed that further battles would follow when he would need a hard-hitting army. Despite this, the defeat of aristocratic Sparta was not at all without political significance since several of the city-states which had been forced into alliance with it broke away and restored their democratic order.

Leuctra ended Spartan hegemony. With the advance of the Theban army under Epaminondas across the Isthmus of Corinth, almost the whole of Greece celebrated the liberation of the helots of Messenia from the harsh yoke of their Spartan rulers. Athens, however, now openly took the side of Sparta to prevent Theban ascendancy at the expense of Sparta. The death of Epaminondas in battle at Mantinea in Arcadia in 362 B.C. made this fear groundless. A state of equilibrium existed among the Greek *poleis* until the Macedonians made up their mind to seize the vacant leadership.

The battle of Leuctra showed that it was possible for a numerically superior army to be beaten by better generalship. The traditional phalanx did indeed remain the most important element but its co-ordination with the cavalry now became a matter of first importance.

It was the limited nature of the Theban reserves of manpower which had obliged Epaminondas to develop a new approach in handling troop formations in order to compensate for this. He thus came to abandon the traditional principle of a uniform distribution of the troops available in a linear formation in favour of the oblique line of battle which he pioneered. Since this time, commanders have diversified the concentration of troops in the front line and have sought to identify the strategic points vital to victory. The defeat of the experienced and more numerous Spartans provided food for thought and encouraged many generals to make a careful study of past battles and analyze their own experience.

Leuctra was the beginning of a new phase in development of the cavalry. Employed hitherto as irregular units for covering the flanks, it became the mobile part of the army and had to acquire the discipline and organization of the latter in order to perform the manoeuvres necessary. At Leuctra, the Theban cavalry of Pelopidas had thrown back their immediate opponent and had brought confusion to the battle-order of the phalanx; nevertheless, the Theban horsemen had operated throughout as a disciplined formation. Their high standard of training enabled them to disengage as a single unit from the battle and to take up a new position.

Epaminondas introduced the idea of a thrust forward in the main direction by a powerful concentration of his own forces whilst at the same time holding back the enemy at other points by forces numerically inferior to those of the opponent. His contribution to military science is to be seen as his well-organized co-ordination of the infantry and cavalry in the battle, the planning of the actions of the two wings before the encounter and the exact execution of the tactics planned. No less than Alexander the Great achieved his military successes on the basis of the tactical principles worked out by Epaminondas.

GAUGAMELA / 331 B.C.

King Philip of Macedonia (356–336 B.C.), after a long struggle, succeeded in uniting all the Greek *poleis* with the exception of Sparta under his patronage in the Corinthian League, which set itself the aim of breaking the power of the Persians and of expelling them from Asia Minor. Following the murder of Philip as the result of an aristocratic plot, the anti-Macedonian party of Greece under the leadership of the great orator Demosthenes of Athens persuaded several cities to break away. Thus it was only after dealing with these and ensuring the strategic defence of his flanks in Illyria and Thrace as far as the Danube that the young King Alexander (336–323 B.C.), was able to devote himself again to the campaign against the Persian Empire. His education by the philosopher Aristotle and his study of Greek military history had awakened an early interest in military affairs in this talented young man. With Macedonia and Greece, he possessed a double reservoir on which to draw for his well-equipped army in which the infantry and the cavalry played the leading roles. Maritime forces were set up only to the extent that he considered necessary for the support of his land army. Chariots and war-elephants were not used in his army. He concentrated on ways of combating them successfully.

In 334 B.C., he started his campaign against the Persians with a force consisting of 30,000 infantry—including 7,000 Greeks—and 5,000 mounted warriors from Thessaly and Macedonia under the experienced command of Parmenio, Perdiccas, Cleitus, Craterus, Antigonus, Ptolemy and the young Hephaestion. Important victories along the River Granicus and at Issus and Tyre did indeed drive the Persians from all the Mediterranean coasts and, with the occupation of Syria and Egypt, Alexander was able to secure protection for his supply lines and communications zone. However, as he advanced towards the heart of the Persian Empire, his troops were once again confronted by a superior army, this time at Gaugamela.

In the Macedonian army, the backbone of the infantry was formed by the free peasants and that of the cavalry by the land-owning aristocracy. The principles of recruitment employed divided the country into districts, each of which represented a military unit. There were six infantry districts and sixteen cavalry districts.

The foot-soldiers were organized as light, medium and heavy units. The light infantry, with their bow and arrow, sling and javelin, opened the hostilities. The medium infantry known as the hypaspists and equipped with lances and large shields, served as a link between the cavalry and the heavy infantry units in combat. The élite troops were the silver shield-bearers; they were similar to the peltasts but did not carry javelins. The main element in the battle-order was the traditional heavy phalanx of the sarissophors, the first six ranks of which were equipped with lances (sarissae) of up to 6 metres in length. They also carried swords, helmets and hexagonal shields. The phalanx was made up of 16,000 to 18,000 warriors and was 8 to 24 shields deep. The smallest unit in the phalanx was the lochos, a file of 16 warriors, i.e., 256 men in all, was called a syntagma. A small phalanx consisted of 16 syntagmas, a large phalanx being made up of four small ones. Thus the large phalanx—although it was a tactical unit in combat—was subdivided for organizational purposes.

The cavalry was likewise divided into light, medium and heavy units. The light units wore no protective clothing and were armed with bow and arrow, a short lance and javelins. They provided cover for the flanks and rear of the battle-array. The medium units were trained to fight on foot or on horseback. The heavy cavalry, equipped with sarissae, swords or scimitars, carried out the main attack. Unlike the older Greek cavalry, the Macedonian force was an independent part of the army and attacked in square, rhomboid or wedge formations.

The exceptional fighting power of the Macedonian army was achieved by its tactical organization and the high degree of manoeuvrability which resulted from this. Individual training, unit exercises and the instruction of the commanders were considered major factors in improving

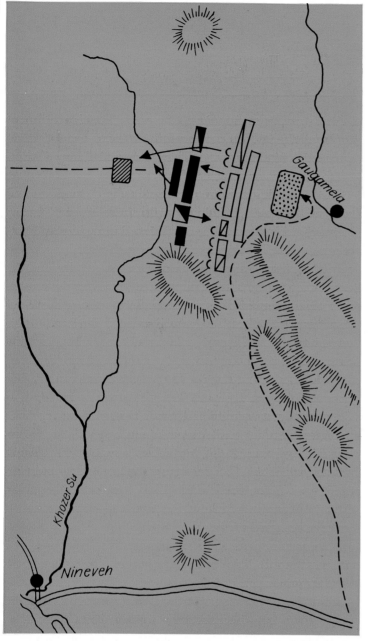

■	Macedonian infantry
◪	Macedonian cavalry
▢	Persian infantry
◩	Persian cavalry
▨	Persian camp
∩∩∩	Persian scythed chariots and elephants
‑ ‑ ‑ ▶	routes of approach
⟶	directions of attack

combat effectiveness. The phalanx was the hard core of the battle-order. The medium infantry, the guard and the heavy infantry were usually located on the right wing while the left consisted of the light infantry and the Thessalian cavalry. Sometimes light infantry units and light cavalry formations were formed up in front of the line of battle to open the action and to deal with chariots and war-elephants. The attack was generally launched on the right wing by the heavy cavalry under the personal leadership of Alexander, the flanks being covered by the phalanx. The hypaspists then advanced through the break in the enemy line. The destruction of the enemy was the task of the heavy infantry while the light cavalry acted as a pursuit force.

Little change had taken place in the Persian army since its first encounters with the Greek city-states. Apart from the King's Guard and the formation of Greek mercenaries, the employment of which had increased during the 4th century B.C., all the branches of the army used irregular combat techniques and relied on their far superior numbers. War-elephants and scythed chariots, developed from those pioneered by the Egyptians and Assyrians, were used in combat but not in a co-ordinated manner. The Persian army did not operate as a coherent unit; the individual generals and satraps did not work together and often pursued their own aims. It was usually the king and his guard that held the army together and when he departed—as at Issus in 333 B.C.—it generally happened that the battle-order disintegrated.

In the spring of 331 B.C., Alexander drew up a strategic plan for the total defeat of the Persian army and for the "march into the interior" in preparation for the occupation of the political and cultural centres of Babylon, Susa, Persepolis and Ecbatana. A major factor was the strategic control of the "King's Road" linking Sardis and Susa.

Alexander advanced from Egypt towards the Persian army, battle being joined at Gaugamela, 400 kilometres north of Babylon. In this, the last and really decisive battle of the war, the two armies operated from fortified camps.

The Persians numbered 60,000 to 80,000 infantry, 12,000 cavalry, 100 scythed chariots and 15 war-elephants. Alexander commanded two large phalanxes 30,000 men strong, two small phalanxes of 10,000 hypaspists and 4,000 to 7,000 horsemen, apart from lightly armed troops.

Darius III had selected the terrain of Gaugamela as the battlefield since he wanted to use part of the King's Road as an approach route and the flat nature of the land was well-suited to his elephants, scythed chariots and large numbers of cavalry. As at Issus, his plan was to encircle the enemy on both wings, these being supported at the front by strong cavalry units and infantry. The king himself was at the centre of this line-up, surrounded by the guard and the best contingents of the Persian infantry, Greek mercenaries, war-elephants and scythed chariots. As an additional precaution foot-traps were laid in front of this disposition. This and other details are known because the king's battle-plan fell into the hands of the victor after the battle. Arrian used it in his expert description of the event in the third book of his *Anabasis*, which is based on the written reports of the two eyewitnesses Ptolemy and Aristobulus (from Cassandraea).

Before the battle, Alexander the Great had made a careful reconnaissance of the terrain and drawn up his tactical plan accordingly. He identified the immediate aim of the Persians to seize his army in a pincer movement and crush it by superiority of numbers. He decided to counter this by a massive concentration of his forces against the Persian centre.

He formed up his army in two wings with a camp at the rear, assigning a reserve unit for the defence of this. He placed the whole of his heavy cavalry on the right wing, the heavy phalanxes covering it on the left flank and light units on the right. Light and medium infantry and cavalry units took up their position on the left wing under the command of Parmenio. The baggage train remained in the camp, in the direct vicinity of the army. By the tactical development of his troops on the wings, mostly cavalry, and the establishment of a second line of Greek units, Alexander counterbalanced the greater numbers of the Persians. By executing a half-turn to the right, he also succeeded in opening up the Persian line, forcing them to re-form.

He was able to convey the impression that he intended to withdraw from the battlefield. Thereupon the Persians attacked his left wing with cavalry and scythed chariots. The Macedonians were able to throw them back, the scythed chariots coming within range of the light infantry units and being forced to withdraw with heavy losses.

It was now that Alexander with his right wing and at the head of his heavy cavalry launched his counter-attack on the Persian centre. After heavy fighting—especially with the King's Guard—he achieved a breakthrough and then swung round to the left. The attack was carried out with such vigour that Alexander came very close to Darius in person who was only saved by the courage of his "Immortals". The Persian king then committed the strategic mistake, however, of once again deserting his army although the battle was not yet irretrievably lost. He withdrew to his

following double page:
Battle-scene between foot-warriors and horsemen, on the Alexander Sarcophagus of Sidon, end of 4th century B.C. Archaeological Museum, Istanbul

base at Arbela, the name by which some authors prefer to call the battle.

In the meantime, the Persian cavalry, after making several attacks on the right wing, broke through the Macedonian left wing, pushed on to the camp at the rear and plundered it. It was only the second line, the Greek reserve units, which were now able to stabilize the front again to some extent. Alexander learnt of the danger to his left wing and had to swing round with his cavalry in order to restore the original battle-order. Thus a battle within a battle was fought by the cavalry formations of the two armies, the outcome of which was decided by the Macedonian units. At the same time, the Persian army learnt that the king had fled. It ceased to function as a single body and disintegrated in the general flight.

Gaugamela was a pitched battle in which both sides were able to deploy their armies in full according to their particular tactical plans. Whereas the Persians operated with a centre and two wings, the Macedonians fought with two wings only, the right one of which, as the stronger, was intended as the spearhead of the counter-attack. The terrain was especially suitable for the cavalry, the phalanxes, the war-elephants and the scythed chariots. Alexander's personal leadership in the battle and his appearance at the head of his troops in dangerous situations influenced the course of the fighting in his favour. Darius III, on the other hand, fearing for his life, prematurely left the battlefield and left his army to its fate at a moment when it even still had a slight chance of success. Although the Macedonians had broken through the Persian centre, fierce resistance was offered, particularly by the King's Guard. The Macedonian phalanxes on the flanks had been unable to keep pace with the rapid cavalry attack so that a gap opened in the front at this point. The phalanxes tried to close up, with the result that they became separated from the left wing, a circumstance which assisted the Persian counter-breakthrough.

The advantage of Alexander's strategy is to be seen in the fact that he reconnoitred the area before the battle, drew up a definite plan of attack with provision for troop movements during the action, kept in touch with the developments which took place and allowed his subordinate commanders freedom of action within the scope of the tasks assigned to them. In contrast to this, the scythed chariots and war-elephants of the Persians were not employed to their full advantage and consequently did not have much effect on the course of the battle.

The victory of Alexander the Great at Gaugamela proved to be more than just a military success and in fact it was the death-blow for the state of the Achaemenidae. From its ruins, a Macedonian world-empire was to emerge, leading to the Hellenistic Age.

CHANG-PING

In the early days of China, during the second millennium B.C., a few great tribes fought for supremacy, the losers being enslaved by the victors. About 1050 B.C., the Chou defeated the Yin at Muye and founded a new dynasty which exercised effective power until the 8th century B.C. After this, the Chou, as the Sacred Emperors ("Sons of Heaven"), were only left with their original homeland as royal demesne, whilst seven principalities succeeded in subjugating about sixty weaker ones by the 5th century B.C. and emerged in actual fact as independent states, the so-called "Quarrelling Realms", according to the chroniclers.

One of these, a tribe of immigrants known as the Ch'in, and controlling the western marches, rapidly achieved an outstanding position. The Ch'in lords, who began to expand their territory after their victory over Wei at the battle of Shao-liang in 418 B.C., were noteworthy for their appreciation of the social changes taking place at that time. The reforms of Shang Yang in the 4th century established a legal basis for the ownership of landed property which had developed in the meantime, promoted peasant smallholdings and encouraged the commodity economy of the emergent towns. The holding of national censuses, the introduction of the cereal duty as a basic tax and the minting of coins assisted in the unification of the administrative apparatus. In 325 B.C., the Ch'in adopted the royal title of "Wang", traditionally the exclusive prerogative of the "Son of Heaven". This "infringement of protocol" was inevitably followed by a military confrontation with the Chou.

As in the Near East, the Chinese armies had infantry, cavalry and chariot units, too. The initially irregular method of combat of the tribal bands was replaced in the 6th century B.C. by a more tightly organized military organization similar to that which existed in the army of Alexander the Great.

A special feature here is the further development and more efficient use of war-chariots. There were two types, differing in construction, equipment, crew and "power unit". These were the general-purpose war-chariot, drawn by four horses, and a heavy vehicle which needed twelve oxen to haul it. The crew of the light and speedy chariot consisted of three heavily armed warriors actually on the vehicle and three sections of infantry providing forward and lateral cover, a total of 75 combatants in all. Thus this type of chariot was not used on its own and, as a strong fighting-unit, played an effective role on the battlefield. These chariots were organized in formations, the smallest numbering five vehicles and the next biggest ten. There were also groups of fifty and a hundred such vehicles, however. The heavy waggons, hauled by oxen, were employed for the transportation of siege equipment and field-works but, if necessary, were also used for defensive actions. In addition, each war-chariot was always accompanied by a transport-waggon with 25 warriors for additional protection.

The cavalry likewise played a significant role. Tactical groups of five, ten, one hundred and two hundred horsemen were used in disciplined formations. They were employed in every kind of military situation—for reconnaissance, attack, defence and the pursuit of a routed enemy. Their equipment and arms were of standardized patterns.

In general, the infantry was not divided into heavily and lightly armed units but was primarily a single formation, this state of affairs resulting from the leading position of the chariot and cavalry units in the order of battle and in military manoeuvres. An infantry unit of five warriors was known as a Wu, 25 as a Liang, 125 as a Tsu, 500 as a Liu, 2,500 as a Si and 12,500 as a Jin. The biggest formation consisted of 37,500 foot-soldiers, i.e., three Jins. Before the battle, each Jin was assigned its task within the framework of the operation as a whole, taking up its position in the centre, in the vanguard or at the rear. Seen as a whole, the function of the foot-soldiers was to provide cover for other units.

Another characteristic of Chinese armies was the highly developed technique of command based on generalized principles of military science. Flags, signs, drums and

War-chariot in the battle of Chang-ping. Painting by Heinz
Zander (1976). Armeemuseum der DDR, Dresden

gongs were employed for the leadership of the troops. Drums were mainly used for the transmission of signals such as the command to attack or retreat to the individual units. Verbal commands were passed on to the smaller formations by dispatch riders.

The battle order of the Chinese armies in the "Period of the Quarrelling Realms" (475–222 B.C.) seems to be a complicated pattern and gives the impression of stagnation similar to that which actually occurred to some extent in the Greek phalanx. Nevertheless, it demonstrates the quality of leadership expected from military commanders who had to co-ordinate chariots, infantry and mounted forces.

As a rule, the order of battle consisted of five parts, the centre with the commander-in-chief, the left and right wings, the vanguard and the rearguard. In principle, each of these five was supposed to consist of a Jin, i.e., 12,500 men. The backbone of the line of battle was always the section centred around a war-chariot, shielded at the front and sides by infantry and followed by a transport waggon.

The battle of Chang-ping—in 280 B.C. or somewhat later—was a land engagement between two almost equally matched armies, that of the Chou and that of the Ch'in under Bo Ch'i. Both were drawn up in the order already mentioned and both consisted of all three types of troops, including the five Jin units specified in the regulations. The Ch'in army had the advantage of being able to operate from a fortified camp while the Chou troops had to attack while on the move. This meant that Bo Ch'i was one-up to start with since the chariot teams in particular needed a camp behind the lines as a supply base and, in addition, it provided reliable protection in the event of a retreat.

The two armies clashed in the classic order of battle. Bo Ch'i showed himself to be an experienced general by the way in which he lured the enemy into the trap with the aid of a trick. He certainly realized that when a battle took place between armies of approximately the same strength, of identical type and with a common battle-order victory could only be achieved by superior tactics. His position was strengthened by the fact that the commander of the Chou army had not reconnoitred the terrain before the battle and had consequently not noticed the Ch'in camp. When Bo Ch'i subsequently withdrew in the direction of his camp, his adversary concluded that he was retreating from the battlefield.

At this, the Chou army speeded up its rate of attack with the result that their ranks spread out and the original line of battle was lost. Already before his withdrawal, Bo Ch'i had laid an ambush, allocating 25,000 troops for this purpose. The advancing Chou troops were suddenly attacked by these units. Before they could recover and reorganize themselves, an attack was launched on their wings by Bo Ch'i's horsemen. Finally, a counter-attack was made by the Ch'in infantry, likewise from the fortified field-encampment. The Chou forces were now surrounded on all sides. It was too late for them to take up an organized defensive position and they suffered a devastating defeat. Since there was no longer any demand for slaves at this time, the prisoners taken were buried alive, the idea of this being to discourage any further resistance.

This battle demonstrated the outstanding generalship of Bo Ch'i, the noteworthy standard of training of his troops and the manoeuvrability of his army. It is evident that the chariot, cavalry and infantry forces as independent branches of the army had mastered the art of tactical co-ordination in large measure. The war-chariots showed their versatility both in attack and defence and, in association with the troops assigned to cover them, as powerful units in the military system. It was in the art of war as practised by the Chinese that this very specific development attained perfection.

As noted already by the great historian Se Ma-tien (145–86 B.C.) in his *Historical Records*, the victory of Bo Ch'i had long-term consequences. The Chou were unable to recover from the blow and the Ch'in annexed their domains. Wang Cheng (or Tsung), who was born in 259 B.C., subsequently subjugated all the other constituent states, expanded China as far as Canton and the South China Sea, linked the border fortifications against the Huns in the North to the Great Wall and as the Emperor Shi Huang Ti (or Ch'in Shih Huang, 221–210 B.C.), also known—not very aptly—as the "Chinese Napoleon", established a great centralized monarchy. Under the next dynasty, the Han, which was of peasant origin, this empire experienced its first classic age as a "state of officials".

A few years ago, water-well builders discovered a pit in the Province of Shensi east of the tomb of Ch'in Shih Huang. This pit, 210 by 60 metres, with a depth of four and a half to seven metres, was paved with bricks and contained very well-preserved clay figures in life size or even larger than life size from the Ch'in dynasty. Their number is estimated at 6,000. These figures evidently represent an army in complete battle-order, warriors with helmets and harness, symmetrically arranged and equipped with real arms, mostly made of bronze, as, for example, bows and arrows, swords, spears and crossbows. The whole is completed by war-chariots drawn by four horses and arranged at equal distances. Up till now only about the tenth part of the warrior figures have been excavated. Yet, once the investigation of the finds by experts is completed, this archaeologically unique treasure will afford us an incomparable insight into Chinese warfare towards the close of the "Period of the Quarrelling Realms" in the 3rd century B.C.

The struggle on the bridge. Idealized representation with foot-warriors, horsemen and war-chariots on both sides. Bas-relief from a burial chamber in Wu-liang-tse, c. A.D. 150.

CANNAE
216 B.C.

By the beginning of the 3rd century B.C., the up-and-coming Roman Republic, which three generations before had occupied only the district of Latium, had completed the subjugation of the Apennine Peninsula. The last independent Greek city, Taranto in Southern Italy, had called on Pyrrhus, king of Epirus, to come to its aid but his efforts were in vain. After initial failures and doubtful successes—hence the term "Pyrrhic victory"—the army of Hellenistic mercenaries had to yield to the redoubtable Romans in 275 B.C. Since, at the same time, Carthage was expanding its sphere of influence in Sicily, struggles between different interests in the city of Messina led to the intervention of both powers, the ultimate result of which was the protracted rivalry between them for supremacy in the western Mediterranean.

In the first of the three Punic Wars (264–241 B.C.), the sea power Carthage and the land power Rome found it difficult to get to grips with each other. It was only when Rome built itself a large fleet and, despite numerous perilous setbacks, eventually achieved victory with its ships equipped with the newly developed boarding-bridges, near the Aegadian Islands that it was able to force its adversary to make peace. This was how Sicily became its first "province" and granary. Naval supremacy had passed to the Romans and they exploited it immediately to establish themselves in Sardinia, Corsica and the Illyrian islands in the Adriatic. On land and utilizing the campaign experience they had acquired, they concerned themselves with the subjugation of the Celtic tribes settling on the plain of the River Po. Carthage looked for means of making up for its losses. Since the terms of the peace treaty prevented it from building a fleet, the Carthaginian general Hamilcar Barca created a broad basis for the re-organization of the army by either subjugating the Iberian tribes or making treaties of alliance with them and incorporating their warriors in the Carthaginian forces. The consolidation of Carthage's "mainland colony" was continued by his son-in-law Hasdrubal and by his son Hannibal (246–183 B.C.) with the intention of recommencing the war against the Romans from here.

The latter were not unaware of what they had in mind and, as a precaution, they forced Carthage to accept a new treaty which prohibited its general from crossing the Ebro. When, however, Rome concluded a provocative alliance with the Greek colony of Sagunto as well, which was situated far to the south of the river, Hannibal was unwilling to hold back any longer. He stormed the besieged city, knowing that this would mean a declaration of war by Rome (218 B.C.).

His plans for the campaign had already been drawn up. Seldom in the history of warfare in Antiquity had such comprehensive plans been prepared. Hannibal's envoys and emissaries streamed out to win potential opponents of Rome for a common action—Macedonians, Illyrians and the Celts of Gaul and the area around the Po. Since the Roman fleet made impossible ambitious undertakings at sea by the enemy, the leaders of Carthage decided in favour of a war on land which obliged the army to set off for Italy across little-known paths over the Pyrenees and the Alps to the River Po—a march of almost 900 kilometres.

Without doubt, Rome was in a better position and had more resources than the aristocratic trade metropolis of Carthage but the Senate's assessment of the situation was too careless. The Roman army had the advantage of fighting on its own ground for the defence of the Republic. Nevertheless, the constantly changing supreme command of two consuls had a detrimental effect on the army, especially since they often held divergent opinions on the conduct of the war. The basic concept for the campaign fluctuated between a direct attack on the city and fortress of Carthage or an offensive against Hannibal's army in the field. Instead of concentrating its troops, Rome actually split up its forces. It was decided that Publius Cornelius Scipio should sail with two legions from Liguria to Iberia, Tiberius Sempronius Longus was to cross from Sicily to Africa with two other legions and Lucius Manlius was to hold

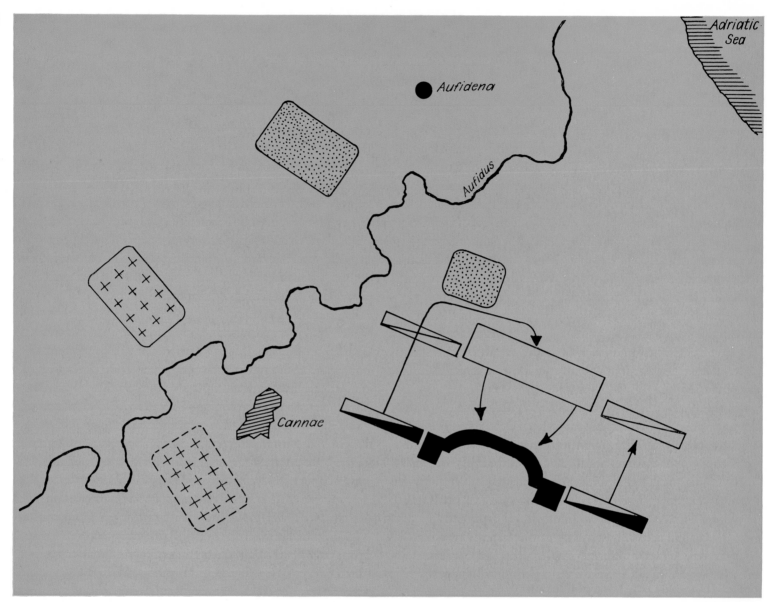

Adriatic
Sea

Aufidena

Aufidus

Cannae

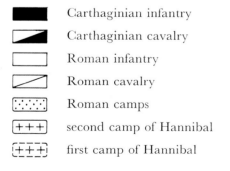

Carthaginian infantry

Carthaginian cavalry

Roman infantry

Roman cavalry

Roman camps

second camp of Hannibal

first camp of Hannibal

back the Gauls. Two legions were left behind for the protection of the capital. The employment of Rome's military resources in such a scattered manner was exactly what Hannibal needed.

The Carthaginian units were divided between the garrison at Carthage with 20,000 men, the reserve in Iberia with 15,000 men and the field army with its 35,000 warriors. It was with these that Hannibal crossed the Ebro in the spring of 218 B.C. and, after minor fighting, reached the plains of the Po at Taurasia.

The memorable "Italian campaign" owed its success to his outstanding powers of organization and his capacity to anticipate the moves of the enemy. Only the vulnerable elephants which Carthage had inherited from the Hellenistic approach to warfare failed to cross the icy and snow-covered paths over the Alps, a march which lasted fifteen days. The Greek trading city of Massalia (Marseilles), which was allied with Rome, had prevented him from marching along the coast and he had thus been obliged to take the more northerly route across the mountains.

Arriving on the plains of Northern Italy, Hannibal defeated a Roman army at the River Ticino and immediately afterwards a second and stronger one at the River Trebia. Most of the Celtic tribes of the area then broke away from Rome and joined Hannibal who stayed among them for the winter. In this way, he acquired a reliable supply-base which was particularly important to him since he was not able to maintain uninterrupted contact with Iberia and Carthage.

The Senate had to give up its intention of sending an expedition to Africa but kept Scipio's troops in Iberia where they harassed the Carthaginian garrisons. Hannibal advanced over the Apennines in 217 B.C. and again defeated his adversary at Lake Trasimeno in Etruria. With the restricted forces at his disposal, he considered that a direct attack on the city of Rome offered little prospect of success and, instead of this, sought to decide events by a pitched battle on a large scale. However, the Roman general Fabius avoided such a confrontation for a lengthy period in order to conserve the combat-efficiency of the legions, this being why he was given the additional name of "Cunctator"— the delayer. This tactic was unpopular with the Romans who had undertaken mighty efforts to reserve the course of the war and in the autumn of 216 B.C. the newly-appointed consuls Lucius Aemilius Paulus and Caius Terentius Varro took the initiative, trusting to their superiority of numbers.

Hannibal had just captured the well-stocked base of Cannae and had established his camp there. Well-rested and in a fortified position, he awaited the approach of the legions who, on completing their approach-march, likewise set up a fortified camp two kilometres away from the enemy.

The Carthaginian army was of extremely varied origin. The Punic troops, apart from the officers, were the least numerous. Carthage, whose citizens also had to serve at sea, had always waged its campaigns with mercenaries and allies from other peoples, including Libyans and Numidians from Northwest Africa, occasionally Greeks and, more recently, Iberians. In addition, Hannibal had replenished his forces with Gauls (Celts) and some reinforcements had got through to him. At his disposal for the battle and including the lightly armed troops, he had 40,000 infantry and 10,000 cavalry. Most of them had seen a great deal of active service and, victorious for many years, their combat-morale was high. Their general, who, far from home, had led them from success to success, enjoyed their unconditional respect and confidence. On the silver hexadrachma coined at New Carthage (present-day Cartagena) in 221 B.C. on the occasion of his appointment to be a general he is a beardless young man of pleasant appearance.

Hannibal was not at all a firebrand. He was an expert in both the Hellenistic and Roman styles of warfare and drew on both in his strategy and tactics. He was well aware of the relationship between war and politics and consequently attached no less importance to diplomacy than to the battle-field. From his earliest childhood on, so it is reported, he devoted his life to avenging the unhappy outcome of the First Punic War. His aim was a political one. To permanently secure the position of the Carthaginian oligarchy as a great power, he considered it necessary to destroy the Roman state in Italy.

This is, as it were, a first-hand information. Hannibal's Greek teacher Sosilos was his first biographer, and the *War Commentaries* of Silenos were translated by Lucius Coelius Antipater into Latin; both authors are mentioned by Cornelius Nepos as his literary sources. Polybius, who lived in the house of Aemilius Paulus two lifetimes after this event and who himself had witnessed the destruction of Car-

The battle of Cannae at the beginning of the Carthaginian
counter-attack on the encircled Roman army. Painting by
Heinz Zander (1973). Armeemuseum der DDR, Dresden

thage by his pupil Publius Scipio Aemilianus, was well versed in the family traditions of Roman leadership. Painstakingly he followed Hannibal's traces from battlefield to battlefield before he put the pen to the paper.

The two Roman consuls had 16 legions at their command, a total of some 80,000 infantry and 6,000 cavalry. The structure of the legions also gave Rome a tactical advantage since they had the best-organized infantry battle-order of the time and were superior to the phalanx in all situtations.

The Roman army had been re-organized at the beginning of the century when the maniples, as the basic units of the legion, had not only been increased in numerical strength but had also been given standard equipment. Each maniple now consisted of *hastati*, *principes* or *triarii*—heavy, medium or light infantry of the first, second and third lines. Each legion was made up of 30 maniples, each with 120 infantry, and ten *turmae* of 30 horsemen each plus 1,200 very lightly armed *velites*. For battle, it was formed up in three lines of ten maniples each. Each maniple, in turn, consisted of twelve rows ten men deep. The space between them was as broad as that occupied by one maniple and was covered at the rear by the second line. The manoeuvrability of the legion was largely achieved by the rapidly performed regroupings of the maniples which were practised in combat-training. In actions against a mounted enemy, the legion took up a circular position with the baggage-train in the centre. Marching was done in three staggered columns, the *velites* providing cover and performing reconnaissance duties. Unlike the hoplite phalanx of the Greeks and Hellenes, the organization of the legion in maniples enabled the Roman army to fight on any kind of terrain. The infantry, drawn from the social class of the free peasantry, formed the backbone of the army. The essential conditions for the creation of a hard-hitting cavalry were lacking and some had to rely on its Italian allies in this respect. The tactical use of the infantry could not always compensate in full for these shortcomings.

The battlefield of Cannae near the River Aufidus was fairly flat and sparsely wooded, permitting good deployment for both sides. With their maniple organization, the legions were able to take up a strong position but the terrain was no less to the liking of Hannibal's superior cavalry. The battle began with skirmishes being launched from both camps but these played no part in the tactical line-up

of the two armies for the main confrontation. The two consuls in command of the Roman army held opposing views on how to fight the battle. Aemilius Paulus wanted to avoid a clash for as long as possible but Terentius Varro favoured immediate action. The latter got his way since he happened to be the commander-in-chief on duty on the day that two armies lined up for battle.

He arrayed the legions in a frontal confrontation along a length of two kilometres in three lines of 12 ranks each, i.e., in a staggered pattern of 36 ranks deep in all. The line-up was covered by the lightly-armed troops and by 4,000 horsemen under Varro himself on the left wing and 2,000 cavalry under Aemilius Paulus on the right. 10,000 troops were assigned to the defence of the camp. With this order of battle, there was the risk that it could be rolled up into a gigantic tangle if attacked from the flanks.

Hannibal placed his troops in a sickle-shaped formation with the weaker units in the centre and the élite contingents and cavalry on the wings. On the extreme right wing, he positioned 2,000 light Numidian cavalry under Hanno and assigned 8,000 heavy African cavalry—mostly Mauretanians—under Hasdrubal to the extreme left. Next to the cavalry units on each wing, there were 6,000 heavily armed Libyans, 16 ranks deep. The 20,000 Gauls and Iberians of the centre were staggered in ten ranks. 8,000 lightly-armed troops provided cover for the line of battle.

The Punic commander expected a concentrated Roman attack on his centre. He had made a thorough study of the tactics of the legions and to some extent had trained his infantry units in their combat techniques. His plan was characterized by a special irony in that after eliminating the numerically and qualitatively inferior Roman cavalry right at the start his idea was to pin down the maniples of the legions in a very confined space und force them to fight as a phalanx.

The great battle began with skirmishes involving the lightly-armed troops of both sides who then withdrew behind their own ranks. The first move took place according to plan when the Carthaginian cavalry attacked the Roman horsemen on both wings and completely routed them. The legions thus lost their cover on the flanks. However, the loss of his mobile units did not particularly worry Varro and he ordered his legions to advance against the Carthaginian centre. In the face of this strong attack, the Iberians

Carthaginian (?) war-elephant, depicted on a Campanian plate of the 3rd century B.C. Villa Giulia, Rome

and Gauls had to fall back, causing a bulge in the Carthaginian line which was occupied by the legions as they followed up. The wings of the Carthaginian army remained in their original position, however, so that the Roman infantry crowded together even more. By this, the legions had lost their advantage of mobility and the initiative passed to Hannibal whose heavily armed Libyans on the left and right flanks now closed in on the Roman flanks. In his attack on the Carthaginian centre at the start, Varro had not been able to break the Carthaginian line but had only forced it to carry out an orderly withdrawal. Hannibal, after achieving a further improvement in his battle-order by closing in the two flanks, was thus able to re-group the units which had withdrawn as well. At the same time, the cavalry under Hasdrubal's command, which was now available again after routing their Roman opposite numbers, were instructed to attack the legions in the rear. The Roman troops were obliged to take up a hopeless, all-round defensive position.

By his tactics, Hannibal had encircled a superior enemy and robbed him of his ability to manoeuvre, rendering him incapable of making a breakthrough in strength in the style of the phalanx. The Romans lost 48,000 killed and 10,000 taken prisoner. 14,000 men, partly cavalry and the rest infantry troops, were able to escape this encirclement, when the Carthaginian centre fell back, by breaking out between this and the flanks. From these units, the military tribune Scipio formed two new legions which were now needed by Rome more urgently than ever before.

Hannibal's victory at Cannae was not simply the result of a successful encirclement of the stronger Roman army but was due above all to the neutralization of the military advantage of manoeuvrability possessed by the legions. The battle demonstrated the great value of first-class cavalry and of a battle-order with additional forces on the extreme flanks. For the Romans, it showed up a weakness of the legion which could only operate at full efficiency when fully deployed. The battle of Cannae refutes the view that an encircling movement carried out on both sides by the weaker force is inadvisable. It rather indicates that even an army with considerably fewer forces than its adversary is capable of winning the day if it uses superior tactics. With the third book of his *History of the World*, on which Titus Livius based his work, Polybius secured for this battle its place in the history of warfare and military theory as a model studied time and again by later commanders.

Down to the present day, scholars have argued about whether Hannibal committed the cardinal error of his life by neglecting to march on Rome after his total victory. Later on he regretted it, but it may be assumed that, in 216 B.C., he doubted rightly the feasibility of taking the city by storm and took the view that a long siege would chain down his forces with ominous results. He believed that he would profit more from the political consequences of Rome's military failure. Some of the Greek cities and the tribes of the Bruttii in Southern Italy did indeed break away from Rome; Syracuse in Sicily and Macedonia, hesitant up till this stage, at last came into the war. However, by this time the spirit of free citizenship was such an integral part of the Roman Republic that it was able to meet this fatal danger by committing all its energy and determination to the struggle. Although the legions did not succeed in defeating Hannibal in Italy, they did destroy the ascendancy of Carthage in Iberia, after which they invaded Africa. At this, the rulers of Carthage recalled their general and his veterans for the defence of their own city. However, despite a daring sea-crossing, Hannibal lost his last battle against Scipio—at Zama, so it is said—and himself recommended a peace treaty which reduced not Rome but Carthage to the status of a minor state.

The "moral censor" Cato (the Elder) used to conclude all his speeches with the words: "As for the rest, it is my opinion that Carthage should be destroyed". After a third Punic War, which may be regarded as an act of aggression on the part of Rome, the pupil of Polybius, acting on the instructions of the Senate, burnt the city down, razed it to the ground, strew salt on its ashes after its struggle for life or death in 146 B.C. and sold the survivors into slavery.

Antique marble bust, said to be portraying Hannibal. Museo Nazionale, Naples

Immediately after the Second Punic War had settled the question of who would control the western Mediterranean, Rome made its presence felt in the eastern part. After some success initially, Hannibal's great plan to mobilize the Hellenistic Diadochi states against Rome as well failed both on account of the rivalries between them and because of the greater social and military potential of the Roman Republic. The Seleucid King Antiochus "the Great" took no part in the Second Macedonian War (200–197 B.C.) and when the Carthaginian general, driven into exile by a Roman ultimatum, later persuaded him, after all, to take up arms, it was the Macedonians who stayed out this time (192–189 B.C.). The consequence was that the realm of the Seleucids soon amounted to no more than Syria while the Macedonians had to withdraw from Greece to their homeland, hand over their fleet, reduce their army to 5,000 men and provide hostages. This harsh peace treaty contained the seeds of a further confrontation and culminated in the Third Macedonian War in 171 B.C.

The political situation in Greece favoured the rearmament carried on by King Perseus in Macedonia. Roman control over the Greek city-states was mainly exercised by supporting oligarchical groups which were unpopular and thus in need of backing. By this, they gave strength to an anti-Roman movement among the democrats reflected in disputes and clashes. Macedonia then offered refuge to all those in Greece persecuted by the "Roman party" and absorbed those capable of bearing arms in its military forces as politically conscious and therefore particularly reliable warriors.

The men of Macedonia capable of bearing arms were now given military training as a matter of course, after which they were transferred to the reserve, from which they could be recalled to active service at any time. Weapons were stockpiled too. At the start of the war, the king had about 21,000 heavy infantry and 4,000 Macedonian and Thracian cavalry at his disposal. Once again, to his great regret, he had to fight unaided by allies.

The Macedonian units used the rigid tactics of the phalanx and were consequently very dependent on the nature of the terrain. Their opportunities in fast-moving warfare lay with the cavalry and for this the tactically superior horsemen of Thrace were particularly suitable. It would have been best to have used them to cut off the Roman lines of communication in the rear and to have conducted a war of attrition by hit-and-run tactics. This was not the course adopted by the king—probably because he considered that the cavalry were needed more urgently to cover the phalanx and the flanks.

The raising and dispatch of the Roman legions took a comparatively long time since there was no sense of urgency about the affair. Nevertheless, by 171 B.C., more than 30,000 legionaries, 10,000 auxiliaries and 40 decked ships plus 10,000 reserve troops had been assembled for the campaign. Despite this concentration of forces, the initial phase was not particularly successful for them. The Macedonian cavalry harassed smaller units and the Roman command could not decide on whether it should seek battle or not. After a while, this was noticed even in Rome and no fewer than three consuls in succession were relieved of their command for not being active enough. On the other hand, the Macedonian military leadership did not continue with their very promising tactics either. In expectation of a decisive encounter, they assigned the cavalry to the phalanx. It was perhaps an error to have concentrated at all on raising infantry units instead of expanding the cavalry still further since Rome had neglected this important branch of the army.

To prevent the legions from suffering further substantial losses from minor actions, the Romans decided that they would have to fight a major battle.

The two armies came face-to-face at Pydna in 168 B.C. The flat terrain favoured both the use of the Macedonian cavalry and phalanx and, on the other hand, the deployment of the legions. The combat area was crossed by a river which separated the two armies. On this battlefield, the Macedonian king concentrated his entire military power, amounting to 40,000 warriors whereas the Romans had only 26,000 men to oppose him. Thus Perseus had the prospect of scoring a victory over the legions of Rome.

The separation of the two armies by the river was a headache for both commanders since they were equally uncertain as to how they should attack. It was only when troops from the two sides came into direct contact with each other whilst watering their horses that fighting broke out. As in the Persian wars, the Macedonian phalanx attacked in close order and had no trouble in driving back the light Roman units deployed in front of the legions. This massive thrust struck the Roman lines with such an impact that even the legionaries had to make a strategic withdrawal, without breaking ranks, however. Due to the low rate of advance of the heavily armed phalanx, the withdrawal of the legions took place as if they were carrying out manoeuvres in their own field-camp with each rank taking the place of the one in front. The greater manoeuvrability of the maniples was able to put a tactically advantageous space between them and the phalanx from which they could mount a new attack.

From their many campaigns, the Roman commanders were already familiar with the strong and weak points of the phalanx and how it operated. It therefore did not escape the notice of the consul Aemilius Paulus (the Younger) that after some time the Macedonian phalanx was no longer advancing in a uniform manner and that gaps had opened in its ranks. He then ordered the maniples of the first two lines to concentrate their attack at these points and instructed the maniples of the third line, the triaries, to attack on the flanks so as to roll up the phalanx from the rear. This second battle-plan took account of the unsystematic use of the enemy cavalry. The Macedonians had given priority to the phalanx and disregarded the experience of Alexander the Great who had always made active use of both kinds of troops, cavalry and infantry. The vastly superior Macedonian cavalry did not attack the legions at Pydna—neither to relieve their own phalanx nor to prevent the execution of the Roman manoeuvre. It is true

Mounted combat. Detail of the Aemilius Paulus base at Delphi, 2nd century B.C. The monument was erected to commemorate the Roman victory over the Macedonians at Pydna.

that they held back the Roman cavalry but did not play their proper part at all at the critical points of the battle and even left the battlefield with all haste when it became apparent that the encircled phalanx would be destroyed. Thus the lack of coordination between the cavalry and the infantry sealed the fate of the superior Macedonian army. 20,000 members of the phalanx were killed and 11,000 were taken prisoner. The fact that the cavalry remained intact was of no use whatsoever to the Macedonian command since, without infantry support, it was incapable of fighting another pitched battle against the legions.

The Roman victory was not, of course, a matter of chance. The Macedonian commanders had not appreciated the advantages of maniple tactics over those of the phalanx. Instead of developing new combat techniques and using the cavalry on a greater scale as a counterweight, they continued to use the outdated techniques from the time of the Persian wars or, at best, of the Diadochi battles, and neglected the co-ordination of the different arms in a criminal manner.

With the victory of the legions over a numerically superior adversary, the battle of Pydna demonstrated that their strategy and tactics represented a significant step forward as compared with the phalanx. In the course of the Punic Wars and afterwards, the Roman military commanders had extended and consolidated their knowledge in this sphere. The deciding factor was not so much the numerical superiority of their army but far more the degree of its manoeuvrability.

An examination of what happened during the battle shows that the massive thrust of the phalanx was still a force to be reckoned with, it is true, but that in the long run, however, it could not survive against infantry formations of greater manoeuvrability such as the legions. The tactical success of the Romans in this battle was the orderly withdrawal of the quicker legions in the face of the slowly advancing phalanx and their re-forming, in the midst of the action, with a revision of the direction of attack. The inactivity of the Macedonian cavalry on the battlefield is an indication that Hellenistic combat-techniques had stagnated. At the beginning of the campaign, the mounted units had waged a kind of guerrilla warfare to good effect against the legions but in the battle they were assigned tasks of second importance providing cover for the phalanx.

While the phalanx of the Macedonians stagnated in its development, constant improvements were made in the equipment, armament and training of the legions on the basis of the experience acquired in the latest campaigns. In Rome, a new generation of commanders emerged who, in the sphere of tactics and strategy and despite the relatively weak cavalry units, proved capable of astonishing achievements. Thus the *res publica Romana* increased its lead over the Hellenistic states in the military sphere, too. The legions were the most highly trained infantry troops of their epoch and had the highest standard of combat readiness, being expert in every kind of attack and defence. They could no longer be outfought by the phalanx. Henceforth the legions could only be beaten by another and more imaginative type of warfare, by even better infantry tactics and more advanced cavalry techniques.

Politically, the defeat at Pydna marked the beginning of the end of the independence not only of Macedonia but of the entire Greek world as well. Macedonia was first of all split up into four helpless mini-states and then converted into a Roman province in 148 B.C., not even retaining the ancient name of the kingdom. Two years later, following the destruction of Corinth by the consul Mummius, the same merciless fate struck Greece. The Roman state expanded as far as Asia and became a new world-empire.

PHARSALUS / 48 B.C.

From the 2nd century B.C. onwards, Rome no longer came up against an opponent which was its equal. Local uprisings in Iberia, Numidia and Asia Minor were put down after protracted hostilities in some cases but these never shook the foundations of the Republic.

A change took place in the structure of Roman society. The old rights of the citizens were hollowed out by slave-ownership on an increasing scale, by the drain on the resources of the conquered provinces, by large-scale trade in the safe waters of the Mediterranean and by usury. The appropriation of the free Italic peasant-holdings by the latifundists broke the back of democracy. Political and social struggles for the leadership of the state were the consequence of this. At the beginning of the 1st century B.C., they reached a climax in the civil wars between the conservative Optimates headed by Sulla and the new-rich Populares under Marius.

The latter was responsible for a reform of the army, which modernized the structure of the legions. The place of the maniple as a tactical unit was taken by the cohort, consisting of three maniples and numbering 600 men. The battle-order of the legions was then ten cohorts in two lines of five ranks each. This improved operational control but there was a loss of manoeuvrability, especially when the terrain was not flat. The cavalry was completely incorporated within the structure of the legion, ceasing to exist as an independent branch of the army. Since the light infantry known as the *velites* was also disbanded, the tactic of skirmishes was no longer used and the determined attack became the sole combat-technique.

Of some military significance were the engineering aspects of the reform. Every legionary now carried not only weapons and personal belongings but also an entrenching tool and other items of pioneer equipment. This naturally resulted in a lower marching speed but the commanders were now able to establish a fortified camp at any time of the day on any type of terrain. The structure of the army was subjected to practical tests and further improved during the wars against the land-hungry Germanic tribes, Mithridates of Pontus, King Tigranes of Armenia and the rebel slaves under Spartacus.

In 60 B.C., in defiance of the political groupings, the generals Crassus, Pompey and Caesar set up the first triumvirate as a step towards a military dictatorship. The Senate was powerless in the face of such a concentration of power which had the whole of the armed forces at its disposal.

When it was the turn of Gaius Julius Caesar to be elected consul in the following year, he used every chance which his function gave to him to expand still further the legions under his command. They reached a rank-and-file strength of up to 4,500 combatants, including the Antique "artillery" assigned to them. This consisted of 55 ballistae firing heavy darts, ten onagers and one catapult. Thus the legions were always capable of capturing even heavily fortified field-camps and could launch an attack while still on the move. Caesar increased the baggage-train which accompanied the legion. This largely consisted of siege equipment and material for establishing a camp transported by 500 mules.

As auxiliary troops, he had archers from Crete and slingers from the Balearic Islands (hence the Latin name). The cavalry attached to the legion had originally consisted of prosperous Roman citizens but mounted Germanic, Iberian and Numidian mercenaries had then taken their place. Caesar increased the manoeuvrability of his army by usually taking 4,000 to 5,000 Gallic horsemen with him.

A change was made in the deployment for the order of battle, the legion being drawn up according to a four-three-three system. The particular feature of this was that the second line served to reinforce the first one whilst the third line, that of the triaries, acted as a reserve for flank attacks or against unexpected enemy breakthroughs in the centre. The creation of a tactical reserve, the establishment of a camp, the provision of cover for his forces whilst on the march and reconnaissance tasks claimed a large part of the military resources at the disposal of the commander.

Caesar devoted particular attention to the order of march. The vanguard consisted of the cavalry and the auxiliary troops, the *auxiliarii*, followed by the main body of the legions with a strong rearguard. Each legion was followed by its baggage-train. The marching speed varied between 25 and 45 kilometres per day, depending on the terrain and the urgency of the situation.

Caesar recognized at an early stage that a command staff was necessary for the leadership of the army. He formed the first organ of command of this kind from the legates and the tribunes and made it responsible at the same time for the training guidance of the commanders at all levels. Thus there was the commander-in-chief and his deputies: the legates, who were the commanders of the legions, the six military tribunes of each legion and the centurions who led the cohorts, the maniples and the centuries. From this time onwards, the commander-in-chief also kept a personal bodyguard at his side. This may be explained, on the

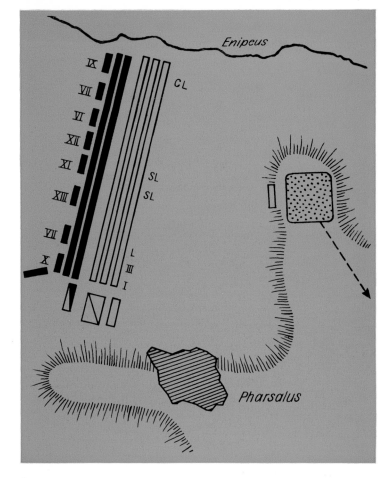

Caesar's infantry

Caesar's cavalry

Pompey's infantry

Pompey's cavalry

Pompey's camp

retreat route of Pompey's defeated troops

I.-L.   legion numbers

S. L.   Syrian legions

C. L.   Cilician legion

one hand, by the rivalries between the commanders which developed from time to time and, on the other, by the occasional reluctance of the auxiliary troops to take part in the battle. Sometimes they even mutinied.

On the basis of the reforms carried out by Marius, Caesar turned the legions into exceptionally hard-hitting combat units and gave them a chain of command which matched the high standard of their equipment and training. He himself engineered the opportunity to test his innovations under campaign conditions by having himself appointed commander-in-chief in Gaul. In a war between 58 and 51 B.C., which he described in glorious prose *(Commentarii de bello Gallico)*, he brought the country under Roman rule, although on one occasion he did indeed meet defeat—by Vercingetorix, chief of the Arverni, at Gergovia.

While Caesar was still in Gaul, Crassus, the greediest of the new-rich of Rome, lost his life in the battle at Carrhae against the Parthians where the Parthian king had the

dead man's mouth stuffed full with gold "so that at last he has enough of it". Unrest broke out in Rome and Pompey was charged with the task of restoring law and order. In the meantime, Caesar's mandate in Gaul, where there was nothing left to conquer, had expired in 49 B.C. and had not been prolonged. The Senate ordered him to disband his legions and demobilize the soldiers. Caesar did not comply with these instructions, which he mistrusted, and concentrated his forces. The Senate then authorized Pompey to enforce its instructions by military means.

The contest had to be fought between the two surviving members of the triumvirate. With the words "alea iacta est" (the die is cast), Caesar crossed the River Rubicon. By this action, he committed high treason in point of law since it was forbidden for army commanders to set foot on Italic soil at the head of their armies in battle order. The inevitable result was a new civil war in which Caesar again furthered his own cause as an eloquent literary witness

Roman warship with legionaries ready for combat, on the fragment of a relief. Museo Vaticano, Rome

(*Commentarii de bello civili* with the battle of Pharsalus in the third book).

After campaigns in various widely dispersed theatres of war, the two generals stood face-to-face in the third phase of this civil war in 48 B.C. at Pharsalus.

Caesar, who had suffered a slight reverse at Dyrrachium which Pompey failed to exploit, marched on Larissa, the residence of Pompey at the time, and at the same time cut off the latter's army from the Syrian legions. Pompey's position deteriorated still further since he was now obliged to move his troops into the interior of the country and consequently lost contact with his powerful fleet. Through his fortified camps on the Adriatic coast, Caesar established a strong basis for the forthcoming campaign and likewise advanced with his forces into the interior of Thessaly where Pompey was intending to link up with Scipio's army.

At Pharsalus not far from Larissa, he erected a fortified camp to bar Caesar's approach. This left the latter with no alternative but to set up a camp himself a few kilometres away from his enemy. The terrain around Pharsalus was flat and excellent for the deployment of the legions.

Caesar drew up his troops in order of battle a number of times to provoke Pompey into joining battle. But the latter's legions stayed in their camp. In this tug-of-war, pay and time played an important role since not every part of the army could be relied on in every situation. After all, the ambitions of the two triumvirs were really a matter of indifference to their troops and whose Republic were they defending for whom? Caesar wanted a quick decision and so he carried out a manoeuvre in the rear of his opponent with the aim of forcing him to deploy his troops. On account of their uncertainty regarding the morale of their soldiers, neither general could afford to be inactive indefinitely and consequently arrayed their forces for the battle. Pompey had 30,000 legionaries and 3,000 horsemen, Caesar likewise 30,000 legionaries and a cavalry force of 2,000. Both sides attached great importance to the deployment of their armies before the start of the action since it was a battle between units with the finest equipment and the highest standard of training.

Pompey drew up his army in three lines with ten ranks each, i.e., in a total depth of 30 ranks. The Cilician legion as the best unit was stationed on the right wing, two Syrian legions formed the centre and the left wing consisted of a

further two legions plus the whole of the cavalry. 2,000 volunteers with a long record of service were distributed along the entire front in the interests of stabilization. The steep banks of the River Enipeus provided protection for the right wing. Pompey took up his position with the cavalry on the left wing. The camp and baggage-train was protected by seven cohorts. With this deployment, his aim was to allow Caesar's legion to open the battle, then to launch a counter-attack and, at the same time, to threaten Caesar's right flank and rear with the cavalry and the lightly armed units.

Caesar likewise arrayed his legions in three lines. His best combat-unit, the Tenth Legion which had won fame in Gaul, was drawn up on the right wing. The Eighth and Ninth Legions, weakened by the preceding actions, formed the left wing which was safeguarded by the river. Light infantry and cavalry provided cover for the right wing while the remaining legions were stationed in the centre. Caesar realized that his right wing was not at all strong, despite the presence of the élite legion, so he took one cohort each from the third line of the legions and, for the first time, created an additional fourth line. Furthermore, six cohorts were instructed to take up a position behind the right wing at right-angles to the front, the others being kept as an operational reserve. The tactic according to the battle-plan was that the six cohorts should go into action together with the cavalry. For the time being, the third line had to take no action and was to take part in the battle only at the personal command of Caesar.

Like Caesar, Pompey had drawn up his legions in the well-tried order of battle but the former's concept revealed superior anticipation and more inventiveness and gave a hint of complex combat-manoeuvres. As Pompey had expected, the battle began with the attack launched by Caesar's legions. They hurled their javelins and then fought with the sword. Pompey's units fought in the same way. Caesar's mounted forces proved unable to withstand a counter-attack by the enemy light units and cavalry and had to give ground.

Caesar did not lose his grasp of the situation and brought up his reserve cohorts to attack the flanks of the advancing forces. His cavalry re-formed and went over to the attack, driving back Pompey's light infantry and mounted units which had become somewhat dispersed in the pursuit of their opponents. As a result, Caesar now threatened the left wing of his adversary who had made no allowance for an operational reserve before the battle. Caesar exploited successful actions of his reserve cohorts and, with them and his cavalry, fell upon the flanks of the enemy. At the same time, he ordered the third line to advance.

The combined frontal and flank attack was delivered in such massive style that the enemy lines disintegrated, the various units finding their own way back to the fortified camp.

Pompey fled the battlefield well before the end in a state of acute depression, leaving his legions—which were still fighting—without a co-ordinating leadership and abandoning them to their fate. The defeated triumvir returned to his camp where he set off with his bodyguard for Larissa and then, without delay, boarded a ship for Egypt.

Caesar made full use of his victory and went on to capture Pompey's fortified camp. The troops who had managed to escape from the battlefield and the camp attempted to flee to Larissa. Leaving four legions to defend the two camps, Caesar set off in pursuit and succeeded in catching up with the retreating units, cutting them off and forcing them to surrender. By this, he totally destroyed Pompey's army in this theatre of war.

Pharsalus was a battle between two Roman legionary armies of approximately the same strength and with the same standard of training. The action developed as a battle fought from two fortified camps, each side using a well-devised plan of deployment based on the tactics of the legion. Caesar won because, unlike Pompey, he always remained in the direct vicinity of his army, initiated all the manoeuvres of his troops himself and displayed great skill in the process.

He showed himself capable of making improvisations on the battlefield, of operating successfully with reserves placed in readiness before the confrontation and of making the right decision at the right moment. It is also worth stressing that Caesar made masterly use of his victory on the battlefield to achieve a strategic advantage. Pharsalus marked a turning point not only in a campaign but also in the civil war and, thus, in the fate of the Republic.

In Ptolemaic Egypt, it was not the support that he expected that the defeated Pompey found but death at the hand of a murderer. The ageing victor, on the other hand, was borne a son by the young Queen Cleopatra who even followed him to Rome. The legions which, after Pompey's death, continued to fight for the old, already questionable constitution of the *res publica Romana* on widely scattered battlefields in Iberia, Asia Minor, and Northwest Africa were beaten one after the other by Caesar, who reported: "Veni, vidi, vici" (I came, I saw, I conquered).

The authority of the aristocratic Senate now seemed irrevocably lost and it appeared ready to accept the leadership of the great general who was as ingenious as he was hungry for power. However, when Caesar threw a warning to the wind and insisted on being given the supreme state power by the "fathers of the Fatherland" at a ceremony on the Capitol, he was stabbed in March 44 B.C. by a group of Republican conspirators whose leaders included his own stepchild Brutus. So it was that the general, who was not altogether surprised by this turn of events, uttered the words "tu quoque, fili?" as he died.

Julius Caesar gave his family name to the seventh month of the reformed calendar introduced by him, and his surname to the title of the supreme ruler of the West, *Kaiser* — although he never became emperor. However, the development of the Roman Republic to a state in which power was concentrated in the hands of one man was already in progress. After another civil war, Caesar's nephew Octavian, who defeated Antony and Cleopatra in the last great sea-battle of Antiquity at Actium in 31 B.C., laid the foundations for the rule of the Julian-Claudian dynasty which ended with Nero and as imperator assumed the name of Augustus.

With the subjugation of Egypt and the advance of the frontiers to the Rhine and the Danube, he considered that the Roman Empire was more or less complete and, in a symbolic gesture, had the Temple of War of the God Janus closed as serving no further purpose. This was not, of course, the beginning of eternal peace. Slaves and unruly tribes in the provinces had to be kept down by force and restless neighbours had to be given a taste of fear. Occasionally, "frontier adjustments" had to be made which met with the resistance of those affected. As a result, Augustus did not disarm his forces but increased his standing army to about 300,000 men.

The legions formed the backbone of the army and, as the principal instrument of Augustus within and without the Empire, remained constantly under arms. He assigned the army to a number of fixed locations but centralized the military administration and command. The largest force, consisting of eight legions, was stationed on the Rhine, there were six legions in the Danube area and another eleven in Syria, Asia Minor, Iberia, Northwest Africa and Egypt. In Italy remained only the twelve cohorts of the Imperial Guard plus the seven cohorts of the Roman Municipal Guard and auxiliary troops.

A legion now consisted of 6,100 infantry, 726 horsemen and auxiliary troops and was headed by a prefect. The tribunes led the cohorts whilst the centurions were commanders of a lower rank. Great attention was paid to training in general and to its engineering and entrenchment aspects in particular. At this time, the Romans were already highly skilled in the construction of fortifications. Apart from simple fortified camps of earth and timber, they also built complete barrack complexes and citadels of stone.

The citadel structures along the Rhine could be used not only as barracks for garrisons but, in time of war, also functioned as almost impregnable strongpoints to bind down enemy forces. They mostly developed from simple fortifications at strategic points such as elevations, river-crossings or positions commanding valleys. The thickness of walls depended on location and military significance.

After Caesar had defeated Ariovistus, the leader of the Suebi, in Alsace in 58 B.C. and had driven him back beyond the Rhine, this river had formed the imperial frontier. Following the subjugation of Rhaetia, Noricum and Pannonia, the Romans also approached the area settled by Germanic tribes along the Upper Danube and began to think about extending their frontiers to the Weser or even to the Elbe to give Gaul better protection from unwelcome surprises. Augustus assigned eight legions to his stepson Drusus for the launching of the operation from the left bank of the Rhine. The campaign in the year 12 B.C. was somewhat in the nature of a reconnaissance action but the next one in the following year penetrated deep into Germanic territory.

Rivalries among the Germanic tribes made it easier for the Romans to move into this area but some of the tribes did recognize the full extent of the danger from Rome and, like the Sugambri and the Chatti, began to form a united front against the common foe. In 9 B.C., Drusus succeeded in reaching the Elbe. After his death, he was replaced as commander-in-chief by his brother Tiberius who was soon made aware of the stiffening resistance. It was only the successful completion of a combined campaign by the army and the North Sea fleet which enabled him to establish the province of Germania in A.D. 5.

To begin with, however, this province existed only on paper. On the right bank of the Rhine, there was a proper administration only in the direct vicinity of the river. The military occupation of the hinterland was limited to a few citadels, easily reached from here by marches lasting not more than a few days. Everything depended on the loyalty of the tribes which were often only formally subjugated or forced into the alliance with Rome.

A deterioration in the position of the Romans took place when the Marcomanni united under King Marbod and brought together, so it is reported, an army of 70,000 infantry and 4,000 cavalry. Then in A.D. 6 a general popular rising against Roman rule broke out in Pannonia and in Illyria under Bato at the same time. Since the Danube legions were unable to deal with this situation unaided, Tiberius was sent to this theatre of war by the emperor, with the result that insurrections also took place in the province of Germania as well.

In this tense situation, Quinctilius Varus toook ver command along the Rhine. His experience had been gained in campaigns in the East and he had made his name by cruel measures of repression. He believed that severity and not diplomacy was the best way to impress the restless Germanic tribes. All that this achieved, however, was to increase their dissatisfaction and to bring them closer together.

The leadership of the coalition of Germanic tribes determined to offer resistance was assumed in A.D. 9 by the 25-year old Arminius, a member of the Cheruscan military nobility. He had served in the Roman army and had even taken part in the Illyrian-Pannonian war as the commander of an auxiliary cavalry unit. For his services, he had been given Roman citizenship and knightly rank. Thus he had an excellent knowledge of the tactics of the legions and knew that at that time the Germanic warriors stood scarcely any chance of defeating them in pitched battle. At the same time, however, he had identified their vulnerability in guerrilla warfare when they were forced to fight on a terrain which prevented their usual tactical deployment. In his endeavours to beat Varus, he was aided by the strong anti-Roman sentiments of the Germanic peasants who were determined to defend their liberty.

It is true that Arminius was numerically equal to his adversary but the differences in arms and equipment were great. Unlike the Romans, the Teutons had no armouries with which to provide their army with standard equipment. Their principal weapon was the *framea*, a spear with a nar-row, short and sharp iron tip which was used for attack and defence. Only part of them had swords, lances, shields, armour and metal and leather helmets. There were also warriors who were equipped with Roman weapons captured as war booty or kept from service with the auxiliary troops. As a whole, they were equipped with many different kinds of weapons.

It was the custom of the Teutons who fought on foot to operate in close collaboration with the cavalry which always attacked as a massed force. The infantry was drawn up in a definite battle-order in a wedge-shaped formation—also known as a "boar's head"—which, however, was only suitable for attack. It was not a standardized formation as the legion and the strength of the force depended on the situation in question. Several "wedges" could be deployed in echelon along the front and they were headed by the bravest warriors. Success or failure in the battle depended on these men since, once the wedge had been driven back, it tended to break up in disorder and re-forming was only seldom possible. The Germanic tribes had an excellent reconnaissance and forward defence system so that the Romans did not often catch them by surprise.

Mixed combat was a special feature of these peoples. Young and lightly-armed warriors went into action simultaneously with the cavalry, hanging on to the manes of the horses as they ran at their side or riding two-up. This Germanic tactic was strenuous and called for much practice.

Arminius, who was fully aware of his weakness in a pitched battle, planned to attack the Roman army on a terrain which was unfavourable for the legions and to gradually destroy it by a series of fairly small encounters. For this purpose, as the site of the confrontation, he chose a path which had been used since prehistoric times and led across wooded slopes, providing concealment for his troops so that they could strike the enemy while on the march without him being able to make effective use of his superior equipment. He was able to include this path in his strategy since the legions had to use a well-trodden route for their march on account of the heavy pioneer equipment they had with them.

Although it was only for a temporary period, Arminius was able to unite the Cherusci, Sugambri, Marsi, Bructeri, Chatti and some smaller tribes under his command. To begin with, he had great difficulty in persuading the allied

tribal leaders to accept the tactics of guerrilla warfare since they preferred a pitched battle and the familiar wedge-formation. Other princes and chiefs were allied with Rome and they learned of the efforts of Arminius to raise an army. Even Segest, his father-in-law, warned Varus and advised him to abandon the idea of a campaign for the time being. Varus, however, disregarded this tip-off and relied on the high strike-capability of his legions.

He was in a fortified camp in the Warburger Börde district when news arrived that tribes were rebelling in the area around present-day Osnabrück whereupon he promptly assembled his forces. The insurrection was just a ruse to entice him out of the camp and on to the terrain in question but Varus fell for it and, in September of A.D. 9, advanced with three legions and nine auxiliary units, 19,000 men in all, into the district of the insurrection. Unfortunately, all the topographical data available must be regarded as un-reliable and this is why many hypotheses exist regarding the location of this momentous battle. It is possible that Varus used the route known as the Eggelängsweg, running from Warburg to Osnabrück via Horn and Detmold. With their great baggage-train, the legions made only slow progress, especially as Varus felt safe from attack as long as the route led through—so he supposed—friendly Cheruscan territory.

Attack by Germanic warriors against the hard-pressed Romans in the battle of the Teutoburger Wald. Painting by Friedrich Gunkel, *c.* 1860.

Roman marble bust of a Germanic warrior, so-called Arminius.

Scarcely any flank protection was considered necessary and little reconnaissance was carried out.

While they were on the march, Arminius kept the legions under constant observation, assessed their strength, assembled his troops along the route and operated according to the weather, the terrain and the time. In this type of warfare in the woods, the Teutons were superior to the Romans. They were armed and clothed according to the conditions there, they had an excellent knowledge of the terrain and they were eager to attack. When the Roman army had covered about half of the route, they were attacked by the Teutons from both sides of the path. The legions were taken completely by surprise and suffered heavy losses already in the initial phase of the battle. They were accustomed to forming up in the well-tried battle-order but they were forced fo fight in a hand-to-hand struggle. The Roman cavalry realized they were in a trap and retreated towards the castellum of Aliso (whose exact position, perhaps on the River Lippe, is also disputed). Most of them were able to escape the Teuton cavalry pursuing them. The legions recovered relatively quickly from the first shock, closed up in small units and even went over to the attack. After their first storm, the Teutons returned to their places of concealment to which the Romans could not pursue

80

them. Continuous attacks by their elusive adversary decimated the legions. Varus destroyed his baggage-train and built a camp—perhaps in the area of present-day Driburg—to enable his army to rest and recover. However, encircled and cut off from supplies, he could not remain indefinitely here and, since the great distance already covered made a return impossible, he decided to continue the march into the dark. After the Romans had left their camp, however, the fighting immediately resumed and continued without a pause until ultimately the entire army perished. Varus, too, lost his life in the final confrontation.

A fairly large number of Romans were taken prisoner. They were either sacrificed to the gods or made slaves. Few succeeded in escaping. The complete arms and equipment of three legions and nine auxiliary units fell into the hands of the Germanic tribes, representing a considerable increase in their defensive capability. They likewise captured the three eagles of the legions and set them up in their sacred groves. They were subsequently recaptured by Germanicus, the son of Drusus, to restore the honour of the Roman army. He also had the mortal remains of the Roman soldiers collected and placed under a burial mound but this was devastated a number of times by the Teutons in the following period.

The battle of Teutoburger Wald consisted of small actions in the forests and clearings of Westphalia and the Sauerland and ended after some days in the total defeat of the Roman infantry. The Teutons succeeded in compensating for their inferiority in arms and equipment by a fast-moving type of warfare on a terrain which favoured this technique, by ambushes, by the attrition of the enemy as a result of constant attack and by hand-to-hand fighting. They forced the Romans to fight in a way which was totally unsuitable for their heavily armed formations and they prevented them from forming up in their customary order of battle. This was a match for the tactics of the legion and their success showed them that they had a good chance of success in the war against Rome to keep their independence. Arminius was unable to take advantage of the strategic significance of his victory, however, since fighting broke out among the Teutons themselves, in the course of which he ultimately lost his life.

The Roman frontier along the Rhine was weakened by the catastrophe and the "province" on the right bank disappeared for ever. The impact of the blow received can even be traced in the accounts by later historians such as Tacitus, Strabo and Dio Cassius. Germanicus was charged with the task of restoring the impaired reputation of the Roman imperium among the tribes on the right bank of the Rhine. This he did in the course of several spectacular campaigns intended to remove the sting of defeat which is also why they were given the full publicity treatment. Nevertheless, on the death of Augustus in A.D. 14, his successor Tiberius decided to gradually go over to the defensive along the Rhine and to reduce costs by having Teutons fight Teutons. He was assisted in this aim by the unceasing quarrels among the Germanic tribes. This was the solution of a realist which, although it did not keep its validity for all time, did give good service to the ageing world empire for the next two or three centuries.

Gravestone of the centurion M. Caelius of Bonomia (Bologna), killed in the battle of the Teutoburger Wald, 1st century A.D.

JERUSALEM / A.D. 70

Thanks to a well-qualified eye-witness, the Judaean historian Flavius Josephus, who was the son of a priest and related on his mother's side to the former royal family of the Hasmonaeans, we possess an exhaustive report of the fighting around the besieged fortress. As the leader of the rebels in Galilee, he defended the rocky fortress of Jotapata but, when it fell, came to an arrrangement with the Roman general, for whom he was said to have prophesied an early accession to the throne. When Vespasian really did become emperor in A.D. 69 and founded the Flavian dynasty, Josephus—who had adopted the name Flavius—accompanied Vespasian's son Titus on the campaign to capture Jerusalem. The historian, who had seen Rome for himself and was convinced of the invincibility of the Roman Empire but nevertheless wanted to commemorate the courage of his fellow Jews, wrote, towards the end of his life and in addition to other works, the seven books about *The Judaean War*.

The Romans had subjugated Judaea and Jerusalem in 63 B.C. and united it with the province of Syria. Under the emperors, they increasingly restricted the partial autonomy initially granted and, at the same time, drastically raised the burden of taxation. Consequently, under Emperor Nero (A.D. 54–68), resistance to this oppression grew and grew. Whereas the aristocratic Sadducees, who were enlightened scholars with Hellenistic views, nevertheless advised collaboration with the Romans, the Pharisees—the traditionally conservative priests who had the support of the urban upper and middle classes—aligned themselves with the Zealots, who were determined to fight and were backed up by the masses of the peasants, the artisans and the urban poor. This alliance created a firm popular foundation for the uprising which spread across the entire country in A.D. 66–67.

The war of liberation began well. The Roman garrison was driven from Jerusalem and a relief army sent to their aid from Syria was thrown back. The country was divided into three areas and the infantry forces organized in units of ten, a hundred and a thousand on the Roman pattern. There was no organized cavalry, however.

In the second phase of the war, Vespasian opened the campaign with three legions and occupied Galilee. The advance was then delayed by the heavy losses sustained by the Roman army in the storming of Jotapata and, apart from this, by the armed tug-of-war following the death of Nero for his succession. On reaching his supreme aim, Vespasian retired from his command in Judaea and his place was taken by Titus, who surrounded Jerusalem in the spring of A.D. 70 to force the rebels to lay down arms.

In the besieged city, there were bitter arguments about the best method of defence, the views of the Zealots ultimately prevailing. To increase their defensive capabilities, they even freed the slaves.

Jerusalem was enclosed by a wall laid out in three sections. The inner wall was three kilometres long and possessed 60 towers. The northern or second wall had 14 towers and formed the outer defences. The new part of the city was protected by the third wall, two kilometres long and guarded by 90 towers. There was a deep trench in front of the northern wall, the other fortifications being largely built on steep ground. The defence was centred around three citadels—the Temple with its four walls, the stronghold of Zion and the Antonia fortification, a great tower surrounded by four smaller ones.

Since the beginning of the siege happened to coincide with the feast of Passover, there were also many country people in the city. This was a disadvantage for the defenders as regards food and other necessities. These people, on the other hand, did represent an important reservoir of manpower for increasing the number of combatants. The fortifications were manned by 24,000 warriors. 15,000 of these under Simon Bar Giora and 60 subordinate commanders defended the north part of the city whilst John of Gishala and Eleazar had more than 9,000 men and 20 subordinate commanders at their disposal for the defence of the Temple and the neighbouring fortifications.

The members of the Christian sect had left Jerusalem two days before the arrival of the Romans, supposedly on account of a prophecy by Jesus. What is certain is that they did not wish to take part in the fighting and moved to the town of Pella, southeast of the Sea of Galilee. Titus had the Vth, Xth, XIth and XVth legions plus 56,000 siege-troops and the cavalry recruited from the allies of Rome. The Romans also had heavy stone-throwing onagers, battering-rams, dart-throwing engines and ballistae.

The cavalry occupied all roads leading to Jerusalem so as to block any attempts to send relief forces to the city. The Xth legion, marching from Jericho and camping on the Mount of Olives, was assigned the task of keeping watch on

The storming of a city stronghold by Roman troops employing ancient siege techniques. Drawing from a lithograph by Carl Votteler, 19th century.

the east wall, which was regarded as impregnable and protected the Temple and the lower part of the city on that side of the deep Kidron Valley. Other Roman camps were set up to the north and northwest of Jerusalem. The vulnerable part of the city fortifications was in the North where there were no gullies and it was here that attacks had been launched by Assyrians, Persians, Macedonians and Parthians in earlier centuries.

Before the commencement of the action, Titus had called upon the insurgents to surrender but this proposal was

Titus on a quadriga during the siege of Jerusalem. Relief on the
Arch of Titus in Rome, A.D. 81.

preceding double page:
Removal of plunder from the captured and sacked city of Jerusalem. Relief on the Arch of Titus in Rome, consecrated by Do-
mitian in A.D. 81 in honour of the victory by Titus at Jerusalem
(A.D. 70).

rejected. Thereupon the first Roman attack was made from the northern spur of the Mount of Olives known as the Scopus. Their powerful artillery destroyed a large part of the northern area of the city. Titus identified the vulnerability of the north wall and cut down all the olive groves and gardens in front of it so as to level the ground up to the wall and establish good positions for his siege machines. The Romans needed two weeks before their great battering-rams were able to smash a large breach in the weakest of the three walls. The defenders tried to set fire to the wooden machines and resisted fiercely. But at the beginning of May the first legionaries fought their way through the breach and into the suburb of Bezetha. The Jews had prepared for house-to-house fighting and the Romans needed several days before they ultimately reached the second wall, the Wall of Hiskia, which was about 700 years old and only 200 metres in front of the Wall of David, which was even more ancient. The Wall of Hiskia began at the western gate of the first wall, extended with sharply angled projections to the stronghold of Antonia and ended at the Golden Gate in the eastern circular wall. After a further five days, the Romans also succeeded in opening a breach in the second wall, heavy siege equipment being used once more. They were then able to force their way into the suburb situated between the Palace of Herod and the Temple. With a spirited counter-attack, the Jews retook the second wall but after a few days it was captured again by the Romans who occupied the new part of the city in the North once and for all.

Flavius Josephus was again instructed by Titus to demand the capitulation of the defenders but they refused. Since the Romans had already sustained heavy losses and the capture of the other fortifications would certainly take their toll, Titus decided to impress the besieged inhabitants with his superiority by a march-past of his troops. The legions appeared in parade-dress, carrying their eagles and followed by the allied peoples with all their colourful equipment. For four days the Romans marched past Titus and his staff in front of the old north wall of the Temple. Furthermore, since he knew that food was short in Jerusalem, he had large quantities of it distributed to his units before the very eyes of the defenders. Flavius Josephus was ordered to negotiate with the defenders yet again but, although he drew attention to the fact that the beauty of the Temple

and a large part of the city was still intact, this had no effect. For them he was a collaborator, bought by the Romans. The parade was a psychological failure.

Titus learned that Jerusalem was being supplied at night with food from the surrounding countryside through secret underground passages and paths. To put a stop to this, he had a high earthen rampart built around the city. Fortified watchtowers along it enabled the entire system of enclosure to be kept under surveillance. After this, the city ran out of supplies.

Despite starvation, the defenders fought on with the courage of despair and with a contempt for death. The embittered legionaries, for their part, crucified the deserters which were caught between the lines. Following a rumour that people fleeing from the city had swallowed gold and jewels in order to get them out of Jerusalem, large numbers of such persons were murdered and then slit open in a single night. Titus took energetic action against such excesses, ordering a plundering auxiliary unit to be ridden down and punishing offenders with the death penalty.

On account of the great quantities of timber needed, the legions had cut down all the wooded areas around Jerusalem. In the city, so many had died of starvation that their bodies had to be cast over the walls and into the space between where they spread a ghastly stench. Fighting still continued with unabated ferocity around the stronghold of Antonia. The legions launched their attacks from the captured suburb between the Walls of Hiskia and David and from the terrain north of the stronghold. The northern part of the Kidron Valley was filled up so that the siege-engines could be brought forward. The attack was now centred on the Wall of David which ran across the city from the Palace of Herod in the West to the centre of the precincts of the Temple.

The defenders made one raid after another and destroyed many of the siege-engines. It was only at the beginning of July that the stronghold of Antonia was stormed, after which the legions turned their main attention to the Temple. Built of marble, gold and rare wood by Herod the Great, this magnificent structure was famed throughout the Roman Empire and Titus would have liked to spare the noble edifice.

The last phase of the siege lasted another month. The wall-breaking machines failed to penetrate the mighty freestone masonry and the defenders, led by John of Gishala and hoping for a miracle to the last, resisted until their dying breath. Only when the wooden outer gates of the Temple were set ablaze and the fire spread, did they fall back. Nevertheless, the legionaries could only advance step-by-step across the great Courtyard of the Gentiles to the Courtyard of the Women, the Courtyard of the Men and ultimately to the Courtyard of the Priests. The fiercest fighting took place on the twelve steps leading to the holy shrine, which still remained unscathed. Behind the great curtain, there burned the oil lamp and there stood the seven-arm chandelier, the table with the twelve loaves of the tribes of Israel and the narrow altar. Behind these, there was the holy of holies, veiled in darkness, which the High Priest was only permitted to enter once a year. A flat stone marked the place where the Ark of the Covenant was believed to have stood during the age of Solomon.

The Temple caught fire from the torches of the legionaries and all the attempts of Titus to save the structure were thwarted by the behaviour of his troops. John of Gishala, together with his remaining warriors, succeeded in breaking out to the upper part of the city in the West which was still protected by Simon Bar Giora, operating from the fortified towers of the Palace of Herod. The attack on this last bastion of the defenders again lasted for weeks and it, too, had to be stormed.

Tacitus, the most famous of Roman historians, certainly had in mind the merciless cruelty of the Judaean War when he wrote the following sentence about another insurrection which took place on the Lower Rhine at approximately the same time: "Romans and Batavians fought humanely, for it was not religion that was at stake." 97,000 Judaeans were taken captive by the Romans and were later sold into slavery. Jerusalem was razed to the ground and only the three towers, known as Phasael, Hippicus and Mariamne, of the Palace of Herod, were kept as accommodation for the Xth legion plus a part of the west wall. In A.D. 71, Titus held a triumphal procession in Rome in which John of Gishala, Simon Bar Giora, the seven-arm chandelier and the table from the Temple were shown to the people.

The battle of Jerusalem was one of the greatest—if not the greatest—military action undertaken by the Roman legions to capture a fortress which was already a system of fortifications. This fortified complex was defended in an active manner by the garrison which launched successful raids and built underground passages to disturb the operations of the enemy. It was impossible to take it in a single action since the fortress was divided into three independent defensive zones protected by mighty citadels. The outstanding military engineering of the Romans, the use of well-tried legions and the inferiority in numbers of the defenders were the reasons which led to the fall and destruction of the city. In addition, the Judaeans suffered from a shortage of food and possessed no mounted units with which to harry the Romans in the rear nor were there any other forces available which could have come to the relief of Jerusalem.

For Rome, the crushing of the insurrection in Judaea was just one more episode and not even the last since it was only after the failure of a second great uprising under Bar-Cochba from A.D. 132 to 135 that the resistance to the alien rule of Rome finally ceased. The destruction of their third temple, however, left a deep mark on the history of the Jewish people. With this national shrine, they lost their religious focal point, even though their dispersion throughout the world and thus the diaspora had been in progress since the age of Hellenism. On the other hand, the destruction of Jerusalem speeded up the total separation of Christianity from Judaism and was a factor in its emergence as an independent world religion.

In the 3rd century, the Imperium Romanum was shaken by a crisis which shook the whole of society. After the spread of the latifundia farming system had initially destroyed the free peasantry, the low productivity of slave labour and the end of a cheap supply of slaves after the end of the wars of expansion led to plots of land from the great estates being made available to small tenant farmers. For their part, however, these *coloni* were fettered to the soil to an increasing extent and were thus the forerunners of the mediaeval serfs. The process of economic shrinkage contrasted with the growth in taxation necessitated by the State administrative apparatus with its swollen bureaucracy. In particular, more resources for the maintenance of the great military machine had to be squeezed out of the population.

The more difficult the situation became in the last decades of the Empire, the greater was the importance of the army for the maintenance of law and order at home and abroad. The consequence of this was that the military dominated the political scene to an ever greater degree. The Pretorian Guard in Rome and the legions on the imperial frontiers competed with each other—and thus in quick succession—in making emperors of their commanders, who usually enjoyed only a short reign. As a result, the fighting qualities of the troops themselves deteriorated. They were now recruited from the poorest strata of the provincial population who sought their fortune in the army. Since the state treasuries were empty, the soldiers were allotted land on which they could settle down with their families and military service often became an hereditary affair. In this way, the military forces were kept up to strength at the expense of quality. The standard of training of the legions deteriorated and the need for economies forced the cancellation of field exercises. The quality of the technical equipment fell, discipline and authority suffered from the lack of capable commanders and the permanent situation of civil war undermined the morale of the troops.

In the middle of the century, the military situation was characterized by the attacks of the Germanic tribes and of various peoples of the Black Sea steppes on the imperial frontiers and by internal unrest. Emperor Decius, known for his opposition to the emergence of Christianity, had discharged many of his long-service veterans for financial reasons and had reduced the strike-capability of the armed forces. He was expecting no unpleasant surprises as he moved along the lower reaches of the Danube with some of the units stationed there in 250 in the direction of Gaul with the intention of crushing a dangerous popular uprising there. However, it was precisely at this time that the Scythians invaded Lower Moesia, now Bulgaria.

For Jordanes, the author of the *History of the Goths*, as for all the other ancient writers, the name "Scythians" was a collective term which was applied to the partly nomadic, partly agricultural Indo-European-Iranian inhabitants of the Pontic steppes. Consequently, the invaders of the year 250 might well have been Sarmatians or other peoples, even the Goths might have taken part in this invasion. All of these peoples operated with mounted forces for the most part and were thus organized for a highly mobile type of warfare, offensive actions being carried out exclusively by the cavalry. The infantry, with both heavy and light units, provided general cover for the army during troop movements, played an active part in defence in pathless areas and participated in the besieging of strongpoints and fortifications. Like all the people living near the frontiers of the imperium, the Scythians were familiar with the Roman military structure and its special features.

They opened the spring campaign of the year 250 with two army groups. The larger of these moved through the valley of the River Laterus whilst the other marched in the direction of Philippopel with the aim of cutting the lines of communication in the Roman rear. Both groups were coordinated, however, and mounted couriers maintained constant contact between them.

The Roman troops under the governor Trebonianus Gallus in Moesia were stationed around Oescus. This strategically important junction of major trade-routes was

Trajanus Decius. Capitol, Rome

Warriors of the Imperial Roman Pretorian Guard, on guard in front of their quarters. Relief, 1st century A.D. Louvre, Paris

protected not only by strong fortifications but also by natural hindrances in the shape of a number of lakes. In this, the Roman troops possessed a strong base for launching attacks on the enemy at any time.

The Scythians made preparations to take the fortress of Novae by storm but had to withdraw to Nicopolis on the Danube where they were defeated in a pitched battle after they had been confronted by a relief army under Gallus. On the other hand, they launched a successful surprise-attack at Beroea and captured Philippopel. The campaign had not produced a decisive advantage for either side but since the legions held their main base of Oescus and the Danube fortifications they were able to stabilize their front, threatening to cut off the retreat of those "Barbarians" who had penetrated the Roman line of defence. During the winter pause Decius, who had hastily left Gaul, reinforced his army by reliable Illyrian units and, in the spring of 251, went over to the offensive. His intention was to encircle and then destroy the enemy formations. Gallus was assigned the task of occupying the banks of the Danube to prevent them escaping while the emperor himself assumed responsibility for the attack on the main concentrations of the enemy forces.

The Scythians under Kniwa had already begun an orderly withdrawal but had lost their mobility on account of their baggage-train being weighed down with plunder. On the plain at Abrittus, they were confronted by Decius and forced to fight. The Romans seized a part of the baggage-train and forced them to sue for peace. The Scythians offered the whole of the plunder they had taken for the right to withdraw without hindrance but the emperor was more interested in a glorious victory, hoping that the news of this would strengthen his shaky political position. This was why he decided in favour of a battle which would lead to the total destruction of the enemy.

There were serious shortcomings in the preparation of the battle and no thorough reconnaissance of the terrain took place. The Roman army was not backed up by a fortress here and, in any case, Decius had no cavalry at his disposal. He also acted unwisely in the way he drew up his forces for the battle since he made no allowance for reserves. He had the whole of his legions form up as a phalanx, planning to destroy the Scythians with the first blow. The latter were fully aware of their weakness in the face of a concentrated Roman onslaught and thus opted for a tactical deployment with the inclusion of marshy terrain. Drawn up in three lines, they awaited the attack of the legions. The first two lines were positioned in front of the marsh whilst the third line, with the main body of their troops, were positioned behind it. The marsh could be crossed only by a few paths and tracks and these were known only to the Scythians. In his calculations, Kniwa allowed for the possible destruction of his first two lines but hoped that they would be able to inflict sufficient losses on the legions in the main action and thus defeat them.

The Romans did indeed break through the first enemy line and decimated the enemy severely, but signs of exhaustion appeared among the legionaries when they had dealt with the second line. Decius allowed them no time to recover their strength but ordered them to attack the third line. Since he had omitted to carry out any reconnaissance, he had no idea of the existence of the marsh. It is even said that the fateful command to attack was given on the advice

of Gallus who cold-bloodedly allowed for a probable catastrophe which would open up the way to the throne for himself. The legions moved forward for the last attack, became bogged down in the marsh and came under intensive fire from arrows and other missiles. A large number of the Romans were killed before the third line of the Scythians was reached who, for their part, now launched flank attacks and encircled the Roman units. Gallus and his units were in a better tactical position at some distance away from the main action and were able to withdraw. His dishonourable calculations proved to be accurate and, after Decius and his son had been killed, he was immediately hailed as emperor by the humiliated troops that remained. The fact that his career was more important to Gallus than the Imperium and the survival of the legions throws a revealing light on the political situation in the disintegration of the Roman Empire. The battle was of decisive importance. In the first phase, the Romans had co-ordinated the actions of their army with the protection available from their fortified base and pursued a successful policy of forward defence. But they failed in pitched battle when they did not keep to their well-tried tactics. Internal struggles for the imperial throne were of no small importance. At Abrittus, the legions fought as a phalanx, their military potential being concentrated in a single, powerful strike. Trapped by the treacherous nature of the ground, they were unable to take up their cohort formation again.

The Scythians fought in a flexible manner and retired in good order. They were also past-masters at adapting their battle-plan to the terrain. Their chief weakness was when they had to assign a part of their forces for the protection of the captured booty since this reduced their manoeuvrability. Emperor Gallus concluded an inglorious peace with the Scythians who agreed to refrain from making further raids in return for annual sums of money. This did not help for very long, however, since already in 274 the Emperor Aurelian was obliged to withdraw for ever from the Trans-Danubian province of Dacia—present-day Rumania—in the face of the advancing Goths.

Battle-scene of Romans and Barbarians on a bronze decoration forming part of a horse harness from the 3rd century. Museo Archeologico, Aosta

The energetic Illyrian emperors Diocletian (284-305) and Constantine (312–337) in particular attempted by institutional and military reforms to halt the decline of the Late Roman Empire.

Diocletian, the son of a freed slave, bound the *coloni* to the soil, imposed the general land tax on Italy, which had enjoyed a privileged position up to this time, and preferred to live in his homeland of Dalmatia. In addition to the frontier army, the *limitanei*, he established an army of territorial militia forces *(comitatenses)* which were used to combat insurgents and the raids by the Barbarian tribes. The army was reorganized and placed directly under the command of the emperor again. With the army under his control, he changed the Augustinian principate into an absolute monarchy on the pattern of the oriental despots.

Constantine the Great, who founded a new dynasty, assured himself of the political support of the Church, the best-functioning organization of his time, when he adopted Christianity and made Byzantium his capital, naming it Constantinople. He abolished the high-handed Pretorian Guard in Rome and replaced it by "court troops" *(palatini)* and a personal bodyguard *(scholae)*. The final separation of the cavalry and infantry proved disappointing, however, since the Roman horsemen, even as an independent force, did not perform their duties with distinction. On the other hand, notable improvements were achieved in the training of officers and in the selection of senior commanders.

In association with a currency reform, the consolidation of the administration of the state did bring about a temporary improvement in the military sphere. Around the middle of the 4th century A.D., the Roman Empire showed once more that it was capable of dealing with insurrections in the provinces, raids by the Sassanid kings of Iran in the East and the invasion of Gaul by powerful Germanic tribes.

The pressure on the frontiers had increased in the second half of the third century after the Alemanni had broken through the fortifications of the limes along the Up-

per Rhine and Rhaetia and thrown the Romans back to the Danube. From time to time, Germanic raiders drove deep into Gaul. In the northeastern parts of the country they even took up permanent positions. In view of this, Constantine II ordered his cousin and "co-emperor" Julian in 355 to sort out the position there by organizing a campaign, for the support of which an army of 25,000 men was to be dispatched from Italy.

The Alemanni, who had been joined by some of the Batavians, had a large reservoir of combatants at their disposal, although there were variations in the degree of training. Their army, led by Chnodomar, still fought in almost the same manner as the Teuton forces of Arminius, using the infantry tactics of the "wedge" formation and a variety of weapons. Their forte lay in their hard-hitting mounted units which possessed a high degree of mobility and could strike at the enemy behind the lines.

Julian, who was equally well versed in Neo-Platonic philosophy and military theory and was a commander of proven ability, realized after a few eventful minor actions that if the campaign were to be a success the army of the Alemanni had to be destroyed at a single blow if the threat that it represented was to be eliminated. He planned to encircle the enemy and, to this end, made extensive preparations in 357 with his troops moving into position from two directions—his own units, consisting of frontier troops and *comitatenses*, on the one hand, and the field-troops coming from Italy on the other. The excellent plan failed to materialize, however, on account of the essential military precautions for its implementation being neglected and due to differences of opinion between the two commanders. The Alemanni got to hear of what was going on, intercepted the army marching from Italy and defeated it in a surprise attack. Julian—to some extent through his own fault—now had to rely on his own resources.

In the meantime, he had not been inactive but had repaired, re-equipped and re-stocked the fortifications of Tabernae (Saverne/Zabern) which had previously been devastated by the Alemanni. He thus possessed a well-protected rear area for his army of only 13,000 men who started out in the direction of Argentoratum (Strasbourg) at the break of dawn. Along the march-route of some 30 kilometres, he took every precaution. The column was headed by the light cavalry, followed by the infantry in legion order and protected by other cavalry units on the flanks. At about mid-day, the battle-array of the Alemanni was sighted on a hill to the west of Argentoratum and east of the Musaubach Valley. Ammianus Marcellinus, who served as a commander under Julian, estimated in his *Res gestae* that the Alemanni were about 35,000 men strong but this figure might have erred on the high side; half that number would probably still be exaggerated.

Julian always endeavoured to utilize the experience and well-proven principles of Roman warfare. To his dismay, he was unable to implement his next measure which was the establishment of a fortified camp surrounded by lookout posts so that his legionaries could rest and recover their strength after the march. He could not do this because his soldiers insisted that battle be joined without delay. This is an indication of the relaxation in Roman military discipline at this time. Since he had to take account of the state of morale of his troops, the only way in which he could achieve victory was by the exploitation of all the tactical features and by the rapid deployment and handling of his forces. He marched into battle with his cavalry on the right wing and the infantry on the left. The legions were organized as a phalanx but with a second and third line. The sec-

ond line consisted of the veterans, the *legio primanorum* (the "young warriors") formed the third line, taking up a position behind the centre. An important aspect was the provision of a small tactical reserve of 200 horsemen and the overall in-depth deployment of the army. Not only the 200 horsemen but also the third line acted as a reserve, since it provided rear cover for the area between the two wings.

Chnodomar deployed his Alemanni in a single line, the infantry units in a wedge formation on the right wing and the cavalry in closed ranks on the left. Apart from his own immediate followers, he made no allowance for a reserve. Instead of this, he laid an ambush on the right wing by concealing armed men in trenches there. The Rhine protected him from a surprise attack in the rear but represented a complication if he were forced fo retreat in the event of defeat. The attack was launched by the advance of the infantry from the Roman left wing. The experienced legionaries spotted the ambush and slowed up their forward movement to avoid being attacked in the rear. When the new situation was reported to Julian, he ordered his tactical reserve of 200 horsemen to attack the Alemanni hiding in the trenches. In the meantime, the cavalry of the Alemanni attacked and routed the Roman mounted units, as was almost to be expected. If it had not been for the tactical battle-order of the Romans, the battle might have been decided at this moment since the enemy horsemen now attacked the Roman infantry from the flank. However, the second line of the legions protected the flank, and halted the Alemanni horsemen.

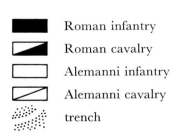

Roman infantry

Roman cavalry

Alemanni infantry

Alemanni cavalry

trench

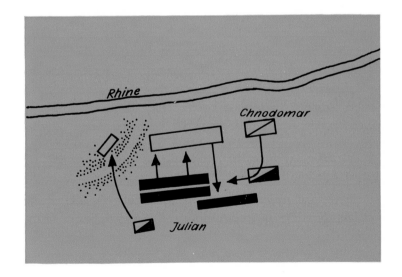

At this critical time, Chnodomar collected his immediate followers together and plunged into the battle at the head of these heavily armed aristocratic warriors in order to force the turn of events in his favour. He broke through the second Roman line but could not overwhelm the *legio primanorum* and the legions were then able to go over to a counter-attack along the entire front. The ranks of the Alemanni were thrown into disorder and they were forced to retreat, still fighting. Many were drowned and only a few reached the far bank of the Rhine unscathed. Julian set out in general pursuit of the routed enemy, who had left 6,000 dead on the field of battle, and captured Chnodomar and 200 of his retinue. Thanks to their carefully prepared and disciplined tactics, the Roman casualties amounted to only 243 soldiers and four senior officers killed and about 1,000 wounded.

The battle of Argentoratum was a pitched battle which was won by using the legions in a style of warfare for which they had been organized and trained although the intended tactic of encirclement could not be implemented in actual fact. Against his will, Julian was forced to open the battle prematurely since he had to consider the mood of his troops and was obliged to take the risk that they might have been excessively weakened by the march. Despite this, he was able to line up the Roman army in a tactical order of battle with a reserve and a deep echelon formation. His cavalry, as nearly always Roman mounted units, was an uncertain factor and was eliminated at an early stage. Despite the phalanx deployment, the three-line echelon stood the test and decided the action when it held firm before the last attack of the Alemanni and proved capable of launching a counter-attack. The legions did not take the initiative but went over to the attack from a posture of active defence —this is illustrated by the defensive strategy here. The Alemannic cavalry was dangerous and aggressive but could not break through the three-line echelon of the enemy infantry. Chnodomar, numerically superior and accustomed to victory, probably underestimated the Roman battle-order and its tactical flexibility; even his personal intervention could not change the course of events. A noteworthy feature of the battle was the preparation of the ambush by the Alemanni, its identification in good time by the legionaries and the immediate commitment of the Roman tactical reserve.

The legions won the battle of Argentoratum by reason of their high standard of training and by the generalship of their commander who was familiar with the best military traditions and combined circumspection with the ability to make rapid decisions. This was Rome's last great victory on the Rhine. Julian kept the Alemanni in check by crossing the river, destroying their settlements along its banks and rebuilding the destroyed Roman fortifications. He came to an amicable agreement with the Franks who also migrated to Gaul. In 361, he became Rome's last "pagan" emperor but he met his death already in 364 in the course of a campaign against the Persian Sassanid King Shahpur II. This was the end of the "Apostate"—the "unfaithful", as he was called by the Christian historians—but new trials and tribulations awaited the Empire.

Combat between Roman legionaries and Germanic warriors (Barbarians?). Side-panel of a sarcophagus, probably 3rd century. Museo Nazionale Romano delle Terme, Rome

The raids of the Franks and Alemanni across the Rhine, alternating with "peaceful" infiltration, were merely the prelude of something far more terrible for the Imperium Romanum. When in 375 the Huns descended on Europe through the Caspian Porte and drove the Goths from the northern areas of the Black Sea, they caused a continental movement of peoples—largely Germanic—which destroyed the cohesion of the fragile Empire. As early as 378, Emperor Valens lost his life in the vicinity of Adrianople in the battle in which his army was defeated by the Visigoths of Fritigern who had fled across the lower reaches of the Danube to Moesia.

He had permitted them to settle there as "allies" (foederati) on condition that they handed over their weapons. Encroachments by officials caused them to rebel whilst at the same time unrest broke out among the overburdened provincial population and even in Constantinople itself. The emperor hurried there with his troops from the Persian frontier and summoned his nephew from Gaul to reinforce him. The union of the two armies was delayed by the Goths blocking the lines of communication. Instead of waiting for the reinforcements in his stronghold at Adrianople, Valens sought battle since his scouts had only sighted advance parties of foot-soldiers.

After an exhausting march, he came upon the Goths who had taken up their position behind a ring of waggons. Fritigern pretended that he was prepared to negotiate but this was only to gain time to assemble his horsemen who had been engaged in foraging and had consequently dispersed. In the meantime, the Roman troops were obliged to stand for hours in the scorching heat of a summer's day. Tormented by thirst, they lost their patience and the light infantry began hostilities on their own initiative. The attack did not get past the ring of waggons but it took the left wing of the cavalry with it and thus threw the whole of the battle-line into confusion. Without an in-depth echelon formation of the legions, with the cavalry fighting in the front line instead of protecting the flanks and without an adequate reserve, the Romans were in a vulnerable state right from the start. Valens now lost his grip on the situation and before he could re-group his army, the strong Gothic cavalry swooped down from between the hills in the North, crushing his troops in an attack from the flank.

Against the background of the growing political and social uncertainty in the hinterland, this grave defeat threw a dramatic light on the decline in the Roman mastery of the art of war and on the shaky state of discipline in the army. The material and moral reserves of the Empire were exhausted and the legions operated as irregular bands in actual fact as a consequence of the ineffectiveness of their commanders. Once an army had been destroyed, it was almost impossible to replace it. The Goths, for their part, demonstrated the ascendance of the mounted units, which, as neighbours of the Scythians in the steppes along the Black Sea, they had brought to a very high level of development, as the main military arm of the future.

Emperor Theodosius, who had concluded peace with Fritigern by ceding him Illyria, finally divided the State into the Western and Eastern Empires when he died in 395. The latter, later known as Byzantium after its capital, lasted another thousand years, whereas the Western Empire was invaded by "Barbarians" who were frequently welcomed by the insurgent coloni and despairing tax payers as liberators from the harsh Roman yoke. In 406, the emperor in the West, Honorius, recalled the frontier-troops from the Rhine for the defence of Italy or at least of his new capital of Ravenna, situated in the safety of swamps. All resistance in the provinces now collapsed. The Visigoths under Alaric plundered the city of Rome and then settled in Southwestern Gaul and Iberia. The Vandals and the Iranian Alani moved through Gaul to Iberia and Northwest Africa, the Burgundians and Alemanni invaded Eastern Gaul and the Franks moved up from the Lower Rhine to Northern Gaul. The two Roman legions in Britain had likewise abandoned the country which was now exposed to the raids of the Angles, Jutes and Saxons.

The Germanic peasant tribes were primarily in search of land on which they could settle. They founded loosely organized state-structures there and were usually recognized as allies by the Western emperor of the day—making a virtue of necessity. He thus retained his formal sovereignty and could also rely on some of them for military assistance. This was especially important since he possessed hardly any troops of his own but soldiers largely recruited from alien tribes who fought in their own manner, once the legion system had disintegrated.

By about the middle of the 5th century, a direct Roman administration outside Italy was still functioning only in Northwest and Northern Gaul between the Loire and the Somme. Even this outpost was threatened when Attila, the king of the Huns who had, up till then, maintained a friendly attitude, quarrelled with the Western Roman emperor about a dowry—in the form of land—which he had been promised but had not received.

Mounted warriors in the battle of the Catalaunian Plains. Painting by Heinz Zander (1973). Armeemuseum der DDR, Dresden

The nomadic tribes of the Huns were horsemen from Central Asia who had frequently descended on Northern China. Some of them had gone southwards towards India whilst others, in the 3rd and 4th centuries, had ridden westwards. They had subjugated the Ostrogoths, the Gepidae, the Herulae and those Alans (now known as Ossets) who did not migrate westwards. Ultimately the Huns settled in the Pannonian plain. Their sphere of influence between the Volga and the Rhine was demarcated by treaties with Eastern Rome.

The principal advantage of the Hun soldiers, who were described by the Roman writers as being very numerous, was their exceptional mobility. They always fought on horseback and were armed with the composite bow, the crossbow, the sword and the throwing spear. They wore fur caps, riding-breeches, riding-jacket and riding-boots. Their army had an extensive baggage-train which included the members of their families. Their tactics were based exclusively on mounted attacks and relied on the weight of numbers. The light equipment and arms of the Huns gave them a high degree of manoeuvrability on the battlefield and they could rapidly change from attack to defence and vice-versa. When attacked by the enemy, they first of all retreated, firing arrows to defend themselves. They were excellent archers and could shoot from any position when mounted, even to the rear. This was a very effective tactic since, as soon as the enemy had sustained heavy losses from this, they turned upon him and attacked with sword and spear.

The military tactics of the Huns had not developed entirely spontaneously but could obviously look back on ancient traditions. These were mainly derived from the teachings of the Chinese general Mao-tun who attached great importance to strict discipline and stressed the role of powerful mounted attacks for outflanking the enemy as a basic principle in pitched battles. The Huns retained this general approach to warfare and also organized an excellent outpost and reconnaissance system. Attila introduced the concept of successive waves of mounted archers and mailed lancers launching an attack. The mailed horsemen, perhaps imitated from the Iranian Sassanids, were necessary since lightly-equipped units alone had great difficulty in dealing with a heavily armed opponent unless they greatly outnumbered him.

In pitched battle on flat terrain, the fast-moving tactics of the Huns were always successful. They did not ride in fixed lines but swarmed over the battlefield, man and horse appearing to form an entity. They either encircled the enemy or, after pushing forward, simulated flight—in the course of which they constantly showered arrows on their adversary—and then suddenly and just as unexpectedly turned upon their foes and resumed the attack.

When the Huns first crossed the Rhine in large numbers in 437, they allied themselves with Rome and destroyed the kingdom of the Burgundians in the area around Worms. This was the event which is reflected in the German epic, the *Nibelungenlied*. In 451, however, Attila invaded Gaul as an enemy. His army included units from the subjugated Germanic tribes. There was a strong contingent of Ostrogoths under their kings Walamir, Theodimir and Widimir and there were Gepidae under their King Ardaric. Like the Huns, these were mounted units and used the same combat methods.

At this time, Western Rome no longer had any legions of the old style. Aetius, the imperial commander in Gaul, was obliged to rely on provincial militia and garrison units, Germanic mercenaries and allies. As the son of an Illyrian general, he had enjoyed a sound military education and was himself a fine rider, archer and lancer. He had begun his career as a scribe with the rank of an officer in the Imperial government and had subsequently spent some time with the Huns as a hostage. These years were not wasted for him since he had the opportunity to make a thorough study of the combat techniques they used. He owed his subsequent successes against the Visigoths and Franks mainly to the Hun horsemen that he had recruited.

He did not have them at his disposal in the momentous days of 451. He therefore concluded peace with the Visigoths and won them over as allies since they likewise felt that the Huns were a threat to their new homeland. Aetius thus commanded the Western Roman units and the army of the Visigoth King Theodorid, whose sons Thorismund and Theodoric were also under arms. Then there were Franks, Sarmatians, Burgundians, Saxons and Germanic units which had already served as auxiliaries.

Jordanes's *History of the Goths* reports that the two armies met on the "Catalaunian Plains"—believed to be near the present-day town of Châlons-sur-Marne. The terrain was

mostly flat but there was a hill of some strategic importance. The numbers quoted are not reliable and Attila certainly did not have the 500,000 men with whom he is credited. However, it is likely indeed that his forces outnumbered the coalition under Aetius. Aetius and Theodorid prevented the Alans under King Sangiban from joining up with the army of Attila. They cut off his approach and, under more or less gentle pressure, persuaded him to change sides and to take up a position with his units in their centre where the new ally could be kept securely under supervision. He did not protest to any extent against such rough treatment since he did not have much to laugh about as a vassal of the Hun king and, at worst, it was simply a case of out of the frying-pan and into the fire.

Attila's battle-plan was based on the general Hun tactic of a mounted attack. The units of Aetius were more heavily armed on average and he deployed his units in such a way that he could rapidly take the hill, the right side of which had been occupied by the Huns before the beginning of the action. The Huns would then have to launch their attack from the plain which would cause their massed horsemen to lose some of their momentum and dash.

In the Western Roman line of battle, the Visigoths were on the right wing, Aetius on the left and the Alans in the centre. The most powerful units were positioned on the flanks. Among the Hun forces, Attila's own troops held the centre with the Ostrogoths and the Gepidae on the wings.

In the hard-fought preliminary encounters, the Gepidae had first measured their strength against the Franks of the Roman coalition. With a vigorous thrust at the beginning of the main battle, Aetius and Thorismund then dislodged the Huns from the hill. Attila counter-attacked in several waves. The Romans withstood this onslaught, however, for, although the Huns broke through the shaky Alan centre and separated the wings, they allowed their own centre to advance too far forward and to expose their wings. The army of Western Rome launched its counter-attack against the enemy flanks and forced most of these units to fight man-to-man. The Huns were thrown back to their ring of waggons, which was practically a fortified position. Forced to take shelter in the ring of waggons, Attila had a bonfire of wooden saddles prepared with the intention of throwing himself in the flames rather than being taken captive in the event of a devastating and dishonourable defeat. At this stage, he had hardly any reserves left.

King Theodorid was killed in the course of the battle which only came to an end when night fell. The Visigoths proclaimed Thorismund as the new king and then returned to their settlements. Aetius himself advised against continuing the action and attempting to wipe out the Huns who still represented a powerful force.

The battle was marked by very bitter fighting, bloody losses on both sides being severe. Mediaeval legend has it that the spirits of the fallen warriors continued to clash throughout the night. The Huns suspected that the withdrawal of the Visigoths was a trick and remained behind the barricades of their encampment. Only when they were convinced that they were in no danger did they begin to retreat. Aetius did not attempt to prevent this since he had no interest in an undue increase in the might of the Visigoths and considered that Attila might be a possible counterweight in this respect. He was primarily concerned with the maintenance of the Empire and political considerations thus prevented him from taking full advantage of his victory.

Although it was a Roman victory, this last great pitched battle signalled the approaching end of the Western Roman Empire. Without a powerful army of its own, Rome was only able to provide some sort of protection for its shrunken frontiers with the aid of temporary and doubtful allies.

Vanquished and victor outlived the battle by only a few years. Attila is said to have died from a haemorrhage in his bridal bed and Aetius was murdered. The state of the Huns was destroyed by tribal feuds even more rapidly than it had arisen and its people disappeared from the historical scene. The Western Roman Empire, only a shadow of its former greatness, became the plaything of mercenary leaders. Even this came to an end when Odoacer forced the 14-year old Emperor Romulus "Augustulus" to abdicate in 476 and did not install a successor. In Northern Gaul, where the battle with the Huns had been fought, the Roman governor Syagrius held out for another ten years on his own until a king of the Franks put an end to the existence of this, the last province of Western Rome.

III

KNIGHTS
AND
MERCE/
NARIES

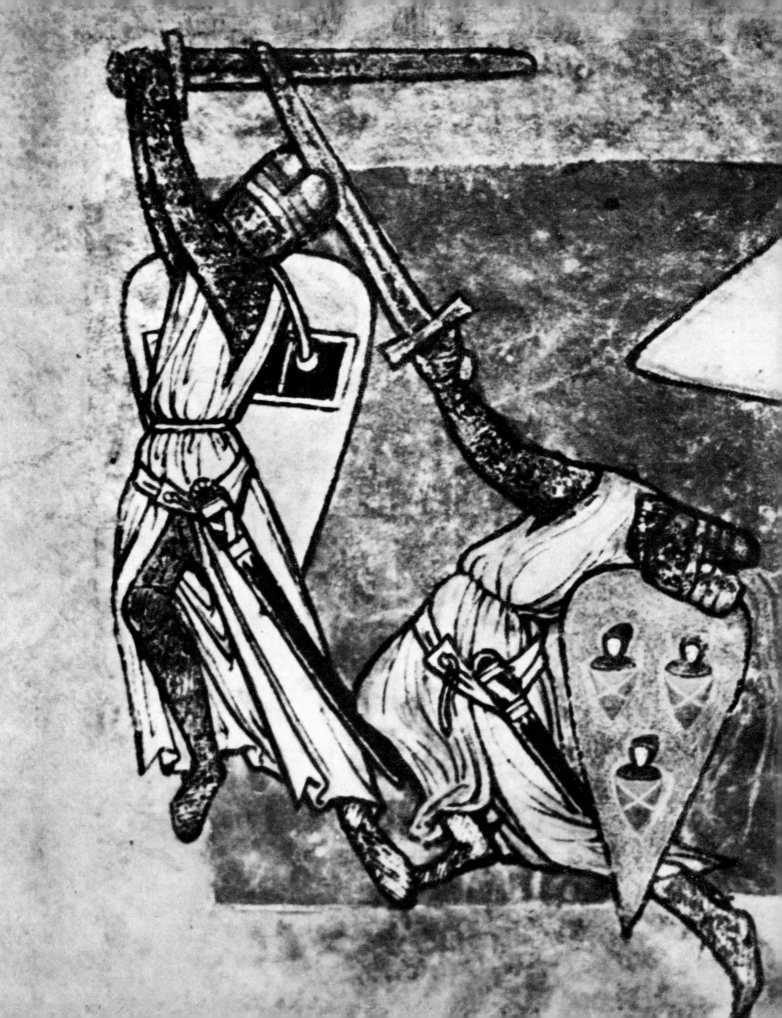

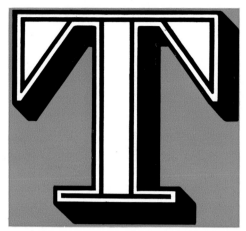

he humanists of the 16th century lauded Renaissance art, the Reformation and the great geographical discoveries which extended their horizons as the beginning of a "new age". Scholars drew their inspiration from the works of Greco-Roman Antiquity and regarded the millennium which then followed as the labyrinth of the "Dark Ages".

The term outlived those who had coined it but this was not the case with their standards. In actual fact, with the Empire of Western Rome, a social order which was already obsolete came to an end on one of the decisive stages of history. Its fund of military experience, together with many achievements of material civilization and culture, passed into oblivion. Germanic and Slav tribes and nomadic peoples of the steppes contented themselves with founding rough-and-ready and mostly shortlived states on the land they conquered and with using a simpler barter economy which answered their needs well enough.

However, only one aspect of the imminent historical process of succession was reflected in the "relapse of the West into Barbarity". On the other hand, it cleared the ground for the development of a civilization whose system of rule, production and exchange was nevertheless superior, in the long term, to that of Antiquity which was largely based on low-productivity slave labour. Furthermore, it was restricted to a specific region. In Eastern Rome and Persia, in China and Japan, there was a transition to a system, which may be described as feudal, this being the result of an uninterrupted movement of social driving forces without any significant influence being exercised from outside.

The manner in which war was waged took account of these changes. Although hereditary monarchies replaced the military and elected kingship of the time of the Barbarian invasions and a class of privileged landowners—including some Roman dignitaries—came into existence, the Germanic states from the 5th to the beginning of the 8th century still relied primarily on the peasant arrière ban of the common freemen, i.e., practically all the menfolk capable of bearing arms of the tribe in question. This made up for the relatively low numbers of the conquerors.

In the confrontations between the Franks, Alemanni, Burgundians, Goths and Suebi and in the wars of the Vandals, Goths and Lombards with Eastern Rome, it was accordingly the Old Germanic tactics and weapons that predominated. It was despair which drove Totila, the young king of the Ostrogoths, to using the subjugated Romans as combatants with the same status as his own warriors for the defence of Italy against the plundering of Imperial officials. After initial successes, this venture failed in the battle of Taginae (553) with the experienced army of the court eunuch Narses, a commander who knew the value of patience.

However, the military arm which was to leave its mark on the late Middle Ages was not developed in Eastern Rome, although it was only here—with the exception of China—that there was still any kind of military theory. The state of the Sassanids outstripped it in military power. The Persians, who had always attached importance to the breeding of horses, learned the art of steel-making in India and, under Khosrau I (531 to 579),

developed in Iran an élite unit of noble cavalry who wore armour and were the forerunners of the *knights*.
It was only after crushing defeats in Europe and Asia that Eastern Rome—or Byzantium as it was more usually called from the 7th century onwards—took account of the change in its situation. However, the repulsion of the Persians, who had advanced as far as the gates of the capital, was due not so much to the efficacy of the "military districts" (Greek: *themata*) established by Heraclius I and defended by conscripted free peasants and lesser nobles as to a strategic surprise-manoeuvre. Together with the Caucasian princes who were his allies, the emperor marched his army from the North through the mountains. In this way, he outflanked the attacking enemy forces, who were strung out from the Sea of Marmora as far as Egypt, and by his victory at *Nineveh* (627) over the weaker covering army of Khosrau II won the long-drawn-out war at a single stroke. The totally unexpected attack cost the Sassanid king not only all the fruits of his offensive but also his throne and his life as well.

It immediately became apparent, however, that both sides were the losers. While they had been tearing each other to pieces, the prophet Mohammed of Mecca had been uniting the tribes of the Arabian peninsula under the banner of Islam, a doctrine which preached submission to the will of Allah. A "divine state" emerged from the umma, the community of the believers. Under the green flag of the Prophet, his successors the caliphs (i.e., deputies) carried the Holy War for the subjugation of the infidels as far as India and the land of the Franks.

It was wrongly imagined that the Arab aggressors were a vast horde of horsemen who annihilated the enemy immediately battle was joined. This was impossible since the aridity of their native deserts did not allow the use of horses over long distances which had to have water. On the other hand, the camels which were used as means of transportation were far too valuable to be sacrificed in large numbers in battle. In actual fact, the victories of the fanatic Moslem warriors with their contempt for death were mostly won on foot to begin with. It was only after the occupation of Persia and the Barbary Coast of North Africa that they learned to appreciate the advantages of hard-riding cavalry troops in battle. If the reports of the chroniclers are correct, these units were even used by the Arab general Abd-al-Rahman in the battle of *Poitiers* (732) against the Franks, although he was still unable to achieve victory.

After this, the Orient and the West achieved equality in military potential. Gifts were exchanged by the two most powerful personages of the time—Charlemagne, who had been crowned Emperor of the West in Rome, and the Abbasid Caliph Harun al-Rashid, who ruled from Baghdad and was the fairytale prince from *A Thousand and One Nights*. Both of their great empires disintegrated between the 9th and the 10th centuries and made room for a greater variety of states. On the political map of Europe, France and Germany were joined by other powers: the Anglo-Saxon realm on the island of Britannia, Poland and the "Rus" of the Grand Dukes of Kiev. Bulgaria emerged as an adversary of Byzantium and the ring of small Christian states in the North of Spain expanded southwards from Córdova at the expense of the Moorish state. The warrior hero of Spanish Christendom, El Cid Campeador, soon caught the imagination of the poets. Hungarian horsemen streamed over the Carpathians and across the Pannonian Plain while in the steppes by the Black Sea the Khazars were driven away by the Pechenegi and these in turn by the Kumans. Sea-robbers, known as Northmen or Vikings, rowed their long boats across the sea from Scandinavia to the coasts of Western Europe and settled in some areas.

The Islamic Orient likewise had its troubles with "new arrivals". While the sciences and the arts flourished and artisan products such as the steel sword-blades of Damascus and Toledo achieved a worldwide reputation, both the caliphs and rebellious governors, the emirs, began to use captured Turkish slaves for military service. As soon as the latter were in the majority, their leaders turned the tables on their masters and themselves seized the power they were supposed to protect. They stripped the caliph of all his powers except his religious authority and, with or without his blessing, founded their own dynasties from the Tajo to the Indus. Mahmud of Ghazni even advanced as far as the Ganges and sacked Delhi.

Feudal structures in society and the army finally became established on either side of the Mediterranean. The great majority of the peasants were reduced to bondsmen or serfs whose person and land were subject to the overlordship of the landowners. The latter alone—together with the clergy—formed "estate" and state which progressed in the form of a fief pyramid. At the top of this pyramid there was the monarch, followed by the great lords, the dukes, earls or margraves. Then came their vassals (such as the barons) and, in turn, the vassals of these latter from the lesser nobility. The fief itself, originally made available in return for services given or promised, then tended to be regarded as a hereditary possession—whether it was a Franco-Norman *bénéfice*, a Russian *kormlenie*, a Byzantine *pronoia* or an Arab *iktaa*.

So as not to be totally dependent on the changeable mood of the great lords, who often carried on feuds between themselves, the monarch maintained a personal retinue. In the economically advanced Orient with its profusion of cities from which he obtained a substantial revenue, the monarch's own guard of well-trained slaves was frequently the principal contingent in campaigns. In the "under-developed" West, the king had neither comparable resources nor effective means of exerting pressure on his vassals. He had to wage a "cheap" war and his authority was accordingly less than that of the Asiatic despots. In the final analysis, it was the real balance of power between the liege-lord and his vassal which decided whether the latter observed his pledge of loyalty to the former.

Under Otto the Great (936–973), this balance was to the advantage of the German king. Although there was nobody far and wide who could rival him in military power, his army numbered only a few thousand horsemen. And, with the poor roads and logistics which were more improvised than organized, it was even difficult to keep these together for more than one campaign during the warm season of the year. A rapid decision, such as that in the battle on the *Lech* against the Hungarians (955) which was won by better weapons and well-considered strategy, was consequently the aim but this was not always achieved.

Otto's mounted warriors from the nobility were not yet knights in full armour since the low level of the Central European smiths did not allow this. At this time, there could still be no question of a marked consciousness of their rank in society. Nevertheless, the organization of the German and other armies was moving in a direction which was to represent the norm in the following two centuries.

While in Scandinavia the Norwegian and Swedish states were consolidating themselves—long after Denmark—the Normans who had settled in France had crossed the Channel and, under William the Conqueror, won the battle of *Hastings* (1066), gaining mastery of the Anglo-Saxons and their kingdom. Other Normans

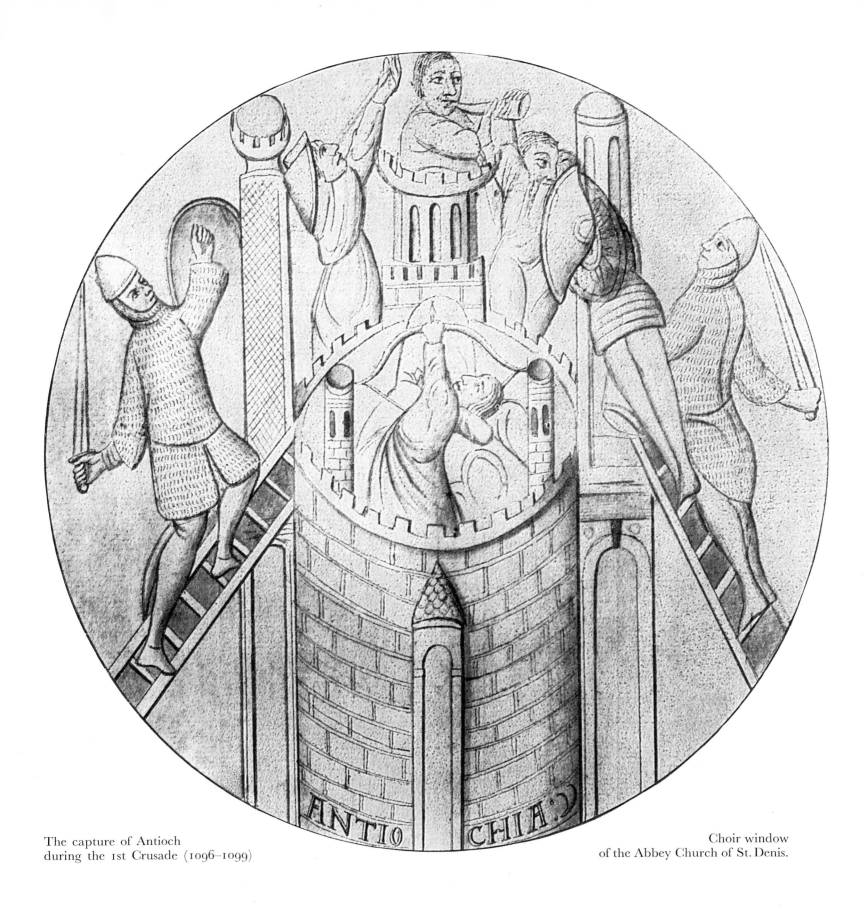

ANTIOCHIA

The capture of Antioch
during the 1st Crusade (1096–1099)

Choir window
of the Abbey Church of St. Denis.

began in Southern Italy on a relatively small scale as princely officials but soon became independent and then, in the struggle with Byzantium and the Arabs in Sicily, established a powerful kingdom. Byzantium, which had regained complete control of the frontier along the Danube after destroying the Slav empire of Ochrid at the battle of Belasitza (1014), unsuccessfully defended its remaining possessions in Italy. It suffered an even more serious defeat at the hands of the Turkish Seljuks who, after capturing Baghdad (1055), advanced to the status of a great Oriental power and, following the victory of Manzikert (1071), occupied Asia Minor. Shortly afterwards, Islam scored a further success with the victory of Yusuf-ibn-Tashfin the Almoravid at the head of a Berber army at the battle of Zallaka (Badajoz; 1086). This delayed the disintegration of the Caliphate of Córdova into small emirates and thus for some time held up the *Reconquista*, the recapture of Spain by the Christians.

The Crusade movement, which united a number of different factors, reacted to this new development in the confrontation between the Orient and the West. Europe, at last becoming stronger economically, increasing in population and enriched by an—initially in Italy—emergent urban bourgeoisie with a lively interest in foreign trade, entered on a new stage in the struggle to control the Mediterranean. Even the first Crusade (1096–1099) took an army of mixed nationality under Godfrey of Bouillon to Jerusalem, the original goal, after surviving many dangers. In the third Crusade (1189–1192), thet wo idols of Western and Oriental chivalry, Richard Cœur de Lion, the daredevil king of England, and Saladin, the astute Ayyubid sultan who won the battle of Hittin in 1187 and recaptured Jerusalem, personally confronted each other and, neither being able to defeat the other, broke off the struggle. With the recognition of their essential similarity and their mutual respect for each other, they were an inexhaustible subject for literature.

In the end, it was the defenders who won. In a contest extending over two centuries, they reduced the Crusader states which had been set up in the "Holy Land" to a narrow coastal strip and then captured one castle after another, the last being at Acre in 1291. In the other theatre of war, the Iberian Peninsula, on the other hand, English Crusaders helped the Portuguese to capture Lisbon in 1147 and the Castilians under Alfonso VIII put an end to the domination of the Moors at Las Navas de Tolosa on 16 July 1212, forcing them to retreat to the mountainous district of Granada, where the enchanting Alhambra is still a reminder of them.

In the 13th century, the Mongols of Genghis Khan as the last wave of mounted archers from Central Asia, swept down almost simultaneously on China, the Orient and Europe. They destroyed the state of Khorezm on the Amu Dar'ya and in Iran and then, in 1223, defeated a combined Russo-Kuman force at the River *Kalka*. Another and even more ambitious campaign took them through the Russian duchies and Poland. At Liegnitz (Legnica), they defeated Henry, the Piast Duke of Silesia, and the German knights who had hastened to his assistance on 9 April 1241. Two days later, Bela IV of Hungary was witness to the destruction of his army at the Sajó on the heath of Móhi by a Mongol army coming from the South. However, since the question of who was to succeed the Great Khan who had died in the meantime had to be decided, the victors withdrew from Central Europe in 1242 as suddenly as they had come. Between the Dnestr and the Urals, however, they established the state of Kipchak, to which the princes of Russia had to pay tribute.

In 1258, the Mongols under Hulagu captured Baghdad. Only the Egyptain Mameluke sultan Baybars, known as the "Sword of Islam", was able to throw them back in the long-drawn-out battle of 'Ain Jalut (1260) at the gates of Damascus and to establish a limit to the power of the Mongol "Il-khans" at the Euphrates.

The conquest of China was completed in 1279 by Kublai Khan with the subjugation of the Sung empire of the South. As the founder of the new Chinese Yüan dynasty, he established his residence in Peking and extended his claims to Korea, Vietnam, Burma and even Japan. Expeditions which he dispatched to *Hakata Bay* in 1274 and 1281 failed to secure recognition of his sovereignty by the Imperial military administrators of the island state, which was administered according to feudal principles but was ruled by a central authority, and were not repeated.

In the final analysis, both the Crusades and the raids by the Mongols led to stronger contacts and cross-fertilization between the principal centres of world culture, to the adoption of forms of military organization such as the knightly orders and to an exchange of goods and experience which was promoted by the trans-continental trade-routes and illustrious travellers such as Marco Polo and Ibn Batutah.

It was already in this epoch that the Golden Age of chivalry which had left its mark in the epics and the minnesong of the 12th and 13th centuries began to decline. Admittedly, both in peace and in war the noble landowner remained the master and the peasant, his vassal from generation to generation, remained his servant. The latter walked in the baggage train while the former rode proudly on his noble steed, rider and horse always being more heavily armoured than his henchman. Accordingly, the army continued to be fairly small and aristocratic with weapons which were essentially conservative in design. To be sure, their craftsmanship never ceased to improve and become more exquisite but there was a lack of new ideas. Full armour gave the knight better protection but rendered him less agile and more dependent on others.

The emergent middle-class, with its demands for greater political power, frequently succeeded by alliances with other forces in freeing itself from the control of the local lords. This confronted the knightly armies with a number of problems. Frederick I Barbarossa, the Hohenstaufen emperor, was the first who had to acknowledge this situation in a wider political context when he attacked an alliance of Lombard towns under the leadership of Milan which were loyal to the pope and was routed by them at *Legnano* in 1176. Admittedly, the circumstances of this were unusual in that Frederick's most powerful vassal, Duke Henry the Lion, broke his oath of fealty and, by refusing to take up arms, greatly weakened the Imperial forces while, on the other hand, the towns were able to put into the field not only militia forces fighting on foot but also knights who took part in the last phase of the battle.

In the 13th century and at the beginning of the 14th, it was not only the Northern Italian cities but also the great Flemish trading and manufacturing centres in particular which were able to raise powerful and very well equipped contingents of infantry and some cavalry units as well from their own resources. In the battle of Courtrai (1302), they defeated the French knights and contributed to the success of the uprising in Ghent under Jacob van Artevelde in 1338. Cologne had already achieved independence at the battle of Worringen (1288) by defeating the forces of its archbishop. In the late 14th century, the cities of the Hanseatic League, with their

Condottiere Bartolomeo Colleoni.
Bronze statue by Andrea del Verrocchio,
unveiled in 1496 in Venice.

resources of ships and pieces of silver, were able to wage wars which were by no means unprofitable against the kings of England, Denmark and Sweden.

Some historians even consider that the 14th century marked the beginning of a new stage in military history but this is for two other reasons: firstly, the appearance of the Swiss peasants on the military scene and secondly the introduction of firearms.

The Alpine peasants from the three original cantons had retained their traditional freedom and had even received a charter to this effect from Emperor Frederick II. The first to question this were the Hapsburgs, in the early days of their career, when they deemed it advisable to consolidate their scattered Alemannic possessions. As it was, the army of knights led by Duke Leopold I of Austria was surprised on the march at Morgarten by the Swiss forces and was badly mauled.

The news of this horrified the aristocracy. Having to fight peasants was bad enough in the first place but being defeated as well was really too much. How this could happen is difficult to say since the pious chronicler, in accordance with the custom of the time, filled in the gaps in the communiqués with borrowings from the *Book of Judith*. For the Swiss patricians of the towns, however, the "rough" peasants were acceptable allies and from the "confederacy of the eight old towns" there emerged a new state. When the Hapsburgs returned to the attack with more powerful forces, they were again elegantly repulsed by the Swiss at *Sempach* in 1386 and at Näfels in 1388.

Did this mark the birth of a new type of military unit? The new aspect which the Swiss certainly introduced was that the infantry was not only massed as a defensive body in battle but was also used for attacking knights in armour, overwhelming them by sheer weight of numbers. This was rapidly appreciated by impartial observers and Swiss mercenaries were in demand everywhere. They were the most popular exports of the Swiss Confederation in the 15th century.

This upgrading of infantry forces was also demonstrated by the Janizaries, the élite troops of the Turkish Osmanli. The Turks had invaded Europe in 1354 at Gallipoli and began to spread over the Balkan Peninsula after victories over the Serbian and other princes at the Maritza (1371) and at the battle of Kosovo Polje (1389). In 1396, they defeated a Crusader army under King Sigismund of Hungary at Nicopolis but were overwhelmed in a catastrophic manner by the Mongol conqueror Timur Leng at Angora in 1402, an event which delayed Turkish ambitions in this area by fifty years. It was only the capture of Constantinople by Mehmed II in 1453 which restored their reputation and power but this time it was even more complete than before.

The Turkish Janizaries were largely recruited from the tribute of children (*devshirme*) exacted by the sultan from subjugated Christian nations while the ranks of the Egyptian Mamelukes were maintained by the purchase of Kurdish and Circassian slaves from other Islamic lands with which friendly relations were maintained. The need of rulers to be able to rely on an obedient body of troops—since these were kept by them and were largely isolated from the general population—instead of on the loyalty of ambitious lords and overburdened vassals—was just as valid on the other side of the Sahara as for the originators of the slave-guards of the Orient. Sunjata Keita had still been able to lay the foundations of the astonishing Mali empire in the battle of Kirina against the kingdom of Suso in 1235 with tribal warriors. But it was with a professional army recruited from slaves and prisoners of war that Sonni Ali (1462–1492) and Askia Mohammed (1493–1528) established the Songhai empire, a force that none of its neighbours could withstand.

However, as long as infantry forces only had the traditional weapons at their disposal, which could only be improved within relatively narrow practical limits—such as the development of the crossbow from the ancient bow or the halberd and pike from the spear, they possessed only a relative superiority over fast-moving mounted units. This situation then experienced a gradual change with the appearance of firearms on the scene. It is true that powder was already known as a means of propulsion for devices of a firework nature before it came into use as "gunpowder" but how and when this happened remains the subject of controversy. The fact that a mixture of saltpeter, sulphur and carbon in certain proportions could be used to shoot heavy objects from a tube was not generally known in Europe before 1300. The earliest credible report of the use of firearms concerns the siege of the town of Cividale in Friuli in 1331, yet the earliest finds date from the last decade of the 14th century. Consequently, little is known of the appearance and design of the original hand-guns and cannon but it is likely that they were invented either in Northern Italy or along the lower reaches of the Rhine. They consisted of a tube 20 centimetres in length at most and having a bore of 1.6 to 3.0 centimetres, closed at one end by a lock fixed to a shaft of iron or wood. To begin with, their range was inferior to that of the crossbow or long bow. Nevertheless, they must have been sufficiently impressive to suggest that gunpowder could help to replace the ancient engines of destruction such as the ballista. The richer cities in particular had great guns built by highly specialized craftsmen. These were known as bombards and were initially forged from iron but it soon became the practice to cast them in bronze. They weighed between three and ten tons, indicating that such cumbersome devices, which could only be moved and set up with very great difficulty, were almost exclusively intended for the besieging or defence of strongholds. In the 15th century, the balls they hurled were made of iron instead of stone as hitherto, the effect of this being to increase the "rate of fire" which could be achieved by a skilled artilleryman by an average of one shot in the course of a day, i.e., from two to three rounds. In particular, the introduction of iron cannonballs enabled the bore to be reduced from an average of 80 centimetres to 10 to 17 centimetres. Finally, the improved composition of gunpowder and constructional modifications to gun-barrels allowed cannon to be used in pitched battles.

To begin with, the artillery was a trade guild. It was not organized in a military manner nor was it regarded as being of the same standing as the other branches of the army. The "warlords" had to "rent" the artillerymen and their cannon and only those who had exceptional resources at their disposal—such as the Teutonic Knights in Prussia—could afford several batteries at the same time. Accordingly it was not guns but the knights' equipment and combat methods of the enemy forces which determined the outcome of the battle at *Grunwald-Tannenberg* (1410) which marked the rise of Poland-Lithuania to the status of a great East European power. The victory of the English over the French at Azincourt (1415), which still caught the imagination of Shakespeare, was primarily won by the yeomen of England with their long bows. On the other hand, a few years later, the rebellious Hussites in Bohemia with its many arts and crafts demonstrated the versatility of the weapon which reduced knights in armour to the status of supernumaries and allowed their attack to be destroyed before it could make contact with the enemy. The fire of "howitzers" from the barricade of waggons caused panic at the battle of *Usti* (Aussig, 1426), as described in vivid words by an eye-witness.

For the first time, the Hussites used large numbers of harquebuses in battle. It was obviously the Bohemian gunmakers with their skill in the working of metal who introduced the hook to absorb the recoil of the weapon and also extended the barrel. From the long arquebus, it was then only a step to the heavier version and to the lighter musket. Both of these were muzzleloaders which were fired by a slow match held in the hand. This meant that two persons were required, one for aiming and one for firing the weapon. About 1440, the matchlock appeared on the scene and needed only *one* person for its operation, the index finger being used to actuate the mechanism which lowered the burning cord into the touch-pan. The maximum range of a crossbow was 135 paces but matchlock muskets could achieve 250 which explains why firearms rapidly came into general use and why musketeers were some of the most respected soldiers up to the time of D'Artagnan. When in use, the musket was supported by a forked stick and the musketeer carried his ammunition in a wide and often elaborate leather bandelier. These lead missiles could cause deep wounds but the harquebusiers and musketeers were unable to defend themselves from attack. Consequently, pikemen were used for their defence and these still had to fight man to man with cold steel.

This does not imply at all that the knight now disappeared from the scene. Even more splendid armour was made in the 15th century and was worn at tournaments with lances. It was more appropriate for the aristocratic sport of jousting than for serious use on the battlefield. Duke Charles the Bold of Burgundy opposed the general trend in more than one sense when he strived to establish an independent power in the centre of Europe despite the resistance of France, Germany and Switzerland. For this purpose, he reorganized his army and once again assigned the knights the principal role. Admittedly, the vigorous prosperity of his cities in the Netherlands allowed him to provide them with the most modern and most powerful artillery ever seen for their support. Up to this time, all culverins had had to be transported on carts but the duke had them made with smaller barrels and fitted to single-axle carriages. These "Burgundian carriages", as the forerunners of gun-carriages, allowed the guns to be manoeuvred during the battle. However, it proved impossible to use them in a tactically effective manner in conjunction with an army of knights. Many noble warriors still considered all firearms to be "hellish falsehood and deceit" and there are credible reports of the slaughter of captured artillerymen by aristocrats furious that "common varlets" could now eliminate heavily armed knights without difficulty before the latter even came within striking distance.

In addition, Charles's unreliable sense of proportion led to his political encirclement so that this time the Swiss attacked the Burgundians not only with the approval of Louis XI of France but even in alliance with Emperor Frederick III. In three hard-fought battles at Grandson and *Murten* (1476) and finally, on foreign land, at Nancy (1477), where the duke was killed, they emerged as the victors.

The fact that the knight then became identified with Franz von Sickingen as a tragic figure, with Falstaff as a comic one and with Don Quixote as a gloomy figure or, in the shape of Ulrich von Hutten, Götz von

The Italian-Spanish fleet defeated the Turks on 5. 10. 1571
in the sea-battle of Lepanto.
Mural by Andrea Vicentino. Palazzo Ducale, Venice

Berlichingen and Florian Geyer, found himself betwixt the class fronts was of course not the fault of the Swiss alone. The tightening of the royal authority weakened the entire feudal system. The state changed into an institution.

The monarchs reduced or even destroyed the "partial sovereignty" of their great vassals while preserving their social privileges. Economic growth, especially within the commercial sphere of the urban middle-class which developed mines, established publishing houses and manufacturing establishments, built fleets and created a powerful banking system, provided the taxation authorities with tax revenues for maintaining an administrative, finance and judiciary system which was solely responsible to the Crown and also for paying a powerful mercenary army in times of war. Accordingly, the part played by feudal service became less and less important in military affairs.

The establishment of a centralized authority did not take place smoothly everywhere and in countries such as Germany or Poland it was even made impossible by the forces opposing it. Nevertheless, even the kings of these countries were obliged to employ mercenaries in accordance with the trend of the time so as not to fall behind the effective strengths of their adversaries.

It was in the small states of Northern Italy which were blessed more generously with hard cash than with voluntary warriors that mercenaries first appeared in an organized form, this being in the 15th century. The recruitment and leadership of the troops was entrusted to private military experts, the condottieri, who usually obtained their "soldiers" from other countries. While Gattamelata and Colleoni were satisfied with magnificent equestrian statues as a reminder of their fame for future generations, the Sforzas in Milan and other mercenary leaders themselves took over the reins of power in the city-states they were supposed to protect and founded miniature dynasties of their own.

Understandably, the mercenaries most in demand were the Swiss who, in this capacity, served the King of France, Venice, Milan, the pope and other potentates. However, since their reserves of manpower were limited and astute agents also forced up the prices charged, a second great mercenary market came into existence at the end of the 15th century in territorially split-up Southern Germany. Here the term *Landsknecht* was coined.

The origin of the word *Landsknecht* has not been completely explained. It is derived from the word "lance" or possibly from "Knecht aus dem Lande" (country boy). It passed into English and French as "lansquenet". The German lansquenets, who were initially recruited from prosperous peasant and middle-class families for the most part, were organized in a kind of guild, like other trades. They themselves chose their commanders and non-commissioned officers and offered their services alternately to the warlords who paid the best wages.

A change took place in the mercenary system in Spain. Its kings, who had finally forced Granada to capitulate in 1492, ruled the Low Countries and Naples, were conquering the Aztec and Inca empires of the New World and lived in a permanent state of war with the Moslems of Northwest Africa, likewise made use of German lansquenets. In addition, however, they also needed troops for longer terms of service and these were drawn from the Spanish peasantry and paid with the silver taken from the American colonies. Their commanders differed from the condottieri and the leaders of the lansquenets in that they were regular officers of the

Crown and their forces were trained for battle in accordance with standing orders. In this way, the *tercios* emerged, regiments of 1000 to 3000 men, largely consisting of pikemen but also already including a considerable number of musketeers. Such a combination made a disciplined unit superior to a group of Swiss mercenaries of equivalent manpower and it can be regarded as the first example of a fully developed infantry formation. Incidentally, the word "infantry" comes from the Spanish.

A convincing demonstration of its capabilities was supplied by the *tercio* in 1525 during the Renaissance Wars (1494–1559) between Spain and France for the domination of Italy at the battle of *Pavia* where the Spanish troops were commanded by Pescara. Not only was King Francis I of France taken captive but the defeat of the Swiss in this battle caused them to lose their pre-eminent position among the mercenaries of Europe.

The political and military hegemony of Spain in Europe, which was supported by its dynastic links with the Holy Roman Empire of the German Nation continued for more than a century. The threat of a Catholic counter-reformation led by a Hapsburg world-power aroused the opposition of a number of very different adversaries. Even under Emperor Charles V (1519–1556), power groupings emerged in which the Protestant "estates" of Germany not only took the side of the king of France but even that of the pope and Sultan Suleiman the Magnificent (1520–1566). France resisted its encirclement and the German princes revenged their defeat in the Schmalkaldic War at Mühlberg (1547) by their counter-attack under Maurice of Saxony in 1552. After the victory at Mohács (1526), the Turks had conquered the greater part of Hungary and had even threatened Vienna in 1529. Their admirals Dragut and Khair ed-Din Barbarossa were hard-fighting opponents of the Imperial admiral, Andrea Doria, Doge of Genoa, and it was only the celebrated victory of the combined Spanish and Venetian fleets under Don John of Austria at Lepanto (1571) which again won a certain freedom of movement, limited though this was, for "Christian seafaring" in the Mediterranean.

Two different lines of development were already apparent at this time: the highest stage of absolutism as a late feudal political form and, in contrast, a round of great revolutions. Both were influenced by the continuing rise of the middle-class which was beginning to develop the features of an independent class. With the emergence of a characteristic and rational mode of production and exchange, based on the freedom of movement of capital and labour and later known as capitalism, this new class came into conflict with the rigid structure of the system of privileges of the estates.

The desire to make their profits within a great national market encouraged the trading and manufacturing bourgeoisie to align themselves with a ruler "answerable only to God" who—in plain language—initiated a standardization of the State administration and, to their mutual advantage, to take the side of an absolute monarchy as one of the main factors in their economic system. When, however, an already self-confident middle-class demanded its share of political power, a clash became unavoidable and heralded a social transformation which had to be implemented with military means.

The first sign of this on the political horizon was the German Peasants' Revolt (1524–1526) which occurred at the height of the Reformation and was condemned by Luther but preached by Thomas Müntzer. The revolt of the Netherlands against alien Spanish rule, obscured at first by the religious dispute and the defence of chartered

Duel between two mounted mercenaries.
Copperplate engraving by J. M. de Jonge, *c.* 1630/40.
Armeemuseum der DDR, Dresden

rights against the inroads of great feudal lords, then displayed in 1572 its real character as a popular revolt of the "Geuzen" on the sea and on land. Despite outstanding generals, such as Alba, Alexander Farnese and Spinola, the Spanish war machine proved incapable of mastering the situation. The long duration of the struggle, which after a truce (1609–1621) continued until 1648, favoured the methodical evaluation of Dutch experience in the field and it was the Dutch school of military strategy—influenced by the study of classic Roman authors—which marked the beginnings of modern European military science. King Gustavus II Adolphus of Sweden applied their theory and practice on the German battlefields of the Thirty Years' War at Breitenfeld (1631) and *Lützen* (1632).

In the Civil Wars of the English Revolution, which have often been inaccurately described as the "Great Rebellion", the Puritan Roundheads were first obliged to establish the appropriate military forces before they could stand up to the Cavaliers of Charles I with their greater combat experience. Oliver Cromwell's *pious* *Ironsides*, mounted volunteers who paid for their own equipment and won the armed struggle of Parliament against the king in the battles of Marston Moor (1644) and Naseby (1645), were aware of what they were fighting for and thus represented the first all-national middle-class peasant and artisan army of history. Nevertheless, the "New Model Army" and its most original creation, the soldier councils which had a voice in the taking of decisions, remained an isolated democratic episode. Converted to the instrument of power of a military dictator—capable though he was—it lost its justification for existing after the settlement between the aristocracy and the upper middle-class in 1660 and again in 1688/89. The English constitutional monarchy returned to the exquisite mercenary army. In addition, it fired golden cannonballs in the direction of the Continent in the form of "subsidies" for its allies. However, it regarded the Royal Navy as its principal weapon and the Fleet swept its rivals from the seas one after another in a series of memorable battles—the Spanish Armada (1588), the illustrious Dutch admirals Tromp and de Ruyter (1652–1654, 1664–1667, 1672–1674) and the French fleet, which after Colbert's reorganization had become a threat to England (La Hogue, 1692).

At approximately the same time, momentous events took place in another direction in distant Asia. In China, the authority of the Ming emperors, who had been put on the throne by a rebellion in 1368 which had swept away the Mongol Yüans, collapsed under the pressure of a protracted peasants' revolt. The "Realm of the Middle" was conquered by the Manchus whose princes took up residence in Peking as Ch'ing Dynasty (1644–1911). Since they were not threatened by any militarily superior neighbours, the principal function of the three-level army, consisting of Chinese district-troops, Chinese provincial forces under Manchurian military governors and the real "Eight-Banner Army" which was exclusively Manchurian and far better equipped, was to maintain the unrestricted power of the Ch'ings over the hundreds of millions of Chinese, the Mongols, the Tibetans, the Uighurs and other subjugated peoples.

In Japan, on the other hand, the powerful daimyos, who governed the provinces of the country and headed the great Buddhist monasteries, vigorously resisted the re-establishment of the centralized state with its hierarchy of officials which had been based on the Chinese model and had disintegrated in the course of the feuds between the local centres of power during the 14th century. The "Sengoku Period" (1479–1577) was a hundred years of civil war with constantly changing fortunes for the sides involved. Eventually, two soldiers who had risen from the ranks, Oda Nobunaga and after him Toyotomi Hideyoshi, were able to halt the disintegration of the central authority and, as autocratic military commanders and with the aid of the muskets which had been adopted from the Portuguese as early as 1543, succeeded in restoring the unity of the State. In the struggle for the position of Hideyoshi's successor, the Daimyo of Edo (Tokio), Tokugawa Ieyasu, defeated his rival at the battle of *Sekigahara* (1600) and was able to bequeath the supreme office of the State, the Shogunate, to his descendants. Thus, he founded the Tokugawa Bakufu (1603–1867), an absolute monarchy of a specifically Japanese kind.

The history of India is characterized by precisely the opposite course. After his victory at Panipat (on 18 April 1526), Babur the Timurid founded an Islamic "Empire of the Great Moguls" which achieved its greatest prosperity under Akbar (1556–1605). The first cracks in this appeared in the second half of the 17th century with the resistance of the Hindu Maratha under Sivaji (1627–1680) while the trading posts of European colonial powers spread like mushrooms along the coast and contributed to the breakaway of the provincial governors from the Mogul in Delhi. The renewal of the Persian state by the Shi'ite Safavids (1501), which under Abbas the Great (1588–1629) was still the worthy adversary of the Ottomans, was wracked by internal feuds and was defeated by the Afghans at Golnabad in 1722. After a last flash of glory under Nadir Shah (1736–1747) it lost its rank as an important Oriental power.

For Turkey, this relaxation in the pressure on its eastern border came too late. To be sure, its military power was still discouragement enough to potential adversaries even a century after Lepanto but it could not keep pace with world developments. Social tension weakened the cohesion and power of the Ottoman Empire. It needed 25 years to wrest Crete from the Venetians (1645–1669). In three wars against Austria, Poland and Russia (1664–1681), energetic Grand Viziers managed to postpone the outcome. Defeats such as that at St. Gotthard (1664) alternated with victory and, as warnings, were consequently not heeded. A great offensive was launched against Imperial Vienna as a remedy for the crisis of the State and it was after the Turks had been defeated in the *Battle of Kahlenberg* (1683) that the catastrophe occurred with Budapest falling in 1686 and Azov in 1697.

Turkey stubbornly defended her European possessions for a long time still but the initiative had passed to the other side. Its continued existence was due less to its army of Janizaries who were not prepared to be reorganized than to the mutual mistrust of the Powers who were not willing to accept a disproportionate division of the legacy of the Ottoman Empire.

Putting the "Oriental Question" on ice as far as possible was only *one* aspect of the policy of a balance of power in Europe initially pursued by England as a trading and maritime power to contain the domination of the Continent by France.

Whenever an unwanted shift in the balance of power seemed imminent, coalitions against the "troublemaker" were formed to restore the equilibrium. Despite all the expertise developed by the cabinets in secret diplomacy, the wars they caused proved exceptionally difficult to end: 1688–1697, 1700–1721, 1701–1714, 1733 to 1738, 1740–1748 and 1756–1763. This was due not least to the circumstance that military organization was largely based on the French model and all armies followed more or less the same rules and used the same textbooks of military theory.

At the end of the 17th and the beginning of the 18th century, the well-established absolute monarchies had more or less completed the further development of the mercenary system and disposed of powerful—and accordingly expensive—military forces. This was already apparent from their outer appearance. The princes had attempted, without very much success, to have at least their personal colours represented in the motley costumes of their lansquenets and other mercenaries but the English Revolutionary Army under Cromwell was the first to wear a standard uniform, the famous Red Coat. Depending on the ability of large manufacturers to supply sufficient quantities of cloth of the same colour at a low price, the wearing of uniforms by the military became the custom in almost all the states of Europe. However, the "King's cloth" was not nearly so attractive as the battle painters of the Baroque period have depicted it and, in fact, it was poorly dyed and coarsely woven. Only the officers, who were mostly from aristocratic families, were better dressed and it was also at this time that standardized insignia of rank came into use, a practice which originated in France, distinguishing lieutenants from captains and generals from marshals.

A constant increase took place in military firepower. The flintlock, of simpler construction than the wheel-lock of the 16th century and thus cheaper to manufacture in large quantities, used a flint as a means of ignition instead of a slow match. Thus the flintlock became the standard infantry weapon and remained so until well into the 19th century. As a muzzle-loader with a smooth bore, two shots a minute were possible, well-drilled soldiers could even achieve three and, when the weather was dry and there was little wind, five shots a minute were not unknown. The pikemen were no longer needed once it had proved possible to fix a knife-like weapon in the barrel or to the side of the gun. However, this "bayonet", which was introduced in the French army in 1687, was not

Kidnapping by Turkish soldiers.
Woodcut by an unknown German master. From: Veit Traut,
"Türkischer Kayser Ankunft, Krieg und Sig", Augsburg 1543.

Fire muskets!
Hand-coloured
copperplate engraving
by Jacob de Gheyn
c. 1597/98.
Armeemuseum der
DDR, Dresden

Uniforms
of the Prussian Army
in the mid-18th century:
artillerymen
and riflemen;
grenadiers;
pioneers; lifeguards.
Coloured lithograph
by W. Bormann,
c. 1850.
Armeemuseum der
DDR, Dresden

so effective as the pike so that infantry had to be given constant protection by cavalry against sudden attacks by enemy mounted units.

The military organized field-artillery with lighter barrels and special gun-carriages became a firmly established arm of the service. A certain standardization of guns and ammunition took place: light cannon ranged from three- to twelve-pounders (from the weight of the iron cannonballs) with heavy siege and fortress guns were twenty-four and forty-eight-pounders, corresponding to calibres between 7 and 17 centimetres. While great reductions were made in the strength of the artillery in times of peace for financial reasons, its numbers were significantly increased in the course of long wars as soon as the fighting power of the infantry and cavalry was affected by irreplaceable losses.

The possibility of increasing taxes whenever they wished, once the inconvenient national assemblies had been eliminated, enabled the kings "by mercy of God" to pursue their political ambitions with military means for long periods at a time. Politics and strategy were aimed at weakening the opponent by a succession of campaigns and ultimately to cut off or exhaust his resources. When the adversaries were of the same standing, this took a long time. Even bloody victories such as those won by Prince Eugene for Austria or the Duke of Marlborough for England, or both together as at *Blenheim* (1704), Oudenaarde (1708) and Malplaquet (1709), over the French, could not end the war. That it would be bourgeois England, with its sense of progress, which in the long run would survive this contest of strength and not the antiquated, late feudal state system of the "most Christian" king of France, first became apparent with the collapse of the *ancien régime* in the Revolution of 1789: "Après moi le déluge"—to quote the words attributed to Louis XV (1715–1774).

All the efforts to avoid abrupt changes in international relations were powerless to change the law of unequal development and it was precisely the 18th century which marked the rise of new great powers: Austria, Russia, Prussia and—"on the edge of the inhabited world"—the United States of America.

In the case of Austria, it is more accurate to talk of a more or less orderly withdrawal of the Hapsburgs from the hotchpotch of the Holy Roman Empire of the German Nation, in which the emperor had less and less say, to their own territory, which extended into Hungary and Italy. Czar Peter I, on the other hand, whose drastic work of reform in the face of conservative resistance made possible an effective reorganization of the military system, won the irrevocable acceptance of Russia as a great European power by his watchful contemporaries on the day in June 1709 on which his regiments at *Poltava* brought down the house of cards of Swedish control of the Baltic.

Prussia, for its part, was vividly described by Franz Mehring as being "not a state with an army but an army with a state". Its foundations had already been laid in the 17th century by the Electors of Brandenburg, after they had inherited the Duchies of Prussia and Pomerania. Under Frederick William I (1711–1740), the cantonal system was introduced which gave each regiment a recruitment area in the country and made the majority of the inhabitants liable for military service throughout their lifetime and they were called up as required.

Regular exercises for three months every year ensured that the Prussian army was a model of well-drilled perfection in comparison with the mercenary armies which were approaching their end at this time. Frederick II

used them as an effective instrument for his ambitious policy of conquest in the two Silesian Wars (1740–1742,
1744/1745) and again in the Seven Years' War (1756–1763). Although the Prussians under his generalship
suffered serious defeats at the hands of the Austrians and Russians, they demonstrated their potential in other
battles, of which *Leuthen* (1757) was a crowning example of a highly developed line tactic in the shape of the
rarely successful "oblique battle order". The course and outcome of the apparently useless war against a superior
coalition nevertheless ensured a place for Prussia among the Great Powers.

At the same time, the Seven Years' War was a first "world war" in which Great Britain eliminated the
French as a rival for colonial power in India and expelled them from North America.

While Hyderabad and Mysore in the South and the Maratha and Afghans in the North were holding each
other in check, Lord Clive's victory over the Nawab of Bengal at Plassey (23 June 1757) laid the foundation
stone for the subjugation of the Indian sub-continent by the British East India Company. On the other side of
the Atlantic, in the dramatic battle of Quebec (1759) in which the commanders of both sides were killed, England
gained control of French Canada, which had been frivolously dismissed by Voltaire as a useless desert of snow.
The real bone of contention, that vast area drained by the Mississippi and its tributaries known at Louisiana,
stuck in the victor's gullet, however. The quarrel about who owned it—and how the costs of the war were to be
paid—fanned the flames of the latent conflict between the Thirteen Colonies on the East Coast and England as
to the degree and extent of their right to an independent taxation system and self-determination, resulting in
the War of Independence (1775–1783).

In the vastness of the American woods, the sophisticated line tactics of the British Redcoats and the mercenaries hired at the courts of German princes proved ineffective against the flexible units of the American settlers
and colonists who were accustomed to using guns and were familiar with the terrain. They fought as confident
revolutionaries for their own cause, as immortalized by the Congress of Philadelphia on 4 July 1776 in the
Declaration of Independence of the United States of America drafted by Thomas Jefferson. The surrender of the
troops of King George III to the popular army of rebels at *Saratoga* (1777) and Yorktown (1781) was an omen
of things to come, marking the end of one epoch and the beginning of a new one.

NINEVEH /627

The Eastern Roman Empire was hard-pressed by the Goths and Huns in the 4th and 5th centuries but it managed to survive. Although the general crisis of the class-society of Antiquity shook its foundations, its civil and military institutions were adapted to the changed conditions of the time with considerable ingenuity in some cases. For the reconquest of Northwest Africa, Italy and Southern Spain, Justinian I (527–565) was again able to mobilize a mighty army of mercenaries, a powerful fleet and "auxiliaries" all of which were vividly described by the historian Procopius of Caesarea.

However, the ambitious but retrogressive Mediterranean policy contrasted sharply with the low military capability of the State which, at the end of the 6th century, had to deal with new aggressors along the Po, Danube and Euphrates. Discipline in the army became slack as the resources allocated for soldiers' pay were reduced by numerous rebellions, defeats and losses of territory and the prospects of booty declined. Following serious social disturbances, troops in Constantinople (or Byzantium) dethroned Emperor Maurice in 602, the same thing happening again in 610 when Emperor Phocas fell from power. To hold back the Lombards, Avars, Slavs and Persians who had advanced far into the territory of the Empire, Heraclius I (610–641), once the governor of distant Carthage, was obliged to undertake a far-reaching and consequently long-drawn-out reform of the army.

The results of this are well known under the term "themes reform". Several small and defenceless provinces were united as a single large district—this was the *thema*—under the command of a *strategus* who possessed both military and administrative authority and a large measure of independence. In addition, as the principal feature of this policy, land was granted to *stratiotes*, free soldier-peasants with hereditary rights, who were pledged to defending the frontier as unpaid foot-soldiers or lightly armoured mounted archers. This was initially done in the four districts of Anatolia which were most endangered. In addition to this, alliances with neighbouring tribes, the "federates" formed an integral part of the imperial defence arrangements. The *thema* army had an efficient organization which, at first sight, displayed several modern features, having the *tagma* (company of 200 to 400 men), *moira* (battalion of about 2,000 men), and the *turma* or *meros* (regiment of 6,000 to 8,000 men corresponding to the earlier legion). These infantry and cavalry units were led by an officer hierarchy headed by the emperor who, in addition, had a well-equipped and well-trained guard at his personal disposal.

The system, which was based on "margravian" practices already tried out in the remote exarchates of Carthage and Ravenna, was completed only in the 8th century under Leo III and it is not known what part it played in its emergent form in Heraclius's great operation against the heart of the Sassanid state in 627. It is possible that he still observed the precepts of a textbook which has been ascribed—incorrectly—to Maurice.

There is no doubt that in some respects the Persians were more advanced compared with the Byzantine emperor. After the bloody repression of a socio-revolutionary religious movement—the Mazdakites—which had seriously disrupted the life of the country, Khosrau I (531–579) of the Sassanid dynasty had initiated a comprehensive programme of reform on several levels which was intended to eliminate this unrest and opposition. The rights of the free peasants were restricted and the position of the lesser nobility considerably strengthened in return. Accordingly, the status of the lightly armed foot-soldiers was far lower than that of the mounted warriors, who were divided into light and heavy cavalry. The light infantry was made up of contingents of small and medium landowners, peasants, herdsmen and members of subjugated tribes. They were armed with a bow, spear and sabre and wore light protective clothing

Great King Khosrau II Parvez in the armour of a Sassanid horseman with helmet, round shield, lance and sword. Taq-e-Bostan. Relief-sculpture from the great grotto in Kermanshah.

Duel with battle-axes between Persian horsemen in armour. Drawing from a 16th-century miniature illustrating the Persian national epic poem Shah-nama of Firdausi (932/43 to 1020-26).

of leather. The mounted archers were the symbol of Persian military power, so to speak, and it was not by chance that the coins of the Sassanid period often carried the figure of such a warrior. In combat, the light cavalry attacked by firing a hail of arrows at the enemy but avoided fighting at close quarters. This was the task of the heavy cavalry which, as an élite force, was equipped with a sword, lance, battle-axe and round shield and scale- or ring-mail—sometimes even made of steel—and wore a helmet. The head and breast of many of their mounts were also protected. The emergence of armoured horsemen who were conscious of their status in society and, under the Great King Khosrau II Parvez (i.e., "the victor"), achieved victory over Byzantium, was already an indication of a trend towards a feudal military system.

In 608, during the reign of Phocas when conditions approaching those of civil war prevailed, the Persians had knocked at the gates of Constantinople for the first time and they did this again in 615. In 614, they captured Jerusalem from which, as followers of Zoroaster, they took its most precious relic, the supposedly Holy Cross of Golgotha, as a

sign of their victory over the lamenting Christians. Alexandria fell to them in 616. Heraclius, to whom it seemed hopeless to force the enemy step by step by an exhausting and protracted campaign from the positions he had won, came to the conclusion that more would be achieved by a military and diplomatic flanking movement from the North with the aid of his fleet which had undisputed mastery of the Black Sea. With the aid of substantial loans from Church funds made available by the Patriarch—and "emperor-maker"—Sergius and after concluding peace with the Avars (621), he opened the campaign against Khosrau in 622/623 from Armenia and the Caucasus. Among the princes of these territories, he found experienced and reliable allies since they were defending their own independence from the Sassanid kings as well as aiding Heraclius. The tribal federation of the Khazars, a nomadic people from the steppes of the Northern Caucasus, also took the side of Byzantium.

With the aid of his allies, Heraclius defeated Rahzad, a general accustomed to victory and known by the title of honour of Shahrbaraz ("Wild Boar of the Kingdom"), at

Tigranocerta in 624. Despite this, he was unable to much progress. While he was marching from Caesarea to Lazica (the ancient Colchis), a storm was brewing at the Bosporus. The Avars under Khan Bayan and in alliance with the southern Slav tribes overran all the frontier defences along the Danube and in 626 advanced as far as Constantinople which they encircled on the land-side on 27 July while the Persians, for the third time, occupied the opposite coast of the Sea of Marmora at Chalcedon.

The merit of Heraclius is perhaps that he still kept to his own plan for the campaign although at that moment three-quarters of the empire was occupied by enemy forces and his capital was practically cut off from the other territory. Byzantium withstood the unco-ordinated siege although it is unlikely that this was with the aid of "Greek fire", the mysterious substance of uncertain composition which was hurled from tubes, ignited in the water and consumed the landing-craft of the invaders. This invention is attributed to a Syrian refugee, the architect Callinicus (c. 673), of a later period. The emperor started out in 627 from the Tiflis area and, in the course of exhausting marches and despite a critical shortage of supplies, crossed the pathless mountains of Armenia. He made a detour around a Persian defensive position at Lake Urmia, came down from the mountains and surprised the enemy in the valley of the Tigris at the beginning of December.

Since the Land of the Two Rivers was a long way from any of the battle fronts, the best troops had been withdrawn from it and it was unprotected. In view of the new threat posed by the enemy troop movement, King Khosrau had Shahrbaraz hurriedly recalled from Asia Minor and given the command over the "home front". After a brief skirmish of no further consequence for the course of the battle, the two armies met on 12 December on the flat terrain near the ruins of the old Assyrian city of Nineveh.

The Persian general had only 12,000 men at his disposal. It is reported that even after the Khazar horsemen, who were not prepared for marches over mountains or winter campaigns, had deserted, Heraclius still had an army of 70,000 men, although it is certain that not all of these were combatants. It is not really possible to say what losses were suffered en route and how many actually fought in the battle. Nevertheless, the numerical superiority of the Byzantines and Caucasians must have been such that even the stubborn resistance of the armoured horsemen was ineffective against them. Half of the Sassanid warriors and their general with them died in the battle. The fact that the survivors of the beaten army immediately regrouped and withdrew in good order to cover the residence of the Great King, which at the time was in the village of Dastagart, is evidence of the soldierly quality of the Persians. When the victors pursued him downstream and arrived there on 6 January 628, Khosrau fled to his winter capital at Ctesiphon where he was then deposed by rebellious lords, imprisoned and executed. His son, Kavadh II concluded peace with Byzantium and returned all the territory conquered in Asia Minor, Syria and Egypt. All this was the result of a single battle in which Heraclius skilfully severed the most sensitive nerve of the enemy. It is unfortunate that only sparse and belated accounts have gone down in recorded history. The notes about Heraclius by the Armenian bishop Sebeos do not contain any military details while the chronicles of Tabari, Theophanes and Nicephorus, the more significant writings on military theory of Emperor Leo VI (886–912) and Firdausi's magnificent epic *Shahnama* date from two centuries and more after the events. On the Persian side, there is a relief sculpture of King Khosrau II in Kermanshah while his wife, the Christian princess Shirin was even a favourite subject of classic Persian poetry.

The true significance of the Nineveh campaign is to be found elsewhere. Both Byzantium, which under Heraclius changed from superficially Roman to an essentially Greek state, and the Persia of the Sassanid kings were, together with their armies, at a critical point in the transition to a new social order which characterized the whole of the Middle Ages. The elements of the old order were already too weak and those of the new not yet strong enough to survive intact such an exhausting trial as the murderous twenty-five years' war. Both sides were confronted with a situation they were powerless to control when, in the deserts of Arabia, a storm arose which had been sown five years before the battle of Nineveh by a prophet called Mohammed who had fled from Mecca to Medina and of whom the outside world had taken little notice.

POITIERS /732

The jihad—the "Holy War"—against the infidels preached by Mohammed drew the attention of the united but poor Arab tribes under his leadership to an enticing aim: the subjugation of the rich lands in the neighbouring regions for the glory of Allah and the gain of the conquerors; those that died for their faith were compensated by the promise that they would qualify for the Seventh Paradise.

The new doctrine, the mainstay of the new state with its expansionist ambitions, impelled the armies of the caliphs, the successors of Mohammed, to make great efforts involving substantial sacrifices. Within a few years of Mohammed's death (632), they had won the battles of Kadisiya (637) and Nahawand (642), defeating the empire of the Sassanids and taking Syria, Palestine, Egypt and Tripoli for ever from the Byzantines. Bloody fighting for the consolidation of the militant Islamic community, from which the dynasty of the Omayyads emerged as victor in 661, reduced for a time the impetus of the attack. It was only at the end of the 7th and the beginning of the 8th century that the caliphate attained its greatest momentum and spread to India, Central Asia and Northwest Africa. It was from here, in 711, that the general Tarik crossed the Mediterranean at the great rock since known as Gibraltar (Jabal-al-Tarik) and after his victory at Jérez de la Frontera destroyed the state founded by the Visigoths in the 5th century. In 720, the Arabs crossed the Pyrenees and marched into France.

The state of the Merovingians, certainly the most important and strongest of those that had emerged in the course of the Great Migration, was struggling with social problems relating to growth at this time. The royal authority was non-existent, the seneschals in charge of the administration of the various parts of the country were fighting among themselves and the rebellious Duke Eudo of Aquitaine was even hoping, at the start, to make political capital out of the advance of the Arabs in Spain. It was only in 732, when they had already captured Bordeaux, that he implored his adversary for help. This was the energetic seneschal of Neustria and Austrasia, Charles Martell, or Charles the "Hammer" as he was subsequently known, the son of Pippin II. For such a divine purpose, he made liberal use of the riches of the Church, assembled a powerful army and crossed the Loire with it at Tours.

Of the battle fought on the south bank of the river, only a very confused picture is available from the early mediaeval sources. Legend has made of it the fateful encounter between Islam and the Christian West. But the details of importance for the history of warfare—such as the place, time and course of the actual fighting—were left vague or are not even mentioned at all. Thus the *Chronicon Moissacense*, the *Gesta abbatum Fontanellensium* and the continuation of Fredegarius Scholasticus contain only sparse notes about the military problems of the battle. Even less is related of the actual intentions of the Arabs—was it a simple raid, did they want to intimidate their Frankish neighbour or were they intending to subjugate the country? On the Arab side, there is only uncertain information of the events and their motivation in the illustrious *Annals* of Tabari which were not written before the 9th or 10th centuries.

What is certain is that in October 732, somewhere between Tours and Poitiers, battle was joined between two armies which were very different in their politico-social structure and military organization. The Arab force, commanded by Abd-al-Rahman, the governor of the Caliph Hisham (724–743) in Córdova, consisted of infantry and light cavalry. The latter unit was armed with lances and swords, wore hardly any protective clothing and, for better manoeuvrability, carried no shields. Their tactics were correspondingly simple: A succession of rapidly executed attacks was intended to bring about the downfall of the enemy. In critical situations, however, they were certainly capable of fighting on foot. Their sense of a religious mission was a

Arabs and Franks in the battle of Poitiers. The warriors of both sides are depicted in knightly armour. 14th-century miniature from the "Grande Chronique de France". Bibliothèque Nationale, Paris

Quant eudes le duc dâqui
taine vit que le prince char
le lot si abatu z hunlie z
qil ne se pourroit vengier
se il ne queroit secours de
augune part il saba aus sarazins dlni

major element of their fighting spirit and was exploited accordingly by their commander. For the offensive against the Frankish empire, Abd-al-Rahman had also recruited a strong contingent of North African nomads from the Berber tribes, hard-riding horsemen and accurate archers.

The Frankish army was made up of contingents from the various counties, mostly consisting of free peasants who had been called up for a specific period of military service in accordance with the usual arrière-ban. These warriors had to provide and maintain their weapons at their own expense, an annual inspection (the March or May Field) being carried out, at least in principle, by royal officials.

In the first half of the 8th century, the Frankish army still consisted, for the most part, of warriors who fought on foot, were armed with spears, swords and battle-axes (known as *franziskas*) and wore no protective clothing apart from a small and usually round shield. Only the more prosperous warriors, the followers of the dukes, counts and great landowners, were mounted and wore a helmet and ring or chain-armour.

The Franks used the "blunt wedge" battle-order of Ancient Germanic origin and repulsed the enemy attack in closed ranks. As soon as their adversary showed signs of weakening, the infantry moved forward, taking care not to lose contact with each other since internal cohesion alone offered protection against a fast-moving enemy. The heavy cavalry, promoted energetically by Charles Martell and used for the support of the infantry, was certainly not solely responsible for the outcome of the battle although it is precisely this which is asserted by tradition which tends to emphasize the role played by noblemen.

The figures quoted for the strength of the two armies vary greatly in the contemporary reports. The "400,000 Arabs" of the Frankish chronicles originated from a vain gloriousness spiced with a vigorous fantasy. Nothing like a force of this size could ever have been put into field at any time by the caliphate and even less could it have been marched for such a great distance. When the material possibilities are considered, the army advancing northwards from Spain could not have numbered more than 40,000 men at the very most and in all likelihood far less. The Frankish army may have been 30,000 to 40,000 men, judging by the social structure already outlined and the accounts in contemporary sources.

Charles Martell in knightly combat with the Arab general Abd-al-Rahman (?) during the battle of Poitiers. Copperplate engraving by Boettger the Elder from a painting by Joh. Jakob Mettenleiter (1750–1825).

Seite 11. N.º 2.

Mettenleiter del. Boettger senior sc. Lips.

Karl Martel schlaegt die Saracenen zwischen Tours und Poitiers im Jahr 732.

For seven days, the main armies faced each other, each waiting for the other's attack and engaging in small-scale skirmishes. It was on the eighth day that the Arabs, whose logistic support was not sufficient to sustain a long period of static warfare, took the initiative and opened the battle. Their attacks failed to break the compact battle-order of the Franks and, although they certainly caused them heavy losses, they were unable to gain a decisive advantage. Isidorus Pacensis described the scene in the following words: "The men from the North stood motionless like a wall. They stood firm like a belt of ice and slew their enemy with the sword. . . . The Austrasians, of powerful physique and with a hand of iron, fought bravely amidst the tumult of battle. They also forced the king of the Saracens to stand and fight and they slew him."

It is possible that the Arabs succeeded in making inroads into the enemy block at some points but they were unable to drive a wedge through it. The defensive capability of the Frankish foot-soldiers proved stronger and ultimately wore down the attackers. An additional factor was the spreading of the false news that the Frankish cavalry had forced their way into their opponents' camp containing all the booty which had already been acquired, at which a part of the Arab army was withdrawn to deal with the situation. Abd-al-Rahman vainly tried to restore order in his ranks before he was suddenly surrounded by Franks and pierced by innumerable spears. The death of the Arab general put the seal on the defeat. The contingents under the green flag of the Prophet fell back and withdrew from the field of battle when evening fell. When Frankish scouts cautiously approached the Arab camp on the following morning, they found it deserted.

The victory won by the Franks from the defensive was perhaps, in the tactical sense, not particularly glorious but it did have significant political consequences. The expansion of the caliphate of the Omayyads, whose troops had already been thrown back at the same time at Byzantium and Covadonga in Asturia between 718 and 722, was halted. This, in turn, caused a further deterioration in the already very serious internal situation of its vast empire and, after the downfall of the dynasty (750) led to a gradual severance of the links with individual provinces. This marked the end of the dream of an Islamic world-state. The realm of the Franks under Charlemagne, the grandson of Charles Mar-

tell, went from strength to strength, becoming the "Empire of the West" (800). It was from this policy that the French and German states emerged when it broke up in the 9th century.

From the military viewpoint, the battle fought between Tours and Poitiers showed that the contingents of free Frankish peasants were still a force to reckon with. A light cavalry formation was not capable of functioning as a hard-hitting tactical instrument and was unable to exploit the superiority of the mounted warrior in the face of infantry drawn up in a firm order of battle. It was after this that the Frankish arrière-ban declined in military importance, its place being taken by a numerically much smaller but very well equipped mounted contingent of noble vassals. Two centuries later, it was this new development in mediaeval military organization which triumphed in unmistakable manner at the battle on the Lech.

BATTLE ON THE LECH /955

The German state which had been formed under King Henry I (919–936) from the revived tribal duchies of the East Frankish empire had no fixed frontiers towards the East. While the temporal and spiritual lords of Lower Saxony were attempting to bring the neighbouring Slav tribes along the Elbe under their sway and thus initiating the easterly German expansion of the Middle Ages, the defence line collapsed along the Danube further to the South.

Towards the end of the 9th century, the nomadic Hungarian or Magyar people had been driven from its pasture lands in the Pontic steppes by the advancing Pechenegi and, like the Huns and the Avars before them, had suddenly appeared on the Pannonian Plain. After the Hungarians—at first in alliance with the East Franks—had defeated the Moravian empire, they defeated the forces of the Bavarian arrière-ban in a battle at Pressburg (Bratislava) in 907 and overran the Carolingian "Eastern Marches" as far as the Enns. From this time on, their terrible swarms of horsemen devastated vast areas of land in the course of lengthy raids which took them beyond the Rhine before the winter forced them to return home, laden with plunder.

In 933, after the construction of the castles along the Saale and a local military success at the Unstrut, Henry I ensured that his own hereditary duchy in Saxony remained unaffected by raids in the following period. This was not the case, however, with Swabia and especially Bavaria, which was a border area. The protection of these regions gained in importance when Henry's successor, Otto the Great (936–973), began casting covetous looks at the Crown of Italy. The sure control of Bavaria, the land of the Danube and the Alps, was an essential condition for any "active" policy in respect of Italy. It is therefore not surprising that King Otto, as soon as news reached him in the early summer of 955 that the Hungarians were again launching an attack on Bavaria, immediately issued a call from Magdeburg to his lords for a campaign against them. This is related in vivid manner by Widukind of Corvey in his *Three Books of Saxon History* and by the monk Gerhard in his biography of Udalrich, Bishop of Augsburg, although they naturally see him from the view-point of clerics prejudiced towards the "heathens".

In compliance with the royal command, the dukes and counts with their vassals appeared on the scene as a body of armoured horsemen. They were armed with swords and lances and, apart from shields, wore armour of an early and still incomplete type. The peasants only helped their lords and did not yet have a specific military function.

The army had been ordered to assemble in the area between Ingolstadt and Neuburg on the Danube and it was here in the course of July that the mounted contingents arrived which are called legions by Widukind. Of these, there were seven in all, consisting of two from Bavaria, which was most directly concerned, two from Swabia, and one each from the king, the Czechs under Duke Boleslav I and the Franks under Duke Konrad. The Saxons were again waging war against the Slavs and therefore considered themselves not available while the Lotharingians, who had formed part of the German kingdom since 925, were assigned the task of covering the area along the upper reaches of the Rhine to prevent a possible break-through of the Hungarians in the direction of Burgundy.

Otto's tactical plan, with his army taking up a position by the Danube to the northeast of Augsburg, posed a threat to the Hungarian lines of retreat and, at the same time, the central location of this area allowed the individual contingents to be brought together relatively quickly and directed in a southerly direction towards Augsburg. It is likely that the army numbered about 7,000 to 8,000 armoured horsemen in all, without counting the members of the baggage train who were not considered as trained warriors, even though they carried arms, and these auxiliary foot-troops did not in fact take part in the battle.

The Hungarian army may have been of the same strength or included a slightly greater number of warriors; even approximate figures in respect of the number of warriors involved are not available for the battle on the Lech either. Without doubt, however, the structure of the Hungarian army differed greatly from that of the German. Its organization reflected the conditions of the gentile society which was gradually disintegrating. It is true that a number of individual commanders, who already called themselves kings, were supported by retinues of well-equipped professional warriors but the great mass of the army consisted of lightly armed horsemen who carried spears, bows, axes and—to a small extent—swords as well. They relied principally on their superior speed. Led by their tribal chiefs, their tactic was to cause confusion in the enemy ranks by launching furious attacks from varying directions. They were expert in simulating flight and retreat and other tricks of war. A very large baggage-train accompanied them on their expeditions, its task being to protect and transport

the plunder taken. In this respect, the Hungarian army led by King Bulcsu in 955 still resembled the armies of the Huns and the Avars at the time of the Barbarian invasions.

Bulcsu did not succeed in taking Augsburg by storm, although the town was only defended by low ramparts without fortified towers. The defenders, led by Bishop Udalrich and Count Diepold of Dillingen, fought off the attacks with determination. According to Gerhard's *Vita*, the bishop, in his clerical vestments and without helmet or armour, himself took an active part in the fighting. A regular siege by the Hungarians was out of the question since they did not have the necessary siege engines at their disposal. Consequently, they probably had to be satisfied with an improvised encirclement. When the army of Otto I approached from the North in August, some of the defenders left the

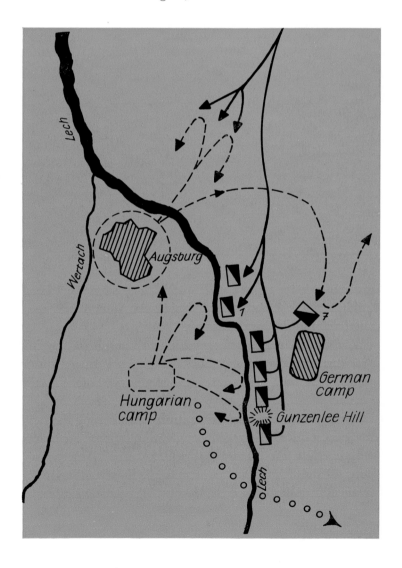

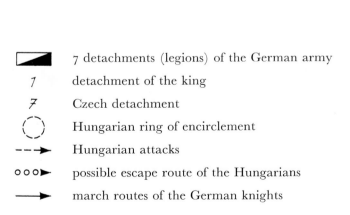

7 detachments (legions) of the German army

7 detachment of the king

7 Czech detachment

Hungarian ring of encirclement

Hungarian attacks

possible escape route of the Hungarians

march routes of the German knights

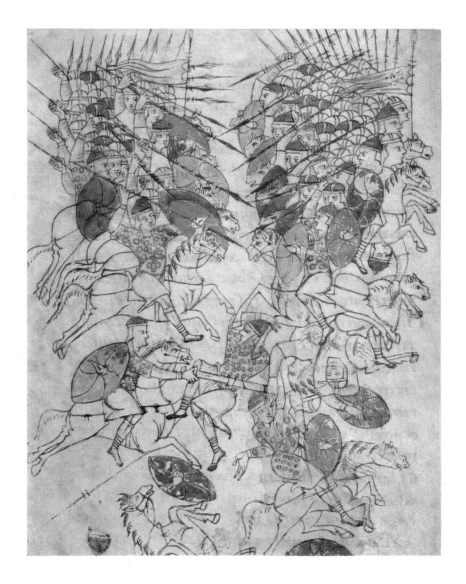

the attempts of the Hungarians to drive their armoured opponents from the field by vigorous attacks and to fight their way over the river and back to the east met with failure. They suffered serious losses and their army was routed. Fleeing warriors drowned in the Lech and others were cut down by the tormented population. Bulcsu and a number of other Hungarians who had been taken captive were hanged by the victor in accordance with the barbaric custom of the period and many others were sent back to their own people after their noses and ears had been cut off as a deterrent.

Battle-scene from the time of the raids by Hungarian horsemen.

Defence of a fortified town attacked by a horde of lightly armed Hungarian (?) horsemen.

Book-illustrations in a manuscript from St. Gallen, *c.* 925. Library of the Rijksuniversiteit, Leiden

town and went out to meet him. At this, the Hungarians abandoned the encirclement, assembled their forces and rode towards the German army.

The actual battle was preceded on the 9th of August by a cavalry engagement. The Hungarians, whose camp was situated on the terrain between the rivers Lech and Wertach south of Augsburg, attacked the Czech cavalry eastwards of the Lech but were thrown back by the latter, who were reinforced by the Franks who hastened to their assistance. On the following day, Otto's main forces, consisting of the Bavarians, the Franks and his own "legion", advanced further to the south to cut off the enemy's retreat. It was here, on the left bank of the Lech and not far from the hill known as the Gunzenlee, that battle was joined. All

The battle on the Lech underlined the superiority of the armoured horsemen both in respect of weapons and tactics and the arrows of the Hungarians proved to be practically useless against protective armour. The close collaboration of the individual contingents of King Otto's force also foiled the Hungarian attack from the rear. The armoured cavalry likewise made clever use of the river as a natural obstacle to absorb the thrusts of the enemy from an advantageous position and then to cut off his escape-route. The battle was fought with fronts reversed which had devastating consequences for the losers. In fact, Otto's tactical plan included the strategic objective of not only repulsing a hostile army but of destroying the Hungarian "nuisance" once and for all in the course of his progress towards the rank of emperor. In this he was successful and in 962 gained the crown which was to bind the German kingdom—until 1806—to a "Holy Roman Empire" and consequently to burden it with a hegemonic position in the "Occident" which was difficult to maintain.

The Ostmark which was revived by Otto I (955) became the nucleus of the state which later became Austria. For the Hungarians, however, the defeat proved to be to their advantage in the long run. Once a drastic end had been put to their profitable expeditions, they were obliged to support themselves from their own land. This caused them to settle down very much more rapidly and enabled the Hungarian people, who had adopted the Roman Catholic faith under their "holy" King Stephen, soon to assume a respected place in the feudal society of Europe.

Armoured horsemen of Otto I fighting in the battle of Lechfeld against lightly armed Hungarian horsemen. Miniature by Hektor Mülich from the chronicle of Sigmund Meisterlin (1457). Staats- und Stadtbibliothek, Augsburg

HASTINGS / 1066

The great island beyond the Channel remained on the edge of the mainstream of history for a long time. The Gauls had called it Albion (the White Island), perhaps because of the chalk cliffs of Dover, while the Roman conquerors named it Britannia, after one of its tribes. After the withdrawal of the legions, waves of Angles, Jutes and Saxons came across the North Sea. The first were responsible for its third name "England" while the latter, in particular, established regional kingdoms as the political organization of the island.

Norman knights with lance and sword attacking the line of battle of the Anglo-Saxon foot-warriors wielding their spears and battle-axes. From the Bayeux Tapestry, 11th century. Musée Tapisserie de la Reine Mathilde, Bayeux

These were united by Egbert of Wessex between 825 and 829, in some cases by force and otherwise in the elegant English manner, while the Scottish Highlands, Wales and Ireland remained in Celtic hands.

A great deal of annoyance was caused by the Vikings of various origins who had settled down along the east coast. At the beginning of the 11th century, it even happened that the whole of England fell under the rule of the Danish king Knut. It is true that Edward the Confessor did succeed in ridding the land again of the invaders but the question of the succession after his death in January 1066 split the ranks of the Anglo-Saxon earls and there was a revolt led by his own brother, Tostig, against Harold II

Godwinsson, who was ultimately crowned king. Two foreign contestants at the same time saw their opportunity to profit from this dispute.

The first to take action was Harald III Hardraade of Norway, an experienced Viking who had won fame in the service of the Grand Duke of Kiev and the Emperor of Constantinople. He landed with a force carried by 300 ships in Northumbria, defeated the contingent of the local earl at Fulford on 20 September 1066, and joined forces with the rebels. However, the main Anglo-Saxon army under King Harold appeared on the scene within five days and cut the surprised and somewhat disorderly enemy forces to pieces at Stamford Bridge. Harald Hardraade and Tostig were slain and the surviving Norwegians departed across the sea.

At almost the same hour, Duke William of Normandy, later known as "the Conqueror", was cruising off the south coast of England. He had carefully planned his expedition well in advance and could reckon with diplomatic support from the German and Danish kings and even from Pope Alexander II while Count Baldwin of Flanders, at the time the regent of France, was his father-in-law.

William's preparations had been in progress since the spring and 450 ships had been assembled at the beginning of August but prevented from sailing by a stiff north wind. King Harold, who had been advised of the former's unfriendly intentions, had arranged in May for a watch to be kept along the coast and had gathered his fleet together at Spithead. However, lulled into a false sense of security by the delay and embarrassed by money and supply difficulties, he dismissed his militia forces on 8 September. The ships were instructed to return to the Thames estuary, some being lost in a storm on the way, and Harold himself hastened from London to the theatre of war in the North, believing that he still had plenty of time at his disposal.

As is was, there was a sudden change in the wind on 27 September and William set out his fleet on the same day from Saint-Valéry-sur-Somme. After landing in Pevensey

142

Norman ships loaded with knights and horses crossing the Channel on their way to Britain. Section from the Bayeux Tapestry, 11th century. Musée Tapisserie de la Reine Mathilde, Bayeux

Bay and meeting with no resistance, he had a fortification built at Hastings and waited for his adversary to take the initiative. Political as well as military reasons may have played a part in this decision. Following the elimination of the Norwegian pretender to the throne, he was uncertain of the attitude of the Anglo-Saxon nobles while at the same time he was obliged to keep his army near the port since a treacherous sea separated him from his base and supplies.

William's Normans, like himself, were the descendants of those sea-robbers who had devastated the coasts of the West Frankish state in the 9th century. Since there was no other way of taming them, they had been given a duchy along the coast on either side of the Seine in 911 as a fief which henceforth bore their name. In the meantime, they became assimilated by the more advanced French nobility and now spoke a Northern French dialect. The organization, equipment and tactics of their military forces was already very similar to the typical mediaeval army of knights.

Between 2,000 and 3,000 knights from a variety of countries had joined the expedition to England, the attraction being the prospect of rich booty. They were not yet equipped with heavy armour but with coats of chain-mail, plus lances, swords, battle-axes and long shields, mostly

pointed at the bottom. Their mounts were unprotected. In addition to the knights, the Norman forces included 3,000 to 4,000 foot-soldiers, including many bowmen.

The Anglo-Saxon army, fired by its brilliant victory of September at Stamford Bridge, made a series of forced marches towards the South and was reinforced on the way by vassals (thanes) who joined it and by contingents of 6,000 to 7,000 peasants. It consisted entirely of warriors who fought on foot, were armed with throwing spears, battle-axes and double-edged swords and used shields for protection. There were small numbers of lightly armed troops who were equipped with bows and arrows or with a sling. The army's nucleus were the "housecarls", the permanent military retinue of the king who were probably equipped with coats of chain-mail and also had better weapons. The strength of the Anglo-Saxon army, which in its organization still resembled that used at the time when the free peasants played the principal part in warfare, was the significant defensive capability of foot-soldiers. It was not the case at all that they were inferior to their Norman adversaries from the very start. When Harold arrived at Hastings on the 13th of October, he took up a position on Senlac hill to ensure that he would not be surprised by the enemy. Deep trenches on the right and left provided protection against attacks from the flanks while at the front the terrain was flat with a downward slope. It was from this direction that the Norman attack was to be expected.

A great deal has been written about this battle which was so eventful for the course of English history. The principal source comes from William of Poitiers, the chaplain of the Duke of Normandy, and his report was written only a few years after the battle and based on eye-witness accounts. A unique document in both the historical and artistic sense is the justly famous Bayeux Tapestry, which is 70 metres long and 50 centimetres wide and depicts the individual events of the battle with an explanation in Latin.

The battle of Hastings was opened by the Norman archers on 14 October 1066. At their heels came the knights and the foot-soldiers. However, the advantage of the Anglo-Saxon position immediately became apparent. The attack lost momentum when the Normans had to advance up the slope and their arrows failed to achieve a break-through. Some of the Normans were driven back down the slope while others fell back of their own accord to gain a respite before renewing the attack or to lure the enemy from the cover of his defences. However, the Anglo-Saxon foot-soldiers refused to come out from the shelter of their shields, which formed a solid wall, and up till mid-day presented no gap through which their adversaries could force their way.

After the Normans had tried for several hours to wear down the opposition, a gradual change began to take place in the situation. Disorder broke out after all at several points in the Anglo-Saxon ranks. Many of their proven warriors were eager for a man-to-man combat when they felt that the Normans were weakening after repeatedly being driven back. They broke ranks to pursue their adversaries down the slope. To be sure, if a battle is to be won, there must come a change from the defensive to the offensive but this was impossible for individual warriors or small groups of men since out in the open the foot-soldier was at a hopeless disadvantage when confronted by an armed horseman. To act in such a manner was to invite disaster. King Harold, who certainly recognized the danger, was no longer able to maintain discipline and close his ranks. So it was that in the afternoon the tide turned in favour of the Normans. The Anglo-Saxon ranks disintegrated and, together with two of his brothers, Harold was killed in the slaughter that followed, an arrow striking him on the forehead. Only the

housecarls in the centre stood firm and for a moment even Duke William himself was in danger. Caught between the enemy bowmen and the knights, they then retreated from the field of battle, suffering severe losses but still maintaining good order in their ranks. It was almost evening before the Normans had overpowered the Anglo-Saxon forces. It is not known what losses were suffered by the latter but it is almost certain that most of the Anglo-Saxon warriors were either slain or taken captive.

The explanation for their defeat cannot solely be sought in the relative backwardness of their military organization or in tactical errors. Then there were the strategic errors which were made by King Harold. It must have been obvious to him that he would have to fight on two fronts and yet he chose the worst possible moment to expose his southern flank, which was even more seriously threatened, in order to deal with the Norwegians. Above all, however, he ruined the second part of the campaign by undue haste. Nothing and nobody obliged him to measure his strength with William within three weeks of Stamford Bridge (unless it was the threat posed by the possible defection of "his" disobedient vassals ...). It has been estimated that he could have mobilized double the number of experienced warriors if he had played for time, although this assumes that they would have answered his summons in actual fact. Finally, it could only have been to the Anglo-Saxon advantage if they had drawn the Normans away from the coast and into the interior of the country instead of hurrying to confront them near the point where they had landed. It was probably the uncertainty of his own political position within the country that made the "upstart" Harold Godwinsson prefer the military risk, with all the haste and lack of forethought that this entailed.

With the victory of the Franco-Norman knights who became the ruling class for the Anglo-Saxon nation and mainly divided up the country among themselves in the shape of fiefs according to the law of conquest, a new chapter in English history began and, for the following centuries, the fate of England was closely linked with that of France, for the better and for the worse. In the long term, however, the conditions also resulted from this which were to lift England for a time to the forefront of social progress in the world.

LEGNANO / 1176

The Italian policy of the Roman-German Emperors was not characterized by an entirely smooth course, although it is true that no other power was able to challenge the supremacy of their position. However, with the growth in the power of the papacy after the reform of Gregory VII (1073–1085), two different directions of development began to emerge which were reflected in a centuries' long struggle between the supreme temporal and spiritual authorities of the Occident—imperium and sacerdotium.

Success favoured now one side, now the other, but it was inevitable that the pope should find allies among all those who felt threatened by Imperial ambitions—not only among the particularistic powers within Germany itself but also among those citizens of the aspiring cities of Lombardy whose prosperity was exploited only too readily by rulers who were always in need of money. Conversely, the latter endeavoured to establish a party which, within the circles of the Italian aristocracy was loyal to the emperor and opposed the political ambitions of the popes or viewed with suspicion the unstoppable rise of the urban middle-class.

The Salian emperors had ended their "investiture controversy" with the papacy in 1122 by the compromise of the Concordat of Worms. However, under the Hohenstaufens, points of contention again appeared and led to even more violent reactions than before. To begin with, events were dominated by Conrad II (1138–1152) and Frederick I Barbarossa. The latter devastated Milan, the centre of the Lombard League in 1162 but was unable to exploit the ad-

Knight (Frederick I Barbarossa) in chain-mail and nose-piece helmet and armed with a mace at the time of the battle of Legnano, followed by foot-warriors carrying swords, spears and shields. Miniature of 1190 from the Annals of Genoa.

vantage gained in the face of increasing resistance and the unyielding attitude of the successor of St. Peter. Campaigns and peace treaties alternated with each other until there was yet another open confrontation between the League and the emperor in 1176 at Legnano.

There are several good accounts of what happened. From the Italian viewpoint, the most significant of these are the *Annales Mediolanenses maiores* or the *Gesta Frederici I Imperatoris in Lombardia*, written by a citizen of Milan, the *Annales Romualdi* by the archbishop of Salerno and the *Vita Alexandri III* by Cardinal Boso. The standpoint of the emperor is related by Godfrey of Viterbo who lived in Italy from 1174 to 1178 and was a tutor of the prince at the court of Frederick I. There are also reports of the battle in the royal chronicle of Cologne and the annals of Magdeburg.

Frederick Barbarossa ("Frederick of the Red Beard"), who had spent the winter in Pavia with a small army, hastened to the Como area on hearing of the approach of the reinforcements summoned from Germany. It was here that the Imperial forces assembled, consisting of the vassals of various temporal and spiritual princes and lords who were obliged by fealty to make the "journey to Rome", i.e., to take part in the Italian campaign. However, in 1175/76, the Guelph Henry the Lion, Duke of Saxony and Bavaria and the most powerful of the German lords, took the part of Pope Alexander III and refused to follow the emperor. Including all those who had joined en route, the Imperial army consequently numbered only 3,000 to 3,500 knights —not counting the vassals on foot who did not take an active part in the battle.

The numerical strength of the Lombard army is less well reported. The figures reported fluctuate wildly between 100,000 men and 12,000 knights whereas a more critical examination and the course of the battle would indicate a force of some 3,000 to 4,000 knights in armour and approximately the same number of foot-soldiers. The army of the Lombard League was made up of contingents from the various cities; its main strength was likewise its body of knights, 50 of whom came from Lodi, 300 from Novara and Vercelli and 200 from Piacenza; other knights from Brescia were still en route at the beginning of the battle. In addition, however, the cities disposed of a substantial force of foot-soldiers, armed with shields and lances. Like the

Knights mounted and on foot attack the standard-carriage which is defended by citizens and mercenaries. Copperplate engraving by Nicola Sanesi.

knights, the infantry was not a tactical force either, and could not carry out tactical operations on the battle-field. Its strength lay in its concentrated mass which was capable of offering prolonged resistance as long as its cohesiveness was maintained. The foot-soldiers of the Lombard League took up their positions around the *carroccio* or flag-carriage on which there was a flag or a bundle of flags and a monstrance with the consecrated host. Unlike the usual military vehicles and carriages, this was consequently not a means of transportation for troops, weapons or supplies or part of a barricade of waggons. The flag-carriage served as a blessed symbol of the pious civil spirit—under the slogan "God with us!", as it were—and was intended to raise the combat morale of the warriors, who were mostly artisans from the guilds, few of whom had any experience of war. The *carroccio*, the communal "substitute" for a royal banner, was not of any direct military importance.

The two armies approached each other at Legnano, three miles to the northwest of Milan whose archbishop possessed a castle here. In the early hours of 29 May 1176, the Lombards sent out a force of 700 knights in the direction of Como to reconnoitre the position of the enemy. This advance party came across a group of about 300 knights of the Imperial army who, for their part, were carrying out a reconnaissance of the Lombard forces. Fighting broke out between the two bodies of knights but the numerical superiority of the Lombards proved of no avail since the main forces of the German army rapidly appeared on the scene and put the Lombard knights to flight. Some of the latter fell back to the main camp but others simply fled as fast as they could from the battlefield. Thus in the first stages it seemed that victory was favouring the Imperial side.

The foot-soldiers gathered around the flag-carriage still offered resistance, however, and they were supported by the knights of the advance guard who had returned here after making contact with the Imperial army. Frederick Barbarossa, who had hoped that his heavily armed troops would score a rapid victory over the Lombard army despite the disloyalty of Henry the Lion, was disappointed in his expectations. He had underestimated the resistance of the militia contingents. In massed ranks, they had faced the enemy with lance and shield at the ready and had repeatedly repulsed the attacks of the German knights, the position of the defenders being favoured by a trench which hampered the onslaughts of the enemy.

In the meantime, there was a major change in the state of affairs away from the battlefield. The Lombard knights who had initially fled from the Imperial army met up with arriving mounted knights of the other towns in the League and returned with them to the scene of the fighting. It was the appearance of these new contingents which determined the outcome of the battle. The emperor's troops proved to be too exhausted to ward off their attack since they had suffered heavy losses in the confrontation with the Lombard militia. Thus the third phase of the battle ended for them with a serious defeat. Many of the German knights were taken prisoner while others took to their heels and were drowned in the River Ticino. The Imperial camp was captured by the Lombards.

Frederick himself escaped to Pavia and drew the correct conclusion from his failure at Legnano. He exchanged the sword for the pen of the diplomat, abandoned his exaggerated claims against the Lombards and concluded peace in neutral Venice with their patron, the pope. Using the freedom of movement he had regained, he broke the power of Henry the Lion in Germany and married his son and successor to the heiress of the wealthy Norman kingdom of Sicily and Naples. His strange death in the waters of the distant River Saleph during the third Crusade (1190) helped to transform the Hohenstaufen emperor into a personage of the Kyffhäuser Saga. The development of the Northern Italian cities, now relieved from direct pressure, took a more prosaic course and, after many challenges in which a second Frederick of the Hohenstaufen dynasty (1212–1250) was not unconcerned, they became the centre of European commerce and manufacturing where early capitalist relations first emerged.

The battle of Legnano was not yet an epoch-making victory of infantry forces over knights. To be sure, the foot-soldiers of the Lombard League, rallying around the flag-carriage, had firmly repulsed an attack by knights but were incapable of resolving the battle by themselves. For this, they were still too inexperienced, they lacked training and their organizational cohesiveness was weak, although the awareness of the city militia that they were fighting for the defence of their rights against the alien Imperial power gave a patriotic flavour to their resistance and certainly strengthened their resolution. The successful defensive action of a body of foot-soldiers which, at Legnano, was also supported by a large number of knights remained for the time being an isolated episode in the history of war. Nevertheless, it anticipated that line of development which, in the 14th and 15th centuries with the Flemish citizens' militia, the Swiss peasants and ultimately the Czech Hussites, led to the independent army of foot-soldiers.

KALKA / 1223

In 1206, the Kurultai, a great assembly of representatives from all the Mongol tribes, elected the "Genghis Khan". The man chosen was Temujin, a man of about fifty years of age who had risen from humble origins but had made a major contribution to the unification of the tribes. The Mongols were in a transitional stage between the gentile order and an early feudal class society of the nomadic type in which they developed surprising power and energy, despite their relatively small numbers. The Great Khan (or "king of the army") was expected to lead these nomadic herdsmen in the conquest of vast new pasture-lands for their great herds.

Temujin surpassed the boldest expectations. To begin with, he invaded China and established himself at the Hwang Ho. He then turned towards the West, taking some Turco-Tartar tribes with him, "dealt with" a few, fairly minor potentates on the way and overwhelmed the great realm of Khorezm in Central Asia and Eastern Iran. Its allies, the Kumans (called Polovtsy by the Russians), were driven back beyond the Volga. It was in the course of pursuing the Kumans, that the Mongols first set foot on European soil, in the steppes of the Caucasian foreland. It was from here, in the spring of the year 1223, that one of their armies—of unknown size—set out under Prince Subedai to deal the death blow to the Kuman state. At the same time, this represented a threat to the principalities of Southern Russia which were linked to the latter by treaties and provided military assistance.

It was to their military organization and their combat techniques in particular that the Mongols owed their ability to achieve sudden victory. It is true that in military organization they made use of Chinese models to some extent (even Temujin's chancellor was Chinese) but otherwise they relied on their own experience. All males capable of carrying weapons were obliged to serve in the army while the subjugated peoples were required to provide auxiliary troops. The army was organized in units of ten, a hundred, a thousand and ten thousand. All were mounted and also took spare horses with them on their campaigns. Travellers, such as Marco Polo, who subsequently visited the Mongol empire, reported that its warriors were excellent horsemen, undemanding, courageous, and, in particular, exceptionally well-disciplined.

Consequently, the principal branch of the Mongol army —and almost the only one—was the cavalry, which was divided into light and heavy units. The lightly armed contingents, equipped with bows and arrows, opened the battle and engaged the enemy in never-ending skirmishes. The heavy cavalry was not identical to the European equivalent. It is true that they wore protective clothing of leather and occasionally iron helmets, as well and were equipped with lances, pikes and curved sabres but they avoided single combat because their tireless horses were of small size and operated in closed formation. This consisted of an advance party, the main army, comprising left and right wings and a centre, and a powerful reserve which could carry out encircling movements or take up the merciless pursuit of a retreating enemy. Such a battle-order—in conjunction with the mobility of the horsemen over almost incredible distances—permitted swift tactics of many kinds.

In their wars of conquest, the Mongol armies were known for their resolute attacks and their aim on the battlefield was the total destruction of the enemy, frequent use being made of diversions and other tricks for this purpose. Since they were always in a hurry—although they were prepared to bring up effective siege-engines of Chinese origin if necessary, they did not like to be delayed by difficult sieges. As a warning to those who were unwilling to capitulate, they destroyed complete cities, together with their inhabitants, and devastated their fields when surrender was refused. In connection with this, G. A. Fedorov-Davydov writes: "The news of the approach of the Mongol hordes travelled faster than the horses of Genghis Khan. It struck terror in the hearts of the people. They expected violence and slaughter, burning and murder, devastation and hunger."

The principalities of Southern Russia which offered resistance to the Mongols mobilized a very powerful army of some 60,000 men (including the Polovtsy). The princes of Kiev, Halicz, Chernigov and Volhynia set out with their own mounted retinue, the Druzhini, and the "polki", the Boyar regiments, which consisted both of cavalry and infantry. From the *Epic of Igor's Expedition*, written by an unknown author at the end of the 12th century and describing a campaign by the Russians against the Kumans, it is possible to draw conclusions as to the weapons and tactics of the Russian army. The mounted warriors would have worn protective armour and helmets and carried sabres, lances and swords while the foot-soldiers were equipped with bows and crossbows. For battle, the army was drawn up in one or two lines which the polki kept intact as a single force. The bowmen advanced in front of the main army, fired their arrows at the enemy and then withdrew immediately.

The Chronicle of Halicz-Volhynia, covering the 13th century, and the *Lay of the Defeat of the Russian Land*, both of which inspired the illustrious *Chronicle of St. Laurentius* of the second half of the 14th century (in Nizhni Novgorod) testify to the first great battle of the Russians against the Mongols —who were known as Tartars to them. According to these great works of literature, the Russian princes and the Polovtsy assembled at the Dnepr. After initial successes against the Mongol advance parties, they moved eastwards and reached the Kalka, a small river, on the 31st of May. However, on account of the rivalry between Mstislav Udaloj of Halicz and Mstislav Romanovich of Kiev, the two most powerful and energetic princes, it was not possible to entrust the command of all the units to a single person; this was to have fateful consequences.

The Prince of Kiev took up a fortified position on a hill near the river with the intention of awaiting an attack by Subedai but Mstislav Udaloj of Halicz, the Volhynians, the men of Chernigov and the Polovtsy crossed the Kalka. After they had advanced only a few kilometres eastwards, they came upon the main Mongol army and were immediately caught up in bitter fighting. The mounted Polovtsy, who were at the front, suffered a defeat, turned to flee and obliged the Russian polki to fall back with them. The battle-order of the main Russian forces collapsed and the Mongols, who now probably had a numerical superiority as well, were able to score a decisive victory even at this early stage.

Portrait of Genghis Khan. Brush drawing. From a private collection.

Tartar and Russian warriors of about 1490. Miniature from a Russian chronicle.

The Prince of Kiev, instead of intervening with his own forces in the battle which was taking place almost in front of him, had watched the defeat of the Polovtsy and the other Russian forces without doing anything. It was now his turn to face the attack of the victorious Mongols. For three days, the men of Kiev were able to resist the onslaught, thanks to the tactical advantages of their position in a hilly terrain. Since the resistance of the defenders could not be broken by military force and Subedai could not afford to lose time by encircling them and starving them out, he resorted to a subterfuge: through a go-between, he offered to allow the Russians to withdraw unmolested in return for ransom money. Mstislav Romanovich trusted this promise and accepted the offer since he saw no other way out of his situation. As soon as the last defenders had left their positions, the

Mongols fell on the withdrawing Russian forces and destroyed them. Mstislav and two other princes in his retinue were strangled.

The battle at the Kalka was a fateful defeat for the princes of Southern Russia and the Kumans. But the Mongols, too, had suffered heavy losses. For the time being, they did not advance any further westwards but moved to the North against the Bulgarians along the Volga and then turned back.

The vanquished did not make use of this breathing-space, however. Eight years after the death of Temujin (1227), the Mongols under his grandson Batu Khan again invaded Europe and with even more powerful forces than on the previous occasion. They burned Kiev and other great cities to the ground and successively defeated the armies of Russian, Polish, German and Hungarian knights who barred their way. By 1241, their advance formations had reached the battlefield of Liegnitz (Legnica) and the Adriatic. In 1242, Batu Khan settled down in Sarai on the lower reaches of the Volga and, with his "Golden Horde", founded the steppe state of Kipchak, to which all the Russian princes were obliged to pay tribute on harsh terms. Even the heroic Alexander Nevsky, who had repulsed the Swedes on the Neva in 1240, defeated the Teutonic Knights on the ice of Lake Peipus in 1242 and had held Novgorod, protected by the marshes around it, against the Mongols, was obliged to kow-tow to the Khan in the interests of his prosperous trading city.

The Golden Horde survived the decline of the Great Mongol Empire and maintained their power for many years afterwards. It was only in 1480 that Grand Duke Ivan III of Moscow, after an indecisive confrontation on the Ugra, succeeded in shaking off once and for all the "Tartar yoke", under which the social development of Russia had been severely restricted for more than two centuries.

Mongol warrior of the army of Genghis Khan. Contemporary Persian illustration.

The power of the Mongols reached its climax under Kublai Khan (1260–1294), the grandson of Temujin. However, the Golden Horde in Russia and the Il-khans in Iran and the Land of the Two Rivers were only nominally subject to the Great Khan who had transferred his capital from Karakorum in Mongolia to Peking. Once he had decided to complete the subjugation of China, which was divided at that time, by conquering the Southern Empire of the Sung, the founder of the Yüan Dynasty followed the ancient Imperial traditions of China and immediately revived the usual claim to sovereignty over the "Barbarians on the frontiers of the empire" in Eastern Asia. The Mongols not only invaded Korea, Vietnam and Burma but also sent several missions with their demands to Japan (1267–1273).

The Japanese royal family, which claimed descent from the goddess Amaterasu and the legendary Jimmu Tenno, had emerged from the tribal aristocracy of the Xamato clan, under whose leadership a tribal federation had been established in Central and Western Japan in the 4th century. After the "Taika Reform" (645–702), which made use of Chinese experience, this became consolidated as a centralized state with its own bureaucracy. Since the 9th century, however, powerful aristocratic families such as the Fujiwara—and after the victory of the feudal military nobles of Northeast Japan under Yoritomo at Dan no ura (1185) the Minamoto—had restricted the authority of the emperor to his function of high priest. He thus became a symbol of the unity of the state and possessed no influence. From 1192, political power had been in the hands of the militarily organized "Bakufu" (government) of Kamakura, led by the Shogun, the "Supreme Commander for actions against the Barbarians", whose status was hereditary and was approximately equivalent to that of a major-domo. Relying on the protection given by the sea, the Bakufu rejected the repeated demands made by Kublai Khan and instructed the young regent Shikken), Hojo Tokimune, from a side line of the Minamoto family, to make preparations for the repulse of the expected attack.

Neither of the adversaries had much experience of such a difficult undertaking. The Mongol horsemen of the steppes had familiarized themselves with all the much more varied techniques of land-warfare of the Chinese, it is true, but they were totally helpless on the water. They consequently forced the king of Koryo, a state occupying part of the territory of Korea and already subject to them, to build in all haste a great fleet for the expedition. It is related that this fleet consisted of 300 warships, 300 military transports and 300 supply vessels, carrying drinking water in particular. The ships were manned by 7,000 seamen.

On 9 November 1274, this armada set out from Masan in South Korea with 20,000 Mongol warriors (including some Chinese troops) and 8,000 Korean auxiliaries on board and after two days at sea reached the island of Tsushima, which was captured after a brief struggle. Landings were also made on the small off-shore islands of Iki and Hirado after which the Mongols disembarked at several points in the Bay of Hakata on Kyushu, the most southwesterly of the large Japanese islands, in the face of vigorous local resistance. Between Hakozaki and Hakata, still in the direct vicinity of the coast, they made contact on the 26th of November with the Japanese army under Shoni Tsunesuke, the commander of the regional forces of the Bakufu, who must have been attentively following the movements of the enemy fleet.

Since the number of Japanese warriors is just as unknown as the exact location of the battlefield and, on the other hand, there is no information as to how many Mongols initially remained with the ships, nothing precise can be said about their respective strengths in the battle. There is no doubt, however, as to the superior weapons and tactics of the invading army. The Mongols had brought a

following double page:
Japanese warriors under the command of Takezaki Suenaga on the march to the coast. The stone ramparts along the coast are already manned by warriors from other provinces. Illustration from a contemporary Japanese scroll.

large number of horses with them so that use could be made of their mounted formations; their bows usually had a greater range than those of the Japanese and poisoned arrows were used. They also had lightly armed Chinese and Korean foot-soldiers at their disposal, who attacked with short bows and long lances. Use was also made by the invaders of a few bombards. These were not really dangerous since they did not fire any missiles but only produced loud explosions, black powder being shaken on to a large priming-pan and ignited by a slow match. However, the roar and flashes of these fiery dragons, which were unknown to the Japanese, was sufficient to terrify horse and horseman alike.

On the Japanese side, Tokimune, in the West of the country, had mobilized all the "gokenin", the knightly vassals of the Bakufu, to take part in the defence. They were reinforced by their illegitimate sons who, by prescriptive right, could hope to receive a fief in return for outstanding military services. For the battle of Hakata, it was mostly the forces of Northern Kyushu which were at Tsunesuke's disposal since it had been possible to assemble these within the brief period of time available. Nevertheless, defenders also arrived from Southern Kyushu and from the chief island of Honshu.

The gokenin were accustomed to fighting with the sword in the manner of the samurai (or bushi); they were the vassals and retainers of the great feudal lords who, in the course of the extension of the northern marches on Honshu and centuries of struggle, had become the warrior caste and accordingly had acquired great experience in the art of war. A tough warrior of this kind wore armour and a helmet and was not unlike his noble contemporaries in Europe or the Orient. He would parade by himself in front of the army on the battlefield, announce his name in a mighty voice and challenge an adversary from the other side to a man-to-man combat. Since the island realm had never been subject to serious attack from outside since history began, its unsuspecting defenders assumed that this manner of fighting was customary everywhere. They were sorely taken aback, if not scandalized, when the Mongol army did not accept their challenge. The latter, regardless of the "samurai spirit" and probably unaware of it, encircled the individual Japanese exponents of the art of single combat by entire groups of soldiers, overpowered them and then not only proceeded to attack the waiting ranks as well but also opened up with "guns". Shaken and bewildered by several hours of fierce fighting of a kind entirely alien to that to which they were accustomed and in which they were accordingly unable to find their feet, the badly mauled Japanese forces withdrew, in the face of massive enemy pressure, to Dazaifu, 15 kilometres further inland.

However, the Mongol army unexpectedly returned to their ships under cover of darkness and no sign of them was to be seen on the following morning. Up to 1945, the tale was told in Japan that a "kamikaze" (divine wind) had sent the ships and those aboard them to the bottom of the sea. Recent metereological research regards this as unlikely since on land there was neither heavy rain nor a storm on that day and the season of the typhoons had long since passed. It may be true, nevertheless, that the fleet, which was not very seaworthy since it had been hastily built in less time than normal at the orders of the Mongols, met with disaster on the return voyage. This might have been due to big waves—perhaps in Korean coastal waters—and one of the contemporary accounts speaks of more than 13,000 men having been lost.

It is also possible that Kublai Khan wanted to teach the uncooperative Japanese a lesson by sending a "punitive expedition" and that the Mongol commander considered that he had done enough with the victory at Hakata to serve this purpose and to maintain the prestige of his master so that the Bakufu would be better disposed towards the Mongols in the future. The somewhat patient dispatch of two further missions in 1275 and 1279 might support this interpretation. The members of both missions were nevertheless put to death by the Japanese, the inevitable consequence of this act being the resumption of the hot war.

In February 1281, when Kublai Khan ordered another landing operation to be mounted, he had even more powerful forces at his disposal than on the previous occasion. The conquest of Southern China, which had been completed in 1279, had increased his military resources so that he was now able to proceed against Japan with two invasion fleets, approaching Japan from different directions.

The "eastern fleet" followed exactly the same course from Masan as in 1274 and the actual expeditionary corps was of a similar composition, consisting of Mongols, Chinese and Koreans, while the "southern fleet" set out from the

Mongol archer of the army of Genghis Khan.
Contemporary Chinese representation.

port of Ningpo to the south of the Yangtze estuary and had only Chinese troops on board. The intention was that they should meet at the island of Iki and then launch a concerted attack on Hakata at the end of July.

As it was, they failed to keep to this arrangement and the eastern fleet arrived at Tsushima already by the end of June and then proceeded to Iki. Without awaiting the arrival of the southern fleet which had left port only after a considerable delay, the eastern fleet sailed to the Bay of Hakata at the beginning of July—i.e, much earlier than planned—to explore the situation there. It was when an attempt was made by a surprise attack to occupy Cape Shikanoshima which dominated the bay that the Mongols met with their first failure.

The Bakufu had made mighty efforts to be better prepared for the danger this time. They had the entire coast of the bay fortified by stone walls extending for almost 20 kilometres and some of these walls are still in existence today. In conjunction with still more extensive earthen ramparts, they hindered the deployment of the mass of the invading troops and enabled the defenders to organize resistance at points exposed to special danger without risk of attack from the rear. In this manner, they were able to absorb the impact of the attack by the enemy, who soon appreciated the situation and withdrew to Iki again.

It was here that they were joined by an advance squadron of the southern fleet. Since in the meantime individual Japanese warriors had crossed to Iki in small boats one after another, and boarded enemy ships and cut down their masts, the fleet did not feel particularly safe from these annoying pin-pricks at Iki. It sailed out in a southwesterly direction to rendezvous with the main squadron of the southern fleet which finally appeared on the 20th of August near the island of Hirado. They then sailed back together to the East, to the Bay of Hakata, to seek a favourable opportunity of landing the troops. Before they could do this, however, they were struck by a devastating typhoon on the 23rd, the entire, unprotected fleet being destroyed. Several thousand men managed to escape from the wrecks and swim to land, reaching the small off-shore island of Takashima where they began to build boats of wood in which to sail home. The Japanese immediately challenged the poorly armed survivors and, after several unequal confrontations, took most of them prisoner. The "battle of Takashima" was consequently more a cleaning-up operation directed against the shipwrecked remnants of the enemy than a real military victory won on the field of battle. The captives were brought to Hakata and, in accordance with ancient customs, publicly executed there as offenders against public order. The "Mongol grave-mound", which can still be seen today, contains the heads of those decapitated.

Thus it was that the second invasion by the Mongols met with failure already in the preliminary stages. In 1281, they had come with far-reaching aims in mind, as is evident from the hoes and ploughs that they brought with them. It may be concluded that they had intended to colonize at least a part of Japan. They were thwarted in this and the catastrophic end of the adventure and the successful resistance of other peoples of Asia to the rule of the Yüan dynasty did not allow a third expedition to be launched against the Japanese islands which were so inaccessible for a continental power.

At the beginning, however, the Bakufu of Kamakura was by no means sure that this was the case and was not prepared to take any risk. The already enormous expenditure on arms was increased still further and represented a heavy burden for the people. They exhausted the resources which were normally used by the government to reward its faithful vassals for the courage displayed in battle. The decline in confidence which resulted from this caused a serious crisis in the feudal order of the Kamakura period and subsequently led to social upheavals which brought the country a long period of "aristocratic anarchy".

The repulse of the Mongol invasion also made such an impact on the historical consciousness of the Japanese people perhaps because it was the last occasion on which a foreign enemy was fought on their native soil. Fortunately, we do not have to rely entirely for our information on the otherwise excellent *Narrative of the Mongol invasions (Hachiman gudo-ki)* and other writings from a later epoch, the accuracy of which is of varying degrees. The vassal Takezaki Suenaga, who himself took part in the actions of 1274 and 1281, had two scrolls painted with battle scenes and accompanying texts in commemoration of the events—and naturally of his own contribution to them. He bequeathed them to an ancestral shrine in his own province of Higo, from where they later passed into the possession of the Emperor Mutsuhito. It was only after the Second World War that the general public and scholars were given access, at the Imperial Higashima Archives of Kyoto, to this document, which is unique both in its artistic execution and in its historical value.

SEMPACH / 1386

The extensive peasant "rural communities" of Uri and Schwyz, which were protected from the direct attentions of great lords by their position in the mountains, were granted the Imperial privilege by Frederick II in 1231 and 1240 respectively. The Hohenstaufen emperor regarded them as the guardians of the newly opened St. Gotthard Pass which linked his possessions in Swabia and Italy and, as such, more dependable than hostile bishops. However, once their neighbours, the counts of Habichtsburg Castle, had achieved royal status in the person of Rudolf I in 1273 and, after a victory over King Ottokar II of Bohemia at the battle of Marchfeld (1278), had acquired Austria as a "vacant Imperial fief" in 1282, the latter endeavoured to take over additional territory to consolidate their possessions and extend their power. The three "forest cantons" of Uri, Schwyz and Nidwalden rightly considered themselves threatened and in 1291 swore "eternal union". This oath, the "Rütlischwur", was not recognized by the Hapsburgs. Although they had temporarily lost the Imperial crown again, they dispatched a small army of knights in 1315 but these were sent home again with bloody heads by the Swiss Confederates after the battle of Morgarten on the 15th of November.

The successful three original cantons were subsequently joined by the cities of Lucerne, Zurich and Berne and then by Zug and Glarus as well. The eight-member confederation had already developed into quite a formidable entity of a special kind and yet the Hapsburgs in Vienna did not abandon their claims. After acquiring the Tyrol by marriage in 1363 and joining it to parts of Vorarlberg which they purchased in 1375, it seemed to them that Switzerland, where they possessed a number of isolated estates, was even more desirable as a link with their territories in Swabia and along the upper reaches of the Rhine. After an incident in 1386 and in view of the calm state of foreign affairs, Duke Leopold III of Austria decided that this was a favourable moment to start a war of aggression.

However, he had made his calculations without consulting the landlord. The Swiss had an excellent military organization, based on the general mobilization of peasants, cowherds and the citizens of the towns. This military tradition, which had its roots in the old rural communities of the peasants and can be traced back to the period of the Great Migration, had not changed to any significant extent in the course of the Middle Ages but had only be-

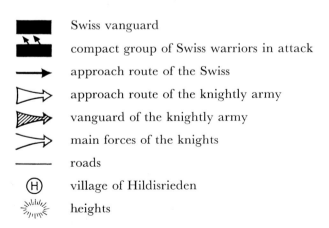

Swiss vanguard

compact group of Swiss warriors in attack

approach route of the Swiss

approach route of the knightly army

vanguard of the knightly army

main forces of the knights

roads

(H) village of Hildisrieden

heights

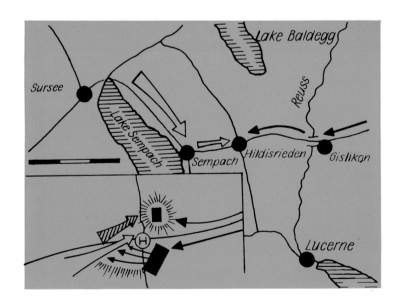

Swiss soldiers equipped with halberds in battle-order. In the foreground the treating of the wounded is depicted. From a woodcut by H. R. Manuel Deutsch, mid-16th century.

Scene from the battle of Sempach. From the World Chronicle of Rudolf of Hohenem. Murhardsche Bibliothek der Stadt Kassel und Landesbibliothek

come adapted to the feudal system, as far as this system had become established in the Alpine region. In the 14th century, the eight "places"—later known as cantons—mobilized certain contingents in time of war, from the total number of those liable for military service and sent them into the field under the command of captains. These captains were usually mayors, senior officials or judges from the rural communities and towns or ennobled citizens who had long served as military commanders and therefore had some experience in the subject.

For battle, the Swiss were organized in three compact groups as a rule—advance party, the main group, consisting of the mass of the men-at-arms, and the rearguard. The battle-order used by the Swiss peasants provided them with a large measure of protection against attacks by mounted knights. They extended their spears and halberds in front of them (the halberd was a combination of a short lance and a battle-axe) and formed a kind of "hedgehog" which could resist practically any attack by enemy horsemen. The decisive new factor in the tactics of the Swiss peasants was that they were not only able to defend themselves but could also take offensive action against armies of knights and were capable of gaining victory by sheer weight of numbers.

The battle of Sempach was recorded in the Swiss chronicles of the 14th and 15th centuries. The accounts are mainly based on the report of Jakob Twinger of Königshofen who evaluated the news brought by Austrian knights who had taken part in the fighting. These and other accounts were included by K. Justinger in his chronicle of Berne, written about 1420, which, in turn, was used by chroniclers from Lucerne, Constance and Zurich as a basis for their own descriptions. Although such numerous sources are worth investigating and comparing, the reconstruction of the actual military events shows that there are not a few contradictions in the information they give.

The Swiss army, which advanced from Zurich and Lucerne, numbered some 6,000 to 8,000 men at the beginning of July 1386 and consisted almost entirely of foot forces armed with edged weapons. Duke Leopold's army was a formation of knights, supported by horsemen and infantry sent by 167 temporal and spiritual lords. In all, it probably numbered no more than 6,000 horsemen and foot-soldiers and was certainly numerically weaker than the Swiss forces. Its strength lay primarily in the knights, armed with lances, from the possessions in Western Austria and the mounted mercenaries who had been recruited.

The Hapsburg ruler decided to march to Sempach and to await the approach of the Swiss army there since he did not wish to be caught in the march like his great-uncle Leopold I at Morgarten. The Swiss, on the other hand, who were advancing from Gislikon, hoped that they could force the knights to fall back towards Lake Sempach. On the 9th of July, the advance guards of the two armies made contact with each other at the village of Hildisrieden. The Swiss vanguard had occupied a hill and it was this that the knights attacked on foot—in the French manner—since it would have been too difficult for their horses to advance up-hill. The Swiss threw back this attack.

Leopold thought that this was the main group of the Swiss army and ordered his knights to attack the hill as they arrived, without first collecting his forces and putting order in their ranks. He himself took part in the storming of the hill. For a short time, the knights were able to force back the Swiss vanguard and even to engage the main group. The banner of Lucerne fell, marking a critical moment in the battle for the Swiss. However, it was only the vanguard that was affected and it was now the turn of the main group to attack. Making full use of the element of surprise, the Swiss attacked the flank of the knights still advancing up the hill and dispersed the forces of Leopold III. The dismounted knights were outnumbered while the squires and servants holding their horses fled in panic, taking with them the other knights and foot-soldiers who had not yet reached the scene of the fighting. According to the Swiss chronicles, the duke himself, two other princes, 28 counts and more than 600 knights and other combatants fell on the Austrian side during the battle while the Swiss losses are said to have been only 120 according to Justinger and 200 in the other reports. It can be assumed that the losses of the confederates were considerably less than those of the Austrians who, incidentally, proved obstinate and only abandoned the contest with the despised "peasants" after a second defeat at Näfels in 1388.

The battle of Sempach again demonstrated the tactical superiority of massed infantry over knights. The latter were much too ponderous and slow in their heavy armour and were unable to charge effectively with their lances against massed foot-troops or repulse an onslaught by them. On the other hand, shortcomings were also apparent in the tactics of the Swiss. In the pursuit of the knights and their followers, not a few of them broke out of the ranks and engaged in plundering without waiting for the end of the battle. It was for this reason that a code of military conduct was introduced in 1393, laying down very severe punishments for disciplinary offences and forbidding soldiers to plunder on their own account. This *Sempach Document* played a great part in the further development of penal and martial law in the mercenary armies.

Sempach went down in history in connection with something else as well. Like no other Swiss battle of the late Middle Ages, it has fired the imagination of later generations with the story of Winkelried. According to legend, one of the Swiss leaders—Arnold von Winkelried—seized the lances outstretched by a number of knights and forced them down with his own body to open up a gap in the enemy line of battle which the Swiss with their halberds were then able to tear apart. This deed, which was later immortalized, in epics and lyric poetry ("Der Freiheit eine Gasse . . ."), belongs to the realm of saga and legend. Arnold von Winkelried did exist but at a time long after Sempach. He was a mercenary commander who was killed in 1522 at Bicocca while attempting to break through the pikes of a line of German lansquenets. The deed passed into the historical narrative tradition and was then transferred to the great struggle for freedom of the Swiss, Arnold becoming a real national hero. Nevertheless, it is certainly possible, in many a battle of that time, that individual heroic figures really did break into an enemy formation in this or a similar manner and lost their lives in the process.

GRUNWALD–TANNENBERG /1410

Like the Knights Templar or the Order of St. John, the Teutonic Order was a product of the Crusades and, like the former, was obliged to seek other fields of activity after the successful Islamic counteroffensive from Egypt. In 1226, after periods spent on Cyprus and in Burzenland in Transylvania, they had responded, with the blessing of the pope, to a call made by Duke Konrad of Mazovia to aid him in his struggle against his warlike neighbours, the "heathen" Pruzzi. They conquered Prussia, built castles and, together with the Livonian Order of the Sword which, coming from Riga, had subjugated and "converted" the Latvian and Estonian tribes, established a mighty state on a clerical basis. This state did not owe allegiance to Mazovian or Polish princes nor did it form part of the Holy Roman Empire. However, while the Teutonic Knights lived in peace with Novgorod following their defeat on the ice of Lake Peipus in 1242, they sought to extend the territory they held to the north of the Niemen which was linked to it solely by the narrow neck of land of Klaipeda (Memel). This was to be at the expense of Lithuania and in 1398 they invaded Samogitia.

The Grand Duchy of Lithuania had acquired vast areas of Western Russia and most of the Ukraine in the course of the 14th century when it had driven the Tartars back to the Black Sea. In 1386, Grand Duke Jagiello (Jagaila)—after embracing the Roman Catholic faith and taking the name of Wladyslaw II—had married Maria, the Queen of Poland and had thus linked the two states by personal union. This was initially a loose arrangement, which probably encouraged the Teutonic Knights in their designs, for the new Polish king did in fact entrust the government of his native land to his younger brother Witold (Vytautas), an experienced military leader. He did not hesitate, however, to repulse a second offensive by the Order in 1409 with the combined forces of both countries, an action which met with the full approval of the Polish nobility.

After the Lithuanian army had joined up with the Polish forces at the beginning of July 1410 near Chervinsk to the northwest of Warsaw, the combined army moved northwards against the Teutonic Knights. The fortresses of Neidenburg (Nidzica), Soldau (Dzialdowo) and Lautenburg (Lidzbark) were taken on the 8th and 9th of July. On the 10th of July, the army reached the small river Drewenz and saw on the other bank the army of the Teutonic Knights taking up an advantageous position with palisades and guns covering their line of battle. In view of the weakness of his position, the Polish king, who was nominally in command, decided not to cross the river but to make a detour at its source and from there to advance further into the territory of the Order. From the 10th to the 14th of July, the two armies moved northwards and finally took up a position east of the village of Grunwald.

The historical record of the great battle which took place here is based mainly on the *Historiae Polonicae*, written in the second half of the 15th century by Jan Długosz, a canon of Cracow cathedral who later became the archbishop there. He examines the history of the kingdom of Poland and the countries on its borders and, in the last sections, deals with the war between the Teutonic Knights and Poland-Lithuania. On the German side, some contemporary reports of the battle are contained in the "Schöppenchronik" of Magdeburg and Detmar's chronicle of Lübeck but there are no eyewitness accounts in the source material.

At the beginning of the 15th century, the Teutonic Order possessed one of the most powerful armies of Europe. Like its state with its clearly defined hierarchical structure, its military organization was also tauter than that of the other countries. The hard core of the army was formed by the armoured cavalry of the regular members and the vassals of the Order who appeared with a mounted retinue. The Grand Master could also mobilize German settlers who had received land in return for the promise to fight in times of war, either on horseback or on foot. The towns on the territory of the Order likewise provided contingents. Through its links with temporal and spiritual authorities in Central and Western Europe, the Order was also able to

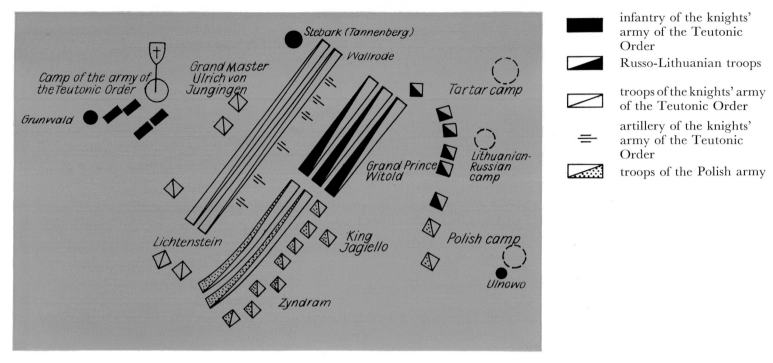

infantry of the knights' army of the Teutonic Order

Russo-Lithuanian troops

troops of the knights' army of the Teutonic Order

artillery of the knights' army of the Teutonic Order

troops of the Polish army

recruit additional mercenary knights for its expeditions. This was the case at that time, too.

The army of the Teutonic Knights at Grunwald numbered about 11,000 men, consisting of about 4,000 knights, 3,000 mounted followers and 4,000 mounted crossbow archers, who dismounted for the battle. The main striking force were the knights who carried lances and swords and wore plate-armour with an iron helmet. The horses were likewise protected by armour in most cases. The mounted forces were organized in troops of some 100 to 200 horsemen. The exact number frequently varied since this was not a tactical unit, man-to-man combat being the rule during battle. The foot forces occupied positions within and around the barricade of waggons during the battle.

At Grunwald (or Tannenberg as the battle was called by the Teutonic Knights), the army of the Order had taken up a battle-order of three lines. Since, however, the front of the Polish-Lithuanian army was broader, the Grand Master Ulrich von Jungingen regrouped the three lines into two longer ones. The right wing consisted of 20 troops under Lichtenstein, the 15 troops on the right wing were commanded by Wallrode while 16 troops remained in reserve. The artillery was placed in front of the line of battle and con-

sisted of heavy cannon, difficult to manoeuvre and firing stone or lead shot.

The organization of the Polish-Lithuanian forces was similar, the armoured cavalry of the Polish nobility and the Lithuanian princes forming the mass of the army. In all, they numbered 16,000 to 17,000 men, comprising 51 troops of Polish knights, 40 Lithuanian units and 3,000 Tartar cavalry. Knights from Bohemia, Moravia, Silesia and Hungary fought in the Polish ranks while the Lithuanian army included a number of Russian units from the regions around Smolensk and Vitebsk which belonged to Lithuania at that time. The Polish-Lithuanian army was drawn up in three lines with the Tartars, Lithuanians and Russians commanded by Grand Duke Witold on the right wing while the Poles under Zyndram of Maszkowice were on the left. The front line extended over some 2.5 kilometres in all.

The battle began at about noon on the 15th of July. Prior to the commencement of the battle, the Grand Master sent the Polish king two swords and, in accordance with an-

Clash of the Teutonic Knights with the Polish-Lithuanian army at the battle of Grunwald-Tannenberg. Miniature from the Chronicle of Diebold Schilling of 1484/85. Burgerbibliothek, Berne

Do man zalt von gottes geburt / M. cccc /
vnd x Jar, vmb Sant Marien Magdalenen
tag / geschach ein grosser streit zu preussen
zwischen dem Teutschen orden an einem / vnd
dem küng von polann an andern teil / Vnd
hatten zu beiden siten vil söldner geworben
vnd sigen dennocht denn mertail zem Teutschen or
den, darinn auch dem mer eren vnd güttes geschach

cient custom, announced the battle. The guns of the Teutonic Knights roared but they had very little effect since a thundery shower had made the powder damp. On the other side, the fighting was opened by the Tartars who galloped up in loose order and discharged a hail of arrows, most of which failed to penetrate the armour of the knights and likewise failed to achieve very much. The left wing of the Teutonic Knights then advanced with lances levelled and put the Tartars to flight. After this, they broke into the line of the right wing of the Polish-Lithuanian army and forced back the Lithuanian and Russian knights after fierce fighting. Some of the Russian units held their positions despite heavy losses.

In the meantime, the other wing had joined in the battle as well. Zyndram's knights held the attack by the Teutonic Knights. Bitter fighting in the first line characterized the climax and the turning point of the battle. When it already seemed that the scales were tipping in favour of the Teutonic Knights, Witold succeeded in bringing up fresh troops of knights from the second and third lines and in reinforcing the resistance of the hard-pressed first line. Ulrich von Jungingen did indeed bring up his reserves to surround the Poles and the Lithuanians and attack them in the rear but the whole of the Polish-Lithuanian third line then moved forward and repulsed the attack. By the late afternoon, the outcome of the battle was clear. The Teutonic Knights fell back and, after their Grand Master had been killed in the turmoil, sought to save their lives by flight. Some of the German forces retreated to the protection of the barricade of waggons but this was stormed by the Poles and Lithuanians. To celebrate the victory, they camped for three days on the battle-field.

Heavy losses were inflicted on both sides but the exact figures are not known. Chroniclers speak of 50,000 and even 100,000 casualties—comprising those killed, wounded or captured—but, as in other medieval sources, these numbers are greatly exaggerated. Nevertheless, they reflect the impressions made on contemporaries that the losses on both sides were without doubt very high.

The foot-soldiers took hardly any part in the fighting at Grunwald. It is true that the new weapon, artillery, was used there. But it had little effect on the course of the battle and, although present in considerable firepower for the standards of the time, it did not save the Teutonic Knights from defeat. In military history, Grunwald comes at the end of the age of chivalry. In Western and Central Europe of the 15th century, it was already apparent that many new developments were taking shape in military organization and tactics. In Eastern Europe, where the feudal order was still largely intact and unaffected by the early forms of capitalist economics, these changes in military affairs came only at a later stage.

The Order of the Teutonic Knights survived this defeat and a mild peace treaty (1411) by more than a century. But its role as a missionary factor and a military power in Northeastern Europe had come to an end. Leadership in this area passed to the powerful Polish-Lithuanian state of the Jagiellos.

USTI NAD LABEM (Aussig)/1426

Bohemia was something of an exception to the rule in the Holy Roman Empire. The Czech nation resisted Germanization and its ruler was the only one, apart from the German monarch, who was entitled to wear a royal crown. The mining of large deposits of silver in the 13th and 14th centuries had made him one of the wealthiest of the princes. On the other hand, the stimulus imparted to trade and commerce by the development of money economy also caused stresses and cracks in the pyramid of the usual feudal system and these were increased still further by the growing numbers of German immigrants. The "Golden Age" of Charles IV of Luxemburg (1346–1378) was followed by a period of social, political and intellectual restlessness which was reflected most clearly in the movement centred around Jan Hus.

The theologian Hus had made himself the spokesman of the Czech national interests and had disseminated the teachings of John Wycliffe, the English "heretic", for which the Council of Constance, breaking the promise of safe conduct given, sent him to the stake on 6th July 1415. The ferment in Bohemia reached a highpoint in 1419 when King Václav (Wenceslas IV) died and his brother Sigismund, king of Hungary since 1387 and king of Germany since 1410, declared his intention of taking his place. As the head of the "Council Party", he was held to be responsible for the murder of Jan Hus. The "Hussites" eliminated the conservative city fathers on the 30th June with the "first defenestration of Prague" and seized power.

The first phase of the Hussite Revolution was characterized in large measure by the humble peasants, subservient to their masters by hereditary right, and by the plebeians of the towns who implemented the early Christian principle of the community of goods already when they founded Tabor. In 1421, however, the radical wing of the "Taborites" lost the leadership of the movement to the middle-class townsfolk and the lesser nobility. Nevertheless, they remained loyal to the leadership and collaborated with it in a highly energetic manner against the enemy from abroad who now attacked the "fortress of Bohemia" from the South, West and North several times for more than ten years.

In 1426, the fighting was concentrated in the area of Northern Bohemia. Prior to this, the Hussites had already won several important military successes over the "Crusaders" of Sigismund and the pope and in 1425 had defeated an attack on Moravia made by Albrecht, Archduke of Austria. In the spring of 1426, the Hussites used the lull before the storm to recapture Northern and Northwestern Bohemia. They laid siege to Usti (Aussig) which had been occupied for years by troops of Saxony.

The Hussite army was an army of the people. Its volunteers were drawn from the peasants and especially from the poor artisans of the towns and countryside who had come to Tabor hoping for a better life. The army also included those members of the Czech nobility who had joined the movement and the citizens' militia of the great city of Prague.

To begin with, the Hussite soldiers—except for the better equipped nobles and burghers—had only their working implements and their hunting weapons. The threshing flail was turned into the fearsome war-flail, the ends of which were lined with iron, while the agricultural scythe became the untempered war-scythe. Then there was the "morning star" and the hooked spears used to pull down riders from their mounts. It was not long, however, before castles and towns furnished the Hussites with crossbows and firearms, the products of Bohemian and Moravian gunsmiths who were famous throughout Europe. In the unceasing struggles of the years after 1419, the Hussites not only improved their weapons but also acquired considerable experience in the art of warfare, particularly in the handling of massed foot-forces against knights and their squires. They put a number of armies into the field, the strength of which varied between 5,000 and 20,000 men.

The mainstay of the entire army was formed by a great barricade of heavy military waggons of new design. From the cover which these provided, the Hussites waited for the enemy to approach and then opened fire with crossbows, arquebuses and small cannon—also known as howitzers—which were mounted on the waggons. Their tactics were based on a co-ordinated combination of defence and counter-attack, launched from specially prepared points in the barricade as soon as the attackers had been sufficiently shaken by the defence. The belief of the Hussites in the divine justice of their cause lent strength to their moral unity and fortified their order and discipline on the field of battle. They called themselves soldiers of Christ and their armies rapidly became the terror of the rulers around them.

Their opponents, the crusading armies, consisted of contingents from individual princes, counts, lords and towns, who sent mounted vassals, equipped with knightly weapons and armour, and foot forces of little military value. These were joined by numerous mercenaries in their contingents since it had already become possible for not a few of the vassals to pay money in lieu of military service. Finally, contingents of peasants and burghers were also mobilized from time to time, since many princes, when faced with a shortage of ready cash and a lack of knights willing to fight, had recourse to the traditional obligation of defence on the part of their rural subjects in times of war. As a consequence, the motley armies of the Crusaders did not represent a cohesive tactical force in their struggle with the "heretics" since their arms, equipment and standards of training varied too greatly for this to have been possible. Many of the knights and mercenaries had only the prospect of rapid plunder in mind. They resented strict military discipline and there was naturally no question at all of any political and moral unity in their ranks. The situation was not much better in the supreme echelons. Command was nominally in the hands of King Sigismund but in practice this function was frequently entrusted to a prince who could count only on the reluctant obedience of the other high-ranking participants in the Crusade.

In June 1426, an army of about 20,000 men assembled in the margraviate of Meissen, crossed the mountains of the Erzgebirge and, on the 15th of that month, marched on the Hussite camp to the west of Usti. The Hussites under the command of Procop the Great (or the Bald) numbered 24,000 to 25,000 men and had built a barricade of waggons on a hill. This was the site of the battle which took place on the 16th of June.

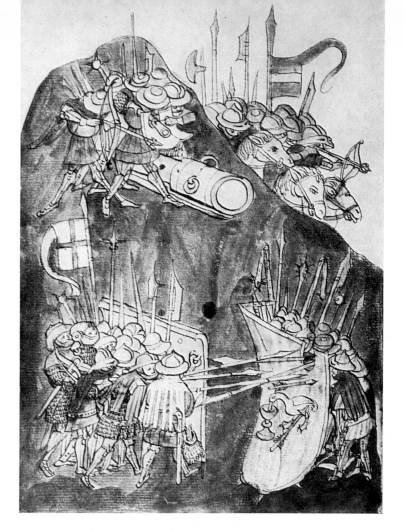

Battle-scene between the Hussites, equipped with firearms and edged weapons, and the feudal contingents of the Crusaders. Miniature, c. 1450. Nationalbibliothek, Vienna

Hussite waggon-barricade, defended by warriors using firearms, crossbows, edged weapons and (in the background) guns. Miniature, c. 1450. Nationalbibliothek, Vienna

There are accounts of the event in contemporary German and Czech chronicles. A collection of sources published by J. B. Mencken in 1733 contains, among others, the impressive description by Johann Rothe of Thuringia and in the *Chronikon* by Hermann Corner, which was likewise published only in the 18th century, there is a picture of the battle. An important light is thrown on the military organization of the Crusaders by the resolutions of the Reichstag at Nuremberg between 1422 and 1427 since they show what contingents of "Glefen", i.e., knights, squires and servants, and how many crossbows and arquebuses had to be provided by the various estates of the Empire. For the Hussites, reliable information is provided by the military code of

1423 of the great Jan Žižka of Trocnov (d. 1424) who had fought already on the Polish side at Grunwald-Tannenberg in 1410. It contains instructions on organization, discipline and tactics and enables important conclusions to be drawn regarding the art of war as developed by the Hussites.

As in previous battles, hostilities were opened at Usti by a cavalry attack on the Hussite barricade. At first, it seemed as if fortune was favouring the Crusaders and they got as far as the first row of waggons. However, as soon as they passed beyond these, they came within range of the cross-bows, arquebuses and cannon. "And now, as the lords, honest men and pious citizens moved up to the barricade of waggons and attempted to break a path through them and many would have therefore shown their excellent and bold manhood and would have gladly injured the heretics, the latter fired their ordnances, which they possessed in countless numbers, and they had long hooks with which they pulled the noble lords and pious men from their horses and slew them. And great dust arose from this, so that the one hardly saw the other and they struck and jostled each other so that many indeed did perish ..." This was the scene as described by Johann Rothe.

While the fighting was going on at the close-packed barricade, some of the Hussite forces broke out from behind it and launched a sudden counter-attack. The knights, mercenaries and foot-soldiers of the Crusader army were unable to withstand the impact of the attack and, after a brief engagement, hastily retreated. Some of the cavalry were encircled in the nearby village of Hrvovice (Herwitz)

and at Předlice (Prödlitz), while the other mounted forces and those fighting on foot endeavoured to escape the enemy by retreating to the North Bohemian frontier. On this the chronicler already mentioned reports: "And by retreating in this manner, the heretics followed them and slew many of the Christians. And many of them found their death from suffocation, since it was very dusty and hot everywhere. And those who managed to escape returned to their homelands in despair. And there was great lamentation in the countries of Meissen, in Thuringia and in Hesse ..."

The battle of Usti was the bloodiest of the Hussite wars and the sources speak of more than 10,000 dead, which is an exaggeration, of course. The Crusaders probably lost between 3,000 and 4,000 men while the Hussite casualties were certainly far less. They won as the result of tactical cohesion, co-ordinated use of edged weapons and firearms from behind the barricade and the interplay of defence and attack.

The Hussites were now able to take the devastating war beyond their borders on an increased scale ("Procop the Bald will have you for his dinner ...") but their internal unity disintegrated in 1431 once the immediate danger from outside had disappeared. The aristocratic faction, which was inclined to come to terms with Sigismund and the pope, destroyed the main nucleus of the popular Taborite forces, led by the two Procops, at the battle of Lipany on 30 May 1434, following the split in the movement. In 1436, the moderate "Calixtines" or "Utraquists" signed the compact of Basle by which they received special rights for their national church. This marked the end of an "early bourgeois" revolution and royal rule returned to Bohemia.

Hussite barricade of waggons

deployment and attack of the Crusader cavalry

attacks of the Hussites

escape of the Crusaders

heights

MURTEN / 1476

The dukes of Burgundy, the descendants of a minor line of the French Valois dynasty, had come into the possession of the wealthy Dutch provinces in the course of the "Hundred Years' War" between England and France (1337–1453) as a result of an adroit changing of sides and the simultaneous end of the House of Luxemburg (1437). Charles the Bold (1467–1477), more noted for rashness than for wisdom, was not content, however, to be the mightiest and most influential of the vassals of both the French and the German monarchs. What he had in mind was the crown of an independent kingdom extending from the North Sea to the Jura mountains. When diplomatic means did not produce the desired result, he resorted to force and occupied Lorraine, "the missing link", which then led to the neighbouring rulers directly affected by his boundless ambitions taking the side of Duke René II of Lorraine, even though there was a great deal of enmity between them.

Trusting to the power of his well-filled treasury and well-equipped knights—the most magnificent of all Europe, Charles picked up the gauntlet thrown down by the Swiss Confederation in 1476. He promptly met with defeat at the hands of the latter on the 2nd of March at Grandson. But he regarded this not as a warning but as a chance accident which could happen to any sturdy soldier. Within a few weeks, he assembled a new army from contingents of Burgundian knights and their squires. Celebrated as an energetic war-lord among the often weak potentates of his time, he had no trouble either in recruiting and maintaining numerous mercenaries—and impoverished knights—from Italy, Brabant, Flanders, England and the German states.

Following the pattern of the French military reform of 1431–1439 under Charles VII, the Burgundian army was organized by the "Statutes of Thionville" (1473), in "ordinance companies" with a complicated military structure. Each company consisted of four squadrons (escadres) of two lances each. Each lance, in turn, comprised one armoured knight, three mounted archers, one crossbowman, one pikeman and a gunner. The latter three soldiers fought on foot and, at most, used horses as a means of transportation on the march. Pay, equipment, discipline and military exercise were also specified in the regulations. Nevertheless, this military organization, extremely modern and flexible in its concept, continued to bear an aristocratic stamp: the nucleus of the army and the actual combatants were solely the noble knights; all the other forces, even if they served in the lance with a knight, were auxiliary troops. In the final analysis, the outcome of the battle was still decided by the knights in man-to-man combat while the foot-soldiers and the mounted marksmen as an "appendage" of the army, were only employed for secondary tasks. This likewise applied to the extremely costly artillery, the already extensive use of which is worth noting. It was due to the invention of the "Burgundian carriage" which allowed the positions of the guns to be changed even while fighting was in progress. This assumed the availability of financial resources on a scale possessed by no other contemporary monarch in Europe—with the possible exception of the Turkish sultan Mehmed II Ghazi (1451–1481) who likewise made vigorous use of his cannon in the battle of Cherdan against the Turkmenians of Uzun Hasan (1473).

On this occasion, the Swiss army did not consist exclusively of contingents from the cantons but also included some Austrian, German and Lotharingian knights together with their mounted retinue who were allied with the Swiss Confederates or had been attracted by the prospect of booty. In the eighty years that had passed since Sempach, no basic change had taken place in the organization and tactics of the Swiss. To be sure, they had acquired a great deal of experience in the field and had a high degree of confidence in their own military power. They enjoyed the reputation of being the best soldiers of the Occident. The army they sent into the field against the Duke of Burgundy numbered about 26,000 men and consisted mainly of foot troops. Paradoxically enough, it was commanded by the Austrian knight Wilhelm Herter since, for political motives, none of the Swiss cantons was prepared to entrust the leadership to any of the others. The individual units were commanded by Swiss captains, however: the advance party of 3,000 men was led by Hans von Halwil of Berne, the compact body of troops by Hans Waldmann of Zurich and the rearguard by Kaspar Hartenstein of Lucerne. The foreign knights, numbering about 1,800, formed a single unit as part of the main body, the intention being that they should provide support in the attack.

There are reports on the battle between the Swiss and the Burgundian army from both sides. Giovanni Pietro Panigarola, the envoy of the Duke of Milan, Galeazzo Maria Sforza, wrote a detailed report of the battle to his master three days later. On the opposing side, Diebold Schilling's chronicle of Berne relates the course, results and consequences of the battle, as they appeared to the Swiss observer. The notes of the eloquent courtier Philippe de Commynes, *Mémoires sur les principaux faits de Louis XI*, are a first-rate source for details of the Burgundian forces.

The Burgundian army, consisting of about 20,000 men, laid siege to the small town of Murten at the beginning of June, the town being defended by 1,580 Swiss under Adrian von Bubenberg. The initial attacks by the Burgundians had proved unsuccessful and the Swiss army was now approaching from the east to relieve the town. To hold up the expected attack, Charles the Bold had a field fortification built about two kilometres to the east of Murten. This "Grünhag", as the position was called, was constructed from wattle, palisades and trenches and protected by cannon. About 2,000 foot-soldiers and 300 lances manned it.

Duke Charles had certainly noted the approach of the enemy but believed that only weak forces had moved up to the Grünhag and that an attack on this 22nd of June was not yet possible. The Swiss also reconnoitred the position of the Burgundian army and observed that their adversary had not yet deployed his forces in battle-order. They consequently reasoned that an immediate attack offered a good prospect of victory.

Their forces advanced from the wood and attacked the Grünhag. The first onslaught was soon halted by a salvo from the Burgundian artillery. This setback was probably due not so much to the actual losses suffered as to the psychological effect caused by the thunder and smoke of the cannon since many of the Swiss must have been quite unaccustomed to this on such a massive scale. The Swiss withdrew and took cover in the undulating terrain. Individual Burgundian knights rode out but were unable to make contact with the Swiss units.

Before the cannon could be reloaded, which was still a very lengthy operation at that time, the Swiss launched another attack, this being from a different direction on this occasion so as to avoid the possibility of a second salvo. In the meantime, the alarm had been raised in the Burgundian camp but before the knights, the bowmen, the pikemen and men-at-arms could arrive—mostly in unorganized groups —the superior Swiss forces had already taken the Grünhag. Its defenders hastily fled back to the camp and ran straight past those hurrying to their assistance. The duke vainly tried to restore order in his confused ranks. The Swiss launched a full-scale attack against the mass struggling to and fro and at the same time the garrison of Murten was able to break out from the town. Only the mounted Burgundians were able to save themselves by flight. Most of the foot troops— English bowmen under Lord Somerset, Lombard gunners and others—were scattered by the Confederates and killed.

Thus was the fate of the Burgundian army decided on 22 June 1476. Charles the Bold fled with the others, of whom only the detachment led by Count Romont was in any condition to fight. The losses were between 6,000 and 8,000 men. "The army was caught unprepared," complained Panigarola from the Burgundian camp, "it was beaten and totally destroyed. I have never seen the duke so bewildered and perplexed as at the moment when he put on his equipment and mounted his horse. ... The artillery is lost ... a gun-park big enough for the greatest campaigns. I will not speak at all of the huts, the tents, waggons, gold and clothing; as I said, the enemy forced his way forward and we were lucky to save even our skins."

There is no authentic data available in respect of the Swiss losses. The envoy from Milan quotes 3,000 men which seems too high just as the figure of 300 dead named by the Swiss must be too low.

Knights in full plate armour with raised swords and knights equipped only with lance and crossbow whose armour consists merely of burgonet, gauntlets and some other parts.

Knights in mail armour with lance, shield and sword, *c.* 1410.

Coloured lithographs, early 19th century. Armeemuseum der DDR, Dresden

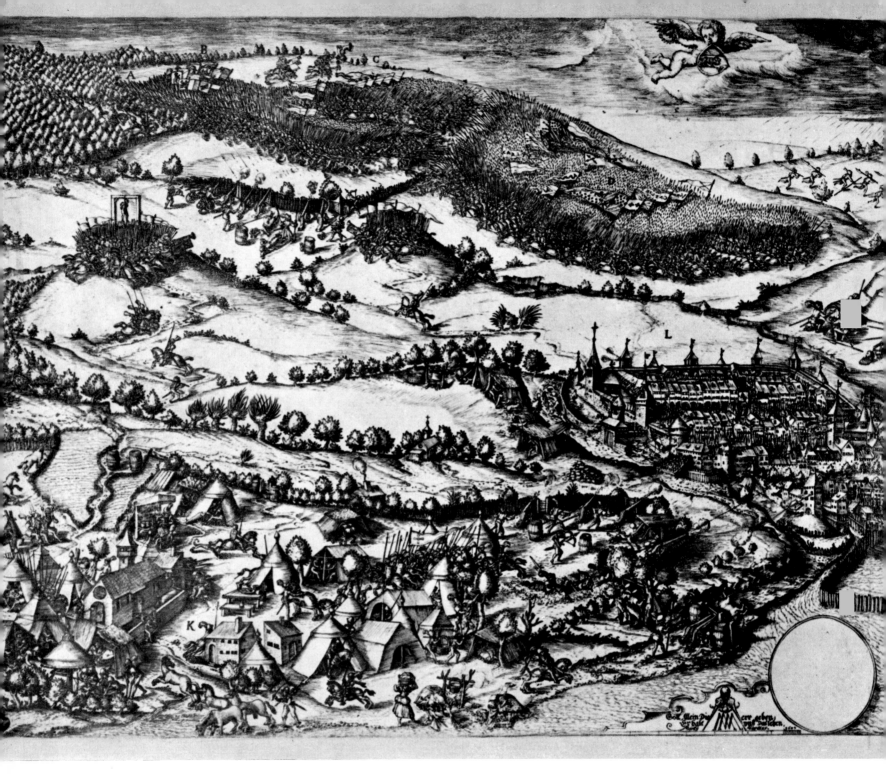

General view of the battle of Murten with the besieged city and
the Burgundian camp. Copper engraving by Martin Martini
from the 16th century. Graphic Collection of the Eidgenössische
Technische Hochschule, Zurich

The war ended in 1477 with a third Swiss victory, on this occasion fought at Nancy, far from their homeland. The prestige of the Confederates was now unlimited and for a time misled them into trying their luck as a great power themselves in Italy's fields. As to the legacy of Charles (killed at Nancy), whose still-admired diamond, the Sancy, rolled unnoticed across the devastated battlefield, there began a quarrel between the Hapsburgs and the Valois which continued on and off for almost a century. It enabled the one to complete the centralization of the French state while the other used it as a dynastic springboard to the Spanish empire "in which the sun never set"—although it was the Dutch, standing on the side-lines, who ultimately proved to be the real beneficiaries.

From the military viewpoint, the Swiss victories over the Burgundians clearly demonstrated the superior combat efficiency of massed foot-troops, equipped with edged weapons, who could attack and destroy armies of knights. These successes showed that the epoch of the individual warrior in heavy armour on horseback was irrevocably coming to an end and that the hour of the "last knight without fear or fault"—whether this was Emperor Maximilian or Bayard—would soon strike. Progress in military organization and warfare was henceforth associated with massed foot-troops, from which the infantry as such was to emerge as the "queen of the battlefield".

Combat scenes from the battle of Murten. Swiss peasants, armed with pikes, halberds and long swords attacking the Burgundian knights and mercenaries. Painting by Ferdinand Hodler (1917). Musée d'Art et d'Histoire, Geneva

PAVIA / 1525

In the 15th century, German hegemony in Italy practically came to an end. Small and medium states had emerged whose material wealth and culture attracted the covetous glances of the French and Spanish sovereigns. The quarrel over the throne of Naples in 1494 set the scene for an open struggle between the two. The French were rapidly compelled to abandon their ambitions in the South but in Northern Italy, where local party politics played a part, the fortunes of war favoured first one and then the other side. The principal cause of dissent was the Lombard Duchy of Milan in the centre of the country.

The French and Spanish had both made considerable progress, although in different ways, in the elimination of aristocratic power within their territory. This allowed the centralized monarchies to take more vigorous action on the international scene and they could not or were not prepared to depend any longer on their politically unreliable and militarily ineffective contingents of the knightly vassals. Since, on the other hand, they did not yet dispose of sufficient revenues for the maintenance of a standing army in times of peace, they were obliged to wage their campaigns largely with mercenaries who fought on foot. These were the troops who determined the profile of the forces of both sides during the "Renaissance Wars".

In time of war, both princes and republics—such as Venice—enlisted renowned mercenary leaders who then recruited an army. It often happened that wealthy "war specialists" themselves advanced the money for this purpose and recovered their expenses in the form of booty in the course of the campaign. In this age, when the military system of the late Middle Ages was in its last throes, cash was consequently the critical question in warfare. An army could only be kept together as long as there was a ready supply of silver dollars. If they didn't receive their pay and plunder was meagre, neither the usual written articles nor promises could keep the mercenaries by the colours for much longer. It was then that mutinies and plundering occurred and armies disintegrated.

The mercenary, who had to provide his own weapons in the 15th and 16th centuries, was usually a professional soldier with combat experience. A distinction was drawn between pikemen who carried a pike or lance of up to 5 metres in length, and marksmen who used an arquebuse or musket. Mercenaries seldom wore any kind of armour. Each dressed himself in clothes as colourful as possible, military motifs being favourite decorations. Contemporary writers frequently complained about these "tipplers" with their "cursing and fighting".

On the battlefield, the mercenaries followed the Swiss pattern and were organized in a number of great "squares". The heart of these formations were the pikemen and in the foremost ranks there also fought particularly strong "double-mercenaries" (i.e., who received twice the usual pay), who were supposed to hack an opening in the enemy line with their two-handed swords of one and a half metre in length. The marksmen took up their positions on the wings and in front of the others before the battle began. The cavalry, who already carried pistols in addition to edged weapons, operated on the flanks.

In 1512, Swiss soldiers had won the day at Ravenna for France, in the following year they fought on their own account *against* France and conquered the canton of Ticino. Defeated in 1515 at Marignano by Francis I (1515–1547) with the aid of German, Italian and even some Swiss mercenaries, they henceforth kept to the French side but were beaten at the Bicocca by the Condottiere Pescara, one of the "fathers" of the Spanish *tercio*. The nucleus of this reasonably mobile formation in regiment strength consisted initially of young countrymen—the sons of peasants who were commanded by officers of the king and given some sort of military training. In their ranks, there were already many marksmen who were equipped with handy matchlocks and, instead of buff-coats, often wore a light cuirass and an iron helmet. They were the best-disciplined troops of their time and could consequently be easily handled by their general.

Despite this, the campaigns of 1523 and 1524 led to setbacks for Spain. The French occupied Milan and besieged Pavia in the winter of 1524/1525. The Hapsburgs did not possess such an impressive war-chest to back up their military activities, although Charles V had added, by way of inheritance, the crowns of Castile, Aragon and Naples to his original possessions in the Low Countries and, after the death of his grandfather Maximilian I in 1519, the crown of the Holy Roman Empire as well—without counting the new discoveries in America. The repayment of his debts after the costly election to Imperial status, the crushing of a major rebellion by Castile cities and knights, the repulse of the Turks, the overcoming of a defeat in the *noche triste* of 1520 during the conquest of Mexico by Hernán Cortés—all this cost money. Thus it was only in January 1525 that a strong Imperial army was assembled at Lodi under the formal command of the Viceroy of Naples, Lannoy, and marched from there to Pavia where the relief of 5,000 German lansquenets and 400 Spaniards under Antonio de Leyva seemed a matter of some urgency. Since all efforts to storm the town had failed, King Francis had decided to starve out the town and the garrison.

The Imperial army consisted of some 12,000 lansquenets, recruited by such famous mercenary leaders as Georg von Frundsberg, Marx Sittich von Embs and Niclas von Salm, 6,000 Spanish musketeers or pikemen, 3,000 Italian mercenaries and 1,500 light cavalry but only 16 cannon. The French army had 53 cannon and 1,200 armoured horsemen, known as *gens d'armes* or men-at-arms, who were accompanied by numerous other horsemen and foot-soldiers. Also on the French payroll were 8,000 Swiss under Johann von Diesbach and the "Black Band", 5,000 Flemish and German lansquenets under Georg Langemantel, the son of a patrician of Augsburg. It was unusual for such a large number to be in the service of the French Crown whose enmity towards "Emperor and Empire" offended many of the lansquenets and their commanders. This was why such mercenary service was generally viewed with contempt and, even years after Pavia, the Imperial general Lazarus von Schwendi had the mercenary captain Vogelsberger condemned to death for recruiting soldiers for France. There was also hatred between the lansquenets and the Swiss—partly because of the competition between them. Thus it was not by chance that the merciless war was declared in 1525 between the mercenaries and was waged ruthlessly.

After the two armies had almost started fighting by accident on account of a herd of cows grazing in a meadow near Pavia, one battle was opened according to plan at dawn on the 24th of February to the north of the town by the Imperial forces. Reports by such mercenary leaders as Frundsberg and Caspar Wintzerer, the Marquis Pescara, letters or communications from diplomatic attachés in the camps of the two armies such as the Abbot of Najera and the ambassador of Siena and not least the autobiographies and memoires of French marshals such as Du Bellay and Montluc provide a reliable picture of what occurred.

Overnight, the Imperial forces had quietly opened up three breaches in the sturdy brick wall surrounding the great park around the castle of the Visconti and some of their troops now streamed across the terrain. Francis I, who had expected the attack from the East, sent his "gendarmes" against the infiltrators and at the same time ordered his artillery to open up. The attack by the heavily armed cavalry was initially successful and the Imperial troops were forced back against the wall which did not allow them to withdraw. It seemed as if the French would win the day. It was at this moment that Pescara ordered his musketeers to fire. They inflicted very heavy losses on the French cav-

Battle of Pavia. Pursuit by the Imperial troops of the Swiss mercenaries in French pay. Tapestry from the 2nd half of the 16th century from the Capodimonte, Naples.

Scene of the battle of Pavia with the precipitate withdrawal of the French across the Ticino and the capture of Francis I. Tapestry from the 2nd half of the 16th century from the Capodimonte, Naples.

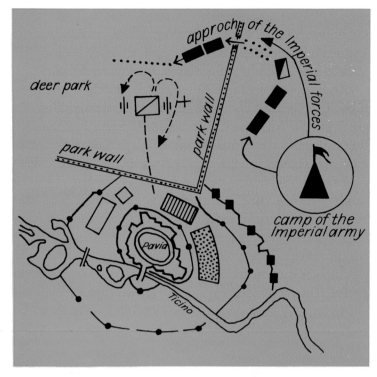

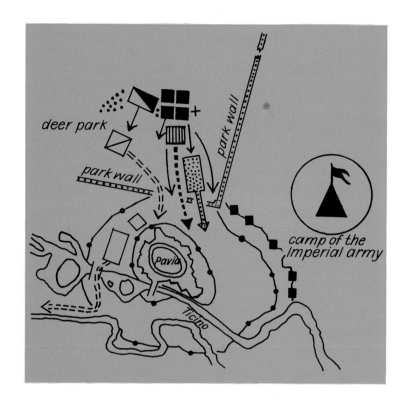

▬	lansquenets
◥	Spanish cavalry
▭	French infantry
▱	French cavalry
⊞	the "Black Band"
▦	Swiss
⬯	encircled garrison
⟶	attacks by the Imperial forces
--→	French attack
===⟹	escape of the French
⋯-→	escape of the "Black Band"
⋯⟹	escape of the Swiss
⩵	French artillery
⋮⋮⋮⋮⋮⋮	Spanish musketeers
⊶■⊷	field position of the Imperial army
●—●—●	lines of encirclement by the French army
✛	Mirabello Castle

alry and shook their morale. "It was a bloody battle," wrote Adam Reissner, "and the French had to fall since the quick Spaniards rapidly surrounded them and everywhere fired lead balls at them, causing fatal wounds. They had not ordinary handguns but long firearms called hooks, arquebusiers being the name of such marksmen. With one shot, they slew many a man and steed so that the entire field was so full of dead horses that the others could not move and did not dare to flee."

When the "Black Band" then appeared on the scene, they were eliminated in a bloody engagement by Frundsberg's lansquenets who outnumbered them by almost two to one and, as the Imperial troops advanced further against the Swiss, the defenders of Pavia came to their aid by making an effective sally in the rear of the French army. Under pressure from two sides, it was now the turn of the Swiss to flee.

The French rearguard had not yet taken any part in the action but in view of the already inevitable defeat the Duke of Alençon ordered it to withdraw across the Ticino and demolish the bridge. In this manner, 4,400 horsemen and infantry troops were able to escape but the great mass of the French army again suffered heavy losses here at the river as it fell back. Many drowned in the rapid waters or were slain and King Francis was taken captive.

The battle, one of the greatest of the century, cost the vanquished more than 6,000 dead, 5,000 prisoners and the loss of all their artillery while it is said that the Imperial army suffered only 500 dead. Tactically, the defeat is to be explained by the fact that the various French units went into action one after the other and in an unco-ordinated manner. First of all, the heavy cavalry was beaten, then the lansquenets and finally the Swiss. The numerical superiority of the French was never exploited in a really effective manner whereas Frundsberg and Pescara synchronized the movements of their forces and won the day despite their lack of artillery support. The enemy, and least of all the knights, had nothing to set against the effective musket-fire.

Henceforth, every tactic had to take account of this as a proven fact.

Pescara marched on Milan. He was immortalized, together with his wife, the Humanist Vittoria Colonna, in the novella by Conrad Ferdinand Meyer. Francis I had to pay a high price for his release with the peace of Madrid in 1526. He broke all the oaths he had sworn, of course, as soon as the pope, who was on his side, gave him permission and the second was followed by a third, fourth and other wars. However, the Swiss were unable to regain their reputation as the best mercenaries of Europe which they had lost at Pavia. It was the lansquenets who now occupied the first rank, a position they rapidly lost to the Spanish infantry, while the proven superiority of hand-held firearms began to revolutionize military tactics.

Lansquenet, armed with pike and sword, and female sutler. Woodcut by Peter Flötner, *c.* 1530. Armeemuseum der DDR, Dresden

SEKIGAHARA / 1600

Towards the end of the 16th century, military leaders who —like many of the condottiere in Europe—had risen to high rank from humble origins made several attempts in feudally divided Japan to enforce the submission of the local lords, the daimyos, to a firm central authority. Oda Nobunaga and—after his murder in 1582—Toyotomi Hideyoshi ruled the land in dictatorial manner and, on account of their modest beginnings, were decried by the old aristocracy as usurpers and tyrants. When Hideyoshi died in 1598 in the castle of Fushimi which he had built, leaving behind three poems on cherry blossoms, he had practically completed the restoration of a central state authority under a military regime. Since, on the one hand, he had made life easier for the most unfortunate of the serfs and on the other had involved the army in ruinous campaigns of conquest in Korea (1592, 1597/98) with the Japanese fleet being badly beaten in four major sea-battles by the iron-clad war-galleys of the great Korean admiral Li Sun-sin, his death was immediately followed once again by the emergence of all the old social contradictions. The self-appointed Imperial general had made his ten most important vassals swear an oath of loyalty to his five-year old son Hideyori but this did not prevent a ruthless struggle from immediately breaking out between them for the highest office of the State which had lost its holder.

Tokugawa Ieyasu was in the best position to start with. The son of a samurai (or "bushi") of medium rank, he had been obliged as one of Nobunaga's paladins to yield to his more fortunate rival Hideyoshi and had been transferred by the latter in 1590 from the then political centre of Osaka to the periphery of the country, to Edo, the present-day Tokyo. Here, however, he had succeeded in establishing a firm position for himself which permitted him much greater freedom of action than the other daimyos who, during this interregnum, had much difficulty in maintaining their authority within their own areas.

In the course of his many journeys across the country, Ieyasu built up an alliance and in particular won over many of the former military retinue of Hideyoshi who were jealous of the five supreme civil officials, the ambitious bugyos, and of their increasing influence on the business of the State and the allocation of sinecures. Of these five, it was Ishida Mitsunari in particular who sensed that danger was imminent and appealed to the daimyos to take their stand around the young Hideyori, who was in his care, as the sworn heir of the more or less legitimate power. Both parties made preparations for armed conflict and it was Ieyasu who proceeded to the attack in July 1600 in the hope that he would find his opponents, between whom there were only loose political links, in a poor state of readiness and that he would be able to defeat them. He assembled an army at Osaka and marched against Uesugi Kagekatsu in Aizu, far away in the Northeast. Another interpretation, however, has it that all this was only a ruse to persuade his opponents to show their true colours during his absence from Osaka and thus enable him to achieve a rapid and final victory. At any rate, the daimyos of the West who were loyal to Mitsunari did indeed take immediate action and overran the castle of Fushimi which was held by Tokugawa forces. At the news of its fall, Ieyasu turned back and marched without haste along the Tokaido road, the principal route of communication of the country, gathering reinforcements on the way, against the "armies of the West". In mid-October, he reached the province of Mino and, a few days later, clashed with the contingents mobilized by Mitsunari and his allies on the hill-lined plain of Sekigahara where three old overland routes crossed.

The battle began at 8 a.m. on 21 October 1600. After heavy rain on the previous day and during the night, thick mist still hung over the flat terrain. The "Eastern armies", firmly under the control of Ieyasu, are said to have numbered 100,000 men whereas there were only 75,000 in the ranks of the "West", which had also established a really effective supreme command. Almost all the daimyos of the land with their followings took part in the battle. As is very often the case in civil wars, both sides used similar

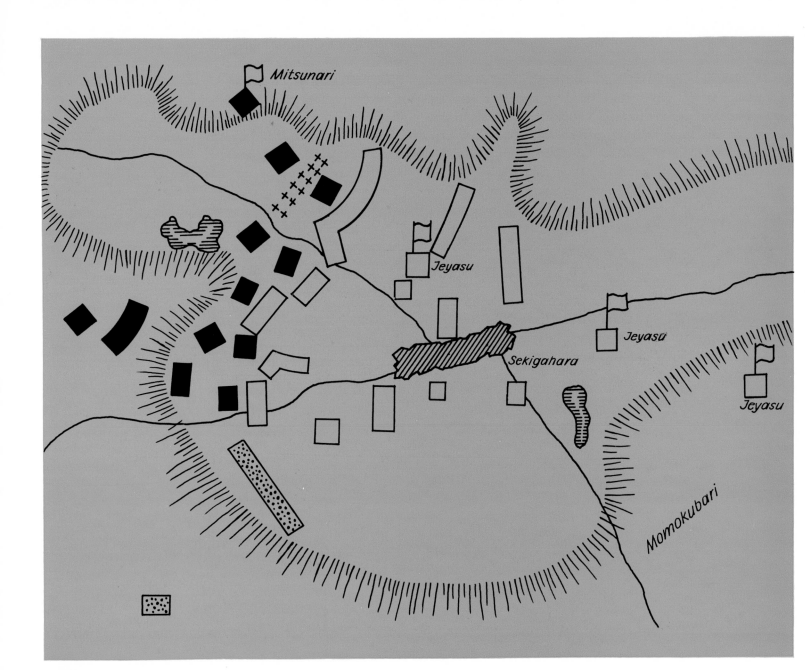

Western forces

"treacherous troops"

Eastern forces

positions of the commanders

ponds

place

+ + + bamboo entanglement

—— overland roads

arms and equipment. Horses were only used by the commanders. The samurai warriors in their helmets and light armour fought with sword and bow or a derivative of the halberd known as the *naginata*, as they had done at the time of the Mongol invasions. The use of the lance was more recent and had become established during the period of the constant internal feuds of the late 15th century with the emergence of large, compact infantry formations. This, in turn, reflected a change in the social composition of military forces. Since the daimyos were no longer able to meet their growing requirements for soldiers from the ranks of their bushi—or samurai, they mobilized the peasants not only, as in the past, for field-works and transportation tasks but also in large numbers as combatants. Since the latter possessed neither helmets nor armour, they suffered by far the highest losses in the battle. Muskets, introduced by the Portuguese, were first used in 1575 at the battle of Nagashino and also played a part—although not a major one—at Sekigahara.

Perhaps with the intention of encircling their enemy, perhaps only following the contours of the terrain, the Western forces took up their positions in a semi-circle, curving inwards and extending loosely from North to South at the foot of the chain of hills limiting the plain towards the West. On the left wing, behind which Mitsunari's command-post was located on an elevation, a hastily erected bamboo barricade cut off a few hundred metres of open terrain. To begin with, Ieyasu issued his orders from some distance away on Momokubari Mountain but then took up a position immediately behind his troops on the plain. He had his troops advance from the West in three lines but only the

Scene from the battle of Sekigahara with the general attack of the Eastern Army under the command of Tokugawa Ieyasu, clearly identified by his black horse. Painting by Kano Tanyo (1602–1672). Toshogu Shrine in Nikko

Japanese warriors in man-to-man combat under the banner of their daimyos during the battle of Sekigahara. Picture on a folding panel. Ihi Museum, Prefecture of Shiga

first of these engaged the opposing forces. Both sides suffered heavy losses in an exhausting conflict which lasted three to four hours but no change took place in their positions.

At about noon, there was an unexpected and sudden development in the situation. The reserves commanded by the daimyo Kobayakawa Hideaki behind the right wing of the Western armies left their positions and attacked the main body of their own side in the rear. As soon as this movement was apparent, the whole of Tokugawa's advanced right wing, which had remained inactive up till now, likewise swung westwards and overwhelmed Mitsunari's last reserves. While the main army in the middle and—with the utmost effort—also on the left wing still stood firm in the face of a now vastly superior enemy, Ieyasu's wing in the South broke into the undefended gap which the changing of sides by the "traitors" had opened up between the remaining loyal troops on the right wing and in the centre of the Western armies. Rolled up in this manner from the South, they were dispersed by Ieyasu's general attack in the early afternoon and practically annihilated. This consequently marked the end of the war. Some of the daimyos on the losing side committed hara-kiri, which was formally known as *seppuku*. Among those who fled from the field were Mitsunari, who maintained his hatred of Ieyasu, and Konishi Yukinaga who, as a Christian, rejected the tradition of honourable suicide. Both were taken captive and together with other leaders, executed.

Sekigahara was a political battle. The "treacherous troops", as they are usually referred to in Japan, or more precisely some of their leading daimyos, had held secret talks with Ieyasu already before the beginning of the battle, so the latter did not even need to deploy any troops against them and could concentrate his attack on the centre and left wing of his adversary. To be quite sure, however, the turncoats had awaited the outcome of the first stages of the battle before openly taking the side of the new star in Japanese politics and thus dealing their erstwhile comrades the deathblow.

The preliminary happenings and the story of the battle were recorded in detail in 1656 by the Confucian scholar Hayashi Razan. Like the papers left by Ieyasu, which were subsequently published, he narrates the course of events from the viewpoint of the victor and states, for instance, that the enemy dead totalled 5,000 but says nothing about the victor's own losses. Kano Tanyo (1602–1672), a member of a respected family and school of artists, was likewise unable, as a painter at the court of the Tokugawas, to depict the event in an unbiased manner and placed Ieyasu on his black war-horse in the centre of his impression of the battle. Nonetheless, his picture in the Toshogu Shrine at Nikko, where Tokugawa Ieyasu was venerated as a divine being, is one of the treasures of world culture.

The battle of Sekigahara is a landmark in Japanese history. Ieyasu, who has been compared with Richelieu, did not use the victory to increase his own personal estates but, in a more far-sighted manner, wisely divided up among his vassals the mighty acquisitions in land and offices taken from the vanquished. He thus succeeded in breaking the backbone of the opposition to the government, in firmly subordinating the daimyos to the central authority and in making the Shogunate or Bakufu—which was transferred to Edo in 1603—the hereditary office of his family with all the proprieties being observed.

Only the Toyotomi, as relatively independent daimyos, were able to maintain their resistance until the capture of their castle in Osaka after two long sieges in 1614 and 1615. From then on, the Tokugawa Shogunate survived unchallenged as the Japanese version of absolute monarchy until 1867. The battle of Sekigahara, which laid the foundation stone of this development, was not merely the greatest but also the last serious battle fought among the Japanese—and at the same time the last battle of any kind on Japanese soil.

LÜTZEN / 1632

This battle, the diorama of which can be seen in the castle of Lützen, was not at all the greatest of the Thirty Years' War in respect of the number of combatants but it was probably the politically most important and had the most significant consequences. A great deal of information about it has survived. The *Theatrum Europaeum* quickly devoted a report to it and a *Warhafft und eygentliche Relation* (A True and Actual Account) was likewise published already in November 1632. In 1633, Laurentius Troupitz published the *Kriegskunst nach Königlich Schwedischer Manier* (The Art of War in the Royal Swedish Manner) and the Swedish historiographer Bogislaw Philipp von Chemnitz printed his book *Königlich Schwedischer in Teutschland geführter Krieg* (The Royal Swedish War Waged in Germany) in 1648.

When the Swedes under King Gustavus II Adolphus Vasa landed in Hither Pomerania in 1630 to head the Ger-

man Protestant "Union", the war had already passed through two phases in twelve years, both of which had been won by the emperor with the aid of the princes of the Catholic League and Spain. After the campaigns of Tilly and Wallenstein against Christian IV of Denmark and the Peace of Lübeck, only the cities of Stralsund and Magdeburg still opposed the "Restitutionsedikt" of 1629 in which Ferdinand II (1619–1637) desired to anchor the victory of Imperial Austria under the Hapsburgs and the Counter-Reformation. Sweden, which had established its ascendancy in the Baltic by successful wars against Russia and Poland, saw this *Dominium maris Baltici* threatened by the Imperial advance to the North and so, for its part, intervened in

Panorama view of the battle of Lützen. Copperplate engraving by Mattäus Merian, mid-17th century. Museum für Geschichte der Stadt Leipzig

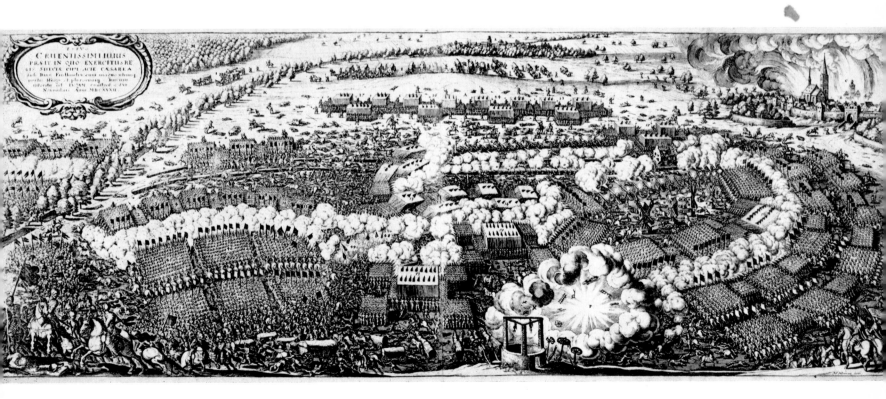

what was going on in Germany. Subsidies offered by Cardinal Richelieu of France facilitated the decision.

Gustavus Adolphus, to whom the Protestant German princes submitted only reluctantly, came too late to save Magdeburg from going up in flames. On 17 September 1631, however, although his Saxon allies on the left wing failed against General Pappenheim, he won a brilliant victory over Tilly at Breitenfeld to the north of Leipzig. This completely changed the situation and Ferdinand was obliged to hurriedly recall Wallenstein, who had been dismissed at the instigation of the jealous princes, and to appoint him supreme commander with an unusual degree of authority.

The wealthy Bohemian Count Albrecht von Waldstein, who also signed his name as Wallenstein, was, by the grace of the emperor, Duke of Friedland and—despite the protest of the princes—of Mecklenburg. He was also the last outstanding condottiere of Europe. He possessed the talent of organization and the gift of command in equal measure and mercenaries flocked to his recruiting agents. Without asking about religion—in a so-called religious war—he faithfully followed the motto that war nourished war—and in particular the warriors. In the summer of 1632, he built at Nuremberg the fortified camp of Zirndorf that the Swedes vainly tried to capture—after a second victory (on the 15th of April at Rain on the Lech) over Tilly, who subsequently died from the wounds received there. While Gustavus Adolphus devastated Bavaria after the indecisive first round against his new opponent, Wallenstein turned towards Saxony, took Leipzig and threatened the Swedish lines of communication to the Baltic. The Swedes had to drive him away at any price and risk a third battle if they were to spend the winter in comfort in Saxony.

In November, the two armies drew near to each other and ultimately took up fortified positions to the east of Weissenfels near Lützen: Wallenstein to the north and Gustavus Adolphus to the south of the old road between Leipzig and Weissenfels. They were consequently facing their own hinterland, with potentially devastating consequences for the loser.

On the morning of the battle, Wallenstein had 12,000 men at his command; reinforcements arrived by noon so that he opened the battle with barely 15,000 troops before Pappenheim's 7,000 cavalry arrived from the Halle area in the late afternoon, but he was certain that they would come

("he knew his Pappenheimers ..."). The centre of the line of battle was held by four mighty tercios; in each of these, musketeers lined the massed ranks of the pikemen, 20 to 30 men, one after another. Tercios of this kind, comprising up to 3,000 men, could offer powerful resistance but were fairly difficult to manoeuvre and vulnerable to artillery fire, presenting an easy target.

The cavalry under Field-Marshal Holck was on the right wing. It was organized in squadrons and regiments which, on the field of battle, were grouped in four powerful formations consisting of lancers, who were still armed knights, cuirassiers who were somewhat more lightly armed and carried swords and pistols or even short carbines, dragoons as mounted musketeers and the troops of Croatian light cavalry. On the left wing, there were two similar lines of cavalry, each consisting of four somewhat weaker formations under General Götz. A trench had been dug in front of the road and this was held by musketeers with seven cannon while the other 14 ordnances were stationed on the right wing at the Mühlenberg.

The King of Sweden was unable to summon in time the mercenaries from Lüneburg and Saxony under Duke George who were still encamped on the other side of the Elbe at Torgau. For the battle, he drew up his 16,000 men in two lines on the south side of the road. Among other things, they differed from the Imperial forces in their social composition: the Swedish soldiers were conscripted free peasants who were subject to strict discipline enforced by severe punishment. Most of them were armed with a musket with an improved matchlock which was easier to use; these had been reduced in weight from seven to five kilograms, enabling the Swedes to dispense with the awkward fork-support. Consequently, only a third of the foot-troops were pikemen while these still accounted for 50 per cent of the Imperial troops. It was only in the following period that matchlock muskets became the standard weapon of European infantry forces. Social structure, high combat morale and more advanced weapons allowed the Swedish forces to use tactics which were superior to the obsolescent Spanish strategy. Gustavus Adolphus consciously based his actions on the precepts of the "school of war" in the bourgeois Netherlands of Maurice of Orange and William Louis of Nassau who had made a systematic study of the Roman military authors and were beginning to practice the "art of war".

The Swedish lines comprised cavalry regiments on the wings and infantry brigades in the centre. Alternate battalions of musketeers and pikemen were deployed within the brigades in such a manner that they provided mutual cover. The infantry also still used the famous "Leather cannon". These guns with light copper barrels and leather reinforcement could accompany the soldiers as they moved forward in battle. They were very manoeuvrable but did not last as long as the heavy cannon. Sixty heavy pieces of artillery were drawn up in front of the army to provide concentrated firepower. The cavalry was deployed in only three

Attack by Swedish cavalry regiments led by King Gustavus Adolphus against the Imperial cuirassiers in the battle of Lützen. Painting by Jan Asselyn (1610–1652). Herzog Anton Ulrich Museum, Brunswick

or four ranks deep so that they could launch a rapid sabre-attack without slowly riding forward and first opening fire with their guns like the Imperial mounted forces. This made better use of the natural manoeuvrability of the cavalry.

When it became clear to Wallenstein, on the evening of the 15th of November, that the enemy was preparing to join battle, he immediately sent a message to Pappenheim:

Hand-drawn battle-sketch by a contemporary
of the deployment of the troops at Lützen.

infantry of Wallenstein's army

cavalry of Wallenstein's army

Swedish-Saxon infantry

Swedish-Saxon cavalry

→ attacks of Wallenstein's army

⇒ Swedish-Saxon attacks

⚌ artillery

✕ death of Gustavus II Adolphus

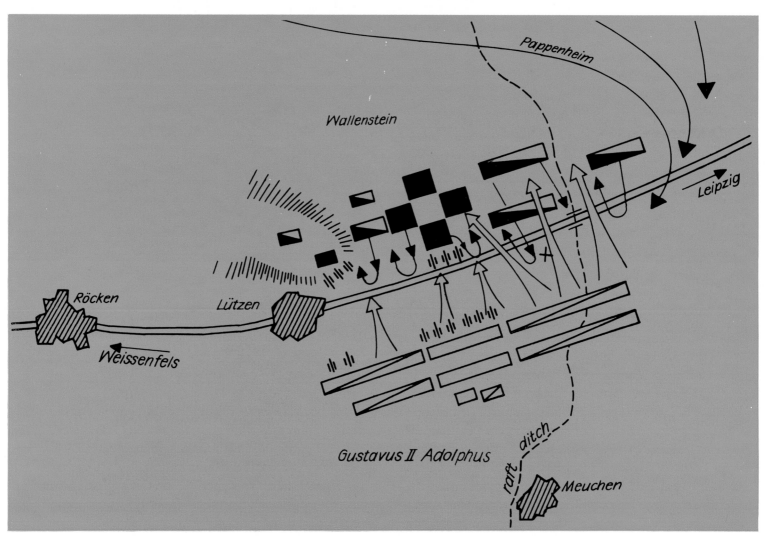

Pappenheim

Wallenstein

Leipzig

Röcken

Lützen

Weissenfels

Gustavus II Adolphus

raft ditch

Meuchen

"Der Herr lasse alles stehen und liegen und incaminire sich darzu, mit allem Volk und Stücken, auf das er morgen früh sich bei uns einfindt." (Leave everything and come with all your men so that you are with us early tomorrow morning.) The general set out that very night.

The morning of the 16th of November 1632—or the 6th according to the Protestant calendar which did not yet take account of Pope Gregory XIII's reform (of 1582)—was overcast and misty. Gustavus Adolphus was obliged to delay the clash until about ten o'clock; a field service was held in the Swedish army and the hymn "A Mighty Fortress is Our God" was sung.

The attack by the Swedish right wing, commanded by the king in person, was successful and the Imperial cavalry was forced back. The centre, under Niclas Brahe, also drove the enemy infantry from the trench, captured the guns and, together with the cavalry, broke up two of the tercios. The left wing, however, where Duke Bernhard of Weimar led five German cavalry regiments, could make no impression on their opponents. Wallenstein, who retained the command over his centre despite an attack of gout, now brought the main forces into the battle, repulsed the Swedes and recaptured his seven cannons.

The Swedish cavalry regiments, reinforced by the second line, made a new charge. Bitter fighting raged between the yielding left wing of the Imperial troops and the right wing of the Swedes and at the trench. The short-sighted king, accompanied by his cousin, the Duke of Lauenburg, his page, Leubelfing, and a few servants, rode somewhat in advance of his men in the turmoil of battle and was hit by a ball in the arm and then by a second one in the back. They were then surprised by Imperial cuirassiers who wounded Leubelfing and, with the duke taking to flight, killed Gustavus Adolphus, who was severely wounded and unknown to them, and his personal servant, Anders Jönsson. It was only when the king's charger, spattered with blood, trotted back to the Swedish cavalry that they learnt of his death.

In the meantime, Pappenheim's eight cavalry regiments arrived on the scene and immediately attacked the Swedish right wing. Once more, the Imperial forces recaptured their artillery in the trench. In the third general attack then launched by the Swedes, in which every man fought with all the strength still remaining, Wallenstein finally lost the tactical initiative, however. Pappenheim was slain, the guns were finally lost after all and the whole of the line of battle began to falter but, despite everything, did not break. When, in the evening, the mist came down again and it became dark, Wallenstein abandoned his baggage train and withdrew to Leipzig. The losses on both sides were very heavy with the Imperial army losing 5,000 dead and wounded and the Swedes 4,000.

The battle, with all its dramatic turns, ended with a tactical victory for the Swedes who held the field and subsequently forced Wallenstein to withdraw his forces from the whole of Saxony. Nevertheless, Lützen did not result in a sensational advantage. It was rather the case that it marked the end of the triumphal progress of the Swedes in a certain sense—and perhaps the end of the dream of a Protestant emperor, too. With the continuation of hostilities, Sweden, with its limited population, began to recruit mercenaries to an increasing extent as well. In 1634, the Swedish army under Bernhard of Weimar, who had taken over command after the death of Gustavus Adolphus, was severely defeated at Nördlingen and it was only in 1648 that the war, which had devastated half of Germany, ended with a victory which admittedly brought the French ally tangible advantages but clearly overtaxed Sweden's more modest resources since it was now obliged to play the role of a great power.

Both the commanders at Lützen have left their mark on the literature of the world, from Schiller to Strindberg. Wallenstein died while seeking a "political solution" to the conflict at the hands of a murderer, the motivation of whom can be traced back to the Hofburg in Vienna. In connection with the death of Gustavus Adolphus, it was rumoured that the second and fatal shot had been fired for personal reasons by Lauenburg or by a servant employed for the purpose by Bernhard. There is no scientific evidence for such legends, which have also been associated with many other fateful battles.

VIENNA-KAHLENBERG /1683

For about 300 years, the Turks were the nightmare of Western Christendom. All the Crusades against them had failed; in 1453, they had captured Constantinople, in 1521 Belgrade and in 1541 Buda. Under Suleiman the Magnificent (1520–1566), their territory stretched from Algiers to Astrakhan and their expeditions and corsairs plundered in the Alps and in Italy. The election of the Austrian Hapsburger Ferdinand I as king of Bohemia and Hungary (1526) was dictated not least by the desire of the estates to establish a united front against their further advance and, in actual fact, after a Turkish defeat in the sea battle of Lepanto in 1571, a precarious state of equilibrium was achieved.

With the halt in their conquests, manifold problems appeared in the despotically ruled multi-national state. While the stream of plunder was drying up and economic life was stagnating as a consequence of the relocation of the world's trade-routes, the high-ranking vassals known as the "spahi" won the right to hold the estates awarded for war services as a hereditary right and consolidated their influence on the provincial administrations. They thus weakened the supervisory function of the sultans who, for a time, became the plaything of rival power-factions and mutinous palace guards. Mehmed IV (1645–1687) endeavoured to find a way out of the crisis by launching vigorous military adventures, despite the increasing number of financial catastrophes. After dearly bought victories against Venice and Poland, he decided to make a major strike against the Imperial city of Vienna. The hope that protection on his flanks would be provided by the French did, in fact, prove vain. It was rather the case that Louis XIV, in his aggressive Rhine policy, allowed himself a breathing space after his occupation of Strasbourg (1681).

The Turkish army led by the Grand Vizier Kara Mustafa set out from the assembly area of Adrianople on 31 March 1683. In Hungary, it was reinforced by Transylvanian, Tartar and other "auxiliary peoples" and, according to contemporary accounts, numbered almost 200,000 men. However, a large number of these were required for the baggage train and included irregular cavalry formations, equipped with long sabres, scimitars, bows and long lances. Accustomed to raids and incursions, they were difficult to use advantageously in a regular battle with rigid discipline and ordered movements. The élite nucleus of the army was made up of the Janizaries, a tactically well-trained professional body of infantry equipped with firearms. Originally a corps recruited from State slaves, they had become a privileged caste—feared even by the sultan on account of their rebellious habits—and were nevertheless always a redoubtable enemy in the field. The cavalry was provided by the spahi who were equipped with lances, scimitars and hand fire-arms and attacked in close order. Finally, there was the famous artillery which was operated by experienced gunners, including specialists from European countries in the service of the sultan. On the way to Vienna, the Turks took about 300 guns of various calibre up the Danube.

The Imperial army of mercenaries was numerically weaker. At the beginning of June it was said to consist of over 21,000 infantry and almost 11,000 cavalry. Another 8,000 troops of both arms were stationed at frontier posts and fortresses in Western Hungary before they withdrew in the face of the Turks. In the course of the summer, troops from the Electorate of Saxony, Bavaria and various South and Southwest German territories arrived so that the strength of the relief army commanded by Duke Charles of Lorraine gradually rose to about 50,000 men. The infantry and cavalry were primarily trained for combat in a definite line of battle. Many had combat experience from the last war against France (1674–1679). The fire from the infantry, deployed in several ranks, and the rapid, closely packed thrust of the cavalry with firearms and edged weapons was the chosen tactic for winning battles.

Poles also took part in the war against the Turks. Under their chivalrous king, Jan III Sobieski, they left their own front in Podolia and hastened to the aid of the hard-pressed —and grateful—city of Vienna. This Polish army consisted largely of the aristocratic cavalry of the Szlachta, who were well acquainted with the Turkish foe. Their arms were similar to those of the mercenary cavalry and they likewise attacked in tight formation. The foot-soldiers were recruited from mercenaries.

Vienna was the centre of the battles. It had already survived a Turkish siege in 1529, yet the defensive fortifications were strengthened only shortly before the new attack. The ring of fortifications comprised a main rampart, twelve metres in height, with twelve bastions, between which strong forward defence positions were located—known as "ravelins". On the bastions there were more than 200 guns. The entire system was enclosed by a trench almost 100 metres in width, in front of which there was also a rampart with built-in positions—"the covered way". It was from here that the infantry and artillery could direct their fire over the flat glacis area which the enemy first had to cross if he wanted to approach the defence line. The siege warfare of that time was waged according to definite rules which specified that the attacker had to destroy the enemy system piece by piece through direct fire and mining, approach the main rampart by crossing the trench and then open up a breach through which the city could be stormed.

By the 16th of July, the Turks had completely encircled Vienna. At this point in time, it had a garrison of about 11,000 men, supplemented by 20 companies of the citizens' militia and three student companies. They were commanded

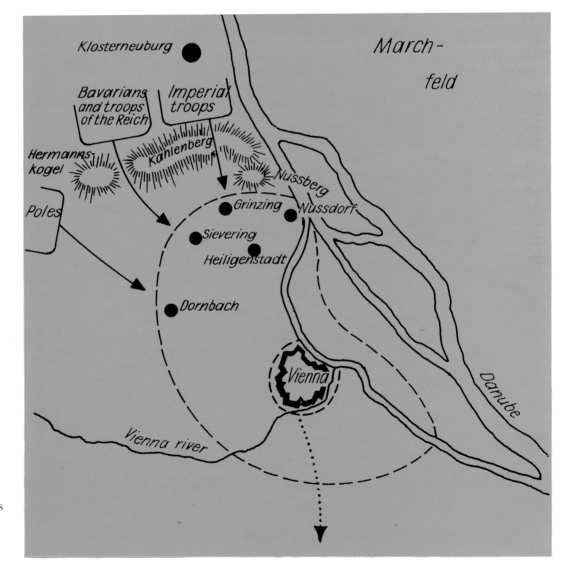

 outer and inner ring of encirclement by the Turks

→ attack of the relief army

⋯▶ escape of the Turks

Attack of the relief army in the battle of Kahlenberg against the Turkish army besieging Vienna. Painting by an unknown artist, *c.* 1683. Heeresgeschichtliches Museum, Vienna

The cavalry attack against the stubbornly defended Turkish camp at Vienna on the 12th of September ended with the defeat of the Turks. Painting by Frans (Francesco) Geffels. Historisches Museum der Stadt Wien

by the Master-General of the Ordnance Ernst Rüdiger, Count Starhemberg. Until he was fatally wounded, the engineering works were directed by the great engineer and military theoretician Georg Rimpler.

The Turks needed almost three weeks to cross the glacis in front of the "covered way". Violent fighting took place around and in the broad trench and around the preliminary defences. Once they had established themselves in the trench and could carry out their excavations from there, the main efforts of the enemy were directed against the bastions known as the Burgbastei and the Löbelbastei in the west part of the defensive ring. The besieged troops made several sallies but, despite local successes, hunger and disease caused a deterioration in their situation in September. The military situation of the Turks also became complicated since they had not succeeded in taking the city within the short time anticipated and could not satisfy the demands for booty of their troops. Disease and a shortage of food due to logistics difficulties undermined discipline. By the middle of September, the Turkish forces had lost about 48,000 men, mainly from the contingents of the "auxiliary forces" who decided to leave.

In the meantime, the relief army of 65,000 men, including the 15,000 Poles, was approaching from the North. On the 11th of September, it occupied the Kahlenberg, an elevation from which it was possible to see Vienna. Battle was joined already on the morning of the 12th. On the left wing, between the Danube and the Kahlenberg, there were 25,000 Imperial and Saxon troops whose attack was given good support by the artillery posted on the mountain. The Bavarian and other German forces in the centre attacked the hilly terrain between the Kahlenberg and the Hermannskogel. On the right flank, they were joined by the Polish cavalry and infantry and by some regiments of the Imperial infantry.

The Turks fought back with their usual stubbornness and made counter-attacks at various points, particularly in the area around the Nussberg. By noon, the relief army had been able to take Nussdorf, Heiligenstadt, Grinzing and Sievering, whereas the right wing had been forced back at Dornbach by superior Turkish forces who had wrongly expected the main attack to come here. Things began to come to a head in the early afternoon. The left wing of the Imperial forces, now advancing rapidly, swung towards the centre and broke the resistance of the enemy who hastily retreated across the Vienna river and abandoned the siege. The Turkish camp, together with the large baggage-train, fell into the hands of the victors. However, it cannot be definitely affirmed that it was then that an enterprising Croatian began the tradition of Viennese coffee-houses with captured coffee beans and "Kipfeln", baked in the shape of the Turkish crescent.

It was only on the other side of the Raab that the Grand Vizier was able to assemble and re-form his remaining forces. After a draconic court-martial, he had eleven commanders executed, who had been too hasty in blowing the retreat and their heads, packed in sacks, sent to the sultan by a courier as a sign of respect. However, this did not help Kara Mustafa to save his own head. Already in December,

he was sent the "silken cord"—the customary demand to accept the blame for the defeat publicly by suicide.

The battle for Vienna demonstrated the increased strength of the defences of a fortified city. The effective support given by the citizens was also a moral factor of some importance in this connection. The besieged inhabitants and troops tied down large Turkish forces and thus facilitated the movements of the relief army. Victory was gained by the skilful co-ordination of the allies. Militarily, it initiated an irreversible turning-point in the armed confrontation between the Ottoman Empire and its European neighbours. Henceforth, it was the Hapsburgs and their allies who took the offensive, forced the Turks to hand back Hungary and, in the course of the 18th century, advanced far into the Balkan Peninsula. It was during these actions that the Austrian "Danube Monarchy" acquired its historical outline.

BLENHEIM - HÖCHSTÄDT / 1704

Absolute monarchy "by the grace of God" achieved its most perfect form in the France of Louis XIV (1643–1715). Louvois, the Minister of War, completed the establishment of a standing army of more than 100,000 men in peacetime which protected the open northeast frontier from behind a triple ring of defences constructed by the engineer Vauban and was based on a outstanding magazin system.

The Peace of the Pyrenees with Spain (1659) had consolidated the political and military hegemony of France in Europe. However, the "Sun King" was not satisfied with the good progress of the mercantile, colonial and fleet policy of Colbert, the General Controller of the Finances and, confident in the superiority of the French military system, did not hesitate to cause one war after another to advance his frontiers or extend his influence, the inevitable result of this being an increase in the number of his enemies. When the Spanish line of the Hapsburgs died out in 1700, he immediately staked the claim of his grandson as their successor and backed this up with military action. England and the Netherlands reacted to this by concluding the "Great Alliance" with the "Emperor and Empire" (Kaiser und Reich), i.e., the Austrian Hapsburgs, as the other potential heir to the Spanish throne. The disputed object was so great that both parties took the then customary strategy of attrition to an extreme, this being a consequence of the manufacturing age. The aim of this was not to decide the matter by a single overwhelming battle but to gradually weaken the adversary by exhausting his resources. However, the courts and their generals were well aware that where interests of such mighty importance were at risk it was also necessary to provoke a battle, even when the heavy losses to be expected were a great risk for the victor as well.

The battle of Blenheim (Blindheim)—known also as the battle of Höchstädt in European literature—was one of the most violent of this war of the Spanish Succession (1701 to 1714). Its fame is due to the two outstanding commanders who were the architects of victory—the Englishman John Churchill, Duke of Marlborough ("Marlborough s'en va't-en guerre ..."), and the Austrian general Prince Eugene of Savoy, the grand-nephew of Cardinal Mazarin and the victor over the Turks at Zenta (1697).

The first signs of an imminent military confrontation began to appear in 1704 in Southern Germany. The Anglo-Dutch forces joined up with the Austrian army to the northeast of Höchstädt in mid-August and took up an almost seven kilometres long defensive position between the Danube at Blindheim and the wooded slopes to the north of the village of Lutzingen. In all, these forces consisted of 66 battalions of infantry, 166 cavalry squadrons and 52 cannon, a total of 52,000 to 53,000 men. Their main strength was on the left wing, commanded by Marlborough.

The Franco-Bavarian troops outnumbered their adversaries and had more artillery but less cavalry. They comprised 81 infantry battalions, 139 squadrons of cavalry and 90 guns and is said to have numbered between 56,000 and 60,000 men, the sources disagreeing as to the exact figure. Its front extended from Blindheim across the village of Oberglauheim to Lutzingen with the brook called the Nebel and its partially marshy terrain between them and the enemy. The Franco-Bavarian forces were divided into two independent formations: one army under Marshal Tallard on the right wing and the more powerful "Armée d'Allemagne" on the left. The latter was under the joint command of the Bavarian Elector Maximilian Emanuel and the newcomer Marshal Marsin, who had replaced the incomparably more capable Villars when the latter fell hopelessly out of favour with the elector. There was no more a supreme command for these two armies than there was with the Austrians and the English but in the latter case the good understanding between the two commanders made up for this shortcoming. On the other hand, the Franco-Bavarian forces largely consisted of long-serving, combat-tested mercenaries whereas the army of the Great Alliance was a motley collection of contingents from standing mercenary armies of widely varying efficiency, training and combat experience. Eugene's army included, among others,

a Prussian infantry corps which had been made available to the emperor by King Frederick I in return for subsidies. It was commanded by the "Old Dessauer"—Prince Leopold of Anhalt-Dessau who had been responsible for introducing the use of the iron ramrod into military service.

A certain risk was involved in attacking the strong Franco-Bavarian defensive positions. Marlborough and Eugene decided to do precisely this, however, although a defeat would have been very damaging for the Coalition, not only militarily but also politically. Both commanders counted on the success of an unexpected first attack with maximum use being made of the superiority of the cavalry. While reconnoitring the enemy positions, they had quickly realized that both Tallard and Marsin and the elector had deployed their armies according to the principle "infantry in the centre, cavalry on the wings" and that accordingly the centre of their line, i. e., the vulnerable "seam" between the two, consisted only of cavalry.

In the early hours of the 13th August, while the morning mist still hung over the terrain, Marlborough's infantry moved forward against the left wing. It was deployed in four lines, the cavalry in two. The French observed the movement and opened up with their artillery. While all this was in progress, Eugene's troops continued to march on the right wing on both sides of the village of Schwennenbach.

Scenes from the battle of Blenheim (Höchstädt): infantry (left) fighting with bayonets and guns, cavalry (centre) attacking the Frenchmen and Prince Eugene (right) ordering his cuirassiers to open the attack. Blenheim Palace, Oxford

He had noted that the enemy front here extended far to the West and likewise moved his infantry and cavalry to the West so as not to be outflanked. His lines were consequently very thin and weaker than those of the enemy.

As soon as they heard that Eugene had engaged the enemy, the English troops under Lord Cutts attacked. Several charges against Blindheim, which was strongly defended, did not achieve any result, it is true, but they did tie down Tallard's forces on his right wing.

In the meantime, the Anglo-Dutch forces under Marlborough crossed the brook under heavy enemy fire and repulsed attacks by the French cavalry. The bloody struggle between Blindheim and Oberglauheim reached its climax. Tallard and Marsin's cavalry launched repeated attacks but the successes they achieved were wiped out again by the fresh troops brought up by Marlborough from the second and third lines.

Eugene had begun his attack in the afternoon but had not been able to gain much ground. The infantry and cavalry of both sides were exhausted and had suffered severe losses. It was now clear that victory would be his who could seize once more the initiative. Without having contacted each other about this, both Marlborough and Eugene simultaneously decided on the attack which won them the day. 109 cavalry squadrons and 19 infantry battalions of Marlborough's army, which were already south of the brook, stormed Tallard's left wing where there were only 44 cavalry squadrons and 9 infantry battalions. Tallard saw what would happen but was powerless to prevent it and his effort to move up reinforcements came too late to prevent the catastrophe. The front was breached and the rest of the cavalry fled to Höchstädt. The marshal was taken prisoner with some of his staff as he attempted to break through to his troops in Blindheim.

While events were taking a decisive and final turn in the centre, Eugene had been unable to achieve a similar

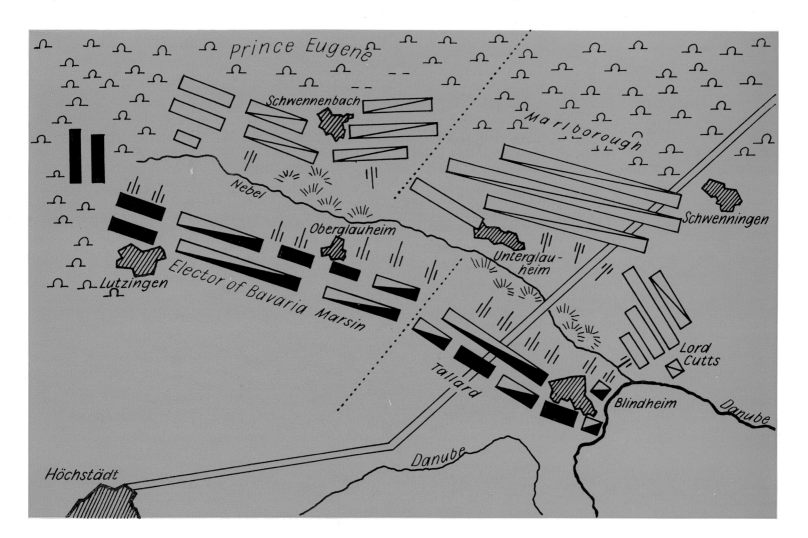

Franco-Bavarian infantry

Franco-Bavarian cavalry

infantry of the "Great Alliance"

cavalry of the "Great Alliance"

artillery

dividing lines between the armies

swamp

forest

result on the right wing. Counter-attacks by the Bavarian cavalry held up his advance and only the Prussian infantry made any progress. It was only when Tallard's defeat was reported that the elector and Marsin decided to retreat. They were pursued by Prince Eugene as soon as he could move up his cavalry but he was not able to seriously hinder the enemy withdrawal. Marlborough was unable to attack from the East since his cavalry was pursuing the enemy in other directions.

Marshal Tallard is brought before the English general Marlborough after being taken prisoner in the battle of Blenheim. At the same time, captured flags, standards and drums are being collected. Blenheim Gobelin. Blenheim Palace, Green Writing Room, Oxford

The mass of Tallard's infantry in Blindheim was lost, however. The Anglo-Dutch troops surrounded the area and shelled it, twenty-seven battalions and twelve squadrons of the French forces surrendering shortly afterwards.

The Franco-Bavarian army suffered a crushing defeat with 12,000 men dead or wounded. Several thousand had deserted, 3,000 of whom are said to have joined the Allies. When the remnants of the army were subsequently collected, they still numbered somewhat more than 20,000 men, i.e., the losses in the course of the battle or during the retreat amounted to almost two-thirds of the original strength. Forty cannon, 3,600 tents and more than 5,400 supply waggons fell into the hands of the victors on the battlefield, to which were subsequently added the 111 heavy guns and two pontoon-bridges of the enemy siege equipment. Marl-

Medal depicting Marlborough in Antique costume, dating from 1703. Heeresgeschichtliches Museum, Vienna

borough's and Eugene's armies also suffered 12,000 casualties in dead and wounded.

The battle was decided by the way in which the two commanders were able to act in unison. Marlborough defeated Tallard because Eugene's troops, numbering only 18,000 men, had tied down half of the enemy forces and stood firm, although outnumbered. Tallard, wrangling with fate, subsequently wrote in his report of the battle that "Two-thirds of the enemy forces were set against our right wing where there was less than a third of our forces." Whereas the Allies already gained an advantage from the well-considered manner in which they opened the battle and co-ordinated their infantry and cavalry units, the advantage of the "stronger battalions" was wasted on the Franco-Bavarian side as a result of the unco-ordinated handling of the various units.

The strategic consequences of the battle were considerable. Bavaria was no longer in the running, which meant that Louis XIV lost his military and political basis in Germany and that the war moved closer and closer to the frontiers of France. The end came only ten years later, after fur-

ther battles of which Malplaquet (1709) was considered to be the greatest of the century, with the division of the Spanish inheritance. Nevertheless, this was no mean testimony to the military performance of the absolute monarchy of France and, although the most powerful of all alliances had put it in its place, it had not been able to break the hegemony of France on the Continent. This was why the 18th century was to remain a "French" one. However, England, as a naval power, saw that its efforts to achieve a "balance of power" in Europe had brought it so many advantages that this policy formed the basis of its foreign policy for another two hundred years.

POLTAVA /1709

France, as the real innovator and protagonist of the modern professional army of modern times, suffered its first defeat in a great land battle at Blenheim in 1704 and it was five years later, at Poltava, that the nimbus of Swedish "invincibility" disappeared in a far more painful manner.

Admittedly, the Swedes had already lost this or that battle—and one recalls Kleist's *Prince of Homburg* at Fehrbellin? in 1675—but they had not lost any of their wars of the 17th century. King Charles XII was therefore not unduly worried when a Russian-Polish-Danish coalition began to question Swedish supremacy in the Baltic in 1700 and—at the same time as the War of the Spanish Succession—started the even more protracted "Nordic War" (1700 to 1721). An unexpected landing on the island of Zealand immediately forced Denmark to back out of the alliance again and a subsequent surprise attack against Czar Peter I (1689–1725) with the victory in a snowstorm at Narva on 30 November 1700 temporarily eliminated the most powerful of the enemy forces.

Not appreciating the Russian potential, which had quietly but steadily increased in the course of the 16th and 17th centuries, and the energetic efforts of the "czar of reform" to modernize his empire which now stretched to the Pacific Ocean, Charles XII devoted the whole of his attention to Poland which had recently become linked with the Electorate of Saxony in a personal union. With the stubbornness which was worthy of a better cause, he pursued Augustus "the Strong" as far as Leipzig and in 1706 forced him to accept the peace of Altranstädt and relinquish his claim to the Polish crown.

> "Polen ist weg, Sachsen ist weg,
> August, der liegt im Dreck.
> O du lieber Augustin,
> alles ist hin . . ."

(Poland is gone, Saxony is gone, Augustus lies in the mire, Oh you dear Augustine, everythin's gone) was the taunt of the ballad-singers.

Peter the Great with depiction of a battle in the background. 18th-century copperplate engraving.

PETRUS ALEXEOWITZ,
Ruſſorum Magnus Cæſar.

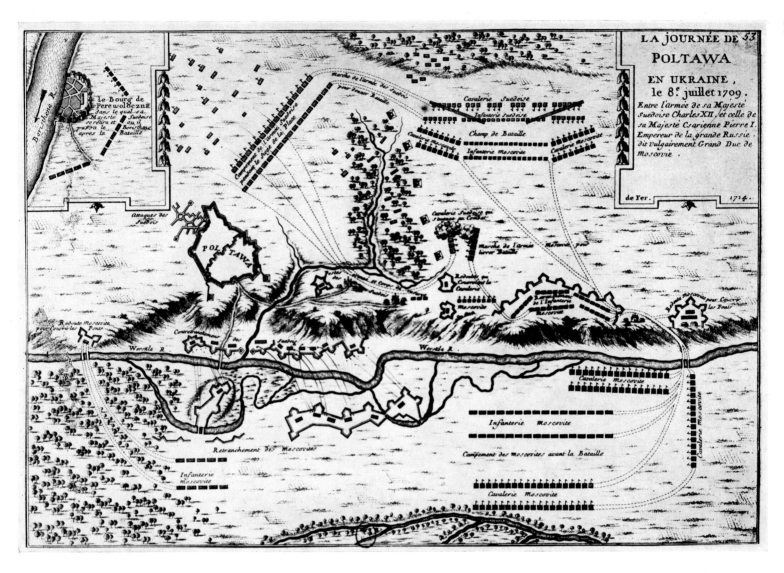

Labels within the map:

La Journée de
POLTAWA
EN UKRAINE,
le 8.ᵉ juillet 1709.
Entre l'armée de sa Majesté
Suedoise Charles XII, et celle de
sa Majesté Czarienne Pierre I.
Empereur de la grande Russie
dit vulgairement Grand Duc de
Moscovie.

de Fer.   1714.

Le Bourg de
Pere wolóczni
dans le quel s a
Majeste Suedoise
se retira et ou il
se Borneme
apres la Bataille

Attaques des
Suedois

POLTAWA

Marche de l'armée des Suedois
pour donner Bataille

Cavalerie Suedoise
Infanterie Suedoise
Champ de Bataille
Cavalerie Moscovite
Infanterie Moscovite
Cavalerie Moscovite

Marche de l'armée Moscovite
pour donner Bataille

Cavalerie Suedoise qui
s'engage au Combat

Redoutes ou Coureront la
Cavallerie

Retrenchemens
de l'Infanterie
Moscovite

Redoute Moscovite
pour Couvrir les Ponts

Borichene R.

Werskla R.   *Werskla R.*

Redoute Moscovite pour Couvrir
les Ponts

Retranchement des Moscovites

Infanterie
moscovite

Cavalerie Moscovite

Infanterie Moscovite

Campement des moscovites avant la Bataille

Cavalerie Moscovite

Cavalerie Moscovite

Efforts by France and England to win over Charles, the will o' the wisp warrior, to their side met with no success. In 1707, he retraced his footsteps and forced back the Russians who, in the meantime, had advanced as far as Courland. Mindful of the unsatisfying outcome of Swedish interference in the problems of the succession on the throne at Moscow at the beginning of the 17th century, he displayed a certain abhorrence for the vastnesses of Russia. At Smolensk, in 1708, he made a sharp turn to the South and it is probable that he had several reasons for this. For one thing, the road to Moscow was blocked by the enemy at several points, the surmounting of which would appreciably delay the march. It was also easier for the troops to live off the country in the fertile Ukraine. On the other hand, Charles

Contemporary plan of the battle of Poltava. Copperplate engraving of 1714 by N. de Fer. Bibliothèque Nationale, Paris

also hoped that his encouraging appearance in the neighbouring steppes would persuade an undecided Turkey to declare war on Russia. Finally, he preferred to attack the enemy capital from the southwest since he reckoned on the support of the Ataman Mazepa who had volunteered to lead the restless frontier people of the Ukrainian Cossacks in an uprising against Peter who only just finished dealing with a revolt of the Don Cossacks under Kondrati Bulavin.

Despite their rapid advance or, more accurately, precisely because of it, the main Swedish army soon found itself in a precarious position. On 27 September 1708, a force

of 16,000 men under General Adam Lewenhaupt, who were bringing reinforcements and supplies from Livonia, were routed at Lesnaya on the River Sosh. At the same time peasant resistance to the invaders flared up in the White Russian forests and King Stanislaw Leszczyński, who had ascended the Polish throne by courtesy of the Swedes, could not persuade "his" nobles to express their gratitude by sending reinforcements. Finally, Ivan Mazepa failed to rouse the mass of the Cossacks and, as a fugitive, arrived in the Swedish camp with 2,000 men. Thus it was that the Swedish army under Charles XII, which had wintered under tolerable conditions in the Northern Ukraine and had been besieging the small fortified city of Poltava since April 1709, was obliged to operate without any lines of communications to its hinterland. On account of disease and the shortage of ammunition, only about two-thirds of his 30,000 men were fully operational. Despite this, the officers and men and, above all, the king himself had the confidence which came from nine years of successive victories without defeat. Of Charles, it was later said by Marlborough, who had met him in 1706, that his ruin was caused by constant success and underestimation of the enemy.

Peter I assembled the Russian army on the east bank of the Vorskla not far from Poltava in June 1709. It differed greatly from the tactically unsure force which had been unable to resist a numerically far inferior enemy at Narva.

Between 1701 and 1709, fundamental changes in the military system had been carried out as a result of Peter's comprehensive state reforms. The place of the aristocratic cavalry and the often unruly foot-soldiers—the privileged "Strelitzi"—had been taken by efficiently organized regiments of dragoons and infantry who had been trained according to strict regulations. Recruits had been drawn from the serfs throughout the country on the basis of three to five per thousand inhabitants who were obliged to spend their whole life in military service. Peter devoted special attention not only to his naval forces but also to the artillery. Monasteries and churches had to contribute their bells from which newly established manufactories in Tula and in the Urals cast cannon, howitzers and mortars. The artillery was reinforced to such an extent that the number of guns at its disposal even surpassed those of the Swedes. By 1706, the number of handguns produced had also risen to 15,000 annually, a figure which was to reach even 40,000 by 1711. By 1709, the re-equipped and re-organized field army included 42 infantry and 31 dragoon regiments, totalling 75,000 to 77,000 men. Another 25,000 were stationed in fortresses and garrisons, especially in the reconquered or newly occupied Baltic areas where the city of St. Petersburg was established at the mouth of the Neva in 1703.

The czar assembled 42,000 men and 72 cannons to oppose the Swedish army in the Ukraine and loyal Cossack

Commemorative medal of the battle of Poltava bearing a stylized picture of the event. 18th century. Bibliothèque Nationale, Paris

Russian infantry and cavalry attacking in the battle of Poltava. Drawing from a mosaic (detail) by L. Lomonossov, 18th century. Academy of Sciences, Leningrad

formations under Ataman Skoropadski covered his flanks on the march. On the 20th of June, the main forces crossed the Vorskla to the north of Poltava, which was defended by 4,200 men and a town militia, and established a fortified camp between the villages of Petrovsk and Semenovsk. A total of ten field-works or redouts, some of which were only provisionally completed to begin with, provided useful support. For the battle, the Russian army was deployed in two lines. The infantry regiments occupied the centre with the cavalry on the wings and the mounted Cossack formations protecting the flanks. A few battalions remained in the camp as a reserve.

The Swedes, who were obliged to force a quick decision on account of their precarious position, moved forward in the early hours of the 27th of June with four infantry columns in the first line and six cavalry columns in the second. Charles XII was only nominally in command. Since he had been wounded in the leg by a Cossack bullet and had to be carried, the operation was handled by General Rehnskjöld in his place.

The right Swedish wing, commanded by Lewenhaupt, captured two of the provisional redouts, penetrated the left wing of the Russians and advanced to the vicinity of their camp. Here, however, it met with heavy artillery and small-arms fire and suffered serious losses. When the Russian cavalry under Peter Menshikov also appeared on the scene, Lewenhaupt withdrew his troops as far as he could, was forced back against the extreme edge of the battle-field and, in this manner, was eliminated before the last phase of the battle began.

In the meantime, the main forces of the two armies had clashed to the west of the Russian camp. Whereas the Swedish infantry and cavalry were still deployed in only one line, Peter kept a battle-order of two lines. As a result, he was able to bring up reinforcements when the Swedes broke through his first line at several points and was able to close the gaps. A merciless bayonet action developed with man against man—the first of such intensity in military history—and the Russians gained the upper hand. The Swedish troops again suffered heavy losses from artillery fire which they were unable to return since, of their 32 cannon, only four light battalion-guns still had powder and ammunition.

Towards noon, it was apparent that the battle had been decided by the Russians, although the Swedes were still resisting in some places and even launching relief attacks but other units had already surrendered. However, during the retreat to the Dnepr to which the king had consented in the evening, the remnants of the exhausted army were at a moral ebb. After Peter had destroyed the river fleet of the Cossacks allied with Mazepa "on the other side of the rapids", the Zaporozhye, which could have represented a last possibility of escape, 15,000 men surrendered on the 28th of June without offering resistance. In all, the Swedes lost more than 9,000 men in dead and wounded and 19,000 were taken prisoner. Only about 1,000 horsemen succeeded in escaping with Charles XII across the Dnepr and reaching Turkish territory. The Russian casualties of 4,600 dead and wounded were far less than those of their enemy. "Phaeton fell from Heaven and the last stone for the founding of St. Petersburg has now been laid with God's help." This was the jubilant reaction of the czar when the full extent of the victory became apparent.

The confused command situation on the Swedish side was due to the highhanded king losing control of the battle from his stretcher and to the inability of his generals to improvise, unaccustomed as they were to taking independent decisions. On the other hand, Poltava provided irrefutable evidence of the combat efficiency of the re-organized Russian army: a new Great Power had presented its visiting card here.

The legendary obstinacy of Charles XII was to prolong the war by many years, even though it had already been lost. After truly astonishing adventures in Turkey, the Swedish king was killed in somewhat mysterious circumstances at the siege of the small Norwegian fortress of Frederikshall. The Peace of Nystad was finally concluded in 1721, marking the end of Swedish supremacy in the Baltic and prompting Peter I to assume the title of emperor as a sign of the change in Russia's status in the world.

LEUTHEN / 1757

Following the end of the male line of the Hapsburgs in 1740, the election of the German emperor again became a matter of dispute—for the first time since 1439. Unchallenged in her domination of the Alpine countries, Bohemia and Hungary, Maria Theresa was able, in the War of the Austrian Succession (1740–1748) and after a Bavarian interlude, to procure the Imperial crown for her husband, Francis Duke of Lorraine and, after 1737 Grand Duke of Tuscany. Frederick II of Prussia (1740–1786) made the most of the opportunity, however, and in two campaigns in 1740–1742 and 1744/45 seized the manufacturing areas of Silesia.

Understandably enough, relations between Potsdam and Schönbrunn remained cool and, when a colonial war broke out between England and France, the king and the empress contributed their own private German quarrel to the world-wide confrontation: Prussia as an ally of England, Austria on the side of France and Russia. As a consequence, in 1756 they found themselves in the Seven Years' War.

Sadder but wiser from the unexpected defeats in the war against the Turks from 1737–1739, Austria began to free itself from the already partially obsolete military principles of Prince Eugene, especially as a serious deterioration in the discipline of the army became apparent after his death (1736). It proved possible to achieve a significant improvement in military organization and an increase in combat efficiency. Its light cavalry—although this was admittedly not an arm of first importance—was even considered to be exemplary in Europe.

On the other hand, Prussia and its junkers had an army which was of an unusual composition. One-third to one-half of its soldiers were conscripted from the country areas and were known as cantonists. From the 1730's, each regiment had its own recruitment area, the canton, and it was here that it enlisted and conscripted its soldiers. They spent the whole of their life in military service but, after basic training, were allowed home-leave for several months every year. It was only during the period of manoeuvres between April and June that the companies were at full strength.

The canton system did not mean that military service was obligatory for everybody since many were exempted from it. But it did offer the Prussian army a series of advantages. To begin with, in the event of war, it could be rapidly increased to nearly 200,000 men. Then there was the saving in pay which would otherwise have been necessary for mercenaries. It was also possible to obtain rapid replacements for losses and desertions and, finally, the cantonist (who was no longer so unreliable) was less inclined to desert than the recruits obtained in other countries by tricks and deception since he had responsibilities and was the family breadwinner.

This canton service was considered an oppressive burden by the peasant and poorer urban strata who were most affected by it and indeed, military service in general was regarded as a punishment and a social disgrace. Thus the Prussian army was also afflicted by the scourge of all mercenary armies: "absence without leave". This was often responsible for more gaps in the ranks than enemy fire, especially during battle and withdrawals when discipline tended to become slacker under the force of the circumstances. For this reason, too, a battle was generally avoided for as long as possible so as to drive the adversary from his position by the art of manoeuvre.

As regards organization, training, leadership and weapons, the Prussian army under Frederick II was one of the most powerful of Europe. It was organized in regiments of ten companies each which were drilled intensively by the company commander and his officers. On the battlefield, the tactical formation was the battalion, which was deployed in three ranks, fire being opened by the platoons with their flintlock rifles. Deployment in long, thin lines and shooting by platoons was practised time and again on drill-squares or at great parades and the army had achieved a high standard of precision in marching exercises which were not easy to carry out. While the infantry fired their volleys, the cavalry attacked their enemy counterparts with cold steel. The artillery was generally used as a "large battery".

Contemporary plan of the battle of Leuthen, clearly showing the approach of the Prussians and the forming of their oblique battle-order.

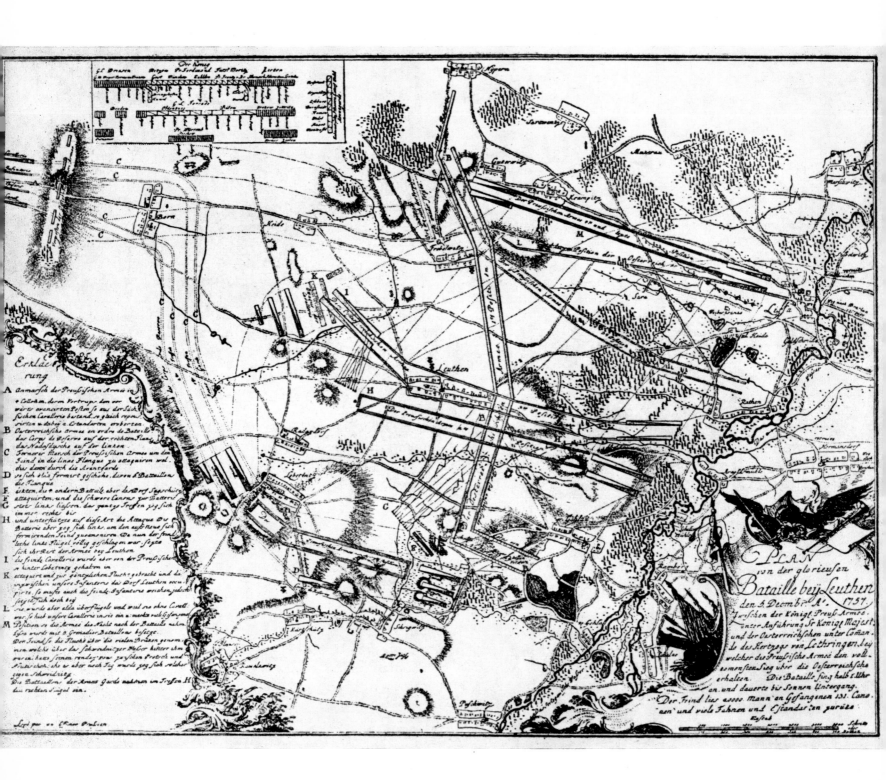

The battle of Leuthen with a cavalry action in the foreground. The artillery duel can also be seen, the infantry being the first to open fire. Painting by an unknown contemporary artist. Former Castle Museum Breslau

It took up its position before the battle since the guns were difficult to handle and, as a rule, were not moved to any other point afterwards. A distinction was drawn between the siege guns and the somewhat lighter field artillery. It was only in the course of the Seven Years' War that a more mobile mounted artillery was developed as well, this being inspired by the Russian model.

Frederick II started the war in 1756 by invading the Electorate of Saxony and advanced as far as Prague. However, after a hard-fought victory before the gates of that city, he lost the battle at Kolin on 18 June 1757 against Field-Marshal von Daun, a cautious tactician, and a Russian army occupied East Prussia, the nobility there hurriedly acknowledging their allegiance to Czarina Elizabeth. The king was forced to evacuate Bohemia but halted the advance of the French troops and an "Imperial army" by an outstanding victory at Rossbach on the 5th of November. However, the mighty fortress of Schweidnitz surrendered on the 12th while on the 22nd of November the Prussians were beaten at Breslau. In view of this situation, Frederick was forced to resort to the "strong medicine" of a fourth great battle in this year for the possession of Silesia

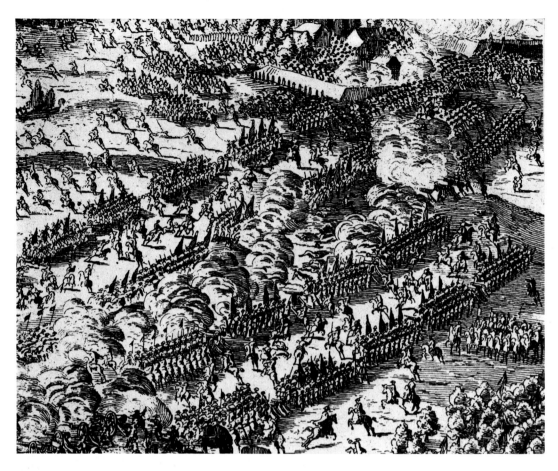

Prussian infantry attacking in the battle of Leuthen. Copperplate engraving (section) by Johann Daniel von Schleuen, 2nd half of 18th century.

Soldiers of the Prussian Infantry Guards of 1786. Coloured lithograph by an unknown artist, c. 1840. Armeemuseum der DDR, Dresden

whose economic and financial resources were of great importance for the continuation of the war. The main Prussian army consequently made a forced march from Thuringia and joined up with the remnants of the units, commanded by the Duke of Bevern, which had retreated at Breslau.

Von Daun, who had been given the "eternal loser", Prince Charles of Lorraine, to assist him in the overall command, was informed of the arrival of Frederick and decided to await his attack in a defensive position nine kilometres long between Leuthen and Nippern. The Austrian army was deployed in the usual manner: 84 infantry battalions in the centre with 144 cavalry squadrons on the wings, a two-line order of battle being employed. In all, there were 66,000 troops and 210 cannon.

On the 5th of December 1757, the day of the battle, the Prussian army numbered 48 infantry battalions and 128 cavalry squadrons with almost 39,000 men. With its 167 guns, the artillery was also numerically inferior to that of the enemy. To begin with, the four columns of

Prussian troops marched head-on against the Austrians. Von Daun had the impression that Frederick was intending to attack at Nippern the powerful right wing and, indeed, the first clashes occurred at the village of Borne. Then, however, the Prussians swung to the South in the cover of several hilly ridges and now also took up the battle-order usual at that time with the cavalry on the wings and the infantry in the centre. Before this new deployment had become apparent to the Austrian commanders, the Prussians attacked the left wing of the Austrians commanded by Franz Leopold von Nadasdy. They gained the upper hand here and were able to drive through the Württemberg regiments. Prince Charles and von Daun were not able to bring up reinforcements in time to strengthen the weakened left wing of their army. It was only on the other side of Leuthen that they were able to form a front facing southwards. However, their new deployment here was up to 100 ranks deep so that the great crowd of soldiers was of no advantage at all since the battle-order was then too

3.tes Bataillon Garde und Flügel-Grenadiere des 1.ten Bataillons
Leib-Garde und des Regiments Garde N.º 15.
1786.

cumbersome. The tightly packed masses were an easy target for the Prussian artillery and the cannonade that followed completed the confusion. The Austrian cavalry on the right wing attempted to relieve the infantry by attacking the Prussian left wing which was apparently exposed. However, their flank was attacked by the Prussian cavalry in turn and they were thrown back. In the course of this they rode through the crowded masses of their own infantry and thus put the final seal on the defeat.

Both sides reported heavy losses. The Austrian army lost 3,000 dead, 6,000 to 7,000 wounded and more than 12,000 prisoners. The enemy captured 131 cannon, nine standards and 46 colours. The Prussian casualties amounted to 6,400 dead and wounded. Von Daun's army hastily withdrew to its winter quarters in Bohemia while the Prussians occupied almost the whole of Silesia again.

The battle of Leuthen marked a high-point in the development of the linear tactics which attained their most sophisticated form under Frederick II within the limits of the feudal-absolutist political order and the military technology of the time. The Prussian king—but this was the only occasion even for him—managed to implement the "oblique battle-order" advocated since the time of Epaminondas. With a reinforced formation of the army in staggered order, he attacked an enemy wing and broke through his opponent's battle-order. The idea of a weaker army defeating a stronger one in this manner was well known to both the generals and the military authors of the 17th and 18th centuries. Its practical implementation presupposed, however, an exceptional degree of manoeuvrability and speed. If the enemy perceived this intention and then modified his own deployment in good time, the attack against the flank again became a frontal battle. Under these conditions, it was only an exceptionally well-drilled army such as the Prussian one against an ineffective enemy which could really exploit the advantage of the oblique battle-order. Then there was the fact that Frederick II as a *roi-connétable* (i. e., his own general) was not obliged to justify his actions to anyone and could take any risk whenever a chance to gain an advantage appeared. In contrast to this, the Austrian generals were bound by the military instructions from the old fogies in the War Council at the Court in Vienna and from Maria Theresa who was strong-willed but far away from where the action was taking place.

For the victor, Leuthen was only a political breathing space which allowed him to continue. In 1759, Frederick II suffered a crushing defeat at the hands of an Austro-Russian army at Kunersdorf and, in 1761, found himself, although a master of the strategy of attrition, on the brink of disaster. However, since Russia under its new ruler withdrew from the Coalition and England proved stronger than France, Prussia was able to end the bloody struggle with a "stalemate", as reflected in the status quo of the Peace of Hubertusburg of 1763. The fact that Prussian militarism managed to survive, despite the manifest disproportion of the forces opposing it, ensured that it henceforth enjoyed the uncontested rank of a European Great Power and, in the Holy Roman Empire, raised the insoluble problem of Austro-Prussian dualism.

SARATOGA/1777

The settlers in the English "Thirteen Colonies" founded between 1607 and 1733 along the Atlantic coast of North America needed military support as long as they were hindered by France as a competing Great Power in their acquisition by force of Indian land. However, when the French lost the whole of their possessions on the mainland from Canada to the mouth of the Mississippi in the Seven Years' War, a complete change took place in this state of affairs. The legislation of the British Crown which did not take account of the new situation and continued to protect the interests of the "mother-country" in a unilateral manner not only stiffened the resistance of the citizens and farmers to colonial rule but even aroused the opposition of some of the powerful planters of Virginia and Carolina who largely owed their prosperity to the forced labour of African slaves. Following the Boston Tea Party of 1773, the first act of open revolt, the conflict rapidly assumed a revolutionary form and emerged as the War of Independence after the initial skirmishes at Lexington and Concord in 1775. On 4 July 1776, the "United States of America" was proclaimed by a congress at Philadelphia. Thereupon, great efforts were made by the colonial power to crush the insurgents who, for their part, were joined by volunteers from Europe such as the Frenchmen Lafayette and Saint-Simon or the Pole Tadeusz Kościuszko, who became George Washington's adjutant, while the Prussian officer von Steuben acted as an instructor to the American army.

The British Crown, which also made use of "subsidiary" troops from German territories, did not succeed in inflicting a decisive defeat on the young republic in 1776. Admittedly, the latter's "campaign of liberation" in the direction of Canada did not come to anything either and English advances led to gains in territory and the capture of New York but a surprise victory by the Americans on the 25th/26th of December against a Hessian corps at Trenton revealed their fighting quality and also their tactical ability. For 1777, the English supreme command planned a major offensive with the objective of cutting off the New England

states in the Northeast from the southern areas and thus decisively weakening the military and political strength of the independence movement. It was planned that the campaign should be launched from three points. An army of about 8,000 under General John Burgoyne was to march to Albany and join up there with the main army under Lord William Howe approaching from New York and a force under Colonel Barry Saint-Leger which was to come from Fort Oswego on Lake Ontario through the Mohawk Valley.

The English troops consisted of 3,000 mercenaries sold by German princes to the British Crown and seven regiments of British "regulars". They had had years of training, were well-equipped and possessed combat experience. On the other hand, by reason of their social structure and their proneness to desert at the drop of a hat, they could only be used in closed formations under the strict command of their officers. They sought to obtain victory by firing diciplined salvoes at the enemy. With the exception of weak Canadian contingents, the British colonial army did not have any lightly armed troops who could fight in scattered order in wooded and impenetrable terrain. This shortcoming had already become apparent in 1775/76 and the military consequences of this became increasingly more serious the longer the war continued.

The American "Continental Army" under George Washington, who had achieved the rank of brigadier general during the Seven Years' War, was recruited from volunteers but these usually only served for a few months at a time. It was intended as the main military force for opposing the British in a pitched battle in the field and was consequently also given tactical training. A role of no small importance in this was played by the militia of the individual states, towns and settlements who had to report when an alarm signal was given—hence their name of "minutemen"—and were immediately available for local operations. Their standards of training, equipment and organization did not allow them to take part in a pitched battle

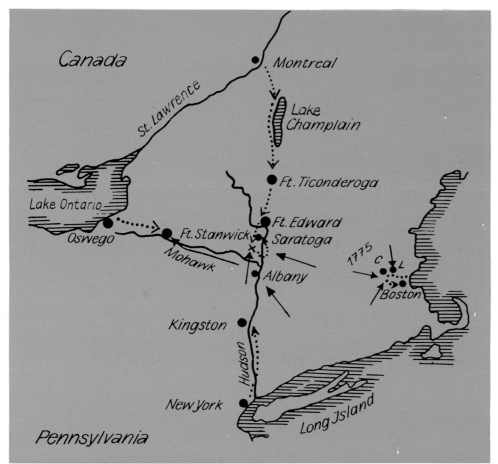

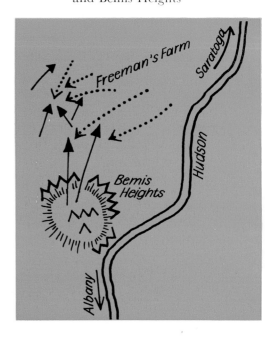

→ manoeuvres and attacks of the Americans

┅┅► British thrusts

position of the Americans
C Concord
L Lexington

× area of Freeman's Farm and Bemis Heights

against a line of mercenaries; they were most effective in skirmishes. Experienced in the use of guns and familiar with the terrain, they made skilled use of the cover available in defence and attack to inflict losses on their more vulnerable opponents by accurate sniping. These advantages were allied with the political and moral awareness that they were fighting for human rights—proclaimed for the first time in 1776. They received considerable support from the general population and had no difficulty in finding new recruits. On the other hand, influential circles of the merchant bourgeoisie and the "plantation barons", the Loyalists as they were known, feared that the "rebellion" would lead to an increase in democracy and, in their own interests, wanted to maintain their profitable links with England, only in a somewhat modified form. To some extent, they even supported the policy of the Crown by raising military units.

In the summer of 1777, Burgoyne's army advanced to Lake Champlain and on the 6th of July occupied Fort Ticonderoga which had been evacuated by the Americans. However, further progress through the wooded areas to the Hudson was accomplished only very slowly and the river at Fort Edward was not reached before the end of the month. It was here that the commander learned that the army stationed in New York had not marched northwards but to the West, to Philadelphia. Consequently, the operational objective was almost certainly doomed to failure even at this stage. The 1,800 men under Saint-Leger had to break off the siege of Fort Stanwick on the 22nd of August and withdraw. At the same time, Burgoyne's army had to surmount increasing difficulties and there was a shortage of food, fodder and horses. A German detachment of 650 men sent out to make requisitions was eliminated by American irregulars. The 4,000 men under General Henry Clinton

General Burgoyne surrendering to the North American general Horatio Gates at Saratoga. Engraving by J. F. Godefroy from a painting by L. F. Fauvel.

who had set out from New York only in September got no further than Kingston and were no longer of any importance for a confrontation further to the north. Despite this, Burgoyne did not consider the possibility of a withdrawal but, after leaving behind a garrison of 1,000 men, crossed the Hudson on the 13th of September to exert "pressure on Albany"—exactly why is not at all clear—and established a camp about 50 kilometres away in the vicinity of Saratoga.

In the meantime, the Americans reinforced their forces unceasingly. Increasing numbers of militiamen flocked to the Albany-Saratoga area and General Horatio Gates took up a position on Bemis Heights seven kilometres away from Burgoyne. Although at a disadvantage numerically, Burgoyne attacked on the 19th September and gained some ground against the militia forces. He dominated the battlefield at Freeman's Farm but was unable to break through the enemy ranks or surround them. Since a large number of his officers were hit by sharpshooters as well, no advantage was derived from this by the English forces.

At the end of September, Burgoyne's already shaky communications with Clinton were cut off completely. Uncertain whether relief forces were to be expected from the South or not, Burgoyne launched a reconnaissance action against the fortified position of Bemis Heights, although it was now a question of 5,000 English soldiers against 11,000 Americans. The latter replied with a counter-attack and defeated the exhausted enemy. It was only now that Burgoyne decided to fall back to Saratoga. This decision came far too late and, after being encircled by almost 20,000 Americans, he was compelled to surrender on 17 October 1777.

Terms of surrender were initially not harsh: the army was to embark in Boston for England on condition that the promise was given not to take any further part in the war. But this pledge existed only on paper. However, the success of the Republican militia forces against the mercenary troops of the British Crown had far-reaching consequences. It placed a major restriction on the operational basis of the English army and, at the same time, was a severe setback for the Loyalists. It attracted the attention of progressive people in many other countries and encouraged them in their struggle against their own despots. On the other hand, it demonstrated that the rebels were worthy allies and in-duced the Bourbons of France and Spain to enter the war on the American side. After a further defeat at Yorktown in 1781, Great Britain had to acknowledge in 1783 that this was the only war that it had lost in modern times.

Militarily, the lamentable outcome of the Saratoga campaign showed that mercenary troops fighting in a rigid line of battle without the protection of light infantry or rifle units on the flanks were defenceless against the fire of sharpshooters and that intolerably heavy losses were inevitable. The experience of the American irregulars thus exercised great influence on subsequent military thinking in Europe. To be sure, most military theorists and officers were initially inclined to regard the new method of warfare as specifically American and to restrict its application to the North American theatre of war. The French Revolutionary Wars were soon to confirm on a more comprehensive scale, however, the significance of this type of warfare which had first appeared for a brief moment on the other side of the Atlantic and which heralded the age of popular armies.

FROM
VALMY

TO
KARLS/
HORST

HE storming of the Bastille on 14 July 1789 by the people of Paris was more than the destruction of a symbol of royal despotism. At the same time, they buried aristocratic rule and monarchy by divine right under the ruins of this mediaeval fortress.

The princes of Europe had no illusions about the explosive nature of the French Revolution and its principles of liberty and equality made thrones, altars and castles tremble. The Hapsburgs and the Hohenzollerns made preparations to hasten to the aid of their Bourbon cousin in the Tuileries at Paris to restore the *ancien régime* before their own realms became infected. The French nation did not fear this challenge and took to arms to defend their revolutionary achievements on 20 April 1792. Nobody suspected at the time that the war—apart from a short interruption in 1802/3—would last for more than twenty years. It was rather the case that the invaders believed, in view of the disintegration of "state authority" in France, that it would be a simple matter to deal with a handful of ill-reputed lawyers and agitators.

However, the experience of the American War of Independence—and on this occasion with truly worldwide consequences—was confirmed that a great people, when fighting with full awareness for a just cause of its own, cannot be subjugated by the mercenaries of a counter-revolutionary royal conspiracy on any terrain at all. What the volunteer battalions lacked in parade skills and manoeuvre practice at the beginning of the campaign was compensated in the long run by their patriotic fighting spirit. Goethe, who was certainly no friend of violent transformations, nevertheless recognized the approach of a totally different period during the campaign in France. At *Valmy*, on 20 September 1792, the "Republican opinion" had stood firm against the Prussian cannonade and had compelled the Duke of Brunswick, whose pompous *Manifesto* had threatened to remove Paris from the face of the Earth, to make a wretched retreat.

As a result of the constraints of the situation, the army at Valmy was still an improvised force of regular troops of the line and volunteers of the newly founded bourgeois National Guard under long-serving generals who were not always above suspicion. In 1793, with the *levée en masse*, introducing general conscription, the Welfare Committee of the Convention established an integrated popular army which proved not only equal but even superior to the military power of the hostile coalition which had been joined by England, the Netherlands and Spain as well. This was due not only to the organizational work, which was the merit of Lazare Carnot, the celebrated "Father of Victory", and his staff but also to the uncompromising political leadership of the Jacobins and especially to the many peasants and artisans who accepted hardship in the hinterland and at the front, who forged the weapons of the Republic which they themselves used. Even in 1793, they crushed a civil war fanned by the counter-revolution. In the decisive battle of Fleurus against the Austrians on 26 June 1794, they reaped the fruits of their common efforts and finally broke the iron ring around the "besieged fortress of France".

Protected frontiers allowed the upper middle-class, with the aid of the guillotine, to free itself from the harsh tutelage of Jacobin dictatorship with the overthrow of Robespierre on the 9th of Thermidor. However, after "the pathos of the Revolution had evaporated" and "its enthusiastic flowers had wilted", the five-man Directoire of the Republic did not succeed in shielding the class-rule of a small leadership of bourgeois notables from the attacks of restoration forces on the one hand and radical democrats on the other. Its efforts to capitalize on the military successes won by the armies of "sansculottes" in the shape of territorial conquests brought the military leadership as well to a point of deadlock in 1796.

It was freed from both these problems—in his own manner—by a military man: Napoleon Bonaparte. The leadership of the twenty-seven-years old artillery officer proved capable, even from the secondary theatre of war in Italy, of breaking up the First Coalition against France in 1797. Bonaparte knew how to exploit the advantages of the popular army which had emerged from the Revolution in the struggle against the miserable hirelings of the courts and led his troops in their campaigns and on the battlefield with a very high degree of consistency and operational clarity. He encouraged the new feeling of responsibility and the creative participation of the non-commissioned officers and other ranks—Republicans in uniform who had to fear the loss of their newly won plots of land if the noble landowners were to return. He used the surprising mobility of reliable lines of riflemen and small columns made possible by this in battle and in bold outflanking manoeuvres. The numbers of deserters and marauders fell to a minimum despite the fact that the rigid depot system had been largely abandoned. Finally, there was the encouragement of efficiency by the prospect of promotion in an army uncomplicated by the restraint of pedantic traditions although it was not at all the case that every soldier carried a marshal's baton in his knapsack as asserted by their commander.

Nevertheless—and Marat had already warned of this—the army was also a danger to the continued existence of the Republic. Around the campfires far from home where the word of the "man in the street" had long since been disregarded, the soldiers sought refuge in *la gloire* and turned to their invincible commander who promised it to them as he gambled with their fate. The victor of Arcole (1796) and Rivoli (1797) could rely on their loyalty and in 1798 they followed him without question into the *battle of the pyramids* in the course of an exotic campaign in Egypt. On the 18th of Brumaire, they carried out a coup d'état against the helplessly vacillating Directoire in Paris which raised Bonaparte to the rank of First Consul in 1799 and to that of Emperor of the French in 1804.

Napoleon I did away with the few democratic institutions in France which still existed when he came to power. For feudal Europe, however, and for England as France's bourgeois rival on the seas, the "Corsican monster" remained the unacceptable heir of the Revolution who forced upon him the hopeless choice of winning victory after victory to the point of exhaustion or of collapse. The emperor's lack of foresight could only favour their position. And so the "Revolutionary wars" against the First and Second Coalitions were followed by the "Napoleonic Wars" against the Third, Fourth, Fifth and Sixth Coalitions with the almost continuous gunfire of *Trafalgar* and *Austerlitz* (1805), Jena (1806) and Friedland (1807), Aspern and Wagram (1809), Borodino and on the Beresina (1812), of Dresden and *Leipzig* (1813) and the spring campaign of 1814—already far back in Champagne—and the dramatic sequel of *Waterloo* in 1815. Ploughing through states and their laws, tossing crowns to and fro like playthings, France's "Grand Army" and the Tricolor advanced in vain to the strains of

The battle of Austerlitz with Napoleon I (to the right)
and his Corps Commanders Soult and Davout. Contemporary
engraving.

preceding double page:
Scenes from the naval battle of Trafalgar. National Maritime
Museum, London

the Marseillaise as far as Madrid and Moscow. Their commander died in exile in 1821 on an African island and, instead of the nations who had courageously opposed the alien rule of Napoleon, it was a "Holy Alliance" of kings who triumphed and reciprocally guaranteed their "legitimacy".

Just as the French Revolution, despite the downfall of its standard bearers, pointed the way for the bourgeois movement for free economic competition and political democracy in the 19th century, the Napoleonic style of warfare set the points for an entire epoch in the military sphere. To be able to oppose it with some prospect of success, even the conservative courts had been obliged to make far-reaching changes in their military systems, changes which could not be restricted to a mere imitation of French models. Not all of these innovations could be grafted on to social relations of a different kind and in some cases, as in Prussia, these social relations themselves had to be modified to provide a more reliable basis for the substantially altered military system.

The "balance of power" envisaged and created by the Congress of Vienna in 1815 proved capable of maintaining peace between the Great Powers for the next four decades. To be sure, the world was not at all pacified and, under an often thin blanket, revolutionary embers continued to smoulder and flickers of flame appeared from time to time all over the world. Spain's colonies on the mainland of America, after a war of independence lasting sixteen years, finally shook off the shackles of the Spanish Crown at the battle of *Ayacucho* (1824) and Brazil freed itself from Portugal in 1822. Revolution, reaction and civil war alternated with each other in the Iberian Peninsula itself. In Italy, patriots rose up against their local despots in 1820/21 and in 1830/31. The Greek struggle for freedom, romantically celebrated by the Philhellenists, achieved victory in 1830 after a combined English, Russian and French force had destroyed the Turkish fleet at Navarino (1827) and the army of Sultan Mahmud had been defeated in the Russo-Turkish War of 1828/29. In the same year, the July Revolution in France drove the Bourbons from the throne—this time for ever. Belgium rid itself of its Dutch monarch while the Polish revolt of 1831, led by the aristocracy, was crushed by the czar's army under General Paskievich.

The time when the maritime powers stole each other's colonial possessions had also passed. Since the battle of Trafalgar, Great Britain was the uncontested mistress of the seas and a frown was sufficient to scare off frivolous challengers. The United Kingdom's military activities were directed against non-European peoples such as the Maratha and Sikhs of India, against Burma, Afghanistan and China, where Hongkong was taken over in the first "Opium War" (1840–1842), against the Xhosa of the Cape territory in South Africa (1847) and the Yoruba of Lagos (1851). In 1830, France began its conquest of Algeria which was to last for decades. It was in the Egypt of Muhammad Ali, the man who subdued the Mamelukes and whose armies under Ibrahim Pasha almost blew apart the Ottoman Empire at the battles of Konya (1832) and Nisib (1839) in the presence of von Moltke, the military adviser to the Turks, that the interests of the powers of the "European Concert" conflicted with each other. Since neither Austria nor the England of Queen Victoria nor Czar Nicholas I of Russia were prepared to accept a rejuvenated and pro-French Egypt as the heir of the "sick man on the Bosporus", they forced it back in 1841 to its original position on the Nile by military pressure in Syria and by exercising diplomatic influence.

However, none of these confrontations was serious enough to necessitate a major re-organization of the military systems and techniques of the Great Powers. The routine resources and methods were good enough to deal with their everyday problems. The changes that took place resulted to a far greater extent from the Industrial Revolution which began in England and, in the course of the 19th century, gradually spread across the Continent.

The Napoleonic Wars had all taken place within the pre-industrial era with regard to the production of arms and armament. Disregarding the successive improvements which took place, well-tried types of guns and cannon survived for many years after the turn of the century. New inventions such as the balloon or Chappe's optical telegraph were not well received; Napoleon rejected Fulton's submarine, correctly estimating that it was not sufficiently well-developed for his purposes. In the lack of activity in foreign affairs after 1815, there were even signs of stagnation in certain areas of the military sphere. After the efforts made during the Wars of the Coalitions, the state budgets had to deal with a heavy burden of national debt and there could scarcely be any question of systematic General Staff work in times of peace. It could not be said at all that strategy and tactics had taken account of all the conclusions drawn from the Napoleonic Wars by such eminent theorists as Jomini and Clausewitz. In some respects, the generals complacently remained at the level achieved at Waterloo. Of the English regulars, in particular, it was said, not without a grain of truth, that they fought under Lord Raglan (known for a dashing way of arranging the sleeves on coats) at Balaklava and Inkerman in 1854 just as bravely and ponderously as they had under Lord Wellington: "Magnificent, but not in the sense of modern warfare" was the malicious comment of a French colleague—which was not quite how the poet Tennyson saw it in *The Charge of the Light Brigade.*

The Industrial Revolution, on the other hand, created conditions previously unknown in the history of warfare. Admittedly, the new technology did not lead to any new weapon at first but it did permit a constant improvement in the materials of war. To enable exchanges of fire to take place whatever the wind and weather, the flintlock was replaced about 1830 by the percussion lock, the pin of which struck a percussion cap usually made from copper and filled with a high-explosive mixture. After 1840, guns were given a rifled barrel and tapered bullets, the rifling leading to increased velocity, range and penetration power. At the same time, the calibre of the rifled muzzle-loader was reduced to 14.5 millimetres. Also about 1840, it proved possible to manufacture a breech-loader suitable for military service, the breech mechanism consisting of a revolving cylinder with a moving percussion-pin. Initially, this weapon had a ballistic performance which was inferior to that of the rifled muzzle-loader but possessed the incomparable advantage of having many times the rate of fire and it could be fired from a prone position. The revolutionary development in hand-guns were followed by innovations in artillery weapons. In the middle of the century, the place of the smooth-bore muzzle-loader was taken by guns with rifled bores and finally by breech-loaders. The use of cast steel instead of bronze for the casting of gun-barrels played a part in this. The long shells fired by these guns were of steel and—with their own fuse and separate cartridge—could be used as explosive or shrapnel missiles.

The manufacture of weapons and equipment by steam power in great factories enabled them to be produced rapidly and in large quantities to uniform standards. In addition, there was the utilization of steam power for purposes of transportation: as locomotives which could rapidly and economically convey entire armies and their supplies on rail networks and even run according to "timetables"; as steamships, permitting gigantic troop and equipment movements even across oceans within a few weeks if not within a matter of days. These and electric means of communication such as the telegraph and later the field telephone created the conditions for the equipment and control of mass armies which allowed general conscription to progress from a principle to actual reality and to extend mobilization to between one-fifth and one quarter of the entire population of a country—including the women, children and old men.

The development of heavy industry led, among other things, to yet another transformation. In the most advanced industrialized countries, the social composition of the men who served in these armies was beginning to change. With the working population becoming increasingly proletarian in nature, an independent class-consciousness began to emerge and more and more worker-soldiers appeared at the side of the peasant soldiers.

Naturally, it was not before the middle of the century that the traits of such a development began to become apparent. The fighting at the barricades of Paris in February and June 1848, the wars of the revolution and counter-revolution of 1848/49 in Italy, Schleswig-Holstein and Hungary, the German "Campaign for the Reich constitution" of 1849 and, to a major extent, the Crimea War of Turkey, France, England and Sardinia against Russia (1853–1856) still took place, by and large, according to old-established ideas of strategy and tactics. Nevertheless, they opened a new round of military confrontation in which pent-up national and international problems demanded a final solution.

Napoleon III, who took advantage of the reputation of his illustrious uncle to force himself on the French people as their emperor in 1852, was subsequently obliged to justify his coup d'état, delightfully satirized by Karl Marx in the *Achtzehnter Brumaire des Louis Bonaparte*, and, as the restorer of the "grandeur of France", out-manoeuvred the Republican opposition. Although he had soothed the anxieties of the population in town and country by proclaiming that the Empire meant peace at home and abroad, he resorted to the instruments of war to upgrade his somewhat hollow imperial status by becoming the referee of Europe. This tactic was still effective at the Paris Congress of 1856 where Russia had to take second place. But the campaign of 1859 against Austria had only a very limited success. Admittedly, the experienced and well-equipped French army at *Solferino* proved superior to the enemy forces under the weak leadership of Emperor Francis Joseph and enabled Napoleon to make a quick and advantageous peace treaty. The right of national self-determination which he advocated to justify his say in matters which did not concern him was then implemented by Italian democrats headed by Garibaldi in a revolutionary manner which was no longer under the control of France. The united Italian state was established in opposition to the will of its "patron" in Paris.

The punitive expedition irresponsibly dispatched by Napoleon III to Mexico in 1861 to collect outstanding debts and help the clerical opposition against the liberal President Benito Juarez developed into a real fiasco. Since it dragged on for years and suffered heavy losses without achieving anything, all it did was to bring disorder into the French military system. In the end, the United States indicated in no uncertain manner that it was high time for the French to get out and so the field was left to the enemy who had "Emperor Maximilian of Mexico", the "front man" of the undertaking, court-martialled and shot in 1867.

Without doubt, it could not have been anticipated in 1861 that American diplomacy would intervene in this way, since at that time the USA itself was engaged in a bitterly fought Civil War between the increasingly industrialized states of the North and the Southern states whose economy was based on slave labour and which, under the leadership of the conservative plantation owners, were intending to secede, i.e., leave the Union. Although at a great disadvantage in the material respect and in the number of inhabitants, the newly formed Confederation of the South proved the stronger side in the military campaign of the first two years of the war. The Confederates had the advantage that most of the officer corps, by reason of their élite background, took their side and influenced many of the experienced troops to do the same. In addition, bearing in mind the vast distance involved in the fighting, there was the significant advantage of the Confederate cavalry.

Time, however, was on the side of the North. By 1863, the war potential of its armaments industry had already far outstripped that of the agricultural South which was also hampered by a sea blockade. The army of the North, in which democratically minded Yankees of all classes and backgrounds served side by side with old "Forty-Eighters" from Europe and former Negro slaves, now numbered almost a million. General Lee realized that only a crushing victory could still give the Confederates any chance of success and he took the risk of launching an offensive which threatened the capital, Washington, and thus forced his adversary to stand and fight. However, after Lee's desperate three-day attack at *Gettysburg* was finally thrown back on 3 July 1863 by the concentrated fire of the defenders, the war reached a turning point and nothing could reverse the course it now took. It was a straight path from here onwards to the surrender of the Secessionists in April 1865 and within a generation the reunited Union was the greatest economic power on Earth.

While France's emperor was becoming entangled in his gambles overseas, Prussia was preparing with a systematic re-organization of its army for the *Prussian* solution to the German question by "blood and iron". Otto von Bismarck, its chief minister, initially formed an alliance with Austria before interfering in a constitutional conflict in Schleswig-Holstein. The two German powers obtained a cheap victory over little Denmark which unexpectedly found itself without supporters. The dispute that immediately flamed up over the "sea-bound duchies with their ethnic links" (as the song went) revealed all the dubiousness of the German Confederation which had been called into life by the Congress of Vienna in 1815 and had disintegrated in 1848, which had been laboriously cemented together again but was irretrievably undermined by the rivalry between Prussia and Austria. Prussia's intention to break the leading position of the Hapsburg emperors in "Greater Germany" by a pseudo-liberal change in the constitution with the aid of general franchise, resulted in the dissolution of the assembly of the German Diet at Frankfort in June 1866 and led to mobilization: the "Bundes-exekution" of the German Confederation brought forward by nine votes to six against Bismarck's "revolution from above". The modern approach to warfare, in which for the first time full account was taken of the industrial age was the work of Helmuth von Moltke, the Chief of the Prussian General Staff. It proved totally successful and already on the 3rd of July resulted in victory at *Königgrätz* (or Sadowa) in Bohemia. Napoleon's efforts to arrange a profitable "mediation" were thwarted by a quick peace treaty wisely arranged on mild terms by the victor. Prussia left Austria untouched and instead annexed small and medium-sized "enemy" states in ample measure. The North German Confederation—in which Austria had no part—was established under Prussian leadership and the independence of the four states south of the river Main was conceded as a consolation prize for Napoleon.

It was clear to all those concerned that the Franco-Prussian part of the match had only been postponed. France undertook greater efforts to improve the state of its army and in fact succeeded in raising the standard of its equipment by a considerable margin—among other things by the introduction of the outstanding Chassepot gun. Despite this, the entire French military system suffered irreparably from the political weakness of an unpopular Bonapartist despotism. Even last-minute concessions to the moderate liberalism of the upper middle-class were incapable of changing this. A cunningly arranged intrigue against the background of the candidature to the Spanish throne of a Hohenzollern prince culminated in the "Ems Telegram" which was edited by Bismarck and used to administer a resounding diplomatic slap in the face. Napoleon did not dare to go against the enraged public opinion of France and stumbled into the trap. The French declaration of war of 19 July 1870 helped Prussia to obtain the assistance of the South German states.

Like the Austro-Prussian War before, the Franco-Prussian War of 1870/71 was decided within a few weeks, between the 6th of August and the 1st of September. Despite the outstanding performance of the individual French soldier and his weapons in the battles of Wörth—Reichshofen, Spichern, Colombey-Neuilly, Vionville—Mars-la-Tour and finally *Gravelotte—St.Privat*, the rottenness of the regime and the incompetent, ill-prepared and arrogant military leadership led to a collapse along the whole of the line. On the 2nd of September, Napoleon III surrendered at Sedan. Two days later, the Republic was proclaimed at Paris.

Both Bismarck and Moltke rejected the Republic's offer of peace without annexations and continued the campaign as a war of conquest for the possession of Alsace-Lorraine. This policy was to have consequences of momentous import. For the time being, of course, the weak Third Republic was unable to repeat the success of the Jacobin contingents of 1793 since the conditions were totally different and finally it had to acknowledge defeat. The second German Empire was proclaimed on 18 January 1871 in the Hall of Mirrors at Versailles, before the gates of the besieged and bombarded city of Paris, and the Peace of Frankfort founded the primacy of the military state of the Hohenzollerns in the "concert" of Europe.

The events of 1871 left deep scars. The first was accurately and realistically characterized by Moltke when he said that the newly conquered "Reichsland" of Alsace-Lorraine would still have to be defended with the sword for another fifty years. "Never speak about it, always think of it" was the attitude of the other side. What the Social Democrat August Bebel had warned against in vain in the first German Reichstag came true: the wound never healed. It remained the most stubborn of the causes of dissent which were soon to split Europe into hostile blocks and it was fanned—on both sides—by vested interests whose business was best served by war and the clamour for war.

1871 was also the year of the seventy days of the Paris Commune in which artisans and workers took the first exploratory steps beyond the latitudes of bourgeois democratic revolutions towards a society founded on socialism developed in the light of the arguments of the different schools of thought. Even though the Communards were defeated on the barricades in the "bloody week of May", they lit an early proletarian flame which was understood not only by those toiling in grey factories but also by the most alert of their adversaries, ranging from Ranke to Bismarck and from Taine and Burckhardt to Nietzsche.

Finally, the international scene allowed Russia in 1871 to delete a few annoying clauses of the Treaty of Paris of 1856 about military restrictions in the Black Sea area and to recover full freedom of movement. However, in the last of the Russo-Turkish wars in 1877/78 which took the Russian troops—after initial difficulties in three hard-fought battles for the fortified city of Pleven—across the Balkan mountains and as far as the Sea of Marmora by Constantinople, the czarist empire proved significantly better in the field than at the green table of the Berlin Congress where it yielded to English pressure and abandoned some of the results which had already been achieved in the campaign.

With the year of 1878, war moved out of Europe and it was only in 1912 that it returned to the "powder barrel" in the Balkans. However, the introduction of conscription on a general scale in all the great continental states and some of the smaller ones and the conclusion of military conventions and alliances, eventually even by Great Britain which, as a maritime power, had always insisted on its traditional policy of non-alliance in times of peace, refute the fairytale of the pacifist role of a civilization based on a property-owning, well-educated bourgeoisie and promoting understanding between nations. Uninhibited rearmament demanded more and more and better and better weapons.

To begin with, the military was somewhat bewildered by the unceasing transformation of the technical fundamentals of warfare. Since almost every weapon was practically outdated before it could be put into mass production and issued to the army, the generals had no idea how they could still keep control of such a rapidly changing state of affairs. After 1871, the introduction of the metal cartridge improved the gas-tight closure of small firearms and allowed their calibre to be reduced yet again to eleven millimetres. As a consequence, the repeater gun, in which a magazine holding between five and ten rounds was arranged in the butt, came into general use. Around 1885, after years of experiments, a smokeless explosive based on cotton cellulose replaced black gunpowder. Quick-firing small-arms were now produced and had a calibre no greater than seven to eight millimetres. Smokeless powder overcame the shortcomings of the first machine-guns, the predecessors of which included "barrel-organ" guns and multi-barrel weapons. In the machine-gun, the gas produced by the explosion of the cartridge was used for the automatic reloading and firing of the weapon. Its rate of fire was so high that the barrel had to be cooled by a water-filled jacket. Smokeless powder likewise led to the development of the first rapid-fire field-guns and high-explosive shells were introduced for dealing with the concrete and armour of military fortifications. Navies utilized screw propulsion at an early stage and in the second half of the century wooden ships were replaced by vessels with hulls built from iron or steel plates. Guns were mounted on swivelling turrets arranged fore and aft and at the sides. Continuous efforts were made to develop torpedoes capable of penetrating the latest armour and armour able to withstand the latest torpedoes.

After a temporary balance of power had once again been established in Europe—ironically described by Bismarck from his vantage-point as the game with the five balls—the Great Powers set about dividing up those parts of the globe still considered to be "available", each endeavouring to gain the maximum advantage and none bothering to ask the opinions of the people most concerned.

Africa was the principal object of the campaigns of conquest approved at the Berlin Congo Conference of 1885. Italy, Germany and Belgium as latecomers in the scramble for Africa wanted parity with the old-established colonial powers of Portugal, Spain, France and England. The social gradient between the aggressors and their victims became so great in the 19th century that there was no possible doubt about the outcome of the colonial wars. Despite all the personal bravery which was shown, the obsolete armies of weak feudal states and in many cases tribesmen armed only with spears could not continue indefinitely their unequal struggle against the economic power and military technology of the highly industrialized capitalist states.

Nevertheless, there are many examples of African peoples resisting the conquest of their territory for an astonishingly long time. Determined leaders imaginatively adapted their inadequate traditional styles of warfare to the strange new conditions, exploited the familiar features of their terrain to wear down the enemy by continual skirmishes and sometimes used the banner of religion to arouse enthusiasm and at the same time maintain discipline in the ranks of their warriors. Thus the French in Algeria were opposed from the rising of Abd-el-Kader in 1832 to the revolt led by the brothers Moqrani in 1871 while in the Western Sudan they were resisted by the Toucouleur leader El-Hadj Omar Saidu Tall from 1854 to 1864. England had to fight three campaigns to subdue the Ashanti and in 1879 was defeated by the Zulu chief Cetewayo at Isandhlwana before making up for this three months later at Ulundi where Cetewayo and the son of Napoleon III—serving as a British officer— lost their lives. And it was even the case that the Malinke state ruled by the commander Samory Touré along the Upper Niger staved off subjugation by the French for three decades, from 1870 to 1898.

Of international importance were the altercations along the valley of the Nile after the opening of the Suez Canal in 1869 which upgraded tremendously the strategic importance of the Mediterranean and of Egypt as the link with Asia. England, principal shareholder in the Suez Canal Company since 1874, did not hesitate to intervene with armed force when a "cabinet of national revolution" was established after a revolt by patriotic officers. Warships bombarded Alexandria and British colonial troops defeated Orabi Pasha at Tell al-Kebir on 13 September 1882, after which they remained in the country as an occupation force. On the other hand, Great Britain proved unable to maintain its position in the Eastern Sudan, which was administered as an Egyptian dependency, in the face of the fiery rebellion led by Mohammed Ahmed, the Mahdi. All efforts failed to relieve the besieged provincial capital of Khartoum and in 1885 the Mahdiya founded a "state of God". It was only after a railway line had been laid across the Nubian desert at the bend in the Nile that the machine-guns of General Kitchener wiped out this state at the battle of Omdourman in 1898.

France attempted to restrict the growth in the sphere of English influence along the Nile but Italy which had only been able to occupy the arid coastal regions of Eritrea and Somalia, endeavoured to extend its position in the evergreen highlands of Ethiopia in the shadow of English power. The picture of internal chaos presented to the outer world by the oldest monarchy of Africa induced the cabinet of Crispi in Rome to aim for the establishment of a protectorate and, with this in mind, it hoped to win support among the Christian lords of the country.

Zulus attacking a British military convoy. Wood-engraving from an illustrated newspaper of 1879.

Sudanese warriors and regular British-Egyptian troops in the battle of Omdourman in 1898. Wood-engraving from an illustrated newspaper.

The Negus, Menelik II, was able to deal with the rebellious lords, however, and after expanding his arsenal of weapons—principally with French assistance—appealed to the sense of liberty of the Amharas, who had never been subjugated, when Italy, after the failure of its "peaceful" offensive, changed from masked to overt aggression in 1894. It was on 1 March 1896, with the crushing defeat at *Adua*, that General Baratieri received the bill for the hasty undertaking which was characterized by both arrogance and imprudence and was understandably criticized by the majority of the Italian people.

As the first great victory won by the natives, despite their inferior equipment, over a "white" colonial army of no less than 20,000 men, Adua made headlines on the one hand and became, on the other, a milestone on the long road of the African liberation movement.

At the turn of the century, which was indeed felt as a *fin de siècle*, the fully developed industrialization society was already moving towards an age which, in its essentials, was first exposed by the English radical economist Hobson and others and given the name "imperialism". Marxists such as Rosa Luxemburg and V.I.Ulyanov, known more familiarly as Lenin, put it in its proper perspective when they recognized it as a last developmental stage of the mode of production and exchange based on the exploitation of "surplus value". As a result of

the uneven acceleration of their growth potentials, the aggravation of their immanent socio-economic contradictions had to lead from free competition to control by mighty economic groups in which industrial, commercial and bank capital was co-ordinated as finance or monopoly capital. In respect of the relations between states, the fact that nearly the whole of the Earth's surface had now been claimed had to lead to a struggle for its redistribution, in the course of which a series of individual crises would lead to a general conflagration which, in turn, could put a socialist revolution on the agenda.

As a result of the process of concentration in the armaments industry which now had mass armies as its customers, some of these giant companies became "world-famous": Krupp, Schneider-Creusot, Vickers and Armstrong, Škoda, Putilov, competitors in the development of weapons and purveyors of war on the international market. In the sphere of hand-held firearms, small-calibre quick-firing weapons and machine-guns finally came

Russo-Japanese War (1904).
The shelling of Port Arthur by the Japanese.
Coloured Japanese woodcut in traditional style, 1904.

into general use and the invention of the recoil brake eliminated the shortcomings which still existed in the design of larger pieces of ordnance. Improved designs enabled the field artillery to be equipped with long-range field-guns and howitzers. High-angle guns of large calibre were used against concrete fortifications which, in turn, were reinforced with steel. Mines were produced for the blocking of overland and sea routes. However, the most significant development from the beginning of the 20th century onwards was the use of powered road vehicles which were initially used only as a means of transportation or haulage. The first armoured vehicles were intended for reconnaissance purposes. Internal combustion engines, fitted with propellers, were also employed for the first aircraft—rigid airships for dropping bombs and aeroplanes for reconnaissance and observation. Within a few years, the aeroplane was developed from a lightly built flying machine to a long-range aircraft, although it remained unarmed to begin with. By the turn of the century, armoured vessels were to be found in almost all the classes of ships in service with the navies of the world. More powerful engines, better fuels, improved grades of steel and changes in hull design now enabled battleships of the "dreadnought" type to be constructed. The experiments made for many decades with boats capable of submerging likewise produced the desired results and submarines were equipped with an improved design of self-propelled torpedo as their principal weapon.

The crises and wars which occurred at the turn of the century largely confirmed the forecasts of the theorists. In 1898, the USA drove the Spaniards from Cuba, Puerto Rico and the Philippines. In the Boer War of 1899–1902, England increased its colonial possessions with the South African Free States of Oranje and Transvaal, containing the richest goldfields of all. In 1900–1901, forces from eight powers under the supreme command of the German general Count Waldersee jointly crushed the Ihotwan movement—contemptuously known as the "Boxer Rebellion"—in the China of the Manchu emperors. The eight powers then agreed on their "spheres of influence" in the most populous country of the world which had proved "indigestible" for any single colonial power.

Nevertheless, the teamwork of the punitive expedition barely disguised the mutual annoyance and the conflicting ulterior motives of those who took part in it. This was especially true of Russia, which remained in Manchuria, and Japan which felt hampered by Russian protests in its colonial subjugation of Korea. The realm of Tenno Mutsuhito had started to develop as a powerful modern state after the Meiji Reform of 1867/68 and had built up land and naval forces which could certainly be compared with any Great Power in Europe. Strengthened by an alliance with Great Britain which raised its international credit-rating, Japan started the Russo-Japanese War with a surprise attack on 8 February 1904.

The defeat of the vast czarist empire was only a surprise for superficial observers. For one thing, the only link with the theatre of war in the Far East was a single railway line. This set a limit to the number of troops and supplies which could be brought to the front while Japan, in control of the sea, could move its troops up by ship to within a few days' march of the actual fighting. Secondly, the autocratic system of government, which had been displaying signs of disintegration for a very long time, was incapable of withstanding the political pressure caused by an exhausting, unpopular and ill-fated war. The weaknesses of the government—incompetence, reluctance to accept responsibility, corruption and old-fashioned thinking—likewise infected the substance and the leadership of the army which was incapable of making optimum use of the steadfastness of the ordinary soldier.

Nevertheless—and despite the surrender of the fortress of Port Arthur, the defeat at *Mukden* and the disastrous sea-battle of Tsushima in 1905—it was not for purely military reasons that the war was lost. It was overtaken by the revolution, the epicentre of which had moved to Russia. To thwart this and save his throne, Nicholas II conducted a "peace of renunciation" and Japan joined the club of the recognized Great Powers.

The Russo-Japanese War was characterized by a few new forms of warfare which were dictated by the effect of rapid-fire weapons. To obtain shelter from weapons of this kind, the armies dug trenches and protected their extended and staggered positions by forward defences of barbed wire. The cavalry was still used for long-distance flanking movements but disappeared from the centre of the battle. Trench warfare took the place of open warfare. For the first and last time, sea-battles were fought by great fleets of coal-fired steamships, oil-fired turbines becoming the pre-eminent means of propulsion shortly afterwards.

On account of the restricted nature of the scenes of action and the limited resources of the combatants, only little use was made of this experience in the Balkan Wars of 1912/13. It was nevertheless applied on a massive scale when the European blocks, the Dual Alliance and the Triple Entente, clashed in the First World War, sparked off by the assassination of the heir to the Austrian throne by Gavrilo Princip in Sarajevo on 28 June 1914.

The scale of this war was far greater than any previous conflict. The armies of Germany and its ally, Austro-Hungary, disposed of a total mobilized force of 6 million men in August 1914 who were opposed by about ten million soldiers put into the field by France, Russia, Great Britain and its empire, Serbia and Belgium. The number of men conscripted in the following years was even greater and more states entered the war. In all, the "Central Powers" headed by Germany—including Turkey and Bulgaria—mobilized more than 25 million troops and the Allies and their associates—including Japan, Italy, Rumania, Portugal, the USA and Greece— about 45 million. More than 20 million guns and 150,000 artillery ordnances were used.

At the beginning of the war, nobody realized that such tremendous numbers of men and such vast quantities of war material would have to be kept in the field for several years or even that this was at all possible. The planners had anticipated a bloody but brief campaign. Since the German army led the world in equipment, organization as well as training and, by reason of its central geographical location, could decide where its principal front would be, it was expected—after German troops had marched through Belgium in violation of its neutrality—that a critical battle would take place in France, the outcome of which—approximately on the 40th day after mobilization—would decide the war. All the strategies of the countries involved—to a greater or lesser extent—took this point as their basis, which was also one of the reasons why England, on this occasion, could not follow the tradition of first watching from the sidelines before becoming involved. In any case, its modest military forces of six divisions would then have been too late.

The actual course of the first phase of the fighting did not correspond in every detail to the forceast but, by and large, it followed the pattern envisaged. The right wing of the German forces deployed in France according

Otto Dix, "Self-portrait as a Soldier".
Pen-drawing, *c.* 1924.

to the "Schlieffen Plan" fought successful frontier battles but was then held and defeated on the *Marne* on the 9th September 1914—the 40th day of mobilization. Against this, everything else was of little importance. From then on, however, the war did not proceed in accordance with the predictions. The fronts stopped moving and millions of men on either side dug in. The "emptiness of the battlefield" celebrated its first triumph.

The Central Powers, which were in a far worse position, could ill-afford a "conflict of resources". The longer the war lasted, the more serious the effect of the economic superiority of the Entente powers on the course of the war would be. The control of the seas permitted them not only to exploit their own resources but also those of their colonies and neutral countries overseas for their war effort while the enemy was restricted to the North Sea and the Mediterranean by a blockade and cut off from the outside world. If the German Reich did not wish to abandon its ambitious war-aims, its supreme military command (OHL) had to think of something to regain the initiative following the failure of its first campaign plan. It was decided that the German army would go over to the defensive on the Western Front and would attempt, after the breakthrough at Gorlice and Tarnów on 2 May 1915 and following a series of co-ordinated offensives, to persuade Russia to withdraw from the war. Despite a significant gain in territory and a weakening of the potential of the czarist forces, the German forces were nevertheless again halted in September along the Riga-Czernowitz line. The occupation of Serbia and the repulse of Anglo-French attacks against the Dardanelles changed the general situation just as little as the opening of new secondary fronts on the Isonzo and before Salonika by the Entente powers.

In 1916, both sides made preparations to bring about a decisive change in the war and Great Britain introduced compulsory military service. Since the Entente countries had greater difficulty in co-ordinating their operations—on account, among other things, of the different war-aims they were pursuing, Germany was able to exploit the advantage of time and on 21 February attacked the fortress of *Verdun* as the cornerstone of the French front with the idea of exhausting the French army. However, the latter maintained its resistance and the losses on both sides in the "hell of Verdun" reached horrifying figures. Finally, with the battle of the Somme, signalled by an artillery bombardment lasting for days, where British troops took over the northern section of the front, and the Russian Brussilov offensive, the success of which in Eastern Galicia induced Rumania to join the Entente in August, the Allies once more regained the initiative. The sea-battle of *Jutland* (Skagerrak) on the 31st of May, although the outcome was indecisive and despite its significance as unique fight between whole fleets of battleships, underlined this state of affairs.

The perplexity of those masterminding the German war effort was reflected in a change in the supreme command of the army, which was entrusted to Hindenburg and Ludendorff who were given wide-ranging powers. The struggle approached its second critical point and the sufferings of the civil population grew worse. Those in power could no longer ignore the growing desire for peace among the masses of the people who were weary of war and the even more profound criticism by revolutionary socialists that the war was motivated by imperialist aims. In the search for a compromise to avoid a social upheaval and to achieve at least some of the original aims of the war, some political groups, in devious ways, investigated the possibility of a separate peace arrangement by persuading this or that power to withdraw from the military pact in question. Their lack of results strengthened the position of the "last ditch" strategists who demanded that the war should be continued until the enemy had been defeated.

At the beginning of 1917, the German command saw a last way of achieving this aim: unrestricted submarine warfare which was intended on this occasion to bring down within about twelve months not France or Russia but the real enemy, England, which was dependent on imports. The German Crown Council was aware of the unreliable basis of these calculations and on the 9th of January State Secretary von Zimmermann said: "Show me the way to a practicable peace and I will abandon this idea! But as things are . . ." It was considered possible that the United States would react to this by entering the war but it was not believed that this would significantly change the situation. At the time, the USA had no army worth mentioning and its forces would have to cross the U-boat infested Atlantic, which meant that it could not make a real contribution to the war within two years at the earliest. By then, however, it was believed that the issue would long since have been decided.

The German calculations were proved wrong in two respects. The declaration of war by the USA on 6 April 1917 was not made as a reprisal for the infringement of international law by the sinking of neutral ships but because it was feared that a victory by Imperial Germany would seriously endanger its own global strategy. President Wilson had to take sides if he wanted to ensure that the debts of the Entente would be repaid and especially if he wanted to thwart the German attempt to achieve world hegemony. Secondly, the U-boat offensive—

"War" (Triptychon) by Otto Dix, 1929/30.
Staatliche Kunstsammlungen, Galerie Neue Meister, Dresden

The First World War at sea.
The "Seydlitz", which took part in the battle of Jutland in
1916, receives a direct hit. Documentary photo

after a giddy 6,000,000 tons of shipping sunk in 1917—was countered much sooner than had been expected and in 1918 not only did the numbers of new ships built in England and America exceed those sunk but an effective convoy system was introduced. Not a single American troopship was sunk and even before the "two-year deadline" had expired one and a half million American troops had been landed on French soil.

On the other hand, the outbreak of the "February Revolution" in Russia on the 12th of March which led to the end of czarist rule prevented the launching of the operations agreed by the Allies for 1917. While the Kerenski offensive failed in the East, the attacks by the Entente in the West resulted in the gain of only a few narrow kilometres of territory, torn by curtain-fire and filled with shell-craters, despite the fact that unheard-of masses of material per man and metre had been used, particularly in Flanders. The great hope first awakened by a local British breakthrough with tanks in the battle of *Cambrai* on the 20th of November did not materialize.

The governments of France, Italy, Germany and Austria were able to suppress the anti-war actions taken by soldiers, sailors and workers following the events in Russia and the "turnip winter". On the other hand, the party of the Bolsheviks in Russia came to power with the socialist October Revolution and, in the "Peace Decree" of the 8th of November, the first Soviet government proposed that the powers involved in the war should open negotiations for a peace without annexations or reparations. This proposal was not well received at all by the Entente powers but Germany concluded a truce on the 5th of December which was then followed by the harsh peace treaty of Brest-Litovsk on 3 March 1918 which established a broad intermediate zone under German influence and German occupation between Finland and the Caucasus. This allowed the Supreme Command of the Army to organize the "great battle in France" after all to snatch a "victorious peace" from the fire in this area, too, before the American divisions irrevocably changed the balance of power.

Nevertheless, despite tactical successes and significant gains in territory, the five offensives launched between 21 March and 17 July 1918 were unable to dislodge the Allies. A French counter-offensive, launched from the flank by Foch, the Allied Commander-in-Chief, at Villers Cotterêts, drove the German troops for the second time—after 1914—from the Marne to the other side of the Aisne. On this occasion, however, their withdrawal was followed by the immediate breakthrough of Allied forces, mainly consisting of British, Australian and Canadian units, through the German defences at Amiens on the 8/9th of August. As a result of this, things started moving along the whole of the Western Front and the German formations were obliged to fall back to the Antwerp-Meuse positions. Their allies, however, collapsed completely and the Salonika front disintegrated on the 15th of September, leading to the capitulation of Bulgaria on the 29th of September. The Turkish army broke up after defeats in Mesopotamia and Palestine and laid down its arms on the 30th of October. Following the defeat at Vittorio Veneto in Italy, it was not only the old "Dual Monarchy" of Austro-Hungary that ceased to exist after the 28th of October but also its army so that the armistice with the Entente of the 3rd November was only of symbolic importance. In Germany, the Supreme Command, now somewhat less vociferous, finally recommended the newly-formed government on the 4th of October to seek an armistice from President Wilson on the basis of his "Fourteen Points" which he had affirmed on the 8th January. Before negotiations could be opened, however, the crews of the High Seas Fleet refused to obey a suicidal command by their admiral to put to sea and, with the revolt of the sailors at Kiel on the 3rd of November, there began the German Revolution of 1918. This led to the proclamation of the Republic on the 9th of November in Berlin and, in the headquarters at Spa, to the flight of William II to the Netherlands. In Marshal Foch's railway carriage, parked on a siding in the woods at Compiègne on the 11th of November, Matthias Erzberger put his signature under the armistice document as the representative of the "Council of the People's Delegates" which, under the chairmanship of the Social Democrat Friedrich Ebert, had sworn to lead the German nation to a better future.

The war caused the loss of some ten million human lives and about double that number were wounded and crippled; it was estimated that it cost 300,000 million gold dollars. The European powers, both victors and vanquished, were left with a mountain of debts, most of which had to be repaid to the USA which emerged from the struggle as the dominating force and creditor of the Old World. The peace treaties which the losers had to agree to in 1919 and 1920 in various suburbs of Paris were far removed from the ideals of a crusade for democracy, the joyous message of which had been proclaimed in apostolic manner by the American president. On the contrary, they were dictated by the overt and rival interests of the centres of economic, political and military power. Their conditions created new dissent and hostility in place of the old and already contained the germs of the next worldwide conflict. They consequently paved the way for those who called for revenge and demagogically quoted the injustice and inconsistencies of the "Versailles System", preparing the ground—knowingly or not—for fascism to thrive on.

The developments in weapon technology which had appeared during the war subsequently came into general military use. The small-arms field was dominated by magazine carbines and light submachine-guns, and also self-loading rifles existed. Mortars of various types increased military firepower and high-explosive shells were developed for anti-tank guns with calibres of 35 to 45 millimetres. Anti-aircraft guns with a flat trajectory and a high rate of fire artillery, the number of tractor-hauled guns increased and experimental self-propelled guns were built. The first rocket launchers appeared, using a circular or a parallel row arrangement. The most obvious example of motorization and mechanization was the tank which acquired a revolving gun-turret, a more powerful engine and a more efficient shape. In aviation, Junkers successfully introduced the all-metal aircraft. Biplanes began to be replaced by cantilever monoplanes which were initially equipped with one or three engines and later with two or four. Rapid improvements followed in operational ceiling, speed, range and payload capability. The battleship continued as the principal naval unit but the aircraft carrier was developed to protect it, the number of planes carried depending on the size and weight of the ship. In addition, flying-boats were built for long-range naval reconnaissance. Particularly rapid progress was made in the development of the size, range, diving depth and armaments of submarines.

The war also accelerated progress in the civilian sector; in aeronautics, radio communications and in the chemical, electrical and optical engineering industries. It resulted in new frontiers and contributed to the emergence of new states in Central Europe, in the Baltic area and in the Orient. Rulers and potentates from Greiz-Schleiz-Lobenstein to Constantinople were overthrown while on the other hand the war led to the creation of new Arab kings and kingdoms. The event which stamped the character of the epoch, however, by attempting to change human society in a truly radical manner, was the appearance of Soviet power in the Russian October Revolution.

Marshal Foch considered that communism was a "disease of defeated nations" and recommended that the centre of the epidemic be isolated by a quarantine belt. In addition, to eradicate it completely, the Entente promptly intervened in Russia and encouraged the counter-revolutionary forces in the country to start a civil war. The Red Army and the "White" forces fought each other from 1918 to 1922 at Petrograd and Archangel, in the Ukraine and in the Caucasus, in Turkestan and the Far East, in Siberia and along the Volga from Kazan to *Tsaritsyn* and Astrakhan. By force of circumstances, the Bolsheviks substituted weapons for words in their critique of imperialism. The military force they created, the Red Workers' and Peasants' Army, proved the stronger in the hard-fought and eventful struggle in Central Russia. By driving their adversary back to Vladivostok, they showed that a new and decisive factor had appeared on the military scene.

Trusting to its ability to establish socialism on a long-term basis by its own resources even in the unfavourable circumstances of a protracted hostile encirclement in a country occupying no less than one-seventh of the total surface of the globe, the Union of Socialist Soviet Republics sought ways of implementing a policy of peaceful coexistence, as conceived by Lenin already before his fatal illness (1922–24), in a world which was henceforth divided into two fundamentally different camps. Although there was little response, it tried to prevent war from developing in the critical situations which became more and more frequent, especially in the atmosphere of the worldwide economic crisis (1929–1933).

Revolts and armed revolutionary uprisings of varying political shades questioned the continued existence of colonial dependence and ranged from China to the Moroccan Riff. Until the 1920's there was hardly any disunity among those interested in maintaining colonial power although, as in the Greek-Turkish War of 1920 to 1922, they occasionally moved different pawns. Their latent disagreements only became apparent, as an open confrontation, when the post-war boom (1924–28) began to decline, threatening their internal stability all around the world and creating the opportunity for aggressive factions to fish in troubled waters. In 1931, the Japanese military considered that the time was ripe, bearing in mind the shaky position of the Western democracies which might have otherwise protested, to occupy Manchuria without hindrance and to start a fire which in 1937 escalated to a state of undeclared war in the heart of China. In 1935, fascist Italy registered its demand for a revision of the political map of the world by launching a massive attack against Ethiopia. In an even more thorough and brutal manner than that in which Mussolini established his "Impero", the National Socialists or "Nazis" of Germany proceeded with the founding of the "Thousand-Year Reich of Greater Germany". They came to power in 1933 and for far too long were dismissed as the expression of a petty bourgeois inferiority complex: "Germany belongs to us today and tomorrow the whole world!"

The fascist "Axis" which had been forged stage by stage between Rome and Berlin regarded Spain, where conspiratorial officers headed by the "Caudillo" Franco had started a countrywide civil war against the Popular Front government which had won the election, both as a terrain for military exercises and as a political arena.

The Axis powers not only tested their weapons for the coming "Great War" but also sounded out the determination of the English and French governments to crush this development in its early stages and found it wanting: a policy of appeasement was followed which cleared the way for the attacker, this time on the other side of the Pyrenees and soon all over the world.

Italian divisions, German weapons and the squadrons of the "Condor Legion" streamed into Spain—not hindered but protected by "non-intervention agreements". Supplies from the Soviet Union and volunteers of various political opinions from many different countries, who hastened to the aid of the government of the Republic and, organized as International Brigades, fought at *Guadalajara* and Brunete, at Teruel and Flix, were unable to make up for the material superiority of the other side. In March 1939, the Spanish people lost the war against the Falangist forces and the two Great Powers that supported them.

By this time, the German Wehrmacht had already gained experience of marching into other countries without being punished for it: in Austria, in "Sudetenland", in Slovakia, in Prague and in Memel-Klaipeda. It was only when Poland was invaded on 1 September 1939 that a point was reached at which England and France could no longer give way without revealing the ineffectiveness of their alliance to the whole world and thus putting themselves at the mercy of the Axis powers. The Second World War began—with all the omens in favour of the aggressor.

This was true, for one thing, of the general political atmosphere. Admittedly, Italy had exhausted its resources to such an extent in Ethiopia and Spain that it took no active part in the war for the time being and Japan, as the third Great Power in the "Anti-Comintern Pact" which was directed against the Soviet Union but was questionable regarding its seriousness, pursued its own war in the "Greater East Asia Co-Prosperity Sphere". On the other side, Belgium failed to renew the defensive alliance with France existing since 1920, the "Little Entente" between Prague-Belgrade-Bucharest, which was orientated on Paris, disintegrated and Turkey avoided any involvement in the military collaboration which had been expected. In the United States, isolationism recalled Wilson's failure in the reorganization of the world and the collapse of the "League of Nations" which had been set up in Geneva with his blessing in 1920; it obliged President Franklin D. Roosevelt (1933–1945) to exercise restraint in pursuing his anti-fascist course. The efforts of the Soviet Union to establish collective security in Europe by means of contractual guarantees were rejected by the Western powers. The way in which the latter carried on the last-minute negotiations aroused the mistrust of the Soviet side which took the view that if Russia became involved in a war with Germany (assuming that the warning shot failed to produce any readiness for compromise by the Germans) it would be the Red Army that would have to bear the brunt of it. It was this which led to the conclusion of a non-aggression pact with Germany in the middle of the crisis in August 1939, Stalin—Chairman of the Council of People's Commissars since May—believing that he could thus avoid the risk of such a confrontation.

The clauses of the Treaty of Versailles specifying unilateral partial disarmament by defeated Germany and the restriction of its Reichswehr to 100,000 men had already been undermined by the Weimar Republic. The rejection of these terms by the Hitlerite government in 1935 and the occupation of the demilitarized Rhineland in 1936 had met with none of the sanctions which had been threatened and thus overcame the last obstacles to rearmament at an unparalleled rate. With the reorganization of the Reichswehr as the "Wehrmacht" use was made of the latest advances in military science and technology. In particular, the importance of a high degree of motorization for gaining the strategic initiative in mobile warfare was correctly assessed. Whereas the French General Staff under Weygand and Gamelin still clung to experience gained in trench warfare and believed, with their defensive attitude, that their "super-Verdun", the Maginot Line, provided adequate safety, the command of the Wehrmacht was already preparing the deployment of self-contained armoured units and their co-ordination with squadrons of military aircraft. The German arsenal of weapons, supplemented by Austrian and Czechoslovak stocks—the latter being particularly valuable—seemed to offer the guarantee of successful "blitzkriegs" in which, from the centre of Europe, enemies in every direction of the compass would be overrun and eliminated one by one.

Without doubt, the element of surprise also represented an initial advantage for the aggressor who could determine the object and the timing of the attack. In the long run, however, the attempt to exterminate the nations of the world or to reduce them to slaves of the "master race" and to impose its will on the world was incompatible with all the laws of history and, in addition, had to fail by reason of the megalomania which was an intrinsic part of it. Even though some governments displayed a readiness to capitulate, such an approach inevitably provoked a reaction of self-defence which could not be suppressed in those threatened by German ambitions. As a consequence, the conflict necessarily hardened and assumed the traits of an anti-fascist, democratic war of liberation in a life or death struggle which directly affected the masses of the people and was not only fought at the fronts but also in the hinterland as partisan warfare.

In an initial phase, the German war-machine—bashfully accompanied at the very last by the more modest Italian counterpart—marched across Poland and the neutral countries of Denmark, Norway, Holland, Luxemburg and Belgium. This took place more or less according to the plans of the General Staff within a few weeks in each case in the course of three campaigns. Finally, after an armoured breakthrough at Carignan and Sedan, German tanks also rolled across France which capitulated on 23 June 1940. From the foot of the Pyrenees to Kirkenes beyond the Nordkap, the most northerly point of Europe, the Wehrmacht maintained a watch on England which, protected by the sea, had to carry the entire burden of the second year of the war in unaccustomed loneliness.

The possibility of surviving this situation was created by the Royal Air Force with its defensive victory in the first great battle fought in the skies of England, the *Battle of Britain*, in August/September 1940. The raids by the numerically far superior German Luftwaffe with the objective of eliminating the RAF, destroying its bases and achieving air superiority over the Channel met with failure, heavy losses being suffered by the aggressors. Göring's terror-bombers, which were supposed to "eradicate" Coventry and other cities and break the morale of the civilian population, achieved the opposite effect. From the unshaken determination of the profoundly embittered British public, the all-party government of Winston Churchill found the strength to withstand this critical phase of the war in 1940/41.

They were helped in this by the self-deception of the German leadership which, assuming that the war in the West had practically been won with the campaign against France, arrogantly supposed, without waiting for the elimination of the enemy in England—which was powerless to intervene on the Continent anyway, that its attention could now be turned to the chief problem, which had always been kept in mind, of "eliminating Eastern Bolshevism". From the late autumn of 1940, the Supreme Command of the Wehrmacht (OKW) had been working out the details of the "Barbarossa" plan for the rapid and total defeat of the Red Army. The dispatch of "military advisers" to Rumania in the autumn of 1940, the "peaceful" occupation of Bulgaria in March 1941, in April the invasion of Yugoslavia and of Greece which had been successfully resisting Italian forces since October 1941, and agreements with Hungary and Finland regarding their participation formed stepping-stones—sometimes improvised—to the invasion of the Soviet Union on 22 June 1941.

The Soviet leadership had not reckoned with a flagrant breach—at least not at this particular time—of the non-aggression pact which was still in force and, before its military preparations could be completed, had to face up to an attack by three German army groups with 175 divisions which outclassed the Red Army in war material and combat experience. The defenders suffered serious defeats and losses. White Russia, Western Russia and the Ukraine were lost and Leningrad was encircled.

Nevertheless, the "Eastern Campaign" of the German Supreme Command was a failure and its strategic objectives were not attained at all. A thousand great factories of decisive importance for the war were saved from the invaders and relocated beyond the Volga, in the Urals, in Siberia or in Central Asia where production started again. In the winter battle at the gates of Moscow, fresh Red Army troops moved over to the counter-offensive on 5 December 1941 and drove the enemy from the approaches to the capital. This first lasting setback for the Wehrmacht plunged it into a crisis. Although it recovered from this by the spring of 1942, the concept of the German "blitzkrieg" was refuted on Russian soil once and for all.

At the same time, the war changed from a European conflict to a worldwide one. In the early hours of 7 December 1941, a Japanese naval task force of battleships, smaller vessels and aircraft carriers with 420 machines on board unexpectedly attacked the American naval base of Pearl Harbor on the Hawaiian island of Oahu, the Americans having failed to take adequate defensive precautions. While Japanese fighters and bombers put the American Army and Navy fliers out of action, many American machines being destroyed on the ground, torpedo planes and dive-bombers sank or damaged most of the Pacific Fleet of the USA. The island empire achieved naval supremacy in the waters of East Asia and exploited this state of affairs to conquer the Philippines, Malaya and Singapore, Burma and Indonesia. Australia and India, as cornerstones of the British Empire, were threatened by the Japanese.

Incendiaries were dropped during
the Battle of Britain
and caused extensive fires in London.
Documentary photo

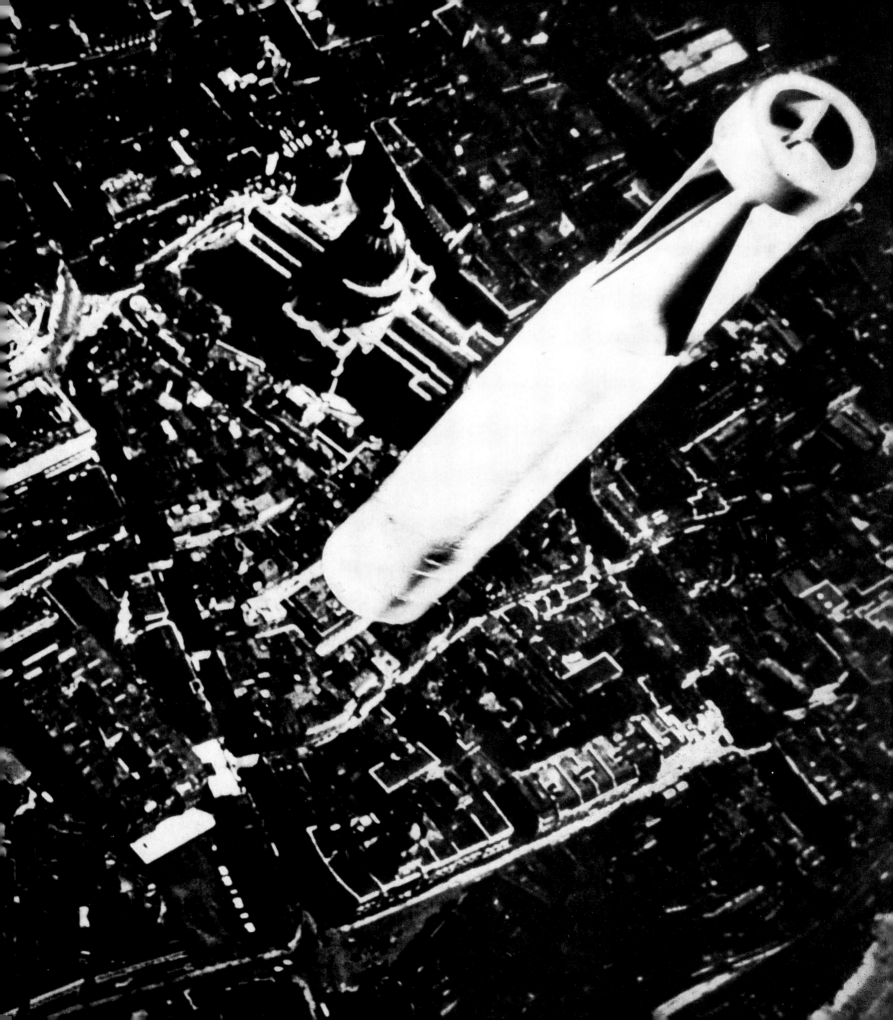

Although the Axis powers presented an impressive sight on the map of the world, the expansion of the areas under Japanese rule was doomed to be just as short-lived as Hitler's "New Order" in Europe. The entry of the United States in the war as a result of the challenge from Japan ended with U.S. industry reaching a level of production which far exceeded that of its foes. Already in the victorious battle of Midway in the Central Pacific from the 3rd to the 7th of June 1942, the reorganized naval and air forces of the USA forced the Japanese into the strategic defensive, the latter losing four aircraft carriers and hundreds of their best pilots.

However, the Allies had still not satisfactorily solved the question of agreement on their common war-aims. In a global confrontation, these necessarily had to be global, too. The USA decided that ten million conscripts— something completely new in American history although far less than the forces raised by the Soviet Union— would be sent in equal numbers to the Pacific and European theatres of war. It was correctly decided that the priority in point of time should be given to the latter since it was here that the turning point in the war would come, the Soviet front tying down the majority of the German divisions. In November 1942, the first American task-force under General Eisenhower landed in Morocco and Algeria while at the same time the British Eighth Army under General Montgomery broke through the German-Italian positions at *El Alamein* in Egypt. The Red Army, the largest military formation in the coalition, not only halted the German summer offensive against the Volga and the Caucasus at the battle of *Stalingrad* but also drove the enemy back from the Terek to the Don and the Donets and forced the encircled German 6th Army under General Paulus to surrender on 31 January and 2 February 1943.

The scales of victory began to tip in favour of the Allies. The survivors of the German "Afrika Korps" surrendered in May 1943 at Tunis and a subsequent Anglo-American landing on Sicily on the 10th of July brought about the overthrow of Mussolini in Rome. In the *Kursk Bend*, the Soviet army broke the offensive power of the Wehrmacht in the greatest tank battle of the war and in the autumn crossed the Dnepr.

Thus a spontaneous synchronization appeared in the operations of the Allies. At their first conference, in Teheran (29 November - 3 December 1943), the "Big Three"—Churchill, Roosevelt and Stalin— also agreed on a co-ordinated strategy for the total defeat of the enemy. This included the opening of a "Second Front" in France which had already been envisaged on several occasions but had always had to be put off for various reasons. For this, the provisional French government under General De Gaulle in Algiers not only offered its own forces but also the full support of the "forces in the interior", the members of the Maquis, the French resistance movement.

The supreme Anglo-American command gave priority to "waterproof" safety for both military and political reasons to exclude any imaginable setback in this great amphibious operation. The success of the undertaking, which had no parallel in history, was to be guaranteed by a tremendous deployment of war material and technical perfection in its execution. When the Allied troops landed on the coast of *Normandy* on the V-Day of 6 June 1944 and smashed the German "Atlantic Wall", these requirements had been met.

An attempt by senior German officers to remove the main obstacle to the ending of the already pointless war and to obtain milder peace conditions for a superficially de-Nazified but largely intact German Reich by

Berlin after the capitulation.
Soviet soldiers hoist the victory flag, May 1945.
Documentary photo

assassinating Hitler met with failure on 20 July 1944. At this point in time, the mighty Belorussian operation had already torn apart the German front in the East at Minsk. In August and September, in the course of new Soviet offensives, Rumania and Bulgaria changed over to the Allied side after the fall of their Fascist collaborators, while in October Soviet forces, together with the Yugoslav Popular Liberation Army which had emerged from Tito's partisans, marched into Belgrade. Allied armoured divisions, after the break-through at Avranches, the second landing on the Mediterranean coast at Cannes and the victory of the popular uprising in Paris, moved up to the German frontier and crossed into Germany at Aachen in September.

Time was now rapidly running out in the bunker of the Reich Chancellery in Berlin. Germany's cities and factories lay in ruins following the Allied air-raids and the Soviet winter offensive reached the Oder in February 1945. Abandoning the territory in the West, the German Supreme Command assembled its last remaining units, still numbering about a million men, for the defence of the capital of the Reich. After the stubborn resistance on the Seelow Heights had been broken on the 17th of April, the Red Army encircled *Berlin* with a pincer movement and, after days of house-to-house fighting, forced its surrender on the 2nd of May. On 8 May 1945, Marshal Zhukov, as the representative of the Allies, accepted the unconditional surrender of Germany at Karlshorst.

The leading statesmen of the Coalition met for the last time at the Potsdam Conference in July/August and called upon Japan to follow the example of Germany and capitulate. Although it was obvious by the autumn of 1944 at the latest, after their defeat in the sea-air battles of the Marianas and *Leyte*, that there was no way out for Japan, its generals still hoped, like the leaders of the "Third Reich" before them—who had since committed suicide, that they could drive a wedge between the Allies. The USSR, which hitherto had not been involved in the hostilities with Japan, put an end to this speculation by making a formal declaration of war on the 8th of August. There was no need for dropping atomic bombs on *Hiroshima* and Nagasaki to persuade Emperor Hirohito to order his forces on 15 August 1945 to cease fighting. In a radio message to the Japanese people, who had been misled by a primitive "keep fighting" propaganda and were now profoundly shocked, he announced the surrender of Japan, which came into force on the 2nd of September.

The Second World War was at an end. More than 50 million people had lost their lives and 35 million had been crippled. These figures included many civilians—the victims of the gas-chambers and the terror of enemy occupation, of bombs and famine from blockades, of street fighting and U-boat warfare. 20 million children had lost their parents and millions of people their homes and homelands. It was estimated that in Europe alone war damage amounted to 260 thousand million dollars while expenditure for military purposes by the countries involved in the war totalled more than 1,100 thousand million dollars.

The price which the nations of the world—and especially the peoples of the Soviet Union which had to bear the heaviest burden of the war—had to pay for the defeat of the aggressors was high. They drew their conclusions. War crimes, crimes against humanity, genocide and military aggression itself met with international condemnation. With the United Nations Organization, a body consisting originally of 51 Allied and neutral states was set up in San Francisco in 1945 which was capable, with all its imperfections, of contributing to the prevention or solving of armed conflicts.

In some of the countries of Europe and Asia, the anti-fascist democratic war of liberation led to a socialist transformation of society. In colonial countries of Asia and soon of Africa, too, national independence movements came to the fore and a "Third World" resulted, of which Latin America, too, considers itself to be a part. This "Third World" is on the threshold between the principles of the capitalist and socialist orders and is on the edge of the two power blocks grouped around the USA and the USSR with their divergent orders of society.

The Second World War revolutionized weapons and equipment to an extent which could not have been anticipated by any military expert at its outbreak. Tanks, guns, aircraft, ships and even personal firearms had increased their destructive power several times over by the end of hostilities and, in turn, raised the supporting services—logistics—to a factor of first-rate military importance. Unmanned aircraft with rocket propulsion, such as the V 1 and the V 2, did not help the German Wehrmacht to turn the tide of war, it is true, but they did announce the arrival on the scene of a new military arm with an unheard-of power of destruction. With nuclear weapons, whose firepower eclipsed even the wildest dreams, it seemed that they would bring about a radical change in the classic pattern of warfare and that wars would henceforth be fought with automatic weapon systems. There was already wild talk of atomic wars being fought by robots. Nevertheless, the "local" wars fought since then have followed the conventional pattern and the military technology used in them has not been fundamentally different to that employed during the Second World War, even though their destructive potential has increased in the course of several generations of weapon systems. But arsenals remain full to bursting point with rockets, nuclear weapons and other means of mass destruction, the scarcely imaginable destructive power of which can only be converted into a productive force for peaceful purposes by a high sense of social responsibility on the part of mankind.

VALMY / 1792

The occurrence of the French Revolution and its continuation caused great dismay at the courts of Europe. It was not only the French princes who had fled before it who beseeched them to take up arms against the advocates of "blasphemous" human and civil rights and to restore the *ancien régime*, the feudal state of affairs which had existed under the absolute monarchy of the Bourbons toppled by the people in 1789. Louis XVI himself and in particular Queen Marie-Antoinette of the House of Hapsburg sent secret appeals for help to their royal brothers and cousins. Since the latter, for various well-founded reasons, did not trust each other on any account and at most only considered the matter from the viewpoint of their own interests, the forming of a great counterrevolutionary coalition took some time to arrange.

On the basically correct assumption that a clash between mutually exclusive social orders was inevitable anyway, the Girondists organized a pro-war party in Paris, a group from the upper middle-class. This faction favoured an attack before the enemy had time to complete the assembly of his forces along the Rhine, Moselle and Meuse. In the hope that the defeat of France would also mean the end of the Revolution, the king gave his assent to this plan and on 20 April 1792 declared war on Austria which was immediately joined by Prussia, the Imperial Diet at Regensburg and the kingdom of Sardinia-Piedmont.

In the first phase of the campaign, it seemed that Louis's double-dealing would bear fruit. Although he himself lost his throne on the 10th of August and was put in prison, the fortresses of Longwy and Verdun were betrayed to the enemy on 23 August and 2 September 1792. The invaders had crossed the French frontier at the end of July but their advance on Paris had been held up more by the muddy roads resulting from torrential downpours and by their bulky baggage-train than by active resistance. About 45,000 Prussian troops, 15,000 Austrians, 6,000 Hessians and 8,000 French emigrants took part in the campaign. The supreme command was in the hands of the Prussian field-marshal Duke Karl Wilhelm Ferdinand of Brunswick. Another Austrian army was stationed in Belgium and was also making preparations to join in the fighting.

The Austrian troops were experienced soldiers but the Prussian regiments were merely well-trained. Their tactics were those of the time of Frederick II and their headquarters, distinguished by the presence of King Frederick William II, followed the principle that victory in any campaign was mainly won by manoeuvres and not by fighting.

The French military command relied on troops of the line in the Northeast and East and on a number of untried volunteer battalions of the National Guard which had been raised as a precaution by the National Assembly in the autumn of 1791. By the beginning of the war, these forces had been organized as the Army of the North of 40,000 to 45,000 men, the Army of Metz of almost equal strength and the Army of the Rhine, likewise consisting of more than 40,000 troops. To a certain extent they were already organized in divisions, some of which consisted of all three types of units, but an efficient command structure was lacking. The Army of the North had tried—although in vain—to gain the strategic initiative in April and May 1792 but the other two formations contented themselves with observing the enemy from Sedan, Metz and Strasbourg.

At the outbreak of hostilities, the French forces were of low fighting power. Pro-Royalist commanders, a shortage of officers due to the emigration of many noblemen, poor discipline in many units, mistrust between patriotic lower ranks and their politically doubtful superiors and tension also between the regular troops and the volunteer battalions—known from their uniform as "white arses" and "blue arses"—initially prevented any vigorous action from being taken in the field. To be sure, the artillery was in excellent order and their guns, mostly four-pounders designed by Gribeauval, had lightweight carriages which made them more mobile. The infantry weapon, the 1777 model, was also the best gun of its type at the time and had a curved butt which allowed aimed shots to be fired at a distance of

The volunteer and line battalions echo the shouts of their commanders—"Vive la nation!" Scene from the battle of Valmy. Part of a lithograph by H. Bellangé (1833).

one hundred metres. Nevertheless, the stocks of firearms were by no means sufficient for the equipment of all the volunteer battalions and for replacements. There was a shortage of uniforms, ammunition and horses.

The Duke of Brunswick called a halt at Verdun to enable the baggage-train to catch up with the rest of his army and so that he could gather a reserve of supplies. This helped General Dumouriez, a prominent favourite of the Girondists, and in June still Minister of War at Paris, in his plan to take most of the Army of the North—which had been reorganized in the meantime—to the Argonne. He was aware that the forced march would probably reduce the number of soldiers at his disposal. At the same time, he ordered the Alsatian General Kellermann to join him with the Army of Metz.

When the Duke of Brunswick learned from his reconnaissance detachments that the passes through the Argonne were held by the French, he decided to make a detour to the North. His intention was first to establish a direct link with Verdun from the West and then to continue the march on Paris. He was convinced that even the fear of being outflanked would make the French commander withdraw from the passes.

In actual fact, Dumouriez did indeed consider such action but abandoned the idea again. If he were to withdraw, there was the possibility that his already exhausted army could no longer be kept intact and he consequently decided to defend the Argonne or, from the flank, to threaten the enemy forces as they marched towards the capital. Reinforced in mid-September to about 36,000 men by the arrival of Kellermann's troops who had been delayed by unfortunate circumstances, the main forces of the two armies occupied the low heights of Sainte-Menehould at the western edge of the Argonne.

Austrian troops succeeded in breaking through the only weakly defended northern passes and capturing Croix-au-Bois on the 12th of September. Following this, Brunswick advanced further to the Southeast with his remaining 34,000 men on the assumption that the French would soon withdraw. Instead of this, his vanguard surprised him on the 19th of September with the news that the enemy was obviously preparing for battle. On the advice of Frederick William II, the Prussian command decided to attack the French troops, who were not considered capable of much resistance. On account of the outflanking manoeuvre executed prior to this, the attack had to be launched in an

French volunteer battalions and troops of the line with their
command staff during the cannonade at the battle of Valmy.
Painting by Horace Vernet. Musée de Versailles

eastward direction, i.e., with a reversed front. Once again, the baggage-train had fallen behind and a lack of food, insufficient sleep and disease undermined the combat efficiency of the Prussian troops.

Following an indecisive artillery duel on the 19th of September in poor weather conditions, Dumouriez and Kellermann advanced towards the enemy as far as the heights of Valmy on the following day. They moved up their 56 guns and opened fire that morning but persistent drizzle prevented anything from being seen at the usual range of 1,200 metres. The Duke of Brunswick likewise undertook nothing more than the cannonade by his 40 guns in the course of the morning.

The mist lifted in the early afternoon but heavy artillery fire appeared to have had no visible effect on the French troops who were deployed in an extended semi-circle. Furthermore, it looked as if the terrain in front of them had been swamped. Frederick Engels considered that a "resolute advance" by the Prussians would have "certainly routed the French volunteers and demoralized regiments" if it had not been for the constant indecision of the allied command. At any rate, the duke countermanded the order to attack when his infantry, in the traditional line of battle had advanced no more than 200 paces. To be sure, some of the French troops faltered at the sight of the well-ordered Prussian ranks, especially when some of the ammunition waggons began to explode. However, their commanders succeeded in banishing the panic which was starting to appear by emotional appeals to their courage and patriotism. It is said that Kellermann waved his hat on the point of his sword and his battle-cry of "Vive la Nation!" echoed from one battalion to the next. The French troops stood their ground, the artillery vehemently continued its fire.

When the Prussians returned to their positions, Dumouriez and Kellermann decided not to counter-attack, the outcome of this probably appearing too doubtful for them. Consequently, the only action was a violent artillery duel until a shortage of ammunition and the renewed onset of rain forced the enemies to cease fire even before nightfall. Since most of the cannon balls fell on wet ground and had no effect, the losses on either side were limited to 200 to 300 dead and wounded.

Since the French remained in their positions on the following days, too, and the Prussians had exhausted their supplies of food, the duke was reluctantly given the authority by the king to negotiate with Dumouriez who allowed him to withdraw through Champagne at the end of September. Finally, by agreeing to surrender Verdun and Longwy, he ensured that the Prussians would be allowed to march back to the frontier unmolested. However, an epidemic of dysentery and a chronic shortage of food resulted in the loss of the tactical coherence of the Prussian forces and they reached their quarters on German soil in almost complete disorder whereas to the east of them the French Army of the Rhine marched into Mainz on the 21st of October and Dumouriez was able to direct the units, which were now available for their purposes, to the northern front where he won a glorious victory at Jemappes on the 6th of November against a smaller Austrian force and occupied the whole of Belgium.

Valmy was not a battle which was fought to the bitter end; the victory won by the French was not a tactical but a moral one, which was far more important. A national people's army, still in the early stages of being organized, had stood firm against the most illustrious mercenary regiments of the time. The invaders had been forced to abandon their dream of snatching King Louis and his "loyal subjects" from the claws of a "black rabble" of terrorists in the course of a military excursion to Paris. They had to admit that it would be no easy task to wear down this incomprehensible revolutionary power.

Goethe, an eye-witness to the event, summed up his impressions in the following terse sentence—and it does not matter whether he really wrote it on the evening after the battle or as a later recollection: "From here and today there begins a new epoch in the history of the world." The victors engraved these words of the "enemy" on the simple monument of Valmy.

The bourgeois French Republic proved victorious on the Continent in the first war of the Coalition against it—thanks, not least, to the Italian campaign of 1796/97 brilliantly fought by General Napoleon Bonaparte. Since the Directoire, which controlled the destiny of France from 1795 to 1799, considered it impossible, however, to defeat the sea-power of England in a similar frontal clash and to obtain a victorious peace in this manner, it attempted to strike at its old rival's most vulnerable point by threatening India as its most profitable colonial possession by establishing French power in Egypt. Bonaparte's somewhat reckless proposal to send an expeditionary force was favourably received and he was given the supreme command of the venture with the responsibility for its failure should this occur. There is the evidence of Talleyrand that an ulterior motive also played a part in this since, at the same time, it was an opportunity to occupy a somewhat too ambitious young commander and his most devoted fire-eaters in an area far removed from France before he became a disturbing factor in internal affairs.

It was naturally impossible to keep the extensive preparations in the spring of 1798 as secret as the presence of *The Sorrows of Werther* in the hand-luggage of the general. On the other hand, there was no reliable "leak" to outsiders of the destination of the seafarers. The surprise was practically complete when, on 2 July 1798 and in the course of the following night, French infantry without artillery support landed at the Egyptian port of Alexandria and immediately stormed it, only slight resistance being offered by its garrison on the derelict city walls. The first ships carrying the expeditionary army under the command of Bonaparte, who immediately prior to this had still been the commander of the forces assembled for the crossing of the English Channel, had left the port of Toulon on the 19th of May. His fleet was also joined by additional vessels from other French and Italian ports.

In all, 15 ships of the line and battleships, 11 frigates, 3 corvettes, 36 brigs and dispatch-boats and 300 troop ships set out. Most of the warships were obsolete vessels and some of them were used solely for the transportation of ammunition, food supplies and equipment. The troops embarked consisted of five infantry divisions of 4,500 men each, 3,000 gunners and 52 pieces of artillery and 2,800 dismounted cavalrymen. 700 horses were also taken for the artillery, baggage and staff requirements. The total numbers of officers and men must have been about 35,000, not including the ships' crews.

The island of Malta, which was ruled by the Knights of St. John, was occupied with hardly any resistance already on the 12th of June and a garrison left there. Unnoticed by the English Mediterranean squadron under Admiral Horatio Nelson, the French fleet then reached the Egyptian coast. Following the capture of Alexandria, the division of General Desaix set out for Cairo already on the 3rd of July, followed on the day after by Reynier's division. A Nile fleet was formed from ships of shallow draft and this set out upstream on the 5th of July. The main force, consisting of Kléber's, Menou's and Bon's divisions, started out on the 7th of July. The first clash occurred on the 10th of July but this did not halt the advance. The enemy did not choose to make any premeditated attack on the individual French divisions which were still strung out.

Since 1517, Egypt had been nominally subject to the suzerainty of the Ottoman Sultan but real power was in the hands of the Mamelukes who had become, in the course of the Middle Ages, the feudal warrior-class and dominated the indigenous population. By tradition, their numbers were maintained by boys bought or taken from outside Egypt who were then raised in the Islamic faith and trained as fanatical warriors. Instead of the Pasha, who was installed in Cairo by the Sultan but had no influence, it was Mameluke Beys who governed the individual provinces. By the end of the 18th century, Ibrahim Bey and Murad Bey were in almost complete control of the country.

Their army of irregulars consisted of not more than 10,000 horsemen but if the entire force had been assembled

at one spot the rest of the country would have been totally unprotected. For every Mameluke rider, there were three servants on average, whose duties were to reload the firearms during battle, to bring up fresh horses, to remove the dead and wounded from the battlefield and to guard the camp. These foot-soldiers were equipped only with relatively simple weapons and, for this reason alone, were of little military importance. The tactics of the Mamelukes were to rapidly ride up to the enemy, fire their guns and then fight with the scimitar. They were accordingly equipped with old flintlocks and pistols, scimitars and, in some cases, with lances as well but they wore no armour, such as a helmet or a cuirasse at all.

At the news that French troops had landed, 3,000 Mamelukes and then 10,000 foot-soldiers were sent to the North. It was only on the 13th of July that they tried to unsettle the enemy by a series of skirmishes near Kobrakit.

The advancing French divisions repulse the attack by the Mamelukes in the battle of the Pyramids. Painting by Lejeune (1806). Musée de Versailles

Since the French command had been unable to provide their still dismounted cavalry with horses, Bonaparte ordered his divisions to form large squares of about ten ranks deep on each side. The non-combatants took refuge in the centre of these improvised squares. These were the civilians from France who had accompanied the expedition, the horseless cavalry, the baggage-train and the staff officers. The field-guns were placed at the corners and between the individual battalions.

Nevertheless, there was no serious fighting on this day and the Mamelukes soon withdrew. A violent clash occurred on the Nile between the two flotillas, the French ships gaining an advantage. The expeditionary army was not bothered on its further march through the arid area. The soldiers let the desert sand run through their fingers and asked Bonaparte: "Is this perhaps the good land that you promised to every one of us?" It was 2 p.m. on the 21st of July, when the divisions, which had been on the march since 2 o'clock that morning, came upon the enemy who had assembled for battle to the west of the pyramids of Gizeh, not far from Cairo. The army of the Mamelukes numbered about 6,000 horsemen and—the figures quoted in the sources vary—between 12,000 and 20,000 foot-soldiers. The horsemen formed a loose front along the left bank of the Nile from Embabeh to Gizeh. The village of Embabeh on the right wing was used as a camp; it was fortified by redouts and protected by forty obsolete guns. The capital lay on the other side of the river.

Bonaparte again formed squares from the five divisions and continued the march in a checkerboard pattern of deployment, the right wing advancing more rapidly to the Southeast so as to seal in the Mamelukes and force them back to the Nile. Conscious of the historical setting, he told those of the soldiers within hearing, who were sweating in the heat of the African summer sun, that forty centuries were looking down on them from the tips of the pyramids. Compact groups of Mamelukes repeatedly rode fierce attacks against the corners of the French formations with the aim of breaking the enemy ranks. However, they were prevented from gaining even the slightest advantage from this

Simple contemporary depiction of the battle. Hand-coloured printed sheet. Musée Carnavalet, Paris

BATAILLE DES PYRAMIDES.

Combat scene showing the superior tactics of the French and the style of fighting of the Mamelukes whose antiquated weapons put them at a disadvantage in the battle of the Pyramids. Wood-engraving by Auguste Pontenier, 19th century.

by the superior artillery and small-arms fire and the extended bayonets of the French troops.

When the envelopment began to take shape at last, advance columns of the French left wing attacked the camp of Embabeh, stormed it after a brief struggle and captured all the cannon. Thus threatened from both flanks, the Mamelukes hurriedly withdrew over the Nile, most of them retreating upstream in the direction of Upper Egypt. By nine o'clock in the evening, the battle was over and the French troops were encamped before the very gates of Cairo. Their casualties were 260 seriously wounded while those of the Mamelukes and their foot-soldiers were 1,000 dead, many of whom had been drowned while crossing the Nile, and 2,000 wounded. On the 22nd of July, the French expeditionary force occupied Cairo without opposition.

When Bonaparte later commented that a victory was always good for something, this was certainly true of the battle of the pyramids which gave the expeditionary army full freedom of movement in Egypt and even allowed it to advance as far as Syria. However, the other part of that half-truth is also demonstrated by this. When Nelson, on the 1st of August, finally tracked down the French fleet which had so often eluded him, it lay unprotected at anchor in the roadstead of Aboukir. By sending it to the bottom of the sea in the battle that followed, he put an end to the strategic objective of the venture. Cut off from France, the expeditionary army was in a trap, a situation which could not be changed even by its subsequent victories over freshly landed Turkish forces at Aboukir (1799) and Heliopolis (1800). Finally, what was left of the army was brought back to France on English ships, in accordance with the terms of an agreement.

For Egypt, which was still at a mediaeval stage, this episode—marking the beginning of the end of Mameluke rule—proved to be the first gateway to a new age filled by the struggle for national independence.

When he heard more details of the outbreak of a second Coalition war and its effects on the situation in France, Bonaparte handed over the command to Kléber and returned alone to France in 1799 on a frigate. Once again he slipped through the enemy naval forces and reached Paris in sufficient time to lead a coup on the 18th of Brumaire against the five members of the Directoire, assuming control of the government as the "First Consul".

TRAFALGAR /1805

The Peace of Amiens, concluded by England and the French Republic in 1802 and based on a compromise, lasted barely a year. When war broke out again on 16 May 1803, the British Cabinet under William Pitt the Younger found itself without allies while Consul Napoleon Bonaparte could count on French "client" states from Holland to Italy and even on Bourbon Spain. These exceptional circumstances led Napoleon, who had been crowned emperor on 2 December 1804, now to begin serious preparations for invading the British Isles, a project which had occasionally been considered before. He had no difficulty in assembling a force in the camp of Boulogne for this purpose. Difficulties first arose when it came to planning the crossing of the Channel, in view of the massive maritime superiority of England.

At this time, England possessed some 115 to 120 ships of the line, about 100 frigates and approximately 300 corvettes and other small ships. The British Admiralty was in a position to raise a significant number of blockade squadrons and keep them as reserves. Thus it could form even other large fleets if necessary or reinforce the existing units without neglecting the defences of its own coasts.

Since the mutiny led by Richard Parker in 1797, the treatment of the ships' crews had improved, they were adequately fed and they received regular pay. The squadron commanders and the commanders of the ships enjoyed greater independence, which led to a considerably higher standard of combat efficiency in the fleet as a whole. It is true that the press-gangs continued to provide most of the recruits and that iron discipline was still maintained with the aid of the "cat o' nine tails" but at the same time care was taken that the seamen acquired a sailor's skills and that the naval officers attained high standards in navigational and tactical ability. The English naval guns had about three times the rate of fire of French or Spanish cannon and English warships were famous for their manoeuvrability.

In France, the naval fleet was still in the process of reconstruction. In 1805, it consisted of 43 ships of the line and a few dozen frigates and smaller ships which were stationed at Brest, Lorient, Rochefort and Toulon and had been blockaded there since 1804. The ships' crews, their officers, commanders and admirals had only limited nautical experience. It was a similar story in Spain which had more than 30 ships of the line—including some large vessels—but did not possess a hard-hitting fleet. Many Spanish officers owed their position to the protection they enjoyed; their tactical and nautical knowledge therefore left much to be desired. The Dutch fleet consisted of 20 ships of the line but nine of these were blockaded off Texel and did not take any active part in the events of 1805.

Since Napoleon knew only too well that the French naval forces were outmatched by the Royal Navy, his problem was to find a way of "enticing" the latter away from the Channel. For this purpose, he worked out a cunning strategy, involving many unknown factors, which recalls a cat-and-mouse game. In March 1805, Admiral Villeneuve was instructed to break out of Toulon and then, by simulating an attack on the Antilles, to lure across the Atlantic the English squadrons blockading Rochefort, Brest and the entrance to the Channel, thus taking them far away from the place where the decisive events would occur. He was to avoid any confrontation with the English ships and was to return home without delay by another route, then making a breakthrough to Rochefort and Brest and joining up with the squadrons there which were now free to put to sea. The naval forces assembled under the command of Admiral Ganteaume of Brest were then to gain control of the Channel "at least for one day" to allow the 2,000 troopships assembled by Napoleon to cross the stretch of water separating England from the Continent.

In the meantime, the British Admiralty kept its forces together and only ordered the Mediterranean Squadron under Nelson in May to keep a watch on Villeneuve, although in actual fact he never caught sight of the latter in the vast areas of the Atlantic. It was only after the French returned to European waters that the reinforced blockade squadron under Admiral Calder tracked down Villeneuve's fleet off Ferrol and fought an indecisive action against it on the 22nd of July off Cape Finisterre on the northwest tip of Spain. While the English ships guarding the Channel and maintaining the blockade had fresh supplies and were well-equipped, Villeneuve's vessels were in a lamentable condition after the long voyage to America. Some of his sailors were in a poor state of health owing to the lack of fresh water and food.

As a consequence of this, the French admiral did not believe he could break through to Rochefort or Brest without going on land first. He initially withdrew to Vigo, where he disembarked his sick sailors, and then proceeded to La Coruña and the neighbouring naval port of El Ferrol to obtain reinforcements from the French and Spanish

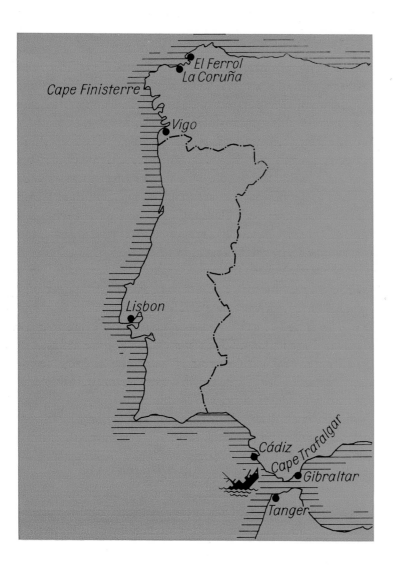

ships at anchor here. However, El Ferrol did not possess facilities either for overhauling and refitting the battle-weary vessels. Despite Napoleon's orders to the contrary and after he had failed to rendezvous with the squadron from Rochefort on the high seas, he decided to set sail on a southern course for Cádiz since this was the only place where he could get sufficient timber, lines, tar, gunpowder and other supplies of vital importance for him. On the 20th of August, he dropped anchor with his 29 ships of the line in the harbour of Cádiz. The numerically weaker blockade squadron under Admiral Collingwood had allowed him free access but had then immediately assumed its former position. Despite his lack of success, Villeneuve intended to set out from Cádiz for the Channel, join up with the Brest squadron and seek battle with the English fleet.

In the meantime, however, Napoleon had had to abandon his plan to invade England since the latter had succeeded in forging a Third Coalition against him with Austria, Russia, Sweden and Naples. On the 14th of September, the emperor instructed the admiral to sail to the Mediterranean to support the transfer of troops from France to Italy.

On the English side, Nelson, who had arrived in Portsmouth after his vain pursuit of Villeneuve across the Atlantic, was given the command of the squadrons lying off Cádiz which now numbered already 29 ships of the line. On arriving there on the 28th of September, he withdrew his forces by 50 sea-miles to persuade his adversary to venture out on the high seas since only in this manner could he be forced to join battle. Nelson stationed his frigates off Cádiz so that they could immediately signal the news, via ships of the line which were entrusted with this specific duty, when the enemy squadrons left port.

On the 10th of October, he drew up his plan of battle which, when they had approached the Franco-Spanish fleet, envisaged the division of his own squadrons into two lines which, sailing parallel to each other, were to attack the enemy line at right-angles and break through it. He thus exposed the leading ships to a great risk since, to begin with, the fire of the entire enemy line of battle would be concentrated on them. Nelson relied on the superior quality of his ships and himself took command of his left line while Collingwood headed the vessels on the right.

On the 19th of October, Villeneuve's fleet of 18 French and 15 Spanish ships of the line of greatly varying quality

Exchange of fire at close range between British and French ships in the battle of Trafalgar. Painting by William Turner (1775 to 1851). National Maritime Museum, London

began to leave Cádiz. A slight wind from west-north-west was blowing when they set course for the Strait of Gibraltar, without paying attention to the English frigates watching from the weather-side. It was only on the following day that the whole of the French and Spanish squadrons were on the high seas, whereupon Nelson immediately set sail for the northeast. It was in the early hours of 21 October 1805 that the two fleets sighted each other off Cape Trafalgar.

When the enemy appeared to leeward, Nelson decided to attack. Villeneuve realized that he could not avoid battle and at 8.30 a.m. ordered his vanguard on the weather-side, the ships sailing in three lines in the centre and the rearguard to put about immediately and to form a closed line of battle. In this way, he took account of the possibility of defeat and made provision for his ships to escape to the near Cádiz. The slight wind, the high swell, confusing signals and the fact that the Spanish admiral Gravina commanding the vanguard—which became the rearguard after putting about—was not bound to obey the tactical instructions of Villeneuve, complicated the turning manoeuvre and led to the break-up of the line-ahead formation.

At about 11 a.m., Nelson, who was steering an east-north course with his squadrons, had the order given to attack and at 11.40 a.m. issued the famous signal: "England expects every man to do his duty." At noon, the centre of the Franco-Spanish fleet opened fire as Collingwood prepared to break through the enemy line with the "Royal Sovereign"; at about 12.30, Nelson's flag-ship, the "Victory" likewise reached the enemy line and broke through it.

By 1.30 p.m., the battle had broken up into numerous individual actions between the vessels involved. On the Franco-Spanish side, there were 33 ships of the line, five frigates and two brigs, accounting for a tonnage of 62,000 tons in all, 2,870 cannon and 27,500 men while the English side numbered 27 ships of the line, 11 frigates and one schooner with a total tonnage of 54,200 tons, 2,230 cannon and 20,500 men. However, as a result of the surprise breakthrough, the better manoeuvrability and the superior rate of fire of the English ships, Nelson succeeded in obtaining a numerical superiority at the decisive moment. The resistance of the Franco-Spanish fleet remained unco-ordinated and the lack of initiative of the commanders of the vanguard and rearguard made it difficult for any effective assistance to be given to the hard-pressed centre. When Villeneuve issued the appropriate orders at 1.50 p.m., the outcome of the battle was already clear. The cannonades began to be heard less frequently at about 3 p.m. and by about 5 p.m. the battle was over.

The Allies lost 18 ships of the line, one of which sank immediately, the other 17 vessels being captured by the English. However, a strong wind which came up from south-south-west in the late evening and increased to hurricane force on the next day drove most of the prizes aground. They were either abandoned by the prize-crews and left to their fate or handed back to their old crews. Villeneuve himself was seriously wounded and taken prisoner. Of the Franco-Spanish squadrons only eleven ships in a scarcely seaworthy or battleworthy condition under Gravina, who was fatally wounded, were able to reach the protection afforded by the harbour of Cádiz.

In contrast to this, the English fleet did not lose a single vessel, even though half of the ships had been badly hit and were temporarily out of commission. Victory cost them 457 dead, 1,243 wounded and the death of Horatio Nelson who, at about 1.30 p.m. during the battle, was hit by the musket-balls of a sharpshooter firing from the fighting-top of the "Redoutable" and died from his wounds three hours later. Nelson's Column in Trafalgar Square in London was erected in his honour by his countrymen.

The battle had no effect on the outcome of the third Coalition War, which ended to Napoleon's advantage, and it did not even prevent the conquest of Naples. Nevertheless, by finally condemning the French Empire to helplessness in the naval sphere, it made England unassailable and gave it the endurance to wait until "Bony" had exhausted his strength on land. It established Great Britain's domination of the "seven seas" which, with all the consequences for its position as a first-rate power in the world, outlasted the century unopposed.

Naval battle of Trafalgar 1805. Painting by Samuel Drummond (1765–1844). National Maritime Museum, London

The two lines of the British Navy attack the Franco-Spanish squadrons sailing in line ahead at Trafalgar. Painting by George Chambers (1803–1840) after a study by Clarkson Stanfield (1793–1867). National Maritime Museum, London

AUSTERLITZ / 1805

The alliance persistently sought by the British Cabinet for the formation of a Third Coalition against France came into being in 1805: it was joined in April by Czar Alexander I of Russia and by Emperor Francis II of Austria in June. However, the opening of hostilities was delayed since the Austrians had to take account of the great distance which had to be covered by their Russian allies and they needed their support. It was only on the 2nd of September that they declared war on Bavaria, the ally of France, Ulm being captured on the 20th of that month.

On the same day, Napoleon completed the concentration of his troops and crossed the Rhine on the 26th of September. Already on the 20th of October, by a surprisingly rapid and wide-ranging movement which was screened by his cavalry, Napoleon succeeded in bringing powerful units up to the Danube, encircling an Austrian army under General Mack at Ulm and compelling it to surrender. More than 25,000 men were immediately taken prisoner, followed by thousands in the operations against the remnants of that army. This was Napoleon's first great military success as emperor, which was crowned a few weeks later by his victory at the battle of Austerlitz (Sladovec).

Since 1803, most of the French forces had been encamped along the north coast in readiness for the intended invasion of England. The opportunity was taken to reorganize the army which had been established during the Revolution and in the course of the first Coalition Wars. Napoleon reformed the divisions as units of approximately the same strength, each consisting of 14 to 16 infantry battalions and an artillery section. As the next-biggest permanent formations, he created the army corps, comprising two, three or five divisions. The cavalry and most of the artillery were partly subject to the orders of the corps commander as a cavalry division or a corps artillery reserve or—and this was usually the case—were organized as a cavalry or artillery reserve under its own independent command.

To begin with, six corps were formed which, together with the Guard and the cavalry and artillery reserve as the "Grande Armée" and consisting of 200,000 to 250,000 men, made up the nucleus of the French military forces. They were under the personal command of the emperor. In the following period, the other parts of the army in France, Italy and Germany were also reorganized as corps formations.

To improve the manoeuvrability of the field artillery, Napoleon greatly increased the numbers of the mounted artillery. In battle, this enabled them to be concentrated in batteries of up to a few dozen guns each. Their fire could be directed with devastating effect in the right direction to support the attack by the reserves who mostly consisted of the Guard or of grenadier battalions taken from the corps or even of one to two corps, depending on the circumstances. Practice with live rounds enabled the artillerymen to fire two rounds a minute instead of one, which was the case hitherto.

For the combat technique of the infantry, the inclusion of the battalion line in two ranks in skirmisher and column tactics was an important innovation. The rapid change from the column to the line and vice-versa gave great flexibility in infantry operations since the advantages of the column—a great power of penetration— and of skirmishing—skilful use of the terrain—were combined with the high firepower of the line. However, the infantry battalions no longer possessed any artillery of their own. On the other hand, every infantryman was supposed to fire two rounds a minute but this was only possible when the weather was dry and there was no wind since the flintlock guns were very sensitive to rain and wind.

The task of the cavalry was to carry out reconnaissance missions over a wide area, to mask the advance of their own troops, to attack breaches in the enemy line of battle and to resolutely pursue the defeated enemy. For this, the cavalry was organized as light and heavy divisions or brigades.

Some changes were also carried out within the Austrian forces. To be sure, the strategic backwardness of their aristocratic military command system still remained, this

being due, to a certain extent, to its dependence on the Court Council of War in Vienna. Nevertheless, their combat methods, and particularly those of the infantry, were gradually adapted to the new requirements within certain limits. In the course of a few years, young recruits took the place of the old soldiers who had been killed or invalided out of the army. There was no time to train these in the artificial and time-consuming forms of line tactics since they had to be sent as replacements to the troops in the field before very long. This was how a more or less radical change took place in the ranks of the ordinary soldiers. It was in accordance with this process when the Recruitment Law of 1802 put an end to lifelong military service, limiting it

Deployment of French troops in the battle of Austerlitz. Contemporary engraving by Basset in Paris.

to ten to twelve years and fixing the maximum age of soldiers at 40 years.

In parallel with this, the severe losses in the ranks of the officers could only be made up by the more frequent commissioning of young men from the middle and even lower middle-class whose training took place more in the field than in the garrisons. Younger officers—favoured by the different nature of the soldiers at their disposal—endeavoured to use mobile forms of warfare, despite the resistance of the old fossils who were their superior commanders.

On the other hand, the Russian army, in which line tactics had never been used in a consistent manner, entered the war of 1805 with hardly any change in its combat techniques. The infantry had already fought for a long time in the massed ranks of battalion columns, their bayonet attacks being prepared by a thin line of troops armed with flintlocks. The massed columns achieved a high degree of penetration in attack and were tough and stubborn in defence but their tight formations were an inviting target for enemy artillery fire. Their battle tactics called for the deployment of several large attacking columns from which the wings, the centre and the reserve were formed. The tactically independent assault columns were each assigned strong artillery units which maintained an effective fire.

General view of the battle of Austerlitz with attacking cavalry and approaching infantry in line order. Copperplate engraving by Carle Vernet. Armeemuseum der DDR, Dresden

In the organizational respect, the Russian army consisted of corps, divisions and brigades but these were not completely identical. In most cases, these units were made up of only one arm. It was a similar situation in the Austrian army and, although a start had been made in organizing divisions and brigades on the French pattern, there was only a superficial resemblance.

Since, in the discussions regarding a joint strategy for the war, the Russian and Austrian negotiators had overlooked the difference of ten days between the Gregorian calendar and the Julian calendar still in general use in Russia, the first Russian formation—despite an impressive performance on the march—only arrived at the River Inn after Mack had already surrendered. General Kutusov then withdrew in the direction of Vienna and afterwards to Olmütz where he intended to join up with the second formation. In the face of the French offensive which followed the Danube downstream, he offered continuing resistance and, in fact, achieved a partial measure of success.

Errors such as this by the local commanders and the movement of the main Austrian forces from Northern Italy, where they had been concentrated on false premises, to the Danube and especially the Prussian preparations for war compelled Napoleon to disperse his corps once again to take account of several operational directions and of his own operational line. Through the use of tricks of war, he was able to secure the crossings over the Danube at Vienna in an intact state after the capital itself had been occupied without resistance.

On the 20th of November, Napoleon was at Brünn (Brno) with only two corps and the Guard, the reserve cavalry under Marshal Murat advanced to Olmütz and

two other corps were one to two day's march away. The temporary inferiority of the main French army led the Allies, at the insistence of Czar Alexander, to go over to the offensive with their 85,000 men, although Kutusov advised against this. According to an Austrian plan, the French vanguard was to be cut off by a surprise movement and Napoleon's main army outflanked by a major manoeuvre, his flanks and rear being attacked and thrown back to the North. It was hoped that an encouraging success would induce the Prussians to enter the war, they were still undecided.

At the first news from his forward troops, Napoleon decided to await the attack in a favourable position since at this time he disposed of 50,000 men at the most. He assembled his forces to the southeast of Brünn and west of the village of Austerlitz on the heights of Sokolnitz and Schlapanitz which were separated by a valley from the plateau of Pratzen and represented an advantageous terrain for his purposes.

On the 1st December, his two corps had already taken up their position: the IVth corps under Marshal Soult formed the centre and the right wing, the Vth corps under

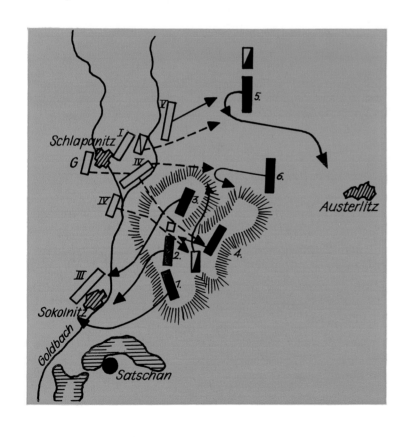

▰	Allies	
◪	Allied cavalry	
▱	Frenchmen	
◩	French cavalry	
⛰	plateau of Pratzen	

1.	Dokturov's Column	⎫ left wing
2.	Langeron's Column	⎬ Buxhouden
3.	Poshibitshevsky's Column	⎭
4.	Kollowrat's Column	centre
5.	Bagration's Column	right wing
6.	Reserve column (Russian Guard)	
I.	Bernadotte's Corps	
III.	Davout's Corps	
IV.	Soult's Corps	
V.	Lannes's Corps	
G	Guard	

Marshal Lannes the left wing. Each had a strength of three divisions and the Guard and the artillery and cavalry reserves were stationed behind the "seam" joining the two corps. In the evening, there also arrived the Ist corps under Marshal Bernadotte after a forced march and this force was deployed behind the centre. The right wing comprised one division only since it was Napoleon's intention to provoke an attack by the enemy against his right flank. When, however, the first battalions of the IIIrd corps under General Davout also arrived in the course of the night, the emperor assigned these to the right wing and brought the division of the IVth corps stationed there closer to the centre.

Kutusov organized his forces in five columns, three of which under Generals Dokturov, Langeron and Poshibitshevsky formed the left wing under the command of General Buxhouden; the centre was held by the column commanded by the Austrian general Kollowrat while on the right wing there was the column headed by General Ba-

gration. The Russian Guard under Grand Duke Constantine acted as the reserve column.

The left wing of the Allies began to move up the plateau of Pratzen already on the 1st of December. It was planned that on the following day it would march down into the valley in front of it and carry out its outflanking manoeuvre. The centre and the right wing continued their advance until they came up against the enemy line of battle. A battle was certainly expected but not in the immediate vicinity. When, in the night between the 1st and the 2nd of December, the French soldiers celebrated the anniversary of the crowning of Napoleon at innumerable bivouac fires, the Allies thought that this was only to conceal the withdrawal of the enemy to another position further westwards.

On the 2nd of December at about 6 a.m., the Russian and Austrian columns moved down into the valley in thick fog, without their commanders realizing that the enemy was not only on the heights opposite but had also received considerable reinforcements. As a result, the Austro-Russian outflanking wing, immediately after it had turned towards the heights of Sokolnitz, quite unexpectedly came upon the enemy who put up a very stubborn resistance. Once the first attacking columns of the Allies had left the plateau and started their outflanking movement and before the next column could begin to deploy for battle, Napoleon, at about 8 a.m., ordered the IVth corps, supported by the concentrated fire of the artillery reserve, to attack the enemy centre. It was at this moment that the morning sun broke through the dark wintry sky—hence the frequently quoted cry of the "sun of Austerlitz".

In advancing against the plateau, Soult came upon the Allied centre column which was taken completely by surprise, overwhelmed it so devastatingly that it retreated in complete disorder and then, swinging round to the right, attacked the assault columns of the enemy left wing in the flank and rear. The French Horse Guards followed but first of all went into action against the reserve column under Constantine which was preparing to counter-attack until the latter, likewise defeated, was forced to make a hasty withdrawal. The cavalry then supported the IVth corps in its successful thrust against the left wing of the Allies whose columns were still launching vigorous attacks against the stubbornly resisting IIIrd corps of Davout. When the French cuirassiers appeared in the rear, Buxhouden ordered his wing to withdraw. The retreat took place across the ponds of Satschan, the artillery had to be abandoned and very heavy losses were suffered.

In the meantime, the Vth corps on the French left wing and the cavalry reserve attacked the weaker column on the Allied right wing. Bagration nevertheless succeeded in escaping this danger and was able to withdraw from the battlefield in good order. He had vainly tried to establish contact with the supreme command which was not to be found anywhere.

By 2 p.m., the French army, of whose 73,000 men only 50,000 had actually taken part in the fighting at this time, was able to break through the battle order of the Allies, overcome their left wing and centre and throw back the right wing. Despite this, Kutusov succeeded in concentrating those parts of the left wing and centre, which had maintained a courageous resistance to the very last, on the roads to Austerlitz and Gödling and fought off all the energetic efforts of the enemy to pursue him.

In all, the "Battle of the Three Emperors" cost the French 2,000 dead and 7,000 wounded whereas the Allies lost 15,000 dead and wounded, 11,300 prisoners, 45 standards and 180 guns. These figures underline the magnitude of the French victory just as much as the request for peace on the following day, by the shaken Court at Vienna. This was signed in Pressburg (Bratislava) on the 26th of December and marked the end of the Third Coalition. Napoleon could now proceed with the crowning of his brothers and sisters and with the establishment of the Confederation of the Rhine. The Holy Roman Empire came to an ignominious end in 1806, at which time the emperor of the French was already preparing to defeat a Fourth Coalition, the theatre of war of which was to extend from Jena and Auerstedt to the Niemen after Prussia joined the coalition.

LEIPZIG / 1813

It was in 1812 that Napoleon finally went too far. He marched on Moscow without first being able to break the resistance of the Spanish people who were supported by English expeditionary forces. The eclipse of the "Grande Armée" in Russia encouraged Prussia to abandon its forced alliance with France and to change sides at the beginning of 1813, while Vienna, in expectation of a change in events, contented itself with an armed neutrality. The Austrians welcomed the truce concluded between the combatants on the 4th of June which included preliminary negotiations for peace. However, since the emperor of the French had to achieve success after success if he wanted to stay on the throne that he himself had created, he rejected the concessions demanded, which amounted to a political defeat, and, after the expiry of the truce on 17 August 1813, had to assume that Austria and Sweden would enter the war.

With the corps stationed along the lower reaches of the Elbe, he had about 427,000 men and 1,268 cannon at his disposal while the Allied forces numbered 512,000 men and 1,381 guns. The lesser numbers of the Napoleonic army were compensated by their integrated command-structure and the possession of the inner line, whereas a united and at the same time flexible leadership on the part of the Allies was complicated not only by unco-ordinated strategic methods but also by political differences.

Admittedly, after the catastrophe of 1812, Napoleon had been able to rapidly build up a new army with which he gained victories at Grossgörschen and Bautzen during the spring campaign but in neither of these actions had he been able to destroy the enemy forces. One reason for this was the reduced fighting strength of the French army. Through the withdrawal of forces from Spain, Italy, the Confederation of the Rhine and the interior of France, Napoleon certainly had enough experienced soldiers for the formation of a large number of units. Nevertheless, these were made up in part of recruits who had been press-ganged by the police and given only a minimum of training. Most of them were scarcely able to withstand the rigours of long marches and a battle. The hospitals were full of wounded soldiers and desertion was rife.

A shortage of horses made it necessary to reduce the numbers of the cavalry and also meant that their mounts had to be treated with care during the campaign which, in turn, led to a reduction in their tactical usefulness. Only the artillery achieved an increase in numbers and strength. With its great firepower, it was always the backbone of the Napoleonic army. During the truce, an improvement took place in this situation but the weaknesses mentioned were not entirely eliminated.

The Russian army, which had likewise not yet been able to make up completely for the losses suffered in 1812, received numerous reinforcements in the summer of 1813. Other reserves were on the march in the early autumn. The recollection of the victory won in the previous year without assistance gave confidence and moral strength to the Russian army. In particular, they now disposed of better weapons, due to the capture of many French arms, the availability of weapons of their own manufacture and deliveries of arms from England.

The Austrian army was faced with great difficulties. Although it had been able to overcome the effects of the defeat of 1809 and despite the improvement in the organization, combat techniques and hitting power of the army as a result of the military reforms carried out under Archduke Charles, there were still many deficiencies in their equipment. The reserves of men and weapons were still insufficient to bring all units up to full strength. This applied especially to the infantry; the cavalry and the numerically small but efficient artillery were in a very good state.

In comparison with its allies, the Prussian army certainly had fewer troops but in combat techniques, organization and morale it led the Sixth Coalition. Thoroughly reorganized and modernized by a reform under the patriot Scharnhorst, it had already displayed its mettle during the spring campaign.

The raising of a militia force in addition to the troops of the line had largely been completed and led to a visible increase in the number of combatants. However, it was only during the War of Liberation that the militia achieved sufficient striking power and discipline and at the beginning it suffered from deficiencies in equipment and had not been thoroughly trained. The use of co-ordinated column and line tactics and the combined deployment of artillery and infantry was characteristic of Prussian combat techniques.

Despite a great deal of friction, the Allies successfully implemented the strategy agreed at Gitschin, Trachenberg and Reichenbach: to approach the principal base of Napoleon on the Elbe by a concentric advance from the North, East and South without exposing any of their three armies —the main or Bohemian Army under Prince Schwarzenberg, the Silesian Army under General Blücher and the Northern Army under the former French marshal Bernadotte, now the Crown Prince of Sweden—to the danger of fighting a decisive battle by itself against the main forces of the enemy.

Conversely, Napoleon tried in vain to prevent them from approaching by destroying them one after another.

Infantry with bayonets fixed and cavalry attacks during the Battle of the Nations at Leipzig. Etching by F. A. Klein and C. Rahl, c. 1815.

His one victory at Dresden on the 27th of August could not make up for the series of defeats suffered by his marshals at Grossbeeren, Dennewitz, at the Katzbach, at Kulm and Wartenburg. He was finally forced to concentrate large forces in the surroundings of Leipzig and hoped, through the exploitation of the inner line which had already become a risky affair by this time, to defeat Schwarzenberg's main army by superior forces and then to deal with the Silesian and Northern armies which in the meantime were to be kept at a distance by smaller forces.

Only an overwhelming victory could help Napoleon in the position in which he now found himself. But he chose not to abandon the crossings over the Elbe by recalling the corps stationed there since, in the event of victory, he wanted to be able to pursue the enemy without delay in the direction of Berlin and Breslau. This meant—in addition to the troops in the already besieged fortresses of the Vistula and Oder—that several ten thousands of men, including

272 complete corps, still in Dresden, Torgau, Magdeburg and Hamburg were excluded from the decisive battle.

On the opposing side, the advance troops of the Silesian Army made the first contact with the main French army on the 13th of October after crossing the Elbe. On the 14th, after a vigorous reconnaissance of the latter at Liebertwolkwitz and Gülden Gossa to the southeast of Leipzig, there resulted the fiercest cavalry engagement of the autumn campaign in which 15,000 horsemen took part on either side, plus the infantry and artillery. After an action lasting seven hours, Murat, the King of Naples and the commander of the French cavalry reserve, was able to maintain the line taken up on the day before. At the same time, however, as a result of the bitter resistance of the enemy, it became evident to the Allies that they had to reckon with a major battle between the two main armies at Leipzig. After it had been found that the marshy terrain to the west of the city did not permit the deployment of large numbers of troops and since the Allied leaders were also worried that Napoleon, after a defeat, would be able to withdraw to the fortresses of the Elbe, it was decided that the main action of the battle should take place around the semi-circle between the southern, easterly and northern directions, only weak forces being deployed in the West.

In all, the Allies on the 16th of October disposed of 205,000 men and 918 guns. Of these, about 100,000 men and 460 guns were stationed east of the Pleisse, and about 30,000 men and 90 guns between the Pleisse and the Elster. Napoleon's forces numbered 190,000 troops and 690 guns, of these he deployed 138,000 men and 488 guns along the southern front, thus indicating his operational intentions.

The assault columns of both sides clashed along the line Liebertwolkwitz-Wachau-Markkleeberg on the morning of the 16th of October. Napoleon's forces achieved a tactical advantage and they not only repulsed the attacks by the Allies but also achieved significant advances. Despite this,

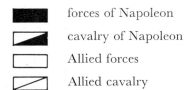

■	forces of Napoleon
◪	cavalry of Napoleon
▢	Allied forces
◨	Allied cavalry

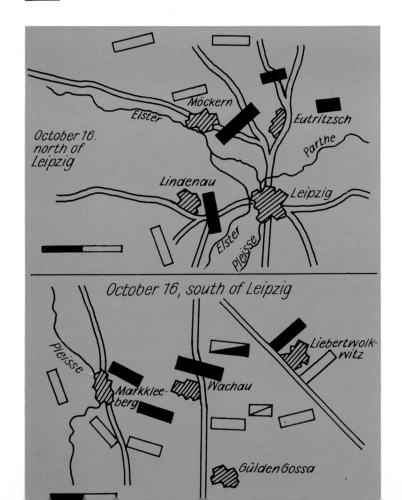

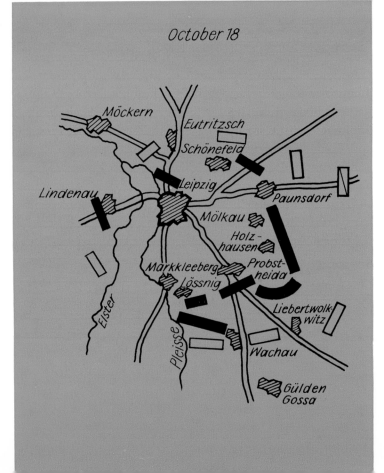

Napoleon hesitated and did not give the order to break through the enemy line of battle, although at mid-day it did not seem possible that the Allies could withstand another attack.

The emperor waited for the divisions from the north of Leipzig which had not yet arrived at Wachau, although they had received strict orders to make a forced march. Only when these reinforcements were at his disposal did Napoleon want to take decisive action. However, it was quite impossible for the corps of Marmont to comply with his orders since in the course of the morning it had been attacked by the Silesian Army at Möckern, tied down and ultimately defeated as well.

When the French counter-attack was finally launched during the afternoon in the direction of Wachau-Gülden

Storming of Leipzig by the Allies. Coloured aquatint etching by J. L. Rugendas from a drawing from nature by J. Wagner, *c.* 1820. Museum für Geschichte der Stadt Leipzig

Gossa, the Allies succeeded in halting it after bitter fighting. Together with the action fought at Möckern, this failure was the decisive event of the day. The Allies could reckon with fairly substantial reinforcements and with the approach of the Northern Army, whereas Napoleon had already deployed the whole of his forces in the first or second echelon of his line of battle and had to make immediate use of newly-arrived troops to keep open his line of retreat through Lindenau in the direction of Weissenfels.

There was no fighting on the 17th of October, which was a rainy Sunday. Both sides used the pause in hostilities for intensive preparations. Against all expectations, Napoleon did not decide already at this stage to begin a general retreat, although it was only possible for him to continue the battle in a defensive posture. For this purpose, he brought his corps closer to Leipzig in order to shorten his battle-line. He still had 160,000 men and 630 guns. The Allies, on the other hand, who had drawn up their forces in six columns, now had 305,000 men and 1,200 guns.

On the 18th of October, violent fighting broke out along the line Connewitz-Lössnig-Probstheida, Holzhausen-Mölkau and Paunsdorf-Schönefeld. For a time, the Allies were in a critical position, following French counter-attacks at Connewitz-Lössnig. Prince Schwarzenberg was obliged to bring up to the southern section the formation deployed to the west of Leipzig and thus remove the only barrier along the French line of retreat, even though further reinforcements were already approaching the battlefield. At Paunsdorf, the Saxon troops changed over to the Allies and other soldiers from the Confederation of the Rhine left the battlefield and set off for home. However, this desertion by small contingents did not have any appreciable effect on the course of the battle and there can be no question at all of "betrayal", although the Napoleonic legend attempted to make this a major reason for the defeat of its hero. It was only in the evening, when it became clear that the positions taken up could no longer be held, that Napoleon gave the order to retreat. Even before this, he had already sent out élite troops to secure the road from Lindenau to Weissenfels. The major part of his army set out in the direction of the Saale during the following night, a strong rearguard remaining behind to defend Leipzig and forcing the Allies to concentrate on the capture of the city. This is what they did, in fact. For the Allies, the battle could only be considered a political victory when Leipzig was in their hands and demonstrated to the rest of Europe the military catastrophe that had overtaken Napoleon. Consequently, their attention was focussed on the storming of the city and prevented them from organizing the energetic pursuit of the enemy already on the same day. This enabled the French troops to gain a head start.

The total losses of the Allies in the "Battle of the Nations" at Leipzig amounted to 53,600 men of whom 22,600 were Russians, 16,000 Prussians, 14,800 Austrians and 200 Swedes. In 1913 a victory monument, more massive than beautiful, with sculptures made by Metzner was dedicated to the memory of those who fought in the battle. This has since become the symbol of Leipzig. The king of Saxony, whose ancestor had placed his wager on the wrong horse, was a somewhat embarrassed participant at the ceremony.

The French army lost 73,000 men or more. Only 60,000 French soldiers were led back across the Rhine to France by Napoleon at the beginning of November after a last victory on German soil when he defeated the Bavarians, who had likewise changed over to the Allies, on the 30th of October at Hanau. This, too, was not of very much help. The imbalance between the forces of the two sides became so crass in 1814 that collaboration between the French Legitimists and the Allies, who had entered Paris in the meantime, forced the emperor, after a winter campaign which once again met with the greatest admiration from his adversary and attentive observer, von Clausewitz, to abdicate and settle on the island of Elba in enforced retirement.

Volunteer riflemen of a Prussian Infantry Guards regiment employed for reconnaissance. Lithograph made between 1840 and 1850. Armeemuseum der DDR, Dresden

Freiwillige Jäger des 1sten Garde-Regiments zu Fuß.

1815.

WATERLOO / 1815

When Napoleon fled from exile on Elba and landed on 1 March 1815 in Golfe Juan not far from Cannes, his assessment of the political situation in France was correct. A triumphal procession, lasting twenty days, took him to Paris but he was mistaken about the extent of the disagreements between the enemy powers concerning the distribution of the spoils at the Congress of Vienna. Their common fear of the "Corsican monster" was far greater and immediately united them again. Already on the 27th of March, he was designated an outlaw. They intended to raise a field army of 700,000 men along the Rhine, in Switzerland and in Italy by the end of June. Many of the troops recalled had to break off their march home to their own garrisons or rejoin the army since they had already been demobilized. This was especially the case in Russia and Austria whose armies had to cover the longest distances to the concentration areas.

Only Prussia had forces in the Rhineland which were rapidly put into the field and moved up into the Belgian part of the Low Countries. By mid-June, the operational army under Field-Marshal Blücher had grown to 113,000 men and 288 guns, organized in four army corps of approximately the same structure. At the same time, English troops were landed and these joined up with the Lowland army and German units from Hanover, Brunswick, Nassau and other parts of Germany, constituting an army of 93,000 men and 204 guns. The supreme command was assumed by the Duke of Wellington who had brilliantly led the victorious Spanish campaign in 1813.

Due to problems regarding supplies and accommodation and to safeguard the long frontiers, the two armies were at a considerable distance from each other. Blücher and Wellington certainly took steps to combine their forces without delay but they considered that a sudden offensive by Napoleon was out of the question and, furthermore, they were confident that they would receive prompt warning of this from their agents in Paris. In the meantime, the emperor was in a difficult situation. Since his return, he had pro-ceeded with rearmament but domestic considerations prevented him from taking drastic measures to raise the forces necessary at short notice for a major war against the Seventh Coalition. Instead of the minimum number of 800,000 men estimated as necessary by him, scarcely 500,000 had been raised by June and of these only 230,000 were ready for immediate service in the field due to a shortage of horses and weapons.

From these and in addition to a few fairly small armies which he assigned to the protection of the frontiers along the Upper Rhine, with Switzerland, Italy and Spain and the coasts, he organized the Northern Army with five corps, four cavalry corps and 300 guns. Admittedly, this army consisted of only 124,000 men but almost all of these were first-class troops and included many veterans who had quickly rejoined the colours as volunteers.

The fact that the two allied armies were widely separated from each other offered Napoleon a splendid opportunity to improve his difficult strategic position at a single stroke. He had to launch separate offensives against the inner lines of Blücher's and Wellington's armies and force them to withdraw as quickly as possible to their own bases: the English to the coast at Antwerp, the Prussians via Liège to the Rhine. He took no account of the fact that after a defeat the two enemy armies could amalgamate their forces by a concentric withdrawal. This was how the emperor, on the one hand, overestimated the internal disagreements within the Coalition and, on the other, underestimated the ability of the enemy troops and their commanders to recover from lost battles. Since he was under extreme pressure in terms of time, he was obliged to act without careful consideration of the potentials of either side and the intentions of the enemy.

Scottish infantry fighting in a square repulse a cavalry attack during the battle of Waterloo. Painting by Félix Philippoteaux (1874). Victoria and Albert Museum, London

Attack by Napoleon's Guard in battalion column against the British battle-line at Waterloo. Coloured lithograph, c. 1830.

On the 14th of June, Napoleon took the initiative and, with 78,000 men and 248 guns, crossed the frontier to the north of Beaumont and east of the Sambre. On the 16th, battle was already joined at Ligny, about 17 kilometres to the west of Namur, with the Prussian army commanded by Field-Marshal Blücher. This force consisted of 82,000 men and 216 guns and had not completed its deployment. In the course of violent local actions, the French troops succeeded in breaking the Prussian line of battle and forcing their adversary to make a hasty withdrawal. Thus the war of 1815 began with a victory by the Napoleonic army which lost 10,000 men whereas the Prussian losses during the battle and in the course of their retreat amounted to no less than 20,000. At the same time, a formation of 40,000 men

■ French infantry

◤ French cavalry

▭ Allied troops

◩ Allied cavalry

= French artillery

┄┄▶ direction of march of the Prussian army corps

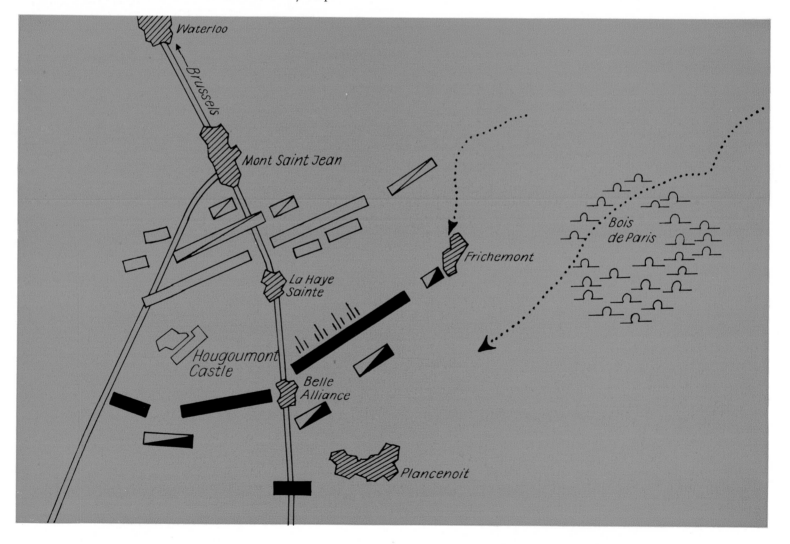

under Marshal Ney advanced along the road from Charleroi to Brussels and at Quatre-Bras, 12 kilometres to the north-west of Ligny, came upon units of hastily assembled Lowland troops who gradually fell back until the French advance was halted by the English battalions brought up by Wellington. Neither commander was able to intervene in the battle at Ligny although Wellington had promised Blücher his help and Ney was urgently directed by the emperor to attack the Prussian flank. The Ist corps under d'Erlon, which had already been separated from the rest of Ney's troops was recalled by the marshal, who was himself in difficulties, with the unfortunate result that in the end it did not take part in either battle, the course of which could have changed decisively by its intervention.

Wellington withdrew from his position on the following day and concentrated his forces on the road to Brussels south of Waterloo. He informed Blücher of his intention of joining battle on the next day, provided that the latter was ready to support him.

Napoleon, who regarded a hasty withdrawal by the beaten Prussians to Liège as certain, assigned two corps and strong cavalry forces to Marshal Grouchy on the 17th of June, the intention being that these should pursue the retreating enemy and prevent the Prussians from taking up new positions. The emperor himself marched to Quatre-Bras with the remaining troops where he joined up with Ney's forces. He regarded his next objective as a second battle against Wellington's troops who had slowly retreated until mid-day of the 17th of June. If he were able to rout Wellington, the road to Brussels would be open, strategic consequences of an occupation of Belgium seemed tremendous.

However, contrary to the expectations of Napoleon, the Prussian supreme command moved its army corps, which had been more or less re-formed, towards Wavre. When the communication arrived from Wellington, Blücher and Gneisenau, his Chief of Staff, agreed to support the Allies on the following day with three army corps and to leave only Tielemann's army corps at Wavre in order to hold back Grouchy. Realizing that a decisive battle could be fought against the enemy if a joint effort were made, the Prussian commanders abandoned their own rearward communications, whereby they took a great but justifiable risk.

Napoleon started out in the direction of Brussels already on the 17th of June. Rain complicated the progress of the artillery in particular and of the ammunition and supply waggons. In the evening, it was discovered by the vanguard that the enemy was no longer retreating.

On the 18th of June, the Anglo-Lowland army occupied a well-chosen and thoroughly reconnoitred position on the ridge of Mont Saint Jean on either side of the road to Brussels. Wellington, who had established his headquarters in the village of Waterloo to the northeast, had 69,000 men and 184 guns at his disposal and fought the battle in the traditional line with battalions and brigades, which was why his assault and penetration capability was less than that of the French. On the other hand, the infantry and artillery had a high rate of fire and thus possessed a very good defensive potential. For the repulse of cavalry attacks, they were very skilled at making a rapid change from the line to battalion squares. The Hanoverian and Brunswick troops, some of whom had already seen service in Spain, were of nearly the same calibre as the English forces.

They were opposed by the 72,000 men and 254 guns brought up by Napoleon from either side of Belle Alliance. Their deployment was hampered, however, by the sodden ground and it was only at about 11.30 a.m. that their left wing advanced with the intention of diverting the enemy. Instead of this, fierce fighting, lasting for an extremely long time, broke out around the park and chateau of Hougoumont. It was this which sapped the strength of the main part of the French army and this was then lacking when the main attack was launched.

Precisely at 1.30 p.m., a line of 80 guns opened fire on Wellington's centre, consisting of Lowland, English and Hanoverian troops. Four divisions, deployed as columns, advanced along the road to La Haye Sainte but, after an initial gain in territory, this movement failed in the face of enemy artillery and small-arms fire. Even an attempt made at 3.30 p.m. to at least capture La Haye Sainte, which was still being stubbornly defended, met with no success.

At 4 o'clock in the afternoon, Ney came to the conclusion that the enemy resistance was weakening and led an attack by 5,000 cavalry, penetrating deep into Wellington's positions. The steadfastness of the infantry, who immediately formed squares, and counter-attacks by English brigades drove back the French cavalry, heavy losses being suffered by both sides. Despite this, Ney repeated the attack with 9,000 horsemen who, on this occasion, were followed by

The climax of the battle of Waterloo with the Prussian thrust
against Napoleon's flank, the attack by the French Guards and
the change to the counter-attack by the British. Painting by William Allan (1843). Victoria and Albert Museum, London

infantry forces. Finally, at about 6 p.m. and after bitter fighting, La Haye Sainte was indeed captured, this representing a key tactical position. Wellington's position was now critical since he had already used all his reserves. At such a moment, it is quite possible that he spoke the oft-quoted words: "I wish it were night or that the Prussians would come," even if the exact utterance was subsequently stylized. In the meantime, the French attack flagged, granting him a respite. In view of the approach of the main Prussian forces reported to him, the English commander was able to transfer fresh troops from his left wing to the exhausted centre.

Even before 3 p.m., Napoleon must have realized his mistake when, instead of Grouchy, who was too far away and had been informed too late, Prussian troops emerged from the wood known as the Bois de Paris and appeared on his right flank at Plancenoit where the first fighting broke out at about 4.30. In the eventful actions that followed, the French certainly held off the Prussian attacks but Napoleon had to reinforce his hard-pressed right wing, which was falling back, by several battalions of the Young Guard forming his reserves in order to resist the pressure.

When the Prussian assault against the flank temporarily weakened and as Wellington had still not been able to consolidate his position, the emperor, now already with the courage of despair, gathered the mass of the Old Guard and all the other operational battalions after 7 p.m. for an attack on the heights of Mont Saint Jean. The assault launched by two columns against the enemy positions was halted by the fire of the defenders but it seemed that the resistance of the enemy was wavering. Shortly afterwards, however, two fresh Prussian corps made inroads in the position at Plancenoit and the artillery opened fire from Frichemont on the close-packed French ranks. Panic broke out in the badly hit French wing at 8 o'clock in the evening and the soldiers even asserted that Grouchy was a traitor and was now fighting against them since they had been assured that he would come yet he had failed to appear. The cry of "Everyone for himself!" spread throughout the entire army. When Wellington launched a counter-attack along the whole of the front, the French troops fled in disorder.

When the Old Guard was surrounded by the enemy and the demand for its surrender was made, Cambronne replied with a curt and soldierly "merde!". Three of its battalions, with Napoleon in their midst, were the last to withdraw in orderly squares from the battlefield at about 9 o'clock in the evening and covered the wild retreat. Following a personal discussion between Wellington and Blücher at Belle Alliance, the less weary Prussians under the command of Gneisenau took up the pursuit of the enemy but exhaustion put an end to this after 20 kilometres.

The French Northern Army lost 33,000 men—including 8,000 prisoners—and 200 guns while Wellington's forces lost 15,000 and the Prussians 7,000 troops.

The outcome of the battle hung on a thread on several occasions: If d'Erlon on the 16th of June had dealt with Blücher at Ligny instead of turning back; if Grouchy on the 17th had been able to find the Prussians straightaway or at least on the 18th had promptly followed the sound of gunfire and the urging of his subordinate commanders . . . ; if the ground had dried out sooner and allowed the battle to be opened in the early hours of the morning . . . Whatever might have happened and even if Napoleon had been able to win the Belgian campaign at Waterloo, he could never have won the war. His last adventure would have lasted somewhat longer than the "Hundred Days" with which it has gone down in history but with the international balance of power existing at the time it was inevitable that he would end up on this or that St. Helena. When he died there in 1821, his death for realist politicians was "news but not an event". A new epoch was about to be confronted with new tasks, new struggles and new symbols.

On the other hand, world literature on this and the other side of the Channel "fought" the battle of Waterloo time and again with a devotion which is characteristic of no other battle. What historian could hope to compete with the descriptions of Stendhal, Balzac, Victor Hugo, Dickens, Thackeray or Stefan Zweig? He would meet his Waterloo. . .

Last action of the Old Guard in the battle of Waterloo. Lithograph by H. Bellangé, *c.* 1830. Bibliothèque Nationale, Paris

H. Bellangé. 1849

Infantryman from the Peruvian Legion of the Patriotic Army.
Contemporary coloured lithograph. Museo del Ejército, Madrid

Plan of the battle of Ayacucho

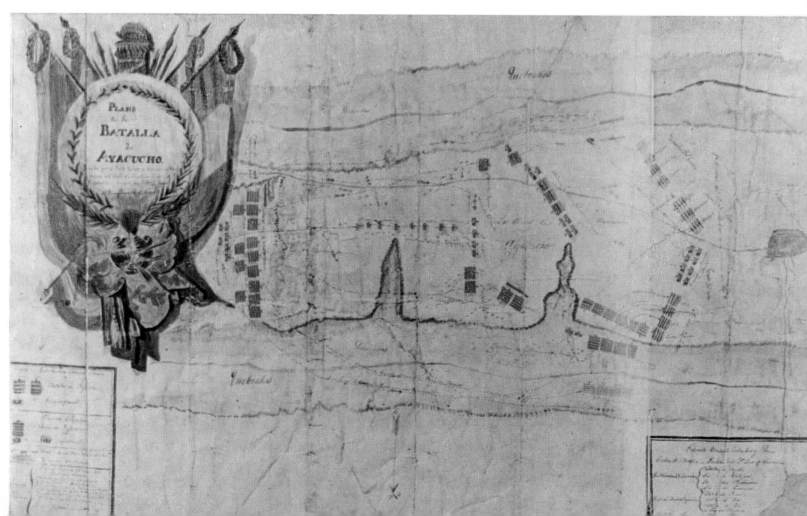

AYACUCHO / 1824

After Napoleon had forced the weak Spanish Bourbons to abdicate in 1808 and placed his brother Joseph on the Spanish throne, a national war broke out throughout the country and—with English support—vigorously attacked the French armies. In Cádiz, a provisional government was set up by a patriotic junta in opposition to that maintained in power by the French and an attempt was made to secure the loyalty of the administrations in the overseas possessions. However, the division of Spain into two camps and the political, military and economic weakness which resulted from this brought the crisis in its colonies in Central and South America, which had already been smouldering for a long time, to a head.

A series of local uprisings culminated in a continental revolution which started in Caracas, "the cradle of Liberty", on 19 May 1810. The political and military leadership of the War of Independence which lasted until 1826 was, with a few exceptions such as Mexico between 1810 and 1815, in the hands of the Creole aristocracy, the outstanding personalities of which included Simón Bolívar y Ponte (1783 to 1830) and José de San Martín (1778–1850).

Ferdinand VII of the House of Bourbon, whose absolute power in Spain was restored in 1814 after the expulsion of the French, sent an expeditionary army under General Pablo Morillo to the coast of Venezuela in 1815. The military superiority of the experienced Spanish troops of the line, struggles between the fractions within the patriotic party and, at the beginning, disappointing support from the lower classes of the people led to the almost complete collapse of the revolution. Only the La Plata district with the centre of Buenos Aires and a few scattered outposts still maintained a successful resistance.

However, a second phase of the War of Independence began in 1816. By the beginning of 1819, the patriots under Bolívar, who assumed the title of honour of "El Libertador", had again brought large areas of Venezuela under their control and in May crossed the Andes in the direction of Columbia. The Royalists here were defeated in the battle of Boyacá on the 7th of August, their resistance in Venezuela finally collapsing after the battle of Carabobo on 24 June 1821. Bolívar now sent an army under Antonio José de Sucre (1795–1830) to the Audiencia district of Quito (Ecuador) and it was this force which inflicted a strategic defeat on the enemy at the foot of the volcano known as Pichincha on 24 May 1822.

In the South, San Martín crossed the Andes from Argentina and joined forces with the Chilean patriot Bernardo O'Higgins. In the battles of Chacabuco (12 February 1817) and Maipú (5 April 1818), not only was the way to Chile cleared but also that to Peru at the same time. A fleet under the command of Lord Cochrane brought most of these forces to the Peruvian port of Pisco in August 1820 and the "Liberator of the South" marched into the capital, Lima, on 12 July 1821. However, the Spanish viceroy, José de Serna, succeeded in avoiding a battle and withdrew into the hinterland with all his troops.

Bolívar and the more conservative San Martín met in Guayaquil on 26 and 27 July 1822. The plan to unite both armies under a single command and completely liberate Spain's last bastion—the viceroyalty of Peru—proved unacceptable and, since the two strategists were unable to come to an agreement, San Martín resigned from all his positions and left Bolívar in sole control.

Although the Spanish Royalist faction, after the overthrow in 1823 of the revolution in Spain which had resulted from the uprising led by Riego in 1820, was split by violent differences of opinion between the Liberals and the advocates of absolutism, Bolívar was initially unable to derive any direct advantage from this. After overcoming very severe geographical and climatic obstacles, the army commanded by Bolívar and Sucre gradually moved forward into the highlands. In the "silent" battle of Junín on 6 August 1824, the patriots, in a man-to-man struggle, defeated a royal army under General Canterac. Not a single shot was fired in the 45 minutes that the action lasted and the battle was won by the sabres of the superior cavalry.

Bolívar marched to the coast with some of his troops to anticipate a possible breakthrough by La Serna. The remaining forces under Sucre remained at the site of the action but initially were not permitted by the supreme commander to engage in any fighting. Only after Bolívar had overcome his reluctance was Sucre allowed to seek a confrontation with the enemy. The delay in joining battle was now due to the Royalists who sought to evade any clash. The troops of the patriotic forces were well-rested, had received reinforcements who had joined the movement in Peru and were well-equipped with supplies. Since the battle of Junín their morale had been very high. This was not affected by the loss of their rearguard which was ambushed at Corpahuayco on the 3rd of December. La Serna, for his part, was well aware of the historical significance of the coming confrontation and made every effort to gain the military superiority necessary by concentrating his forces.

The two sides took up their positions in the pampa of Ayacucho on the 7th and 8th of December, 1824. The name of this place in the Quechuan language means "dead corner" and recalls a massacre from the period of the Conquista, the Spanish colonial conquest.

The first skirmishes between patrols occurred already on the 8th of December. It was characteristic of the often unconventional practices of Sucre and his general Córdoba that in the following night they had all the musicians in their army suddenly play a serenade for the Spaniards, this "serenata" being combined with violent small-arms fire and causing considerable confusion on the other side.

The site of the battlefield in the eastern Cordilleras was 3,600 metres above sea-level—a slightly sloping plateau at the foot of Condorcanquí mountain, broken up by hills in the West and delimited by abrupt gorges in the East. It measured about 1,200 metres from East to West and between 600 and 800 metres from North to South.

Sucre's "United Army for the Liberation of Peru" was in the eastern part, not far from the spot known as Quinua, and could march towards Huamanga at any time. The Royalists took up their position on the rugged slopes of the Condorcanquí so that they could make full use of their artillery. The fateful tactical disadvantage of this deployment was that it was impossible to make a rapid descent nor could the cavalry spread out on a massive scale; there was practically no line of retreat. A washed-out waterless river-bed with occasional steep banks ran through the no man's land and through the centres of the forces on either side.

On the morning of the 9th of December, under a cloudless sky, 5,780 patriots faced 9,310—or, according to Spanish sources, 7,936—Royalists. However, the latter were largely Peruvians—Indios—recruited by force or even former prisoners-of-war who had been persuaded to change sides. The number of Spaniards, almost entirely officers and NCO's, did not exceed 500. The weapons on both sides resembled those of the Napoleonic Wars but there were far fewer cannon. The relatively low number of combatants gives an indication of the particular difficulties of warfare in remote colonial areas.

The army commanded by Lieut. General José Canterac, the chief of the Viceroyal General Staff, consisted of three infantry divisions and two cavalry brigades; it also had 14 cannon. The "vanguard division" under General Jerónimo Valdés together with four battalions, three squadrons of hussars and four mountain-guns was stationed on the advanced right wing at the foot of Condorcanquí. The 1st Division, commanded by General Juan Antonio Monet and consisting of five battalions, occupied the centre while General Alejandro González Villalobos with the five battalions of the 2nd Division and three squadrons formed the left wing. The viceroy with the small élite unit of the "Halberdiers of the King" took up a position on the right wing immediately behind Valdés's division. On the other hand, Canterac's headquarters and reserves—ten cavalry squadrons and seven guns—were placed behind the seam between Monet's and Villalobos's divisions and this subsequently complicated the co-ordination between the two command-centres to an exceptional degree. The three divisions, whose artillery was concentrated on the two wings, formed a slightly curved semi-circle. The tactical plan called for an initial advance from the wings, where gorges prevented the enemy from being able to retreat. The decisive assault was to be launched from the centre as a breakthrough.

The "United Army for the Liberation of Peru" was made up of three infantry divisions and eight cavalry squadrons. After the setback of Corpahuayco, they still had one complete cannon of their original two and this was in the charge of Lieut.-Colonel Fuentes. The left wing was covered by the 1st Division under General La Mar, consisting of the Peruvian Legion, three battalions of partisans—partly

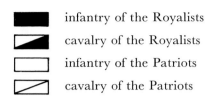

infantry of the Royalists

cavalry of the Royalists

infantry of the Patriots

cavalry of the Patriots

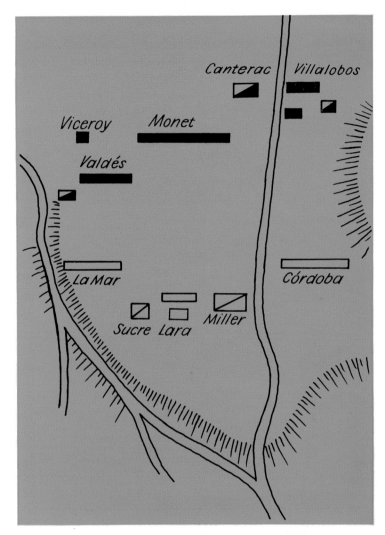

mestizos and Indians—known as the "Montoneros" under Marcelino Carreno. The right wing was occupied by the four Columbian battalions of the 3rd Division led by General Córdoba.

There was no centre as such. Five squadrons—Columbian grenadiers and hussars and grenadiers from San Martín's Andes Army—under Brigade-General William Miller, an experienced English soldier, were drawn up slightly behind but in close proximity to Córdoba while Sucre held the 2nd Division under the Columbian general Jacinto Lara in reserve to the left of Miller. The headquarters, with squadrons of "hussars from Junín", was between Lara and La Mar and allowed the supreme commander to operate without restriction in any direction.

Before the battle began, he acceded to the wish of some of his officers who walked into the area separating the two armies and shouted a last greeting to their friends, former comrades and even relations on the other side. Sucre then rode along the front on a chestnut stallion and roused his soldiers in Napoleonic manner: "You accompanied me in Quito, were victorious in Pichincha, brought freedom to Columbia! Today you are in Ayacucho at my side. You will be victorious here, too, bringing liberation for Peru and thus ensuring the independence of America for all time!"

The battle, which has been described in no less than nine detailed reports—some contradictory—by participants from both sides, began at 10 a.m. The Spanish left wing under Villalobos moved forward against Córdoba's divi-

General view of the battle of Ayacucho with the attack by the Volunteers' Battalions of the patriots.

sion. Since the artillery did not come into action to the extent anticipated fighting broke out at close quarters on either side. The outcome hung in the balance but it became apparent that the Royalists had unexpectedly suffered heavier losses. On the other hand, the right wing under Valdés, with systematic artillery and cavalry support, succeeded in forcing back the lines of La Mar's division and gaining ground. At this moment, when the flank attack by the Royalists was proving successful on at least one side, Sucre brought up some of his reserves to the threatened section, enabling La Mar to stabilize his line, although he was unable to repulse the enemy entirely.

From Canterac's viewpoint, there was a particularly serious deterioration in the situation of Villalobos's division since the guns there had not been moved up into the position envisaged so that a major factor in the plan of battle could no longer be exploited. Instead of utilizing the tactical advantages achieved by Valdés for a breakthrough or even an encirclement, he ordered the centre to move forward so as to relieve Villalobos in particular and at the same time destroy the cohesion of the enemy divisions. However, before Monet's division could deploy for an attack, it had to cross the deep trenches which resulted in its lines becoming unduly extended. In the course of this difficult manoeuvre, it was counter-attacked by the patriotic forces. Sucre gave the order for General Miller's cavalry, which had been waiting in readiness, to proceed to the attack and, at the same time, Córdoba's division moved forward against the left flank of the enemy. At the moment that the counter-attack was launched, General Córdoba shot his horse to symbolize to his soldiers that there was no going back now. The slogan was now "Forward with victorious step!" As a result of this attack and with the advance of further cavalry units, the full initiative was regained on both wings. Canterac in person now led his reserves in support of Valdés and his division but the battle had already taken an irrevocable turn. Miller's cavalry and Córdoba's infantrymen drove the enemy further back against the mountain slopes. La Serna vainly tried to re-form his fleeing troops. By about 1 p.m., the battle was over. Spain's last army of any importance on the American continent had ceased to exist.

The pursuit of the defeated enemy lasted until the evening. Not a few of those who escaped capture lost their lives in the thunderstorm which followed during the night. The viceroy and sixty generals and senior officers had to hand over their swords. More than a thousand soldiers were taken prisoner and more than 2,500 small-arms and the entire artillery captured. 2,109 dead—1,800 Royalists and 309 patriots, were left on the field of battle.

Simón Bolívar paid tribute to the services rendered by Sucre in the final defeat of Spanish rule by appointing him "Grand Marshal of Ayacucho".

The capitulation signed by Canterac on the 10th of December ordered the unconditional surrender of all the garrisons on the territory of the Viceroyalty. This instruction was disobeyed only by two centres of resistance. In Southern Peru, General Olañeta established a terrorist regime loyal to King Ferdinand and the second Spanish restoration. He suffered a crushing defeat at the hands of Sucre on 2 April 1825 at Tumusla and, on the 6th of August, Southern Peru became officially known as Bolivia in honour of Bolívar. Sucre, whose name is still borne by the capital, became its first president.

The commandant of the Peruvian port of Callao, Brigade-General José Ramón Rodil, likewise refused to surrender with the words: "Let those surrender who allow themselves to be beaten! Not I!" Simón Bolívar replied to this with the thread of a merciless strategy of destruction against the "rebels". Callao nevertheless held out for a year and twenty days before the last 400 Royalists, "looking like ghosts", laid down their weapons on 23 January 1826.

Of its American imperium, Spain retained—until the end of the century—only the islands of Cuba and Puerto Rico. On the mainland, the victorious War of Independence brought forth a new configuration of states which, in many respects, inherited a fateful legacy from their colonial past. On the other hand, it was one of their notable characteristics that they seldom resorted to war as a continuation of their policies with other means.

SOLFERINO / 1859

The Holy Alliance formed in 1815 by the rulers of Europe to deal with attempts to topple thrones gradually lost its cohesions in the period that followed. Nevertheless, peace between the Great Powers was outwardly maintained until the Revolution 1848/49 brought new factors into play. Napoleon III, who had seized the crown of France in 1852, hoped that "glorious deeds" would make people forget the loss of their Republican liberties. In association with England, he made use of the smouldering oriental question, to achieve supremacy on the Continent at the expense of Russia as a result of the Crimean War (1853–1856). In the same manner, he simulated an interest in the right to national self-determination to snatch Italy from the oppressive Austrian yoke. In 1858, he concluded an agreement with Piedmont-Sardinia, which, by itself, had been defeated by the army of Field-Marshal Radetzky at Custozza in 1848 and at Novara in 1849, and, more or less unexpectedly, declared war on Emperor Francis Joseph I in the spring of 1859.

In accordance with the trend of the time, Austria had extended conscription to all sections of the population in 1848/49 but the more prosperous classes could still purchase exemption and provide a substitute. In principle, the period of active military service lasted eight years but the permanent financial difficulties of the Monarchy reduced this in actual practice to two to three years, the soldiers being allowed home leave for the rest of the time. With the exception of the 2nd Army in Italy, the Austrian units were consequently at a low strength which limited their military effectiveness. Although the peacetime strength of the army was 334,000 men on paper and could theoretically be brought up to 674,000 in the event of war, only about 240,000 men were under arms at any one time.

The Hapsburg policy of national suppression did not allow the corps to be permanently stationed in their recruitment areas. This always caused delays in mobilization. If war broke out, Austria could only gradually put its forces into the field and only after some considerable time could they appear in the theatre of war at maximum strength.

The Ministry of War had begun to re-equip the infantry with the Lorenz muzzle-loader rifle in 1856. Lack of money and a low production capability meant that by 1859 only the troops of the line in the 2nd Army were in possession of the new weapon. The reinforcements sent to Northern Italy and the reservists and troops recalled from leave were hurriedly equipped with the Lorenz gun but not given any thorough training with it. The tactical requirements resulting from the greater range were likewise left to the discretion of the individual commanders.

Nevertheless, the Court and the Army Command believed that the Lorenz weapon enabled the Austrians to outfight the French and Piedmontese troops. As a result, they neglected the urgently necessary replacement of the obsolete artillery guns by muzzle-loaders with rifled bores although this weapon was far superior, merely by its great range, to the smooth-bore gun.

No change was made in the combat formations. The commanders still adhered to the traditional tactics of retaining strong reserves and safeguarding the flanks by separate detachments. This reduced the firepower and penetration capability of the front whereas in most cases in combat it was precisely a question of exploiting all the firepower available.

The French army was likewise based on conscription and substitution. The period of active service was six years (two of which were usually spent on leave) followed by one year with the reserve. Due to the use of substitution, the army contained a large number of long-serving soldiers which certainly increased its reliability from the viewpoint of internal affairs. On the other hand, it also meant that there was a lack of trained reserves since not enough soldiers were discharged every year and not enough recruits called up. Although the veterans who had completed several periods of service displayed great élan in battle, they proved to be less suitable for rapid and tiring marches.

The army administration had made a start with the introduction of the Minié-type muzzle-loading rifle and

rifled-bore muzzle-loading artillery gun. Whereas the re-equipment of the artillery had almost been completed by 1859, only the Corps of Guards and the rifle battalions had been fitted out with the Minié gun. Bearing in mind the greater range of the Austrian Lorenz rifle, Napoleon III advised his infantry to run under the enemy fire and attack with the bayonet.

A promising start to the campaign was made by the French and the Piedmontese. Master of the Ordnance Gyulai, the commander of the 2nd Austrian Army, regarded the battle of Magenta on 4 June 1859 as lost even before it had reached a critical point. He evacuated Lombardy and

Austrian cavalry attack against the vigorous resistance of the French infantry in the battle of Solferino. Painting, attributed to Anton Strassgschwandter. Heeresgeschichtliches Museum, Vienna

Milan and withdrew his corps to the left bank of the Chiese. The French Supreme Command under Napoleon III likewise failed to deploy all its forces at Magenta. Surprised by the easy and unexpected success, it advanced only hesitatingly to the Chiese, the advance guard reaching the river on the 18th of June.

In the meantime, the Austrian reinforcements had been mobilized and had arrived in the area. Francis Joseph himself took command with Master of the Ordnance Hess as his chief of staff. In addition to the 2nd Army with four corps, a 1st Army was established with three corps. Three other corps were stationed to the north and south to protect the flanks of the main army. The levels of command between the Imperial headquarters and the two army commands were not clearly defined. Since the emperor, whose military abilities were no better than average, received advice from every possible quarter, consistent leadership was lacking. Moltke, the chief of the Prussian General Staff described this situation as follows: "Let a commander be surrounded with a number of independent men, the greater their numbers, the more exalted, the more intelligent they are, the worse it is. Now he heeds the advice of one, now that of another; he carries out what is basically a reasonable action up to a certain point, then an even more reasonable one in another direction, after which he recog-

nizes the certainly justified objections of a third and the remedy proposed by a fourth, so it can be wagered by a hundred to one that with perhaps perfectly well-motivated measures he will lose his campaign."

Francis Joseph and Hess decided do withdraw the corps of the 2nd Army which were still between the Chiese and the Mincio to the "fortress square", as it was termed. When both were then assembled east of the Mincio on the 21st of June, other advisers persuaded them to change over to the other bank once more and to take the offensive. A cavalry detachment had reconnoitred the other bank of the river, to be sure, and had noted the presence of powerful enemy forces but had not been able to find out anything about their intentions.

The Mincio was crossed on the 23rd of June. The two armies were assigned only three bridges for their main forces and only a few roads for their further advance. The corps

■	Austrian corps
◪	Austrian cavalry divisions
▭	French corps
◩	French cavalry divisions
▭ s	Sardinian-Piedmontese divisions
▬	railway-line
⚑	Austrian army commands

consequently marched one behind the other which must have been a tremendous hindrance to their rapid deployment for battle. On the evening of the 23rd of June, the vanguard reached the line Guidizzolo—Solferino—Pozzolengo. A further advance was planned for the 24th. The Austrian Supreme Command did not expect a battle on this side of the Chiese. Reports that the enemy had already crossed the river were discounted as inaccurate or not important.

Napoleon III, who did not wish to endanger the reputation for generalship implied by his name, did indeed halt at the Chiese at first, unsure of what action he should take. However, most of his troops crossed the river on the 21st of June and on the 22nd the Ist, IInd and IVth Corps, the Guard and the three Piedmontese divisions joined up on the left bank of the Chiese along the line Carpenedolo—Castiglione. Only the IIIrd Corps, which was following the main army as a reserve, was still on the right bank of the river. A rest was planned for the 23rd of June, the intention being to continue the march towards the Mincio on the

24th. From a balloon specially sent up for this purpose, the main command received vague reports on the 23rd of June about Austrian troop movements in the direction of Solferino but these were interpreted only as the deployment of detachments protecting the flanks. A renewed advance by the whole of the enemy army was not expected and it was assumed that the next battle was more likely to occur only east of the Mincio.

Since the French troops had been given a hot meal in the evening and, apart from this, were provided with tinned food so that the time-consuming cooking of food in camp was not necessary, they were ready to move off already by 2 a.m. on the 24th of June. Despite the reports from the balloon, the Supreme Command had failed to send out the cavalry to reconnoitre the area in a thorough manner. Nevertheless, the corps were each assigned separate roads so that rapid deployment was possible. The first contact with the Austrian vanguard was made between 3 and 4 a.m. to the southwest of Solferino. Only when fairly powerful formations became involved in the action were reports sent to the two headquarters but these did not present a clear picture.

Napoleon was the first to realize that a battle was about to develop. He ordered the centre, consisting of the Ist and IInd Corps and the Guard, to attack in the direction of Solferino and take possession of the heights there. The right wing with the IVth Corps, supported by the following IIIrd Corps, was to advance to Guidizzolo and tie down the Austrian troops there. The Piedmontese divisions advancing on the left wing were instructed to outflank the enemy to the south of Lake Garda. The artillery reserve was ordered to take their guns to the Campo di Medole.

It was only after long hesitation that the Austrian headquarters made up its mind to order the 1st Army on the left wing to attack and defeat the enemy reported to the west of Guidizzolo and then to advance against the flank of the main enemy force moving in the direction of Solferino. By then, the 2nd Army, forming the Austrian centre, had to be in control of the heights of Solferino. The task assigned to the right wing, which consisted of only one corps, was merely to hold the section between the centre and Lake Garda. All corps were ordered to stop the preparation of the meal which was still in progress, to get ready for combat and to absorb the vanguard troops who were already in action. As a result, most of the soldiers had to go into battle with an empty stomach. In the course of the morning, it was also found that the artillery could not compete with the long range of the French guns and could therefore only give support to their infantry at close quarters.

The battle came as a surprise for both sides. The Austrian headquarters and its two army commands failed completely. They were unable to gain a clear picture of what was happening nor were they able to lead their troops in a concentrated manner. The Austrian troops entered the battle one detachment after another, were given no artillery support in most cases and, after suffering severe losses, began to fall back already in the afternoon.

The 1st Army proved itself to be incapable of carrying out the mission assigned to it. Instead of defeating the enemy, it was itself obliged to withdraw to the Mincio.

Between 2 and 3 p.m., the main French forces, supported by the 80 guns on the Campo di Medole, stormed the heights of Solferino and captured the actual village. Having sustained heavy losses, the 2nd Austrian army likewise began to withdraw. Francis Joseph's headquarters acknowledged defeat and ordered their troops to withdraw across the Mincio. Only the right wing under Benedek—which had no effect on the outcome of the battle—maintained its ground against all the frontal attacks of the Piedmontese divisions.

Without any real determination, the victors changed over to the pursuit of the defeated army. Like the two Austrian armies, the allied forces had suffered severe losses and it was first a question of finding replacements for these. Between 160,000 and 170,000 men had taken part in the fighting on either side; about 15 per cent of the other ranks and 25 per cent of the officers were lost in the battle. This shows that Solferino was one of the bloodiest battles in the history of modern warfare. The lasting impression made on the Swiss Henri Dunant by the misery of the many wounded led him to found the "Red Cross" in 1864.

The two monarchs lost no time in concluding peace in order to anticipate the possible intervention of Prussia. Austria's hegemony in Italy was at an end but Napoleon III was likewise not satisfied with the results of his victory. To be sure, France gained Savoy and Nice but a fiery national uprising from the Po to Sicily prevented the emperor from acting as an arbitrator in a divided Italy, a position which he had reserved for himself, and led to the emergence of a national state under a central government. This claimed the status of an independent Great Power and soon demanded papal Rome as well—to the defence of which a French division was summoned!

The battle came as a surprise for both sides. The Austrian headquarters and its two army commands failed completely. They were unable to gain a clear picture of what was happening nor were they able to lead their troops in a concentrated manner. The Austrian troops entered the battle one detachment after another, were given no artillery support in most cases and, after suffering severe losses, began to fall back already in the afternoon.

The 1st Army proved itself to be incapable of carrying out the mission assigned to it. Instead of defeating the enemy, it was itself obliged to withdraw to the Mincio.

GETTYSBURG/1863

The election victory in 1860 of Abraham Lincoln, the Presidential candidate of the Republican Party, heralded to the delighted citizens, farmers and workers of the United States of America the end of the long political domination of the slave-owning "plantation barons". The losers, on the other hand, did not hesitate to withdraw from the Union the Southern states under their control and to form their own confederation. The Federal Government contested their right to "secession" and in 1861 accepted the military challenge by the rebels. This was the beginning of a civil war lasting four years between the North and the South.

Neither the Unionists nor the Secessionists were able to achieve a resounding success in the first two years. Nevertheless, the Southern states reached the limits of their potential in 1863 when they had 350,000 men under arms—six per cent of the white population. In contrast to this, the Federal Government was easily able to raise an army of 600,000 men on account of the much greater population of the North. Whereas the supreme command of the Confederates organized their regiments only temporarily as divisions and corps, those on the Union side formed part of permanent divisions and 23 numbered corps. Their weakness was that new recruits were not assigned to existing units but to new regiments.

In the winter of 1862/63, important military decisions were taken by the administration of President Lincoln. They concerned the raising of more effective cavalry forces with the aim of putting an end to the dangerous raids of the Confederate cavalry and of themselves carrying on long-range reconnaissance; general conscription was introduced, at first with the right of substitution, later without this; provision was made for the arming of the Negro population in specially organized regiments and divisions. Improvements were constantly achieved in the equipment and material support of the armed forces thanks to the highly developed industry of the Northern states.

The improvised militia armies of 1861 and even the armed forces of 1862 were mainly equipped with small arms from Europe. Due to the re-equipment with rifles there, large stocks of mostly smooth-bore muzzle-loaders were available for purchase but the variety of different models caused difficulties in the field. This is why the factories specially built for the purpose accelerated the manufacture of firearms whose high quality resulted from the use of industrialized production methods. It is true that most of these weapons were muzzle-loaders with rifled barrels but breech-loading field-guns and rifles were also produced. Even repeaters and rapid-fire guns, such as the legendary "Henry Stutzen" and simple machine-guns were part of the production programme.

Civil inventions were used on a wide scale for military purposes—balloons for artillery observation, the telegraph and especially the railways. Troop movements, the supply of weapons and ammunition and the removal of the wounded and prisoners of war were handled by the new means of transportation. Construction gangs extended the rail network, built junctions and handling facilities and rapidly repaired the damage caused by the enemy cavalry. Bridges and roads were built which were notable engineering achievements.

To keep up with the North, the Southern states likewise equipped their army with rifles. Since they did not have the industrial base for manufacturing their own weapons, they had to rely on imports. As a result of the blockade by the Union fleet which became more effective with every year, this supply became less and less which in turn resulted in high prices being paid for goods brought through the blockade. The Southern states were also either incapable of exploiting technical progress in other spheres or unable to utilize it to the extent required by the demands of war. An expansion of the rail system was out of the question and the lines already in service proved extremely vulnerable once the Union as well was able to send mobile cavalry units behind the enemy lines.

Only in the art of military leadership did the Southern states maintain their advantage: in the concentrated use of

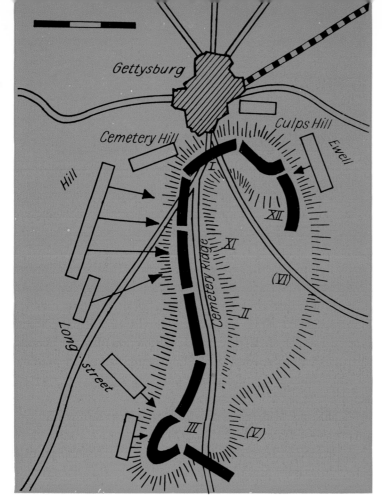

troops at points of strategic importance and in the determination with which operations were mounted. The standard of training of their field army was superior to that of the Union army, which suffered from a severe shortage of trained military personnel. The leaders of the Union still continued to employ their forces in a scattered manner and hesitated when it was a question of major operations. There was also too little mutual support and co-ordination beween their armies. Nevertheless, all these shortcomings were compensated by the fact that the troops outgrew their original militia character without losing the features of a democratic national army and their increasing military experience helped to overcome tactical weaknesses.

By reason of the predominant use of muzzle-loaders on both sides, the principal combat-formation was the serried battalion or company column. In combat, they could nevertheless rapidly take up lines of fire and the assault column likewise advanced in fairly loose formation. Wide use was made of trenches by the infantry who, in this manner, increased their defensive power. Artillery was employed on a massive scale in close tactical co-ordination with the infantry. The reconnaissance of the vast areas where fighting was in progress and long-distance raids were characteristic of the cavalry. They were given support by mounted artillery units to raise their operational tactical potential.

It was not possible to establish a unified front over a distance of some 4,000 kilometres. The alternating theatres of war in Texas, along the lower reaches of the Mississippi, along the Tennessee, in the Alleghenies and in Virginia were only loosely connected with each other, if at all. The main forces of the two armies were concentrated, however, in the relatively narrow area of the Northeast between the two capitals of Washington and Richmond on the Potomac, the river which formed the frontier.

With the battle of Chancellorsville from the 2nd to the 5th of May 1863, the attempt by the Potomac Army under General Hooker on the right bank of the Rappahannock failed to defeat the main forces of the Confederates under General Robert E. Lee. Their defeat cost the Union troops 17,000 casualties while Lee's army lost only 12,000 men.

Hooker withdrew across the river and his opponent concluded that the time was right to launch an offensive on the territory of the Union.

However, with his 75,000 men and 172 guns, Lee did not succeed in making a surprise invasion of Pennsylvania along the upper reaches of the Rappahannock. Already on the 8th and 9th of June, Union cavalry observed powerful Confederate forces marching towards the North. Hooker followed them with the Potomac Army, comprising seven corps with 90,000 men and 220 guns, with the intention of outflanking them. However, the Government forced him to dispatch units in different directions to cover various positions, thus breaking up the cohesion of his army and, on the 28th of June, it even replaced him by General Meade since it was not satisfied with his leadership.

Most of Lee's cavalry under the famous cavalry leader Stuart, far in advance of the rest of his army, began a raid on Baltimore and Washington. As a result, Lee had no accurate information about the movements of the enemy. At the end of June, he concentrated three powerful corps, which were likewise tending to move apart, in the direction of the road-junction of Gettysburg. The first clash with Union cavalry took place west of here on the 30th of June. For the following day, Lee ordered Hill's corps to carry out a forced reconnaissance in the direction of Gettysburg.

Limbering up of Union guns and the attack by Confederate infantry on the positions of the Union troops during the battle of Gettysburg. Part of the panorama by Dominique Philippoteaux. National Military Park, Gettysburg

Although it was not the intention of either commander, this developed into a battle involving the main forces of both sides.

In the meantime, the Ist Corps of the Union had likewise reached Gettysburg and joined up with Buford's cavalry. After being reinforced by the XIth Corps, it considered itself strong enough to defend the town on the 1st of July. However, at about 3 p.m. and under the severe pressure of Early's Confederate division on their northeast flank, the two units were obliged to carry out a precipitate withdrawal and evacuate Gettysburg. They lost half of their men, 5,000 of whom were taken captive. Defensive

positions were hurriedly dug by the survivors at Cemetery Hill, to the south of the town. The Secessionists, who on this day were still numerically superior with their 30,000 men and 90 guns, preferred not to develop their initial success straightaway since Lee did not know for certain the position of the main enemy forces.

On the following day, the IInd, IIIrd and XIIth Corps of the Union army took up a position on the elevated terrain extending over Culp's Hill, Cemetery Hill and Cemetery Ridge to the south of Gettysburg; the Vth and VIth Corps were still marching towards the battlefield. It was only at about 4 o'clock in the afternoon—as the result of differences

Field positions, exploiting the natural features of the terrain, in the battle of Gettysburg. Documentary photo

An amputation in a field hospital of the Unionists during the battle of Gettysburg. Documentary photo

The battlefield of Gettysburg after the withdrawal of the Confederate army. Documentary photo

of opinion between the corps commanders—that the Confederates, whose three corps had arrived in the meantime, attacked the Unionist IIIrd Corps with the Confederate right wing under General Longstreet after preliminary artillery fire, forcing it back to the Vth Corps just arriving on the scene. The unco-ordinated attempt of the corps in the centre, a whole two hours later, to break through the Unionist centre, had no effect as a whole, despite local successes. An attack launched from the North likewise produced no tangible result.

After the unsatisfying course of the actions up to this point, Lee ordered a massive attack against the Unionist centre for the 3rd of July, exploiting the territory won on the previous day. Before this took place, however, a surprise attack was made that morning from the East against the Unionist right wing. Despite all the efforts made, the XIIth Corps stood firm and when the first detachments of Stuart's cavalry arrived at last they were too tired to bring about a change in the situation at this stage.

At about 1 p.m., Lee's 150 guns opened up, this being answered immediately by Meade's artillery. At three o'clock, Longstreet launched his massed attack—which has incorrectly gone down in American history as "Pickett's Charge" —against the stone wall of the defenders, 15,000 men taking part in this. Attacks and counter-attacks over 1,200 metres of open terrain led to bloody hand-to-hand fighting. The Unionist artillery took an active part in the action by shelling the enemy troop-concentrations and their flanks as they advanced and the only Confederate assault-group which, on the right wing of the attack, succeeded in reaching Cemetery Ridge, could not be reinforced. Finally, the attack by the Secessionists collapsed in the face of the fire by the defenders and, although badly hit, they withdrew in good order to their original positions.

On the following day, neither side made any effort to resume the battle. It was only in the night of the 5th of July that Lee, who had lost 20,000 men, started out on the retreat to Virginia. Meade, who had suffered no less than 23,000 casualties, was content to observe the enemy withdrawal from a respectful distance.

Even today, opinions vary as to whether Gettysburg was a tactical draw, a successfully repulsed attack or a defeat for Lee. Either way, this battle—together with the capture at the same time of Vicksburg on the Mississippi by General Grant, splitting the territory of the Confederation—marked the turning point of the war.

Lee fought this battle with the political aim of threatening Washington and thus inducing the European powers to establish diplomatic relations with the rebels and strengthening the position of those "Copperheads" in Congress who advocated peace based on a compromise. The result showed that the Southern states no longer had the strength to deliver a decisive blow against the Union and consequently had the opposite effect. After losing the initiative, the Confederates were condemned to passive resistance and it was only a question of time before they had to lay down their arms. Time was entirely on the side of the industrial North which represented the logic historical progress in this epoch.

In his Gettysburg Address of 19 November 1863 at Cemetery Hill for those slain in the battle, Lincoln correctly understood this and advocated a radical interpretation of a broad American democracy in the bourgeois sense. He did not live to see the end of the Civil War: as one of its last victims, he died on 15 April 1865, at the hand of the assassin, William Booth, five days after the surrender of General Robert E. Lee.

KÖNIGGRÄTZ (Sadowa)/1866

In June 1866, Prussian-Austrian dualism split the German Confederation which had been restored with much effort after the Revolution of 1848/49. The two powers had fought a joint war against Denmark for Schleswig-Holstein as late as 1864 in order that the spoils should not be enjoyed by one side alone and to gain the support of public opinion which was concerned about national unity. However, relying on its military strength, the Prussian government under Otto von Bismarck—which was also faced with an internal constitutional conflict—used the crisis to solve the German question to its advantage in June 1866. Saxony, Bavaria and four other states of the German Confederation joined Austria, but the kingdom of Italy declared war on the latter, the intention being to liberate Venetia from Austrian rule. To be sure, the Italians were immediately defeated, right at the beginning, at Custozza on 24 June 1866 but the Southern railway, which had just been completed, was only able to transport the Austrian troops which were now available to the North at a time when the events there had already been decided.

Between the 26th and 29th of June, the individual corps of the Austrian Northern Army and its Saxon allies, who had withdrawn to Bohemia, suffered several defeats; only the Xth Corps won a victory over the Prussian Ist Army Corps at Trautenau on the 27th of June. Master of the Ordnance Benedek withdrew the shaken Imperial and Saxon forces to the heights northwest of the fortress of Königgrätz (Hradec Králové) behind the Bistritza on the 1st of July.

The Austrian military chiefs had learnt something from the war lost in 1859. An extreme form of shock tactics was introduced using serried battalions formed up in columns and dispensing with aimed small-arms fire to a large extent, and the artillery was re-equipped with rifled-bore muzzle-loaders. However, many of the old military weaknesses were rooted in the backward social and political conditions of the Monarchy and survived despite all the efforts to reform the military system. This included, above all, the disregard by the leading members of the military hierarchy of the need to carry out practical military training in peace time and to apply the principles of military theory to generalship in times of war. It is true that there were frequent discussions of the experience gained from the last campaign in Italy of the shortcomings in the activities of the military command but insufficient account was taken of this. The General Staff, which was fully responsible both for the strategic preparation of the war and for the direction of the operations was not organized along modern lines. The relations between the commanders in the field and the Chief of Staff were still largely those of the Napoleonic style of leadership.

The Prussian army was based on the principle of general conscription. The negative elements which had accumulated in the system over the years were largely eliminated by a re-organization carried out at the beginning of the 1860's. The infantry were equipped with the needle-gun, the most advanced type of rifle, and great importance was attached to rifle training and the handling of weapons. However, the conservative thinking of the generals prevented the adoption of a combat formation in keeping with the features of the breech-loading gun although numerous proposals were made in this connection. Only with reference to the basic formation was a start made with the use of the company line and column, together with the battalion line and column. At this time, a start was made with the re-equipment of the artillery with the breech-loading field-gun of cast steel. By 1866, only the Guards and one or two artillery regiments had been fitted out with the new guns, most batteries still being equipped with the smooth-bore muzzle-loader.

From 1864, the General Staff had sole responsibility for planning the initial deployment of the troops and for the determination of the operational objectives. In addition to the full utilization—for the first time—of the railways for mobilization and for bringing units to strategic points, a significant innovation was the march technique along a wide-ranging front developed by Helmuth von Moltke, the

Chief of the General Staff. The fact that the older territorial troops had left the active army helped to raise the marching speed and the principles of leadership of the General Staff enabled all units to be concentrated for battle within one day despite the widely spaced approach-march.

Following the victories won along the Upper Elbe and at the Iser, the three Prussian armies moved towards each other at Königinhof until they could be co-ordinated as a single operational entity. They lost contact with the enemy, however, and it was only on the 2nd of July 1866 that cavalry units on reconnaissance discovered that enemy forces had taken up positions on the other side of the Bistritza. Although their exact strength was not known and it was assumed that these were only strong rearguard units cover-

ing the withdrawal of Benedek's main army to the fortress of Olmütz, the Prussian command decided to attack.

It feared, however, that when faced with a frontal attack by superior Prussian forces the enemy would immediately withdraw across the Elbe to Pardubitz. Consequently, Moltke deployed his armies so that they could join up on the battlefield after a separate approach. The Ist Army of Prince Frederick Charles with the IInd, IIIrd and IVth Army Corps and a cavalry corps were instructed to mount an attack across the Bistritza and for the time being tie down the enemy forces occupying the heights. In the meantime, the IInd Army of the Crown Prince Frederick William with the Ist, Vth and VIth Army Corps and the Guards were to make a detour around the right flank of the enemy and cut it off from the crossings over the Elbe. Finally, the numerically much smaller Elbe Army was instructed to encircle the enemy left wing. Only after the encirclement of the enemy on both sides had been established was the 1st Army to go over to the attack with all the resources at its disposal.

In the transmission of these orders, it became apparent that the telegraph line laid between the headquarters and the army command centres was out of order. It was only long after midnight that ordnance officers brought Moltke's instructions, resulting in a considerable loss of time for the two armies on the wings.

After the serious losses in the battles along the frontier, Benedek scarcely dared to hope that a favourable end to the war was still possible and was perplexed by the situation. He would have preferred to make an immediate retreat but he was not able to bring the bulk of his supporting units over the bridges across the Elbe at Königgrätz in sufficient time. His cavalry was unable to provide him with re-

liable information about the enemy and his probable intentions. Consequently, on the 2nd of July Benedek still assumed that an enemy attack was not to be expected on the following day either. However, so as not to be surprised, he deployed the assembled corps in a curve opening to the rear in preparation for a defensive battle.

Battery positions were built and the artillery assigned definite lines of fire. The bridges over the marshy valley of the Bistritza were destroyed, making the Austrian front on the heights behind it practically unassailable. The right wing was held by the IInd and IVth Corps, the centre by the IIIrd and Xth and the left wing by the Saxon army. Benedek formed the reserve from the Ist, VIth and VIIIth Corps and from the cavalry. In view of the advantages of his position, he became increasingly more confident that he could fight a good defensive action against the Prussians and then withdraw without hindrance from them.

In all, the Northern Army still disposed of more than 206,000 men and 650 guns. The Lorenz muzzle-loading rifles of the infantry were inferior to the needle-guns of the Prussians but Benedek hoped to make up for this by closely co-ordinating his infantry tactics with those of his artillery which were equipped with rifled-bore muzzle-loaders-

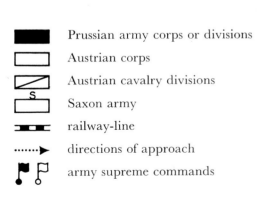

Prussian army corps or divisions

Austrian corps

Austrian cavalry divisions

Saxon army

railway-line

directions of approach

army supreme commands

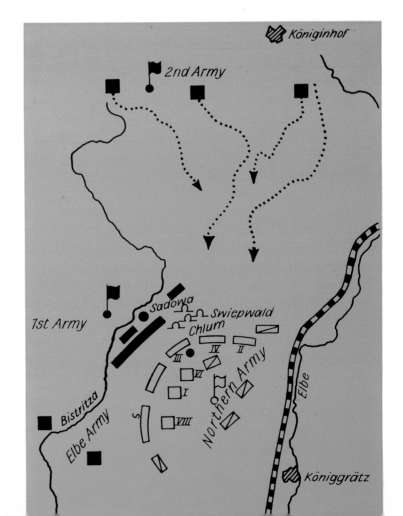

Prussian infantry, advancing in battalion column and under artillery fire across the Bistritza, and the Prussian headquarters during the battle of Königgrätz. Lithograph by Friedrich Kaiser and F. Hartwich, *c.* 1870.

Rest, good food and intensive preparations for the battle helped to restore the self-confidence of the troops after their defeats in previous actions.

On the Prussian side, the 1st Army had 85,000 men, the 2nd 97,000 and the Elbe Army 39,000. In all, they had 702 guns at their disposal. The first attack was launched across the Bistritza in the early hours of the 3rd of July by two army corps of the army of Prince Frederick Charles. It proved impossible to advance against the strongly fortified heights and it was only on the left wing that anything was achieved, Swiepwald wood being occupied. The attacking troops did, however, draw the entire attention of the enemy to the Bistritza front. The two Austrian corps forming the right wing left the front facing north, although they had not been instructed to do this, and swung round towards Swiepwald wood.

Since the Prussian infantry, which had been given practically no artillery support, had suffered severe losses and had even withdrawn to some extent, Benedek saw the moment coming when he could counter-attack. He was not aware that only a part of Frederick Charles's army had

been under fire and that it still had strong reserves. Before Benedek could give the order to attack, however, reports reached him about the approach of more Prussian troops from the North. With great difficulty, he managed to extricate the two corps on the wing, which had already been badly mauled, from the fighting for Swiepwald wood and return them to their old positions on either side of Chlum.

The crown prince's army was held up by the marshy approaches and as a result its arrival on the battlefield was delayed. However, instead of immediately outflanking the enemy, his army corps fought their way to the hard-pressed left flank of the 1st Army, establishing a tactical link with it at about 2 p.m. Bitter fighting took place for possession of the heights of Chlum. Instead of leading them to a victorious counter-attack, Benedek was forced to throw his reserves, one after another, into the battle on his right wing. Despite repeated Austrian counter-attacks, Chlum finally remained in Prussian hands. After destroying the enemy corps fighting here, the army of the crown prince forced its way irresistably into the rear of the Austrian forces holding the Bistritza heights.

The Elbe Army had also failed to encircle the enemy left wing and, instead of this, had launched a frontal attack against the Saxons. Fierce fighting took place here for several hours without either side gaining an advantage until in the afternoon, at about three o'clock, the Saxons were obliged to retreat.

Once his right wing had disintegrated and withdrawn from the battlefield, Benedek ordered the still undefeated corps in the centre at 4 p.m. to fall back to the bridges across the Elbe. The Prussian supreme command noticed the enemy movement and ordered its troops to make every effort to prevent the enemy from executing a disciplined retreat. The massed Prussian cavalry were held up, however, by the selfless courage of Austrian squadrons. A line of 180 field-guns which had been deployed in the meantime stopped any further advance by the Prussians. Since the Prussian units had also got mixed up with each other, a general order to halt was issued. Admittedly, the vanquished were able to withdraw without hindrance from their adversary but it was in a chaotic state that they crossed the Elbe and re-formed as well as they could on the other bank.

It was only while the battle was in progress that the Prussian supreme command realized that the whole of the

Northern Army was in action. Not enough room had been allowed in the encircling manoeuvre for this event. Through this and the endeavours of the two armies on the wings to join up with the 1st Army fighting in the centre, Moltke was unable to implement his intention of cutting off the enemy from his lines of retreat and destroying him. Despite this, the Prussians won a devastating victory, suffering only 9,000 casualties against the 43,000 Austrians killed, wounded or taken prisoner.

Once more, the needle-gun had reaped a terrible harvest, although not on the same scale as in the previous actions, owing to the skilful use made of the Austrian artillery and the renunciation of the suicidal assault tactics. The fighting strength of the Northern Army was broken for some time to come, although the Prussian army was itself in no position to make an immediate pursuit and first had to rest and re-form.

Disorderly withdrawal of the defeated Northern Army across the bridges at Königgrätz. Lithograph by Friedrich Kaiser, *c.* 1870. Heeresgeschichtliches Museum, Vienna

However, no further battle was fought. Neither from the military nor from the political viewpoint was it Prussia's wish to wage a war of destruction against a power which—when handled carefully—could prove a useful ally for the future. In addition, Bismarck had to hurry with the conclusion of peace in order to prevent diplomatic "mediation" being offered by France and welcomed by Austria. The peace treaty did not call on the Danube Monarchy to yield any of its territory but did allow Prussia to annex Hanover, the Electorate of Hesse, Hesse-Nassau, Frankfort and, of course, the subject of the dispute—Schleswig-Holstein. In 1867, it assumed the leadership of the newly-established North German Confederation.

GRAVELOTTE - ST. PRIVAT /1870

The Franco-Prussian War of 1870/71 was a logical continuation of the policy adopted by Prussia in 1866 of "unifying the Reich from the top downward" and without Austria. Following the defeat of the Hapsburgs in Vienna, it was now the time for military force to be used in eliminating the opposition of Napoleon III, who regarded himself as the guarantor of the "Main line" (i.e., the River Main), to such a drastic change in the balance of power in Europe. Bismarck succeeded in provoking the Emperor of the French into declaring war on 19 July 1870, whereupon the South German states took the side of Prussia as the "injured party", enabling the latter to enter the war with a significantly greater number of troops.

After defeats in Alsace and at the Saar between the 4th and 6th of August, the French Army of the Rhine was badly hit and forced to retreat. The main force, consisting of the IInd, IIIrd and IVth Corps and the Guards was gathered around the fortress of Metz where it was also joined by the VIth Corps. On the 12th of August, Marshal Bazaine took over command in place of the emperor who was suffering from a bladder complaint. The three corps of the army group stationed in the South under Marshal Mac Mahon withdrew right back to the camp at Châlons-sur-Marne to collect reinforcements and then to rejoin the main force.

Of the three German armies, the 3rd Army of the Crown Prince of Prussia, consisting of five army corps of Prussian and South German troops, followed Mac Mahon. The 1st Army, commanded by General Steinmetz with the Ist, VIIth and VIIIth Army Corps, and the 2nd Army of Prince Frederick Charles with the IInd, IIIrd, IVth, IXth, Xth and XIIth Army Corps and the Prussian Guards advanced without delay to the crossings over the Moselle below and above Metz.

Although the war of 1859 had already revealed many shortcomings in the organization of the French military system such as the sluggish mobilization of the field-troops or the lack of reserve facilities, it was only the Prussian victory of 1866 over Austria and the failure of the reckless French intervention in Mexico (1861–1867) that led to the reforms initiated by Marshal Niel whose name is better known in connection with a noble species of rose rather than for his contribution to military history since he died already in 1869. The Chassepot breech-loading rifle was issued to the infantry in 1867 and the re-equipment of the artillery with rifled-bore muzzle-loaders was completed. Furthermore, in the course of a liberal political "relaxation", the National Guard was re-established and improvements were made in the system of raising reserves.

Nevertheless, many weaknesses still remained. These included the contradiction between the organization of the army in peace and in war since divisions and corps were only raised after mobilization; the lack of agreement between the places where the troops of the line were stationed and the districts from which recruits were obtained; the outdated system of substitution with its unfavourable effects on the availability of trained reserves; finally and above all, the corruption caused by Bonapartist inefficiency in the military administration. As in Austria, the advances in military theory resulting from recent wars were disregarded. The system of command was outmoded and the French General Staff had likewise not been developed into a modern instrument of military planning and leadership. Since the Chassepot rifle with its calibre of 11 mm and its range of 1,200 metres was superior to the needle-gun with its 15.43-mm-calibre and a range of only 600 metres, the French generals considered that this outstanding infantry weapon was best used for defence. They recommended urgently that the enemy should first be allowed to attack and only after he had been repulsed should the French troops go over to the offensive. As a result, the initiative was practically presented to the enemy on a plate.

The military authorities of the North German Confederation had taken heed of the tactical and strategic experiences from the war of 1866. Improvements were made in military training and the company column and line, together with the half-battalion in column formation, became the

main combat unit. At Königgrätz, individual company-columns had already formed scattered groups of riflemen and it was this new mode of combat alone which was suited to an action in which the enemy was also equipped with breechloading rifles. In this respect, however, the conservative thinking of the Junker generals prevented the full exploitation of the revolutionary significance of the breech-loading rifle for tactics with all its consequences.

The re-equipment of the artillery with rifled-bore cast-steel guns with breech-loading was completed and attention paid to the co-ordination of the two arms. Opinions remained divided as to the cavalry. The campaign in Bohemia brought new experience in this connection but the traditional aristocratic ideas of the role of the cavalry as a decisive element in battles remained. The demand of the General Staff that the cavalry should be employed primarily for reconnaissance and pursuit was accepted in prin-

Attack by Prussian cavalry against French infantry and machine-gun fire at Mars-la-Tour. Lithograph by J. Wendler from a picture by Friedrich Kaiser.

ciple, to be sure, but not enough attention was paid to it in training.

The General Staff also improved the planning of approach-marches and also the technique of marching on a broad front.

Its aim was to encircle the enemy by making a speedy offensive advance on the wings with the centre remaining firm, the enemy thus being encircled and destroyed in a concentric operation. However, most of the army and corps commanders did not understand this objective and—as in 1866—endeavoured to keep very close to each other.

After the frontier battles at Weissenburg, Wörth and Spichern, which had not been envisaged by the German headquarters, the German command did not know for certain the location of the French Army of the Rhine. Admittedly, the scanty information supplied by reconnaissance parties indicated that Mac Mahon was falling back to Châlons but nothing was known about the probable further movements of the main French forces. On the 14th of August, violent fighting broke out at Colombey-Neuilly to the east of Metz but the Prussian headquarters were unable to deduce very much from this.

On account of the unsatisfactory state of its defences, Bazaine had planned to evacuate Metz and likewise withdraw to Châlons via Verdun. He was just about to leave when news reached him that enemy cavalry units had crossed the Moselle. The battle at Colombey-Neuilly had only a slight effect on his intentions. Instead of energetically continuing the preparations for the withdrawal or alternatively making every effort to defend Metz, he displayed a strange indecision and more or less left it to the corps commanders to march to Verdun or otherwise, as they thought best.

In the meantime, not only cavalry divisions but also two, and later three, enemy army corps had crossed the river below Metz. The rapid progress of the German advance-troops resulted on the 16th of August in a surprise attack on the long columns of the French forces on the march. A battle developed along the line Rezonville—Vionville—Mars-la-Tour, powerful cavalry attacks being launched by both the Germans and the French. The fact that both sides each suffered losses of 16,000 to 17,000 men is an indication of the bitter fighting that took place here. Although the enemy attacks were repulsed and the road to Verdun remained open, Bazaine ordered the troops to march back to Metz on the following day.

On the 17th of August, neither the supreme command of the Army of the Rhine nor the Prussian headquarters had an accurate idea of what the enemy would do next. Bazaine made up his mind to lead his army with the IInd, IIIrd, IVth and VIth Corps—leaving the Guards behind as a reserve—to a position northeast of Gravelotte, marching along the ridge from Amanvilliers to the west of Metz and preparing for a battle here with a reversed front. On terrain offering many advantages for his purpose, he intended to clear the road to Verdun and to inflict such a defeat on the German armies that they would have to break off their offensive. Trenches were dug along the ridge in the course of the evening and night, battery positions were established to give protection to the machine-guns which had only been issued to the troops at the beginning of the war and had not yet achieved a satisfactory standard of technical perfection and the villages cleared by the engineers in readiness for local actions. While all this was in progress, the line of defence which joined up with the left flank at the Moselle was extended to St. Privat and Roncourt south of the Orne by advancing the positions of the French corps. In all, the front covered a length of 11 to 12 kilometres.

The Prussian headquarters decided to exploit the positions gained on the 16th August and to deploy its main forces of the 1st and the 2nd Armies with seven army corps and one army corps as a reserve along the road from Metz to Verdun. Since the French positions ran roughly from south to north, the troops of the two opposing armies found themselves at right-angles to each other on the morning of the 18th of August. Still unsure as to whether Bazaine would attempt to march off to Verdun or maintain his positions at Metz, the Chief of the Prussian General Staff instructed his army corps to move forward in a staggered formation in a northeasterly direction.

By this, Moltke wanted to take account of both possibilities. Only when he had obtained further information about the enemy in the course of the day did he endeavour to set up a pincer movement with the army corps fighting on the extreme wings but this failed completely on the left and only led to a flank attack on the right wing.

Steinmetz, of whose three army corps only the VIIth and the VIIIth were on the west bank of the Moselle, did not understand the instructions given, which were couched in very general terms, ordering him to keep in close touch with the movements of the 2nd Army. When at noon on the 18th of August the first gunfire was heard from the direction of Amanvilliers, he ordered the VIIIth Army Corps to move forward at Gravelotte and also used the artillery of the VIIth Army Corps to provide support. Until the afternoon and apart from slight local successes, all the frontal attacks failed in the face of superior French fire. Due to the severe losses suffered and after almost all the officers had been killed or badly wounded, some of the Prussian troops panicked and fled as fast as they could.

With the 2nd Army, where the IXth and XIIth Army Corps and the Guards manned the first line and with the

IIIrd and Xth Army Corps, still licking their wounds from the 16th of August, occupying the second, the IXth Army Corps moved forward over a considerable distance and began the artillery action at about noon to the southwest of Amanvilliers. It was not long before the infantry, who likewise suffered severe losses, had to cover the batteries which had been brought up or protect their limbers. The Chassepot rifles and the machine-guns again reaped a bloody harvest and prevented every attempt to gain a respite by attack. The Guards advancing on the left also had to content themselves with an artillery action until the XIIth Army Corps, carrying out an encircling movement, was able to attack the enemy flank across Roncourt and St. Privat.

However, instead of waiting for this flank attack by the Saxons, the Guards launched an assault against St. Privat in the late afternoon when the French gunfire ceased for a time. The frontal attack by half-battalion and company columns was immediately answered by enemy fire and within a short time the artillery and the Chassepot guns with their

Attack by Saxon troops on an elevation occupied by French Turkos and Zouaves. Painting by Th. Götz (1878). Armeemuseum der DDR, Dresden

long range had accounted for 8,000 men. Once again, this included a large number of officers since they refused to obey an imperial order of the 18th August to dismount or even lay down with their soldiers. The gain in terrain finally won at St. Privat was consequently bought at a blood toll disproportionate to the result.

Only when the XIIth Army Corps moved forward via Roncourt in the direction of St. Privat at 7 o'clock in the evening were the Guards able to resume their attack against the village high above. In street and house-to-house fighting, they succeeded in defeating the French VIth Corps, which had exhausted its stocks of ammunition, and capturing St. Privat. Bazaine had refused to bring up his reserves in good time and to reinforce the troops fighting there.

Steinmetz, too, resumed the general attack at Gravelotte in the evening with the VIIIth and VIIth Army Corps.

Prussian-North German army corps

Prussian-North German cavalry

French corps

French cavalry

fortifications

railway-line

railway-line under construction

directions of approach and attack

army supreme commands

When this failed once again, he was assigned the IInd Army Corps—the only reserves at the disposal of headquarters. This night-attack was likewise repulsed by the enemy fire and proved to be a senseless waste of human lives.

The approach of nightfall ended the recurrent actions in this great frontal battle. However, by the following morning, the French corps, which throughout the day had made brief counter-attacks but largely restricted itself to a destructive defensive fire, left its positions and withdrew to the real fortification area of Metz. As a consequence, Bazaine abandoned all his operational intentions although his corps had largely proved successful on the battlefield. The German armies had not been able to destroy the Army of the Rhine but the latter allowed itself to be confined to Metz, thus enabling Moltke, after a breathing space, to reorganize his forces and continue the offensive towards the

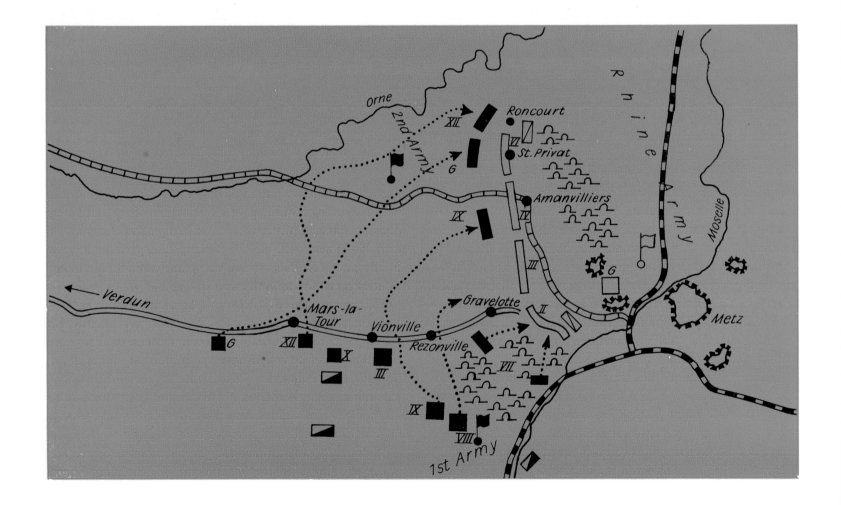

interior of France. It was the end of the Second Empire when Napoleon was taken prisoner at Sedan two weeks later.

Some sources state that 180,000 men fought on either side at the battle of Gravelotte—St. Privat. Others quote figures of 220,000 Germans, of whom 110,000 with 600 guns were involved in the actual fighting while the French forces numbered 140,000, of whom 84,000 with 400 guns took part in the battle. The French lost between 12,000 and 13,000 men in dead and wounded, while 5,000 were taken prisoner but the two German armies suffered 20,000 casualties. The main reason for this was the antiquated combat formation whose weaknesses were made even more apparent by the terrain which was unsuitable for a frontal attack. Faced with the devastating French fire, the company columns dispersed spontaneously after the first shock. To a much greater extent

Street and house-to-house fighting on the evening of the battle of St. Privat and Gravelotte. Lithograph by an unknown artist, c. 1880.

than at Königgrätz, the soldiers themselves took the initiative in forming groups and lines of riflemen, using the natural features of the terrain for cover and firing from a prone position. This represented a major change in tactics which was to survive by many years the founding of the "Second" German Reich at Versailles on 18 January 1871 and its annexation of Alsace and Lorraine.

ADUA/1896

Italy, which completed its unification as a national state only with the occupation of Rome on 20 September 1870, was—like Germany—a late arrival on the colonial scene. As a result, it only secured a slight part of the spoils—along the coasts of the Red Sea and Somaliland—in the "scramble for Africa" at the end of the 19th century. However, it seemed that it had a good chance of extending its possessions in the direction of the interior since the neighbouring Christian feudal monarchy of Ethiopia was affected by internal chaos which weakened its defensive potential. To gain time, Emperor Menelik II was ready to sign the treaty of friendship of Ucciali on 2 May 1889 after he had ascended the throne but the discriminating interpretation of this by Italy led to the outbreak of war again already in 1894. The English government, which was taking action against the Mahdi state in the Sudan at this time, gave diplomatic support to Italy while France and Russia—the latter primarily for religious reasons—provided Ethiopia with some material assistance.

After suffering minor defeats at the beginning, Menelik was able to achieve a significant increase in the numbers of his forces by the end of 1895 and to improve their equipment. He now crossed the frontier between the North of Ethiopia and Eritrea arbitrarily fixed by the Italian colonial administration. His advance guard under Ras Makonnen destroyed an Italian advance detachment under Major Toselli at Amba Alege on 7 December 1895. Fort Makale was then besieged and its garrison surrendered at the end of January 1896. These two successes raised the morale of the Ethiopian troops and contributed to the development of a popular war against the Italian occupation forces in the province of Tigre.

Only a small part of the Ethiopian forces, which are clearly shown by illustrations to have consisted of several tribal formations, was organized in a systematic manner. In addition to a hard core of 30,000 men, including a mounted bodyguard of 3,000 troops, and 32 guns, there were the provincial contingents raised by the princely governors, the "Ras", the strength and fighting efficiency of which varied greatly. The Ethiopian army, whose leaders mostly came from the Amharic aristocracy, numbered about 80,000 men, 8,600 horses and 42 guns at the beginning of 1896. The foot-troops of these peasant warriors were armed with guns or spears. The firearms included both ancient flintlocks and modern repeating-rifles. The ordnances were all quick-firing field-guns but were not usually used in battle, being more frequently employed for siege purposes and military parades. The guns obviously included some Maxim and Nordenfeld machine-guns but these, like the field-guns, were hardly ever used. The mounted units—some of whom were drawn from the Galla tribes—fought with sabres and were famous for their fine horses.

Their attacks were opened by fire from long lines of riflemen whose task was to tie down the enemy while spearmen encircled the enemy positions at the same time and attacked them from the flanks and the rear. As soon as the enemy began to withdraw, the cavalry likewise attacked the flanks and turned the retreat into a rout, making any further resistance impossible. Although they advanced in large, tightly packed groups, the infantry knew how to exploit the cover offered by the terrain. Natural features such as valleys, elevations and rocks were used to surprise the enemy and launch hand-to-hand actions.

It was clear that tactics such as these could not prevail against regular troops equipped with the latest weapons who had sufficient ammunition and were capable of adapting their combat techniques to the terrain in question and to the irregular methods of fighting of their opponents, even though the latter outnumbered them several times over. This was why Menelik organized a quite outstanding espionage system which provided him with accurate information about all the intentions of the enemy, his probable movements, strength, weapons and stocks of ammunition.

Siege and storming of Makale by Ethiopian troops. Lithograph from an illustrated newspaper.

Symbolic Ethiopian representation of the battle of Adua.
Private collection of Prof. Dr. Franz Ansprenger, Berlin (West).

He was adroit at providing the enemy reconnaissance forces with false news to unsettle the enemy and induce him to take ill-considered action.

After the defeat at Amba Alege, the Italian colonial army was reinforced to corps strength and in February 1896 consisted of four brigades, three of which consisted of regular Italian troops while the other was recruited from Eritrean mercenaries. The infantry were equipped with modified Vetterli-Vitali magazine-rifles which had been supplied to the Italian army only after 1887. Like all modified firearms, they tended to jam when used for long periods and then they could only be used as single-shot weapons, assuming that they did not fail completely. The artillery had 32 mountain-guns of 75-mm calibre, 12 rapid-fire guns of 42-mm calibre and eight older pieces of artillery which were manned by Eritreans.

In all, there were 20,170 men in the expeditionary corps. In addition, the detachments guarding the ammunition stores and important areas of terrain in the strength of a regiment or battalion totalled 5,830. Reinforcements from Italy were on the way by the sea-route and were expected at Massawa between the end of February and mid-March.

The governor of the colony and the commander of the expeditionary corps was General Baratieri, the last active associate of Garibaldi still serving. The Crispi government, angered by the defeats, stripped him of his functions on the 22nd of February and appointed General Baldissera as his successor but at the same time neglected to advise the person most concerned of his dismissal. He, in turn, who had hitherto been content to move his troops in parallel with those of the enemy, felt obliged by the reproachful dispatches from Rome to display greater activity. His intention was to occupy an area of terrain offering a tactical advantage and force Menelik to attack him there. He was certain that the enemy could be repulsed and heavy losses inflicted, inducing him to open negotiations, the results of which would correspond to the interests of Italian colonial policy.

After his success at Makale, Menelik continued his advance in a northerly direction but, after reaching the heights of Sauria, turned back again towards Adua, the capital of Tigre, to obtain supplies of food. He assembled his forces here in several camps. His spies spread convincing rumours about alleged disagreements between the Ethiopian leaders and the low combat morale of their army.

The Italian troops likewise reached the heights of Sauria in mid-February and prepared defensive positions there. However, their commander was unable to establish reliable communications with the base in Eritrea to ensure the delivery of supplies and food. Baratieri was thus confronted with the alternative of either retreating in the direction of Massawa or, by the occupation of Adua, attempting to improve his supply situation on his own initiative. He had decided in favour of marching back on the 23rd of February but had to change this decision on the following day when informed that Ethiopian militia forces were seriously threatening the only possible line of retreat. Under these circumstances, Baratieri considered it more advisable to advance on Adua and force the enemy either to attack him or to withdraw to the interior of the country.

Baratieri's hesitation for several days raised a protest from his brigade commanders who confidently asserted that an attack on the allegedly totally demoralized Ethiopian forces at Adua offered the prospect of a great victory. After a council of war, the supreme commander did decide to advance in the direction of Adua but halted at the half-way stage to occupy a ridge which seemed to offer a particularly favourable defensive position from which to await the Ethiopian attack. Since the Italians had no maps and the designation of the areas of terrain was vague, there were obviously misunderstandings between Baratieri and his brigade commanders as to the line to be reached. Consequently, those commanders who did not approve of what they considered the weak leadership of the general saw no reason and without formally deviating from the order given—why they should not advance so far with their brigade that they could dare to make a surprise attack on the Ethiopian camps.

A march during the night of the 29th of February/1st of March to Adua across unfamiliar territory led to the first trouble between the four columns. When the line designated by Baratieri was reached during the early hours of the morning, the column on the left wing continued to move on and, with its advance detachment, attacked the Ethiopian camp which was directly in the vicinity. The column in the centre and the reserve column remained in the position they had been assigned and made preparations for its defence but their left flank was now exposed. The column on the right wing, which had initially halted, then began to move forward again and lost contact with the centre. It unexpectedly clashed with a stronger enemy formation which immediately opened fire and practically wiped out the isolated Italian brigade.

Menelik had been advised by his scouts that the enemy was marching in his direction. He assumed that an attack would be made on his camps and instructed the subordinate commanders to take the appropriate measures but to leave the camps apparently unprepared and undefended. The perimeter guards were to hastily retire and thus provoke the enemy into pursuing them without taking the usual precautions. Menelik planned to launch a counter-attack and for this purpose dispatched a fairly strong force, including the whole of his cavalry, to take up concealed positions near the area which the flanks of the enemy were expected to cross. The emperor's calculations proved correct, particularly on account of the Italian brigade commanders taking independent action, continuing their advance and thus thwarting the intentions of their general.

In the attempt to beat off the Ethiopian counter-attack provoked by its advance attachment, the Italian column on the left wing completely disintegrated even before it could be deployed in any combat formation at all. Its withdrawal became a panic-stricken flight immediately Ethiopian cavalry appeared on the flank. In the meantime, the Ethiopians had gone over to the attack on a broad front and had already begun to encircle the enemy centre. When Baratieri tried to cover the two flanks of the centre with his reserve column, he found that this was almost completely tied down. The artillery likewise proved to be incapable of holding up the enemy since they had rapidly exhausted their ammunition and it had become impossible in the meantime to bring up further supplies from the rear. Directly the artillery moved to the rear with the guns still in their possession, they were followed by the rest of the Italian forces. Baratieri certainly endeavoured to organize an orderly retreat at about noon but he did not even succeed in forming an effective rearguard. The Italian battalions lost all tactical cohesion, discipline broke up and a disorderly flight was the result. Weapons and every other item of equipment were thrown away and the expeditionary corps became a horde of men in uniform with only one aim in mind—to save their skins at any price. The legend that was circulating everywhere at the time and according to which the Ethiopians usually emasculated their captives may have contributed to this.

Baratieri and other officers tried in vain to at least guide the flight to their own fortified camp. However, fear of the cavalry which was sighted time and again on the right flank drove the fleeing troops to the Northeast, i.e., in the direction of the coast, although the way there was unknown and local guides were not available. The situation of the Italian troops was alleviated to some extent by the fact that the enemy first stormed the camp on the height of Sauria and only made a half-hearted pursuit. Menelik made no effort to cut off the disappearing enemy and completely destroy his forces. It was only on the 3rd of March that Baratieri, who had now learnt of his dismissal at last, was able to collect the survivors and re-organize them. He found that only 3,520 officers and other ranks were left of the original 20,000 troops in the expeditionary corps.

The defeat by itself did not mean the end of the war. The fall of the Crispi cabinet which resulted from it and which had based its actions on the Triple Alliance with Germany and Austria, brought about a change in the Italian policy of "transformism" which ultimately led to Italy joining the Entente Powers in 1915 and fighting against its former Allies.

On the other hand, Adua was not the first victory of African forces over European colonial troops in the late 19th century. The Zulus in South Africa, Samory Touré in Mandingo Land in West Africa, the Mahdi, Mohammed Ahmed ibn-Abdullah, in the Sudan and others had been able to defeat the invaders on various occasions. However, the victory which caught the attention of an entire oppressed continent and gave it new courage was won by Ethiopian soldiers on that 1st of March in 1896.

MUKDEN/1905

In the division of China into "spheres of influences" by the Great Powers, Japan considered that not enough attention had been paid to its interests. In 1894/95, it had won a war against the "Empire of the Centre" but, in the face of protests by Germany, Russia and France, had not been able to enforce the terms of the Peace of Shimonoseki. After the suppression of the revolutionary Chinese Ihotwan movement—known in Europe as the "Boxer Rebellion"—by an international expeditionary force in 1900/01, a head-on clash occurred between the Russians and Japanese in Manchuria and Korea. In the night of 8th/9th February 1904, Japan, which was backed up by an alliance signed with England in 1902, opened hostilities without a formal declaration of war by attacking the Russian fleet anchored off Port Arthur.

The only link between Russia and the theatre of war was the Trans-Siberian railway, which had been completed in 1903 but had only one track. The Russian forces could not exploit their superiority on land whereas Japan could make full use of the easily won command of the sea in Far East waters. The campaign of 1904 favoured the Japanese but this did not determine the outcome of the war. Following an indecisive battle at the Shaho in October, the Russians had gone over to a static form of warfare. Widely distributed trench systems were constructed along a front of 90 kilometres, making it very difficult if not completely impossible to launch frontal attacks with a subsequent breakthrough. After a vain attempt by the Russian Supreme Command to gain the initiative at San-de-pu between the 25th and the 28th January 1905, before all the Japanese armies to the south of Mukden (now known as Shen-yang) could join up with each other, both sides made preparations for a decisive battle not far from the old residential city of the Manchu rulers.

Within a few decades, Japan had totally modernized its feudal military system and, with the aid of French and, later, German instructors, established powerful military forces. The military system was based on the Prussian model and many of its officers studied at the Military Academy in Berlin and gained practical experience in military leadership by serving in the Hohenzollern army. Its industry was already able to produce all the equipment for military operations on land with exception of large-calibre guns and optical instruments which were imported from Europe. The Japanese army was equipped with small-calibre magazine rifles for the infantry, quick-firing field- and mountain-guns for the artillery and a considerable number of machine-guns. In addition, it was well supplied with communications and engineering equipment.

At the beginning of the war, there were 13 divisions on active service, the rapid mobilization of which was favoured by the fact that their depots were located in the areas from which their recruits were raised. Each division had two infantry brigades of two regiments each, an artillery regiment with 36 guns, a cavalry regiment, an engineering battalion, a supply battalion and a telegraph section. The thoroughly prepared and thus rapid raising of 15 reserve brigades was carried out in the divisional districts and it was this which enabled the Supreme Command to operate in Manchuria with far more powerful forces than had been expected by the enemy.

After the surrender of the Russian fortress at Port Arthur on 2 January 1905, the siege troops no longer required were transported to Mukden. After their arrival, Field-Marshal Prince Oyama—Minister of War and Chief of the General Staff for many years and Commander-in-Chief in the war against China in 1894/95—had five armies, or army corps in actual fact, at his disposal. With a total strength of 350,000 men, there were at least 300,000 under arms, which was only possible through forcing Chinese coolies to bring up ammunition and supplies. Firepower was provided by about 1,000 guns, including 170 big and very big models, howitzers of up to 28-cm-calibre and about 200 machine-guns.

Although it had almost always been successful in the previous battles, the losses sustained in men and material

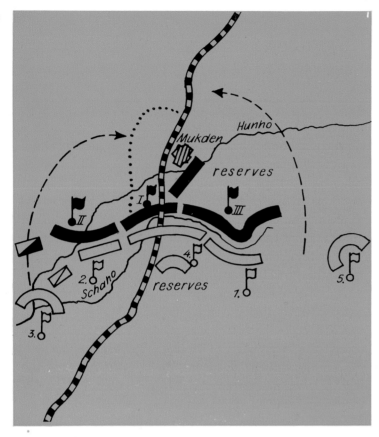

were intolerable for the Japanese army over a long period. The Court and the government consequently insisted on an end to the protracted and exhausting static warfare by an offensive to bring about a decisive turn in the fighting. To improve the prospects of success, the Supreme Command made efforts to achieve a fundamental improvement in its assault tactics, especially by co-ordinating the infantry and the artillery. Every Japanese attack against permanent defensive systems was to be preceded by sufficient artillery fire. The infantry was instructed to advance in small, open groups and in short, sharp movements against the enemy trenches, the task of the artillery being to give them continuous support and to use the indirect aim method for this.

Oyama realized that the enemy was constantly receiving reinforcements and would soon achieve absolute superiority. However, he relied on the energy of his officers and on the total discipline and courage of the soldiers whose confidence had been increased by the previous victories over the "Whites". This was why he decided in the second half of February in favour of an offensive battle.

The Russian commander-in-chief and one-time Minister of War, General Kuropatkin, had at his disposal, it is true, the whole of the so-called Manchurian Army with some 500,000 men but the total strength of the three armies which fought along the Shaho front was only 305,000 as regards the actual combatants. Numerous units guarded the vital South Manchurian railway, which branched off from the Trans-Siberian line at Harbin since this was subject to unceasing attacks by Japanese cavalry forces. Other detachments were used for supply duties or were scattered over wide areas to ensure protection of the flanks.

Due to the outdated social relations and the backward political system, the re-organization of the czarist military system carried out in the 1860's and 1870's had not been able to eliminate the sluggishness of the military apparatus, although some improvement had been achieved. The corrupt and incapable military bureaucracy—which made up for these deficiencies by its arrogance—was not affected by these reforms. With the adoption of general conscription in 1874, the Russian army was numerically the strongest of the world. This mass-army necessitated certain changes in the military apparatus and in the organization of its levels of command but only the establishment of military districts and an improvement in the training of officers produced a positive effect.

A shortcoming of a special kind was the strict separation of Guard units from the troops of the line. The General Staff did not maintain close contacts with actual military practice and was unfamiliar with the many requirements of effective leadership. As a result, Kuropatkin's staff considered the timely organization of an espionage service behind the Japanese lines as beneath its dignity and left this matter to the secret police. It had likewise neglected to obtain maps in good time for the areas in Manchuria where the next fighting would take place or to place these at the disposal of the commanders in the field, as they had reckoned with a campaign in Korea.

The infantry and the artillery were equipped with modern weapons but there were no high-explosive shells for the excellent 7.62-cm field-guns so that they could only fire shrapnel shells. There were hardly any howitzers or mountain-guns at the Shaho which had particularly serious consequences on positional warfare. The batteries only moved up into exposed positions in the field for the direct bombardment of the enemy and bayonet attacks were preferred for infantry actions. Attacks were still launched in tightly-packed formations which represented an easy target for the enemy artillery even before they could reach the enemy lines.

In mid-February, the Manchurian Army nevertheless numbered twelve army corps with two infantry divisions each. These, in turn, consisted of two infantry brigades, one cavalry brigade and an artillery brigade of 48 or 64 guns, a pioneer company and the communications and supply services. In addition to these forces, Kuropatkin had some independent rifle brigades and a strong contingent of Cossack cavalry. The artillery had 1,439 guns, 226 of these being large-calibre ordnances. However, there were only 52 machine-guns and there was also a serious shortage of communications equipment.

The reinforcements which arrived after a journey of several weeks on the Trans-Siberian railway were mostly units of thirty-to forty-years old reservists. Mindful of the approaching revolutionary crisis and not wishing to un-duly weaken Russia's position in the system of European military blocks, the Court and government did not dare to send active units of the line from the western military districts to the theatre of war in the Far East, although only these could have brought about a decisive change in the situation. The soldiers were indeed brave and prepared to bear hardship but the war aims, which were totally alien to them, the succession of defeats, and the shortage of food —bread in particular—, ammunition and medical supplies caused a deterioration in their combat morale. The many religious services in the numerous tent-churches could not change this situation. The officers lost their illusions about a dashing colonial war against an allegedly semi-barbarian people and the sobering effect of all this even affected the generals.

On the 19th of February, a council of war decided to anticipate the Japanese attack which was to be expected following the capture of Port Arthur by opening an offensive on the right wing. The IInd Army was assigned the execution of this task and the operational reserve was placed at its disposal. On that very day, however, Oyama had already completed the re-grouping of his troops and the 5th Army on his right wing and the 3rd Army on his left were about to undertake far-ranging encircling manoeuvres. The 5th Army began to move forward on the 20th of February and was followed on the 24th by the 1st Army.

The pressure on his left flank forced Kuropatkin on the 24th of February to cancel the attack by the IInd Army planned for the following day and to immediately move the reserves deployed there to the east, towards the threatened left wing. In actual fact, the Russians were able to withstand the Japanese attack although the Russian IIIrd Army had to fight a major artillery action. However, Oyama's principal objective with his advance on the east wing was to divert the enemy's attention from the main attack and to provoke him into making premature use of his reserves.

Really decisive fighting commenced on the 27th of February when the Japanese 3rd Army began to encircle the Russian right wing in a manoeuvre covering a large area. Taken by surprise and incapable of organizing effective counter-measures, the command of the Russian IInd Army withdrew its troops from the Shaho. It was only on the 2nd of March, when the Japanese cavalry from the Northwest were already reported via Mukden, that Kuropatkin took a large number of units from the Ist Army in the centre and from the IIIrd, which was involved in bitter fighting with enemy forces, in order to reinforce with these troops the IInd Army which in the meantime had occupied a prepared line of defence 20 kilometres to the west of Mukden. However, the counter-attacks by numerically superior forces on the 6th of March were carried out in a scattered manner and consequently did not achieve anything. Oyama rapidly brought up reinforcements to support the wing making the encircling movement to the west which had been attacked.

Since the weakened defensive capability of the IIIrd and Ist Armies was unable to throw back the Japanese attack which had now been launched along the entire front, Kuropatkin ordered his troops on the 7th of March to withdraw from the Shaho to the other side of the Hunho. To remove the continuing pressure on Mukden, he assembled a large number of battalions from all the army corps and with these forces on the curved right wing started a new counter-attack on the 9th of March against the advancing Japanese 3rd Army. However, this counter-attack, too,

was rendered ineffective by a subsequent shortage of ammunition and by a violent winter sandstorm.

On the same day, the Japanese 5th Army broke through the front at the Hunho to the east of Mukden, when it became evident that the Manchurian Army was threatened by a pincer movement. In view of this critical development. Kuropatkin immediately broke off the battle and his armies began to retreat already on the 10th of March. Crowded into a corridor 10 kilometres wide and exposed to violent Japanese artillery fire on both flanks, they followed the railway for several days, covered by the stubbornly resisting rearguard forces.

On the 9th of March, Japanese cavalry units entered Mukden and two days later the 3rd and the 5th Army joined up to the north of the city. However, only rearguard troops and stragglers fell into the hands of the Japanese, the main Russian forces being able to escape encirclement. Since the three weeks of fighting under very severe winter conditions had also exhausted the Japanese troops, Oyama was unable to organize an effective pursuit of the enemy, all his reserves having already been committed. Nevertheless, this was a notable Japanese victory against a numer-

Japanese infantry in action in the trenches at Shaho. Documentary photo

ically superior enemy. The Manchurian Army left 92,000 dead, wounded and prisoners on the battlefield while the victor lost 40,000 men.

The battle of Mukden illustrated the new dimensions in warfare with massed armies: creeping barrages, trench positions behind barbed wire, battlefields covering a vast area and fighting over a long period of time. In the Russo-Japanese War, this type of warfare was not taken any further since Oyama did not dare to attack the switch line at Ch'ang-ch'un and Tokyo's Anglo-Saxon creditors were beginning to become nervous. The czar's primary concern was to anticipate the revolution already shown to be imminent by the sailors of the battle-cruiser "Potemkin" and

Russian infantry attacking in close lines of battle and without covering fire. Painting by François Roubaud (1907).

by the barricades of Lodz. Consequently, after the sinking of his "Second Pacific Squadron" in the sea-battle of Tsushima (on the 27th/28th of May), he hastily signed the Peace of Portsmouth (USA) on 5 September 1905, ending the war in which Japan, by force of arms, was admitted to the circle of the imperialist Great Powers.

BATTLE OF THE MARNE / 1914

On 3 September 1914, news reached General Galliéni, the Governor of Paris, that the German columns, instead of marching on the French capital, were marching past it at about 40 kilometres to the east. He advised General Joffre, the commander-in-chief of this and instructed the 6th Army, which had been newly raised in Paris, to prepare to launch an attack on the enemy flank. This was the beginning of the battle of the Marne which was to be an event of decisive importance in the course of the world war which had broken out a month before.

Since the 18th of August, five German armies had been marching towards Northeast France—deliberately infringing the neutrality of Luxemburg and Belgium—with the aim of advancing via Paris to the Swiss border so as to destroy the main French forces in an envelopment battle of gigantic dimensions. The originator of this plan of campaign, which was as dangerous as it was unrealistic, was Count Schlieffen, Chief of the General Staff in Berlin from 1891 to 1906. Colonel-General von Moltke, the nephew of the victor of Königgrätz and Sedan, had retained the main principles of the Schlieffen plan, apart from a few changes, although this, in the version of 1905 when Russia was militarily engaged in the Far East, did not have to take account of a serious war on two fronts. Moltke, who headed the General Staff at the headquarters of the field-army in Luxemburg, hoped to complete the campaign with his concentric operation in about six weeks. After this, the victorious divisions were to be transported to the eastern theatre of war where, in the meantime, a single army was defending East Prussia against the northwest front of the numerically superior Russian field-army since, in the opinion of the General Staff, it could be assumed that the enemy offensive here would commence only after a very long delay.

In "Plan No. XVII", which had been drawn up in 1913, the French General Staff anticipated a German advance through Belgium but with its right flank along the Sambre —Meuse line and had consequently deployed in 1914 at Verdun an assault group of three armies whose task was to split up and destroy the enemy force executing the wheeling movement. However, in the calculation of the enemy forces, it had assumed that only active units would be used in the first wave whereas in reality the Germans used their reserve corps in the very front line and were thus able to extend the wheeling movement to the territory beyond the Sambre—Meuse line. This was a very unpleasant surprise for the General Staffs of the Entente Powers and was one reason why the frontier battles in Northeast France were lost by the French and the six English divisions which had arrived on the scene in the meantime.

The military systems of the Great Powers had been subject to massive changes in the decade before 1914. Based on millions of trained men, they consisted in times of war of several independent armies, organized in corps and divisions. The most important unit was the infantry division which usually consisted of two infantry brigades of two infantry regiments each, a cavalry regiment (most of whose troops were posted to the cavalry divisions in the event of war), an artillery regiment, pioneer troops and supply units. Depending on the country, the numerical strength of these divisions ranged from 16,000 to 21,000 men. Since the end of the 19th century, a great change had taken place in the firepower of a division. In addition to magazine rifles, the infantry also had machine-guns although these were admittedly not very numerous; all artillery units were equipped with field-guns of 75 to 77 millimetres calibre with a range of seven to eight kilometres. There were also light field mortars and a few heavy howitzers and field-guns with calibres of more than 100 millimetres. The German army entered the war with the largest number of heavy field-guns which proved to be of great value in the elimination of fortified positions.

All the countries involved expected a war of short duration with a rapid victory through encirclement, pincer movements and the subsequent destruction of the main enemy forces. The leading generals based this view on the tremendous assault potential of their armies by reason of their increased fire-power, overlooking the fact that the defensive capability of the troops in the field had risen by a similar degree and that losses could rapidly be replaced by the millions of trained men in the reserve units.

The 1st, 2nd, 3rd, 4th and 5th Armies making up the arm of the German forces executing the wheeling manoeuvre—the 6th and 7th Armies were fighting in Lorraine and Alsace—were held up by the resistance of the Belgian population, it is true, and weakened by the need to assign units for the protection of the supply lines but were able to gain the initiative in the main direction of advance. The tactics of the aggressors proved superior to those of the defenders but only frontal battles were fought, these causing very heavy losses to the Germans while those of the enemy were limited. This was why few prisoners and weapons were captured. Nevertheless, the German headquarters considered that the frontier battles had largely ensured victory and ordered two army corps to be sent to the East where the Russian offensive had been unexpectedly launched already in the middle of August and had put the 8th Army in a critical situation. It had originally been planned that two corps should follow the 1st and 2nd Armies on the right wing to reinforce them if necessary. After the frontier battles, the German battalions marched up to 40 kilometres every day in the scorching sun and this led to considerable numbers of soldiers becoming unfit and to difficulties with supplies. Their combat strengths dropped to between 60 and 50 per cent. Serious damage to the rail network in Belgium and Northern France by civilian actions in Wallonia and by the retreating units of the Entente Powers prevented German forces from the 6th and 7th Armies from being moved to the right wing in time.

By the end of August, all the French and English troops fighting to the northwest of Verdun were retreating to the Seine. On the 2nd of September, the government of the Republic left the capital and moved to Bordeaux which caused the population to anxiously recall the events of 1870. The morale of the troops was affected by this. Desertion increased among the troops in the field and some demoralized units even disintegrated. Nevertheless, the French were able to avoid the destruction of their main forces. With every day, they drew closer to the reserves which had been raised whereas the Germans moved further and further away from their bases. Joffre and his staff restored disci-

pline by replacing 33 generals, ranging in rank from army commander to brigade commander, and setting up court-martial which suppressed desertion, conduct leading to panic and cowardice by imposing punishments of a very severe nature.

Although Joffre had decided to go over to the counter-offensive within the next few days, he was initially sceptical when he heard Galliéni's news. He had only shortly before learned of the Russian defeat at Tannenberg-Soldau in East Prussia at the end of August and he also knew that Field-Marshal Sir John French, the cautious commander-in-chief of the British Expeditionary Force, was in favour of retreating to suitable ports of embarkation. On the other hand, it had also been observed that the assault and combat strength of the enemy was declining. The French 75-mm field-gun had proved superior to the German equivalent and contributed to the steep rise in German battle-

"Close combat". Woodcut by Max Unold (1914).

casualties. So it was that Joffre decided, after all, to go over to the counter-offensive on the 6th of September along the entire front from Paris to Verdun and to use all the forces at his disposal for this. He was able to convince Sir John French of the expediency of his decision and to ensure that the English would collaborate.

In view of the increasing French resistance, the German 1st and 2nd Armies were obliged to abandon the march on Paris at the beginning of September and to divert their direction of the Marne, which they began to cross on the 3rd of September. Contrary to the instructions received from headquarters, however, the 1st Army was a whole day's march in advance of the 2nd Army, which meant that the flank of the right wing, and thus the entire army carrying out the wheeling movement, was unprotected. Only one reserve corps was available and when this undertook a reconnaissance manoeuvre in the direction of Paris on the 5th of September, it became entangled with the advancing French 6th Army at the Ourcq.

The violent fighting which immediately began forced the 1st Army to withdraw the army corps already south of the Marne and to deploy them to the east of Paris. The action at the Ourcq continued with unabated ferocity until the 9th of September and caused Galliéni, among other things, to have five infantry battalions brought to the front in taxicabs which he had requisitioned for the purpose. This subsequently led to the ironical comment that the battle of the Marne had been won by a car parade. Through the withdrawal of the left wing of the 1st Army to the Ourcq, a gap of 40 to 50 kilometres resulted between it and the 2nd Army and, since this gap was held only by cavalry forces in a makeshift manner, it represented a favourable opportunity for the Allied divisions.

On the 6th of September, there began the Allied coun-

ter-offensive along the Marne, extending as far as the bend in the Meuse at Verdun, i.e., against all the German forces involved in the wheeling manoeuvre. While the French forces stubbornly held the enemy forces intent on advancing at any price, English divisions cautiously but irresistibly moved forward into the "Rebais gap". On the 9th of September, together with the still weak French forces, they crossed the Marne so as to advance simultaneously against the flank of the German 2nd Army and the rear of the 1st Army.

At the beginning of September, Moltke had ordered both armies to make an immediate start with the development of a defensive front facing Paris in order to anticipate French attempts to outflank the right wing. In actual fact, this meant the abandonment of the original plan for the campaign. As a result, he was now confronted with a situation which was anything but clear. There were no

Badly-hit horse-drawn supply column of the British Expeditionary Force at the Marne. Documentary photo

Temporary bridge built by German pioneer troops during the advance to the Marne. Documentary photo

reserves within a reasonable distance which were available for rapidly closing the gap and the reports that were arriving were at variance with each other. Lieut. Colonel Hentsch, the General Staff officer sent by him to the front for the second time, finally found that the 2nd and also the 1st Army were in serious danger although this had not been realized to the full extent by their commanders. Since there was no radio link with headquarters, Hentsch had to take a decision on Moltke's behalf: he strengthened the supreme command of the 2nd Army in his opinion to retreat to a more favourable position and advised the first army command to make a withdrawal without loss of time.

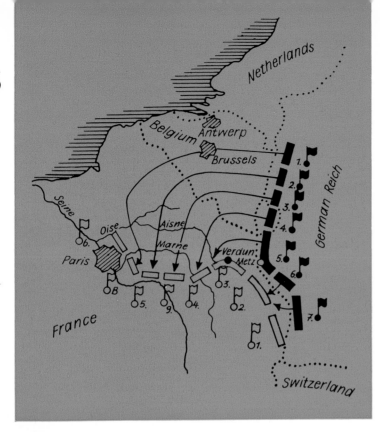
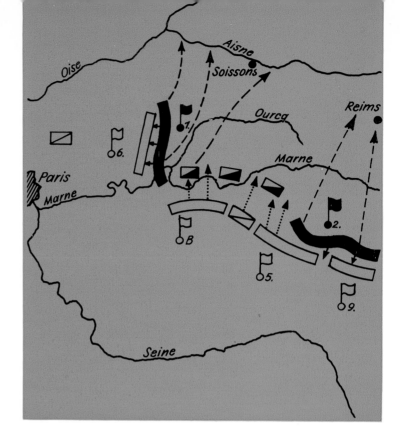

German troops

German cavalry

Allied troops

Allied cavalry

German directions of approach

German retreat on Sept. 10, 1914

directions of attack of the Allies on Sept. 9, 1914

army supreme commands

supreme command of the British expeditionary corps

The contradiction between the tactical position, which in the meantime had taken a favourable turn, along the Ourcq and further eastwards opposite the French 9th Army under General Foch which had just been brought into the line here and, on the other hand, the dangerous overall strategic situation of which only a few officers were aware provided the militarist propaganda of later years with the excuse to interpret the outcome of the battle of the Marne as a "riddle", "destiny" or "miracle". Hentsch and Moltke were blamed for everything and it was openly asserted that unbeaten troops had been abruptly halted in their triumphal progress and forced to withdraw by unjustified orders because the two officers lacked the necessary strength of character and belief in victory.

In actual fact, the Allied armies had already obtained the initiative in the principal directions and tactical successes won by the Germans at the Ourcq and at La Fère Champenoise could not alter this. Retreat was the only reliable way of still avoiding the encirclement which was already taking shape. To be sure, this implied that the strategy of the short war against France had failed. Therefore legions of historians and military authors in Germany rejected for decades with a lack of discernment the doubts that were raised as to the feasibility of the Schlieffen plan.

Nevertheless, the bare facts are quite clear. At the climax of the battle of the Marne, the exhausted and decimated German infantry and cavalry divisions were confronted with superior Allied divisions which were mostly at full strength. The German Western Army ran out of breath when it was at the culminating point of its offensive. As a result, the battle begun on the 5th of September had to be broken off after five days of fierce fighting, at least escaping a catastrophe, even though a strategic defeat could not be avoided.

Since the Germans began their retreat in the night of the 9th/10th of September, the French and the English were at first bewildered by this development since their commands had reckoned with further heavy fighting along the Ourcq—Marne—Meuse line. Their hesitation in moving forward allowed the five armies of the group originally charged with the execution of the wheeling manoeuvre to withdraw in an orderly manner and to take up defensive po-

sitions north of the river Aisne. Allied attempts in the following days to break through these positions did not succeed. The Germans and the Allies went over to trench warfare after several attempts to outflank each other to the north in a "race to the sea" by both sides failed.

Five German armies with 1.1 million men and six Allied armies with 1.3 million men fought in the battle of the Marne, this military turning-point in the First World War which was to have such fateful consequences. In the course of the withdrawal, the Germans left behind 200 guns and about 40,000 of their troops were taken prisoner. These are the only reliable figures which can be quoted in connection with the actual battle. Otherwise all that is known is that the Entente lost about 380,000 men dead, wounded or taken prisoner from the outbreak of the war until the pursuit to the Aisne. It can be assumed that the German losses were of the same magnitude.

German soldiers killed
in the battle of the Marne.
Documentary photo

VERDUN / 1916

When the German artillery, with more than a thousand guns, opened fire on the fortifications and positions at Verdun in the early hours of 21 February 1916, it was the beginning of the first of the long-drawn-out and senseless "firepower battles". On the assumption that the Russian armies in the East would be paralyzed after the crippling campaign of 1915 and that the French forces in the West would be weakened to a large extent, the German Command had set itself the aim of "exhausting" France by an attack along a narrow front and thus forcing it to sue for peace. General von Falkenhayn, Chief of the General Staff of the field army following Moltke's dismissal after the battle of the Marne, had voted for Verdun since he calculated that the French would use the whole of their reserves without regard to the losses sustained in order to hold this cornerstone of their front. It was the first offensive by the German Western Army since the failure of the campaign of 1914 and, once again, the Army Supreme Command headquarters (OHL) pursued aims of decisive importance for the war with this offensive battle.

No fierce fighting had occurred on the front at Verdun since the middle of 1915. The terrain of the fortress, with a total periphery of about 50 kilometres, consisted of the citadel with the ramparts around the town, the inner belt with 20 modern armoured forts as the main line of defences and 40 intermediate fortifications and outer forts. The latter formed the backbone of the field positions which had been built since the beginning of the war. They were in a staggered layout of considerable depth, were well-camouflaged and ran across steep and heavily wooded gorges and elevations. The strength of the "fortified region of Verdun", as it was officially described, was based on a skilful combination of field positions and fortifications but it was manned by only small numbers of infantry and artillery troops. The French headquarters in 1914/15 had frequently drawn on the troops and weapons stationed here for use as reserves. This was how 43 batteries of heavy artillery and even more field-artillery batteries had come to be withdrawn from this area. The forts still possessed the guns permanently installed under their armoured turrets but they had practically no infantry troops now that these had to man the field positions. The distance between the actual fortifications and the German trenches was six to eight kilometres.

The enemy forces on the other side consisted of the German 5th Army under the command of the German crown prince. Since 1914, it had been deployed around the fortress in a "two-thirds" circle which was open to the southwest. Prince William and his Chief of Staff, General Schmidt von Knobelsdorf, had long been eager to launch an attack along both banks of the Meuse against Verdun, a bulwark famed for many centuries. Falkenhayn certainly acceded to their insistent requests but he ordered that the attack should be restricted to a section 13 kilometres wide along the right river bank, although flanking artillery fire from the other bank of the Meuse would have to be reckoned with. The first objective laid down by headquarters was the exceptionally well-fortified northeast front of the fortress, dominated by Fort Douaumont. Six and a half divisions were brought up to the section to be attacked. These were to be supported by 850 guns, including 576 heavy guns and more than 200 mortars of various sizes, representing a concentration of artillery firepower on a scale unparalleled in the history of warfare.

Since the beginning of the war, there had been a further increase in the firepower and combat strength of the infantry divisions. Although the numerical strength per division had declined, the infantry had considerably more machine-guns and hand-grenades at its disposal and, for trench warfare, was supported in a variety of ways by mortars and mine-throwers. The assault divisions assembled for Verdun were also equipped with flame-throwers which had been specially developed for attacks at close quarters against fortifications. There had been a steady increase in the calibre, range and penetration of the artillery, particularly the heavy guns with a flat trajectory, and a tremendous rise in the number of guns in service had taken place.

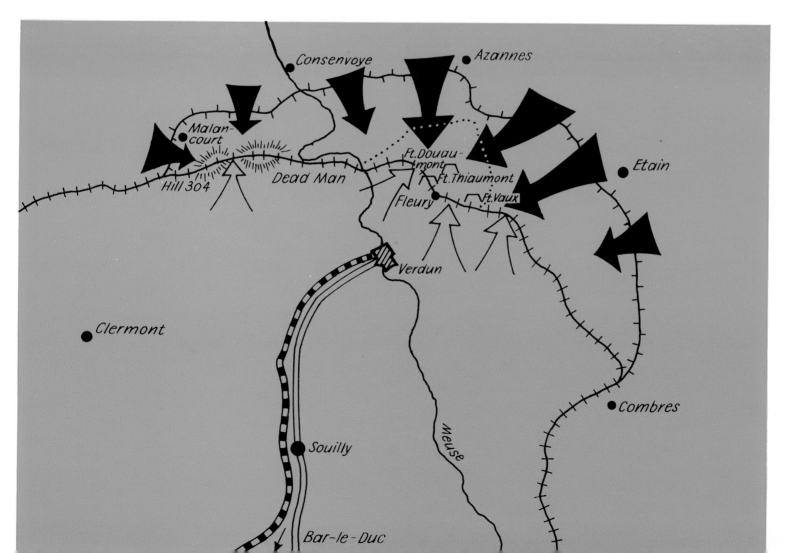

Gas-shells were to be seen in ever-increasing numbers in the vast ammunition dumps, following the introduction of this horrifying chemical weapon by German headquarters in 1915 in flagrant violation of humanitarian considerations.

Aviation, which had been used almost exclusively for reconnaissance purposes at the beginning of the war, had likewise experienced many changes. In addition to fighters, bombers, observation and long-range reconnaissance planes, low-level strike aircraft for the support of the troops in the front line also appeared at Verdun for the first time. After the signal and telephone systems had proved unreliable in the face of the massive artillery barrages, small portable radio-sets came into use for communications, allowing units in the trenches to establish radio links with the HQ's und the artillery. There was even a change in the outer appearance of the soldiers. Those fighting at the front wore steel helmets and always carried a gas mask. The Germans had been wearing field-grey uniforms and the English khaki-brown ones since 1914 and now the red trousers of the French soldiers were replaced by blue-grey ones.

Although vain attempts to make a breakthrough by Allied divisions in 1915 had already provided a convincing demonstration of the destructive firepower of massed weapons for defensive purposes, both headquarters and the Supreme Command of the 5th Army considered that the forces scheduled for this were sufficient to attack the fortified front successfully, despite their differences with regard to the use of the reserves. On account of the unfavourable weather, the battle had to be put off on a number of occasions from the 12th of February onwards. It was then opened nine days later with an artillery barrage by the German guns which lasted for eight hours. The infantry, together

329

	front line by mid-February 1916		armoured forts
	front line in early July 1916		German directions of attack
	front line in late December 1916		French counter-attacks

The armoured fort of
Vaux shortly before it
was stormed by German
troops during the battle
of Verdun. Documen-
tary photo

Landscape destroyed by
an artillery barrage lasting for weeks during the
battle of Verdun. Aerial
photo

with pioneer and flame-thrower detachments and under the command of senior officers in some cases, moved forward to the strains of the Yorck March and "Prussia's Glory", not expecting to encounter any serious resistance from the heavily shelled field-positions. However, despite their heavy casualties, the French displayed no signs of retreating and their stubborn resistance very quickly forced the German assault troops to take cover again on and in the ground.

The French headquarters were certainly aware of the carefully concealed and camouflaged preparations by the Germans for the attack but had been unable to form a clear idea of the purpose and timing of it. On the one hand, it was not prepared to disturb its own preparations for a large-scale offensive in the central section of the Western Front but on the other it was also unwilling to abandon a bastion, whose military value was the subject of argument among military experts, without offering stiff resistance. This was

why Marshal Joffre issued orders for Verdun to be held at all costs. The suggestion by the competent Army Group Command at the start of the battle that the right bank of the Meuse be abandoned was rejected. The new commander of this section of the front, General Pétain (known later for his unfortunate collaboration with the Nazis during the occupation of France) was instructed to hold the terrain around the fortress at all costs and was assigned another army for the purpose, although this was still in the process of being assembled.

Falkenhayn's expectations in regard to a powerful concentration of French forces which had "only to be bled to death" were more or less justified. When the German artillery, during the very first days of the battle, destroyed the only standard-gauge railway track to Verdun and the narrow-gauge line between Bar-le-Duc and Verdun proved inadequate, the French headquarters brought up 3,500 trucks.

"Skirmish".
Chalk drawing by Otto Dix (1917).

"The Death of Clery".
Aquarelle by Otto Griebel (1923).
Kupferstichkabinett, Berlin

Throughout the entire battle, these vehicles transported men and materials along the "Holy Road" from Bar-le-Duc via Souilly to Verdun and it was with their help and the quantities of ammunition they brought that the French could gradually change the situation in their favour.

In the first stage of the battle, lasting until the 29th of February, the attackers only penetrated the defence system by a distance of up to three kilometres along a strip about ten kilometres long. Nevertheless, they unexpectedly cap-

tured the powerful fortification of Fort Douaumont and were able to hold it despite vigorous counter-attacks. However, the German troops suffered badly from the enemy artillery fire from the west bank of the Meuse and their élan was increasingly affected. It was only with great difficulty that they could fight their way forward, yard by yard, until the attack lost its momentum completely.

On the 5th of March, the second stage of the battle was initiated by the 5th Army, which received reinforcements in the meantime, with a massive expenditure of ammunition. Its assault divisions now advanced along the west bank of the Meuse as well, the objective being to storm the elevations known as Hill "304" and "Dead Man" in order to eliminate the artillery fire from the flank. Every success had to be won at a high price in the face of constantly increasing fire from the defenders. The totally exhausted German troops finally ceased their attacks on the 30th of March after suffering very heavy losses. Nevertheless, Falkenhayn, headquarters and the crown prince refused to break off the battle even after its failure. They still advocated the presumptuous idea that Verdun would drain the life-blood from the enemy.

The two sides were locked in struggle from the beginning of April until the beginning of June and incredible quantities of ammunition were expended to obtain possession of individual points of the terrain. It was a battle dominated by the use of machines, equipment and ammunition. For weeks on end, the soldiers were forced to vegetate in muddy craters under constant artillery and mortar fire. A hail of "green cross" gas-shells, filled initially with chlorine and after the middle of May with phosgene as well, compelled them to spend hour after hour fighting for breath in their gas-masks. The penetrating odour of rotting human flesh completed the "hell of Verdun". But whereas the French Supreme Command replaced its tired divisions regularly after some weeks at the front, the German troops received few replacements—mostly very young recruits or elderly landwehr men—and they were withdrawn from the front only when they were completely worn-out.

Without having learnt anything from their previous experience, the Germans started a third major offensive at the beginning of June with the objective of penetrating the inner belt of forts from the outer fortification of Thiaumont to the village of Fleury. They succeeded in capturing the battered Fort Vaux and Thiaumont and reaching Fleury. But then the attack was halted, even though continuous cover was provided by the German artillery. In the night of the 22nd/23rd of June alone, it fired 110,000 gas-shells filled with phosgene, the sole purpose of this being to silence the enemy guns. With the effective support of their superior aircraft, the French were nevertheless able to throw back the German advance by making violent counter-attacks. When the Allied armies, in turn, opened an offensive further to the north against Bapaume, Combles and Péronne, the fighting at Verdun declined in intensity since the German headquarters soon had to withdraw troops and equipment from here for use as reserves in the battle of the Somme. No troops could be transferred from the Eastern Front after the Russian "Brussilov offensive" on the 4th of June had broken through the Austrian positions at Luzk. This notwithstanding, individual German attacks still continued until the end of August. It was only after the declaration of war by Rumania on the 27th of August and the resignation of Falkenhayn that his successors in headquarters, Field-Marshal von Hindenburg and General Ludendorff, on the 2nd of September, ordered that no further attacks should be made at Verdun.

However, the new Supreme Army Command still wanted to hold the small area of the fortress that had been captured, this being mainly for prestige reasons. They refused to withdraw the troops to better lines of defence since they were unwilling to admit defeat to the rest of the world. So it was that further violent fighting took place at the end of October when the French launched a brief but determined attack. Within a few hours, they had driven the German battalions from sections and bases which, in some cases, had been in German hands since February. These included the edge of the village Fleury, Fort Douaumont and, a few days later, Fort Vaux as well. The German headquarters, which at first ordered the recapture of the lost positions, had to cancel these instructions since their troops were no longer in a position to implement them. By the middle of December, there followed a second major attack by the French, again of limited duration, to the northeast of Verdun and on this occasion the enemy was driven from the remaining positions still held on the terrain of the fortress. After a struggle lasting ten months, the battle of Verdun thus ended with a decisive German defeat. The French soldiers, the *poilus*, had kept their word: "Ils ne passeront pas" —they shall not pass!

Official sources state that the French lost 377,231 men, including 162,308 dead and missing. The figures for the German losses vary between 337,000 and 373,000 men. Recent calculations indicate a total of 420,000 French and German dead, plus a total of some 800,000 wounded and poisoned by gas for both sides. Unrecognizable human remains and skeletons are still being discovered at Verdun.

JUTLAND /1916

The positional war on land was also continued at sea, so to speak. The Royal Navy "swept" the seas of the world. On 8 December 1914, off the Falkland Islands, it sank the German cruiser squadron under Count Spee which had previously achieved victory at Coronel; together with French naval forces, it bottled up the Austrian fleet in the Adriatic and restricted the Turkish navy, which had been reinforced by two German vessels, to the Black Sea. The blockade specifically directed against Germany extended around the North Sea from the Channel via the Orkney and Shetland Islands to the Norwegian coast. In the view of the Admiralty, the mere "presence" of the superior Grand Fleet (as the "fleet in being") was basically enough to prevent the enemy fleet from leaving the "mousetrap" of the German Bight for the Atlantic, thus enabling full use to be made of the resources of the worldwide empire and allowing them to be brought to the fronts without hindrance: "We have the ships, we have the men, we have the money, too!" A whole series of circumstances was first necessary before the two battle-fleets nevertheless clashed with each other on the high seas in 1916.

Within the space of a few hours, the British Grand Fleet left Scapa Flow after 10.30 p.m. (CET) on the 30th of May and the other Scottish bases at about 11 p.m. and the German High Seas Fleet set out at 3.20 a.m. on the 31st of May in the direction of the Skagerrak from its bases on the Jade and the Elbe. The German scout vessels were already at sea and the British cruiser squadrons were already steaming eastwards. After almost two years of inactivity, it seemed as if the decisive sea-battle between mighty battleships so often envisaged by the pre-war politicians and naval theorists was about to take place. Admittedly, since the outbreak of war, there had been several actions fought by cruiser squadrons, as—with a clear advantage for England—at Heligoland on 28 August 1914 and at the Dogger Bank on 24 January 1915, but there had been no confrontation between the battle-fleets, although this had seemed a possibility on several occasions. Contrary to the assertions which sup-

posedly justified the mad pace of naval rearmament and the laying down of bigger and better battleships, it was not the latter but the cruisers and the light naval vessels, particularly the U-boats and their blockade of the trade routes which determined the course of the war at sea.

The launching in 1906 of the British battleship "Dreadnought" of 22,500 tons announced that a new dimension had been reached in the construction of warships. The leaders in this sphere of activity were Great Britain and Germany which, in a fierce race between their naval construction programmes, replaced their ships of the line and armoured cruisers by an increasing number of battleships. Before the appearance of the Dreadnought class, the largest ships displaced 14,000 tons but now the shipyards began building battleships of up to 31,000 tons, battle-cruisers of up to 25,000 tons and even light cruisers of 3,500 to 6,000 tons. With the use of turbines, designers were able to raise the speed of battle-ships to 21.5 to 23 knots and that of battle-cruisers to even 25 to 30 knots. Depending on the type, the new battleships had between eight and twelve heavy guns which were mounted in nests of two or three in armoured turrets and were of 28 to 38 centimetres (11"–15") calibre. Their maximum range was 20 kilometres and normal range in action 15 to 18 kilometres. The armour of the battleships was 10 to 35 centimetres (4"–14") thick while that of the battle-cruisers was somewhat less, in the interests of greater speed. At the outbreak of war, Great Britain possessed 29 and Germany 16 of these floating fortresses; their shipyards lost no time in the construction of such vessels but other countries proceeded with the re-equipment of their fleets at a more leisurely pace. The older and tactically outclassed battleships and armoured cruisers were nevertheless still kept in service or formed reserve squadrons since admiralty staffs continued to believe that they had a necessary part to play in sea-battles.

The declaration of war by Great Britain and its strategic view of the war at sea as primarily a long-distance blockade torpedoed the infamous "risk" concept of the Ger-

man naval staff under Admiral Tirpitz. On account of the restricted radius of action of their battleships and their lack of powerful cruiser formations for protection and scouting tasks, an attack by the ships of the German battle-fleet on the British naval bases in the North of Scotland was not really feasible. It was for this reason that Admiral Scheer, who became the commander of the German High Seas Fleet in 1916, increased the attacks on the English coasts which had already been carried out repeatedly in 1915 by battle-cruisers, light naval units and naval airships—the "zeppe-

The German battle-cruisers "Seydlitz" and "Von der Tann" changing course at the beginning of the naval battle of Jutland. Documentary aerial photo

lins". The idea behind this was to provoke the British into sending a part of the Grand Fleet out into the North Sea for a confrontation. In actual fact, the German raids did cause unrest in Great Britain. At the same time, the Russian government, after the severe losses during the fighting on land in the course of the 1915 campaign, urgently requested their allies to obtain command of the sea in the Baltic. To be sure, Admiral Jellicoe, in command of the British fleet since the beginning of the war, rejected every suggestion that his main forces should move into the Baltic but he declared his readiness for offensive operations by the Grand Fleet in the North Sea as far as the Kattegat and the mine-fields of the German Bight. As a result, there was similarity between the operational concepts of the two naval commands although neither was aware of this.

In the spring of 1916, the British Grand Fleet had 28 battleships, nine battle-cruisers, 26 light cruisers and eight obsolete armoured cruisers. The Germans, on the other hand, possessed 16 battleships, five battle-cruisers, six obsolete ships of the line and eleven light cruisers. In addition to their superiority in numbers, the British ships were characterized by greater range, higher speed and bigger guns while the advantages of the German vessels were their armour, ruggedness, accuracy of fire and armour-piercing shells.

An attack by the German cruiser formation originally planned for the end of May against the English and then, however, against the Norwegian coast with backing from

the battle-fleet was intended to bring about a confrontation. U-boats had already been lying in wait off the English bases for several days. In accordance with the operational orders of the 30th of May, the reconnaissance force under Admiral Hipper with five battle-cruisers, five light cruisers and 30 torpedo-boats left port at 2 a.m. on the following day. They were followed at a distance of 50 sea-miles by the main force under Scheer with 16 battleships, six older ships of the line, six light cruisers and 31 torpedo-boats. By 3 p.m., the reconnaissance forces of the two sides were already within 15 sea-miles of each other at the southwest exit of the Skagerrak.

The British naval command had planned to send a force of small ships into the Kattegat at the beginning of June. This was to provoke a sortie by the big ships of the enemy fleet which would then find themselves up against the Grand Fleet which would be at action stations in the North Sea, the destruction of the enemy then ensuing. Alerted by the presence of German U-boats, the Fleet Command received the alarming news from the naval radio monitoring

Battleship in action during the battle of Jutland. Documentary photo

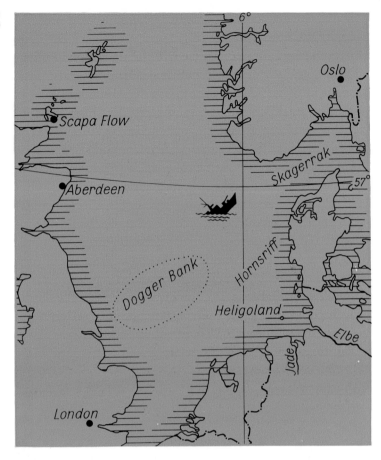

service that the enemy had been sent radio signals on the 30th of May indicating a manoeuvre in the North Sea. Jellicoe decided to put to sea at once and ordered his ships to rendezvous 100 sea-miles to the east of Aberdeen. When he learned on the following day that enemy forces had left the Jade and the Elbe on a course north-west by north but that Admiral Scheer's flag-ship had not been identified among the vessels monitored, Jellicoe assumed that he only had to deal with the German cruisers. As it happened, the German flagship, "Friedrich der Grosse", had exchanged its call-signal with that of a land-station shortly before and it was this which tricked the British radio operators.

The commander of the battle-cruiser squadron, Admiral Beatty, was about 70 sea-miles to the southeast of his own main force and was heading towards the coast of Jutland on the afternoon of the 31st of May. At about 3.20 p.m., the cruiser "Galatea" sighted two German torpedo-boats investigating a Danish ship which they had stopped. The exchange of fire which then followed with these vessels was

the start of the battle of Jutland. Alerted by this, Beatty turned south-south-east with his six battle-cruisers, 14 light cruisers, the seaplane-carrier "Engadine" and 27 destroyers to prevent the enemy craft from escaping. Hipper therefore broke off his operation and withdrew with the intention of drawing the British ships towards his own main force.

At 4.10 p.m., the first reconnaissance aircraft ever involved in a sea-battle took off from the "Engadine". At about 4.22 p.m., the two battle-cruiser squadrons sighted each other on a parallel course and at 4.48 p.m. the "Lützow" opened fire at a distance of 15.4 kilometres, the English ships replying three minutes later. The German ships rapidly found the range of the enemy and between 5.05 and 5.30 p.m. sank two of the enemy battle-cruisers. In the meantime, the four British battleships assigned to Beatty also appeared on the scene. From a distance of 17.5 kilometres, they joined in the battle with their thirty-two 38.1-cm guns. After each side had made a torpedo-boat and destroyer attack, the German battle-fleet came in sight at

5.38 p.m. so that it was now Beatty who decided to retire to the Northwest in the direction of the rest of the Grand Fleet. Hipper took up the pursuit in poor visibility and was followed in line-ahead formation by the main German force. Intent in destroying his much weaker opponent, Scheer did not realize that Beatty wanted to draw him towards the main British force. When this appeared in the vicinity at about 7 p.m. with 24 battleships, three battle-cruisers, eleven light cruisers, eight old armoured cruisers and 45 destroyers, the wild chase had ruined the tactical cohesion of the German High Seas Fleet and initially made it impossible for it to take up an effective battle-formation.

Due to the unfortunate leadership of his adversary, Jellicoe was able, between 7.16 and 7.38 p.m., to put his ships on a south-east-to-east course, despite his hesitation in taking an immediate decision. They were thus at right-angles to the German course and enclosed the leading German ships in a semi-circle. This was the classic manoeuvre known as "crossing the T". From this excellent position, the British battle-fleet concentrated the whole of its fire on the first ten ships of the enemy line, the already damaged battle-cruisers being among these. To avoid the imminent destruction of his leading ships under the disastrous force of the British broadsides, Scheer ordered his ships to put about at 7.33 p.m. A torpedo-boat attack was launched and smoke-screens laid to facilitate this difficult manoeuvre. However, instead of taking up a better tactical position in which all his battleships could bring their guns to bear on the enemy fleet, Scheer issued the order to turn about a second time so that he voluntarily returned to the hellish fire of the "crossed T". The German admiral was intent on recovering the initiative at all costs but, in view of the superior British fire, had to order his ships to put about for the third time at

The obsolete German battleship "Schleswig-Holstein" in the naval battle of Jutland. Documentary photo

8.18 p.m., the manoeuvre being covered by a torpedo attack carried out jointly by the battle-cruisers and the torpedo-boats. Scheer broke up the hopeless battle and left the battle-field to the superior enemy.

The British ships altered course to evade the torpedoes and lost contact with the enemy. It was only at about 9 p.m. that the two fleets headed towards each other again, a further exchange of fire taking place at 9.15 p.m., but this ended after about ten minutes by Jellicoe turning southwest and south. He preferred to avoid the uncertainties of a battle at night and wanted to be ready to continue the action the next morning at Hornsriff, near the entrance to the German Bight. Although the courses of the two fleets crossed at a quarter past midnight, only a part of the main German force and the rearguard of the British fleet were involved in the clashes occurring between 2 and 3 a.m. These resulted, however, in the loss of many ships by both sides. Jellicoe, who had great difficulty in keeping his squadrons together during the night, turned towards the North at about 4 a. m. after a last torpedo attack by his 12th Destroyer Flotilla (at 3.10 a.m.) but did not find the enemy. Before leaving the scene of the engagement, he searched the area for survivors and damaged ships but made no attempt to penetrate the German mine-fields to the south. The High Seas Fleet assembled at Hornsriff where Scheer correctly decided not to seek a further encounter with the Grand Fleet on his own initiative. Since a continuation of the battle was not to be expected, he issued the order to return to port at 5.07 a.m. Jellicoe instructed his ships to do likewise 25 minutes later. The commanders of both fleets were quite sure that victory was theirs.

With a tonnage of 1,900,000 tons (compared with perhaps 230,000 at Lepanto in 1571 and 380,000 at Tsushima in 1905), Jutland was the greatest sea-battle of history up to this time and has remained the only one fought between entire fleets of battleships. The British had the heavier losses—although most of these were suffered during the preliminary engagement: three battle-cruisers, three old armoured cruisers, one light cruiser and seven destroyers, a total of 115,025 tons plus 6,094 killed or missing and 674 wounded. The Germans lost one battle-cruiser, an old ship of the line, four light cruisers and five torpedo-boats, totalling 61,180 tons plus 2,551 killed or missing and 507 wounded. Although the figures indicate a limited tactical success for the numerically weaker German High Seas Fleet, the battle was not really won by either side. The performance of the battleships, not one of which was sunk, explains why the maritime powers continued to have faith in them under quite different conditions—resulting for the most part from the increasing danger from the air—and continued to build new ones even when the concept of these vessels was outdated. On the other hand, the battle of Jutland influenced neither the course of the war nor the strategic balance of power—including the blockade situation—and thus emphatically refuted the doctrine of the decisive role of powerful battle-fleets.

Henceforth, the admiralties of both sides "saved up" their big ships and the next chapter of naval history was dominated by unrestricted U-boat warfare—again on the recommendation of Admiral Scheer. These tactics were pursued by Germany as from 1 February 1917 and, after causing the United States of America to enter the war much sooner than anticipated, proved to be a failure in 1918, despite the initial successes which had been won. On the big ships of the German High Seas Fleet, however, the mutiny of their crews marked the beginning of the German November Revolution.

CAMBRAI/1917

In the late autumn of 1917, the British headquarters under Field-Marshal Haig had to bear, for a time, the main burden of the war following the failure of the French spring offensive in Champagne. It had valid political and military reasons for wishing to achieve a convincing success before the end of the year. After all the attempts to break through the German Western Front, where vast quantities of ammunition and equipment had been expended in the battles fought there, had failed to bring about any change in the preceding months, Haig and his staff examined various proposals to use smaller forces along a restricted part of the front. In connection with this, the question was also raised concerning the further use of the Tank Corps. Some leading officers proposed that it should be disbanded while others favoured its further development, were opposed to disbanding it and wanted it to be given a task which corresponded to the specific features of this new weapon.

To be sure, the "tanks"—the original code name—first went into action on 15 September 1916 on the Somme but this premiere was not very encouraging. Of the 49 vehicles made available, 17 broke down on the way to the front, another 18 failed at the start of the action and of the 14 which made the attack five were destroyed by enemy fire. It was a similar story in 1917 at Arras and on the Aisne and hampered the further development of armoured vehicles as an independent branch of the army. As a result, widely varying and even opposing views were held as to their military usefulness. Leading politicians and generals of the Entente Powers believed that the combination of fire-power, armour and mobility could have a decisive influence on the course of the war. On the other hand, practically all the German commanders rejected the tank as a misguided development. For their part, the technicians and protagonists of the tank argued that the lack of success was due to the many design-faults of the first tanks and their use in a manner unsuited to their characteristics. They considered that outstanding results could be achieved with a properly developed track-laying vehicle and the right tactics.

By the autumn of 1917, the British Tank Corps had received the Mark IV model which retained the rhomboid form of its predecessor, was eight metres long and four metres wide, weighed 28 tons and had armour 12 mm thick at the front. It could effortlessly crush barbed wire defences of any depth, destroy defensive positions and cross trenches of up to three metres wide. The Mark IV was built in two versions, a "male" version with two 57-mm cannon and four machine-guns and a "female" one with six machine-guns, and was characterized by great firepower. Depending on the terrain, the 105 hp Daimler engine gave it a speed of 3–6 kph (2–4 mph) and a range of up to 24 kilometres (15 miles). Four of the crew of eight were needed exclusively for the driving and steering of the vehicle. On account of the noise, heat, abrupt shocks (no springs were fitted to alleviate this) and the see-saw movement, the crews suffered from an exceptional degree of physical stress which limited the time they could spend in combat.

The commanders of the British Tank Corps, including the Chief of Staff, J. F. C. Fuller, who later became known as a military theorist, proposed to Haig that a massed attack should be made by all the tanks which could be assembled. To ensure a suitable terrain, concentration and the element of surprise, they carefully selected a narrow section of the front to the southwest of Cambrai. The ground had not been torn apart by weeks of artillery fire and there were no serious obstacles to the tanks on this terrain. It was also known that this section was manned only by three battle-weary German divisions which were scarcely capable of offering serious resistance to an unexpected attack by massed tank forces. To make the surprise complete, there was to be no preliminary artillery fire along the twelve kilometres of the front where the attack was to be launched. However, the command of the Tank Corps insisted that the tanks should return to their base within twelve hours at the latest of the beginning of the attack.

The British headquarters certainly accepted the proposal but increased the scope of its objective. After the tactical breakthrough of the Tank Corps, the success was to be exploited by a cavalry force which was to advance into the enemy hinterland and eliminate Cambrai as an important traffic junction. In addition to the 476 tanks in three brigades of three batallions each, of which 378 were the actual strike-vehicles and the other 98 supply-tanks, and the three divisions of the cavalry corps, headquarters gave the command of the 3rd Army, which headed the attack, another six infantry divisions and several squadrons of aircraft, totalling 400 planes. Deployment took place with complete separation of the different arms and thorough use of camouflage.

These precautions were so effective that even the French headquarters only learned of the attack planned by its allies shortly before the tanks went into action. Since he considered the forces used to be inadequate, the French Commander-in-Chief, Foch, offered his British colleagues the services of a rapidly assembled task-force but they declined this.

Warned by statements taken from prisoners, the Supreme Command of the German 2nd Army and of the competent Army Group under Crown Prince Rupprecht of Bavaria ordered full combat readiness for the divisions

Mark IV tanks passing a British artillery position at Cambrai.
Documentary photo

"Male" Mark IV tank with side-mounted 57-mm gun captured
by German troops during the battle of Cambrai. Documentary
photo

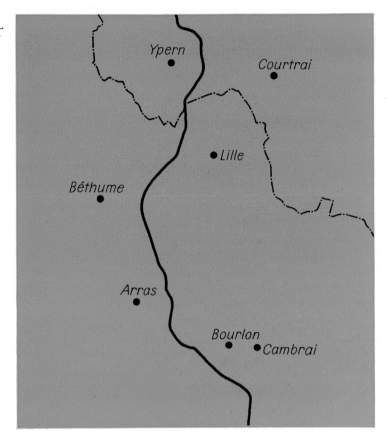

along the front. The limited reserves immediately available were mobilized and the positions behind the front line were manned. Since there was no information about the concentration of the British armoured forces near the front, the command staffs reckoned only with an assault by infantry forces. For this event, the Germans rightly considered that the system of defences built in March 1917 after the withdrawal behind the "Siegfried Line" were impregnable. A preliminary zone, about 1,000 metres deep and containing barbed wire resistance points at regular intervals, extended in front of the first trenches, which were three to four metres wide. Behind these at 200 to 300 metres, there was the second line of trenches, protected by a barbed wire zone 25 to 30 metres wide and reinforced with numerous strong-points. About two kilometres further to the rear, there were the intermediate positions of similar layout but not yet complete in every detail.

Early on the 20th of November, at about 7 a.m., in overcast and foggy weather, the first wave of 204 tanks penetrated the German preliminary zone, followed by in-

fantry forces. A few minutes later, about 1,000 British guns began to put down a rolling barrage, preceding the tanks and seriously hindering the defenders over a distance of nine to ten kilometres. When the steel leviathans emerged from the fog which had been made even thicker by smoke-shells, the German troops were caught totally by surprise. They were paralyzed by the fear that the tanks inspired and even the curtain-fire of the batteries far back had little effect. The tanks overcame all the obstacles with hardly any effort, cleared paths for the infantry following them and, with their own guns, destroyed the advanced batteries of the enemy. The tanks rapidly repulsed German counter-attacks, causing great losses.

After the second line of 114 tanks and the third with another 24 had joined in the battle, the British succeeded in capturing about ten kilometres of territory by mid-day as a result of this tactical breakthrough. With aircraft support, the leading tanks destroyed the German artillery positions to a depth of eight kilometres and turned towards Cambrai. Only a thin line of infantry, backed up by field-guns and machine-guns, desperately held up the operational development of the British breakthrough. Fairly strong reserves of the German 2nd Army had been on the march to the area since before mid-day but they only joined in the battle towards the evening.

The impetus of the attack by the tanks, which had outpaced the infantry accompanying them and no longer had the rolling barrage of their own artillery to support them, now began to decline as well. Direct hits from the enemy artillery unexpectedly caused heavy losses. The involvement of the cavalry corps, the approach of which was held up by many obstacles, was delayed by several precious hours. When it finally advanced on Cambrai—without any co-ordination with the infantry and artillery—its attack collapsed in the fire of the German machine-guns. The situation now became critical for the British command and this was exploited by the Germans to set up a new line of defences on both sides of Bourlon, in front of Cambrai and along the Scheldt.

When British headquarters, which still saw a tremendous victory within its grasp, ordered the attack against the three apparently defeated German divisions to be continued on the following day, it soon discovered its mistake. On the first day of the attack, the Tank Corps had been obliged to use all its resources to consolidate the success achieved and consequently was only able to put 49 tanks into action on the 21st of November and not more than 67 on the day after. Since the elements of surprise no longer applied, the tanks no longer had the effect that they had had at first. The British armoured vehicles were unable to break through the newly organized defences at any point. In these circumstances, Haig was obliged to break off the attack on the 22nd of November.

Since it was not yet possible to service the tanks on the battlefield and the corps had also lost 60 of its vehicles, its removal from the front began on the 27th of November. Three days later, a counter-attack was launched by the German 2nd Army with three assault formations and it was now the turn of the British troops to be taken by surprise. The Germans attacked with 18 divisions which were supported by about 1,240 guns and many aircraft. All the Mark IV tanks still at the front had to be used for its defence. Without being able to effectively hold up the advance of the enemy, many were again put out of action. By the 6th of December, the German assault formations had recaptured a good half of the territory lost. Their impetus was then exhausted by the stubborn resistance of the British reserves hurriedly brought to the front. Trench warfare again became the order of the day for both sides. Since the 20th of November, the Germans had lost about 41,000 men in dead, wounded and prisoners and the British about 45,000, plus 120 tanks, most of which—even if they were wrecked or burnt out—fell into the hands of the enemy.

The tank battle of Cambrai did not bring the "limited" but spectacular victory expected by its protagonists of the Entente and the further course of the war was only influenced by it to an indirect extent. Its real significance was that the 20th of November 1917 marked the day when tanks passed their first real test and, as a new branch of the army, showed that they were capable of bringing movement into the rigid fronts of trench warfare. In the bloody battle of Flanders, the British troops had needed 90 days to penetrate a whole nine kilometres but the tanks achieved a breakthrough of the same extent at Cambrai in not more than half a day. Admittedly, it was also shown that they were not a wonder-weapon as such and that they could only successfully complete their task when co-ordinated with infantry and artillery, whose degree of mobility was still inadequate, however, and with supporting aircraft.

TSARITSYN/1919/20

The Russian February Revolution of 1917 had ended czarist rule, it is true, but it had not been able to overcome the more profound social and political afflictions of the country nor had it brought peace to the masses of the people who were weary of the war with its alien aims, the heavy losses and its unending hardship. It needed the October Revolution, won by the Bolshevist party with its advocacy of socialist principles, the establishment of the power of the Soviets and the adoption of a decree on peace by the IInd All-Russian Soviet Congress in November 1917 before the guns on the Eastern Front were silenced. The czarist army was demobilized; the peasant soldiers hastened to their villages to take over the land the Revolution had won for them.

Since the Central Powers continued to exercise military pressure to force acceptance of a dictated peace and the signs of an armed intervention by the Entente were likewise increasing, the Council of the People's Commissars under the chairmanship of V. I. Lenin issued a decree on 28 January 1918 concerning the formation of a voluntary workers' and peasants' army, the nucleus of the first formations being provided by the Red Guards of the workers already in existence in the towns and by the Red Sailors of the Baltic Fleet.

The newly established armed forces were immediately confronted with severe tasks. After the Peace of Brest-Litovsk (on 3 March 1918), both the Central Powers and the Entente not only acted as occupation forces but also gave support to the counter-revolutionary forces which assembled in the South and East in particular and also in the Baltic areas and in the North.

After the defeat of Germany and the armistice of Compiègne (11 November 1918), the Entente Powers intervened to an increasing extent and, with their surplus stocks of weapons which were rapidly becoming outdated, ensured that the civil war waged by various "Whites" against the Soviet regime was kept going.

In the fighting of 1919, the control of the Volga line played an outstanding part. There had been fighting taking place at and around Tsaritsyn (Volgograd) since 1918 which had developed into several separate actions with varying results. Although these covered a period of more than a year, they were nevertheless equivalent in importance to a battle from which the Red Army ultimately emerged as the victor.

The strategic significance of the city on the Volga, its importance as the seat of political, administrative and military authorities, a junction of trade routes and communications and an industrial centre, explains the repeated attempts by counter-revolutionary forces to take Tsaritsyn by storm and its stubborn defence by the Red Army with the heroic support of the workers. Even in mid-January 1919, the commander of the White Don Army of Cossacks, General Krasnov, decided not to move towards Voronezh again but once more made a vain attempt to break through the positions of the Red 10th Army at Tsaritsyn. Serious defeats of the Don Army along all the sections of the front in the winter of 1918/19 enabled the 10th Army under the command of A. I. Yegorov to join the offensive successfully opened by the 8th and 9th Armies at the beginning of January 1919 in the direction of the lower Don and Donets.

The advancing Southern Front under the command of P. P. Sytin drove the demoralized Don Army from vast areas and led to its almost complete disintegration. Some of the Cossack regiments stopped fighting of their own accord and returned to their villages and hamlets along the Don. However, since the Red Army had only a few cavalry units, unlike the White Guard forces, the Southern Front could not act with sufficient mobility. Their advance became noticeably slower and was ultimately halted by the "Volunteer Army" formed by General Denikin with the aid of material support from the Entente powers. The difficult military situation of the young Soviet Republic in the spring of 1919 as a result of the intervention of the Entente powers

Soldiers and commanders of the Red 1st Cavalry Army on the march to the front. Documentary photo

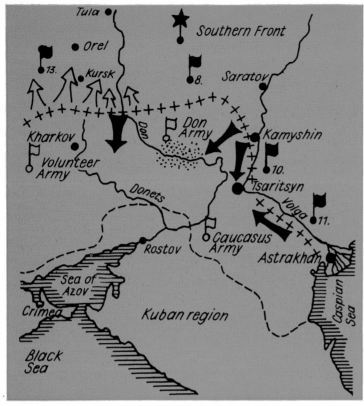

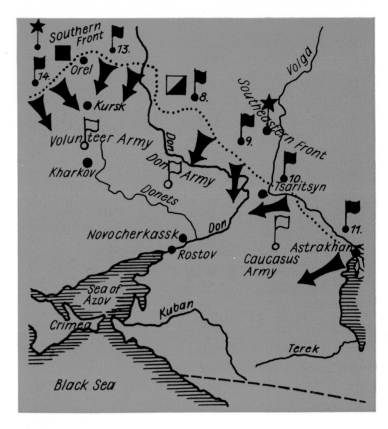

region of Cossack uprising	

<table>

Legend left column:

:.:.: region of Cossack uprising

_ _ _ _ front line at the end of May 1919

++++ front line in August 1919

▶ attacks by the Red Army
in August/September 1919

▷ attacks by the troops of Denikin in September 1919

♪ ⚐ army staffs

★ Red front commands

Legend right column:

■ combat patrol of the Red Army

◪ cavalry units of the Red Army

_ _ _ _ front line in March 1920

.... front line in mid-October 1919

▶ attacks by the Red Army
in November/December 1919

from Archangel to Baku and the dangerous advance of the "Supreme Regent of Russia", Admiral Kolchak, from the Urals to the Volga prevented an immediate reinforcement of the Red forces on the Southern Front. Their combat strength was already very limited due to the heavy losses suffered during the preceding autumn and winter campaigns. They were subjected to another severe test when the Cossacks along the middle reaches of the Don rose against them. To deal with the latter, the command of the Southern Front was obliged to withdraw fairly powerful forces from the sections along the lower Don and the Donets.

Fierce fighting broke out in the South in April and May. After the flight of Krasnov, Denikin raised a new Don Army and this, together with the Volunteer Army, drove the Red troops from the Donets region and the lower Don and reached the area of the Don Cossack insurrection at the beginning of July. The retreating Red forces of the Southern Front launched repeated counter-attacks against the White Guard forces who had more powerful cavalry formations, in particular. To join up with Kolchak's armies which, however, had suffered a severe defeat in June and were beginning to withdraw in a poor state to Siberia, Denikin extended his offensive in the direction of Tsaritsyn. In addition, the Caucasus Army under General Wrangel which had been raised in the Kuban region in the meantime launched an attack along the Don. After bitter fighting, it broke through the positions of the Red 10th Army at several points and then reached the Volga. The Red troops evacuated the city on the 30th of June after the working population had given them every possible assistance to the very last moment. Since the latter had to fear the appropriate reprisals from the enemy, they also left the city together with the troops. However, attempts by the Caucasus Army to break through from the east bank of the Volga, where it had established itself, to the White Cossacks of Uralsk and Orenburg and to Kolchak's left wing failed in the face of the resistance of the 10th Army and of the 11th Army stationed at Astrakhan. It was only to the north of Tsaritsyn that the White Guard troops achieved limited successes in the direction of Kamyshin by exploting once again the mobility of their powerful cavalry units.

The White Guards and the Entente powers regarded the capture of Tsaritsyn as a great victory. This was why Denikin issued his infamous *Moscow Directive* here on the 3rd of July in which he, as the commander-in chief, ordered the "Armed Forces of Southern Russia" to capture Moscow by the autumn after a concentric offensive and to eliminate the Soviet state once and for all. In the course of the continued advance, the main direction of Denikin's armies was now towards Voronezh and Kursk. In exhausting struggles but with their will to resist unbroken, the units of the Southern Front gradually withdrew towards the North. At the proposal of the Chairman of the Council for Workers' and Peasants' Defence, V. I. Lenin, the letter "All for the fight against Denikin" was published on the 9th of July by the Central Committee of the Communist Party and pointed out in frank words the danger hanging over the Soviet Republic.

The Entente powers supplied Denikin with vast quantities of military equipment via the Black Sea ports. In 1919, they sent 380,000 rifles, about 3,000 machine-guns, 217 field-guns, about, 1,000 tanks, 194 aircraft and 1,335 motor vehicles. In addition, he was given artillery and infantry ammunition, uniforms, medical supplies and other goods. However, all this did not make up for the politico-social weakness of the White armies. The Caucasus and the Don armies were recruited mainly from the conservative Cossacks who feared that they would lose their traditional privileges and the land and animals that they owned and were consequently opposed to the Soviet order. The Voluntary Army was made up almost exclusively of czarist professional and reservist officers, officer cadets and sons of the upper bourgeoisie and the prosperous peasants. Working people suspected of sympathizing with the Revolution were treated without mercy by Denikin's troops. Communists, members of the local Soviets, commissars and officers of the Red Army and also ordinary workers and soldiers were shot without exception when they fell in their hands.

The moral superiority was on the side of the Red Workers' and Peasants' Army which in 1919 developed into a well-organized mass army of regular troops. Supported by the working class and the poor of the cities and villages, it felt that it was fighting a just war of liberation under the leadership of the Communist Party. The blockade of Soviet Russia by the Entente powers, which drew a clear line between the forces involved, only strengthened the troops in this belief. In all the units of the army, it was the Bolshevists who inspired the others with their bravery and courage. In the factories, the workers who were themselves tortured by hunger sacrificed their strength to produce weapons, ammunition and other equipment for the troops at the front and for the newly raised reserves. Despite this, there were not enough military supplies to ensure a steady and adequate stream of ammunition and equipment for all the fronts and armies. Consequently, these supplies had to be used for particularly important objectives according to the main strategic direction at any particular time.

The Southern Front was increased from 86,000 to 171,600 men and for a time it was able to hold up the attack by Denikin's troops who numbered 151,900 men and still had superior cavalry forces at their disposal. On the 23rd of July, the Supreme Commander of the Red Army, S. S. Kamenev, ordered the command of the Southern Front, which in the meantime had been entrusted to Yegorov, to open a counter-offensive and, on the left wing, to launch an attack with a powerful assault-group on Tsaritsyn and the lower Don. This major strike against Denikin's base was to be supported by a secondary attack by a smaller assault-group from Voronezh and Kursk in the direction of the Donets region. Due to delays in the initial

"The Death of the Commissar".
Painting by Petrov-Vodkin (1927).
State Tretyakov Gallery, Moscow

concentration of these forces, it was only on the 14th/15th of August that these attacks by the Southern Front forces were belatedly launched. They consequently came as no surprise to the enemy and Denikin was able to take the appropriate measures in good time. The cavalry corps of General Mamontov was able to break through the seam between the 8th and 9th Armies already on the 10th of August and to advance into the hinterland of the Red Southern Front. To deal with this, both assault groups had to make considerable reserves available, especially cavalry units, of which there were too few already. These units, which included the 1st Cavalry Corps under the command of S. M. Budenny, were then lacking when the assault groups had to make their own attack.

Despite this, the Eastern assault group under the command of V. I. Shorin and consisting of the 9th and 10th Armies launched its attack along the Don and on Tsaritsyn and achieved an advance of up to 100 and 150 kilometres. In close tactical co-ordination with the 11th Army of the Turkestan Front, which was advancing from Astrakhan along the Volga in a northerly direction, they fought their way to the approaches of Tsaritsyn. However, counter-attacks by the Whites prevented the direct capture of the city. The assault group suffered from a lack of powerful mobile units with which to extend the numerous breaches made in the positions of the Don and Caucasus Armies and develop them into breakthroughs, thus achieving a permanent advantage. At the end of September, it was re-organized as the Southeastern Front under the command of Shorin and had to cease its attack for the time being.

The disappointing result was on the one hand due to the lack of reserves but also, on the other, because of the failure of the second assault group which had not been able to overcome the positions of the Volunteer Army despite some initial successes. For their part, the White Guard troops continued their offensive on the 12th of September and achieved rapid progress. The Volunteer Army under General Mai-Mayevsky advanced speedily in the direction of Kharkov—Kursk—Orel. Their élite force, the officers corps of General Kutepov reached Kursk on the 20th September and threatened Orel and Tula. At almost the same time, the cavalry corps of Generals Mamontov and Shkuro moved on Voronezh and occupied the city. Thus

in the autumn of 1919, the decisive strategic operations in the South shifted from the Don and Tsaritsyn to the region of Orel, Tula and Voronezh. This meant that Moscow, the capital, was in a position of deadly earnestness.

It was in this direction that exceptionally severe and eventful fighting developed in Central Russia, ending only at the approach of winter in November with a total defeat of the scattered White Guard forces and with a victory for the Red Southern Front. The cavalry units raised in the meantime played an important part in this. They included Budenny's legendary 1st Cavalry Army, immortalized by the realistic description in the works of Isaac Babel, and the Combined Cavalry Corps under B. M. Dumenko. When the Southern Front again launched a counter-offensive on the 17th of November, the Southeastern Front resumed its attack. Reinforced by the 11th Army, it advanced against the desperately resisting Don and Caucasus Armies. While the 11th Army destroyed the White Cossack units at Astrakhan, the 9th Army moved against Novocherkassk and the 10th Army to the south and north of the great bend in the river Don in the direction of Tsaritsyn. The forces of Denikin stationed here were either destroyed or forced to make a precipitate withdrawal and on the 3rd of January, 1920 the Red Army troops entered the city on the Volga which had so long been the subject of dispute. On the 7th of January, the Combined Cavalry Corps was able to make a rapid advance and capture Novocherkassk as well. Thus the Southeast Front carried out the task set and defeated the Don and Caucasus Armies. Its units were then re-organized as the Caucasus Front and reinforced by the 1st Cavalry Army. They then pursued the enemy forces, which were now beginning to disintegrate, to the Kuban region, to the coast of the Black Sea and to the Terek. The Civil War encouraged by the Entente powers entered its final phase and the soldiers sang:

From Siberia to the British Sea
The Red Army is the strongest army!

GUADALAJARA/1937

The world economic crisis, which since 1929 had been gradually destroying the comforting idea that bourgeois society was again experiencing a profitable upswing, despite the world war and the Socialist Revolution in Russia, made its presence known at many doors. Nor did it spare Spain, which was rather burdened with its historical backwardness. Incapable of finding an answer to its consequences, the dictator Primo de Rivera abandoned ship in 1930 and in the following year a coalition of democratic parties overthrew the throne of the last of the Bourbons. Bitter disputes over the political and social content of the Republic proclaimed on 16 February 1936 culminated in the election victory of the "Frente Popular", the Popular Front, which formed a Left-Liberal government with the participation of the Socialists. Thereupon, fascist, monarchist and clerical groups prepared for civil war. On the 18th of July, a conspiracy headed by Franco, Queipo de Llano, Mola and other generals openly defied the Republic.

Although it was joined by most of the professional officers, this military coup d'état was only a local success. In by far the rest of the country, workers and peasants took up arms in defence of the Republic. Under the Socialist Largo Caballero, the government was placed on a broad basis, the central region prepared for an all-round defence against the mutineers who advanced on it from all sides in the autumn, their pincer movement repulsed and the Fifth Column—this was where the term originated—brought under control.

After their venture threatened to collapse in the face of the resistance displayed by the people, the insurgents hoped to achieve a rapid victory at the beginning of 1937 with the aid of Italian expeditionary troops in compact formations. Immediately after the capture of the strategically unimportant town of Malaga in the South, they prepared the main strike in the central section of the front which, in various bulges, ran right across Spain.

It was 7 a.m. on the 8th of March, 1937 when the Republican positions along both sides of the national road Madrid-Zaragoza-French frontier a good 50 kilometres to the northeast of Guadalajara were subjected to heavy artillery fire for 40 minutes. The main road between Siguenza and Guadalajara passed across a plateau from where it reached the road to Valencia at Alcalé de Henares. This was the only road along which supplies could be brought to the capital and it was thus of vital importance for the whole of the Madrid front. The plateau was at a height of 1,000 to 1,200 metres; its central part, which was ten kilometres wide on average, was bounded on both sides by gorges of about 200 metres in depth. This was why it was of unique strategic value.

Despite this, the section of the front here was protected only by weak Republican forces from the Guadalajara division in scattered and badly chosen positions. Apart from a few self-willed militia troops of the Anarchosyndicalists, there were no reserves of any kind nor any prepared rear positions in the hinterland. The battalions were poorly armed, had little training and did not know how, by mobile defence, they could resist an attack by superior forces. Their officers were certainly determined but had little tactical knowledge. The competent staffs scarcely concerned themselves with the combat readiness of their units and the reconnaissance arrangements were in a sorry state. The consequence of this was that the enemy was able to bring up powerful forces without really being noticed.

Following the failure of the third attempt at the Jarama in February 1937 to take the capital by a frontal assault from the West and the South, Franco's headquarters wanted to break through the Republican positions at Guadalajara, which were known to be weak, and push forward to Alcalé de Henares. After the breakthrough had been made, the troops stationed on the Jarama front were also to resume their attack, join up with the forces coming from the North and together capture Madrid which would then be surrounded on all sides. At the insistence of Mussolini, the Italian Legionary Corps under General Roatta which had been newly raised in February was used for the attack along

"The Fight of the Thälmann Brigade".
Painting by Willi Sitte (1956).
Armeemuseum der DDR, Dresden

both sides of the Madrid-Zaragoza national road. This force consisted of four motorized divisions with a total of 40,000 men, about 250 guns and 140 light tanks. It was to have powerful air support, provided by units which also included the German squadrons commanded by Lieut. General Sperrle.

General Roatta and his so-called "Staff of the Volunteer Troops" were not aware of the climatic conditions on the Castilian plateau where, in March, wintry conditions could return at any time and consequently took no precautions for this eventuality. It was rather the case that they planned to advance along the national road and the neighbouring roads so that their troops would reach Alcalé de Henares on the seventh day of the attack and unite there with the forces coming from the Jarama. The right flank was covered by the Francoist division "Soria" which had 20,000 men and used horse-drawn vehicles. The beginning of the attack was postponed a number of times and was finally fixed for the 8th of March.

When the offensive by the Fascists began with an unexpected artillery bombardment, panic broke out in the positions under fire. However, in the villages in the immediate hinterland, the retreating Republican battalions were able to offer fierce resistance and thus prevented the enemy from achieving immediate success. It was only on the second day of the attack that it became apparent that the numerically superior and better-armed Legionary corps had made a breakthrough with the Republicans only continuing to resist at scattered points. Two Legionary divisions advanced towards Trijueque and Brihuega along the national road and the roads branching off it. However, on this 9th of March, the temperature fell to zero. The drenched roads became icy and thus made it impossible for the motorized columns to advance as planned across the inhospitable plateau as far as Torija, near Guadalajara. Apart from a few thousand Blackshirts and the officers, the Legionaries were recruited from soldiers returning from the war in Ethiopia, unemployed workers and impoverished agricultural labourers. They naturally lacked any

Struggle for the Madrid – Zaragoza national road during the battle of Guadalajara. Documentary photo

élan of their own and the initiative did not usually come from their company officers. As a result, they allowed the defenders an involuntary breathing-space.

In the meantime, the Supreme Command of the Spanish Popular Army, whose regular units were stubbornly defending Madrid, withdrew the XIth and XIIth International Brigades from there and several brigades from other sections of the front and threw them into the fighting at Guadalajara. As a result of the heavy losses suffered at the gates of Madrid, the two International Brigades were only at a very low combat-strength. However, like all the International Brigades, they consisted of volunteers who, as anti-fascists of many different opinions—communists, socialists or bourgeois democrats and humanists, had come to Spain since the late autumn of 1936 to defend the Republic and the cause of liberty against the Francoist generals and their German and Italian accomplices. Accordingly, the soldiers and officers of the International Brigades, in whose ranks there were also many Spaniards, were distinguished by political consciousness, efficient discipline and leadership and the ability to use the weapons at their disposal.

The units of the old Spanish army which had remained loyal to the Republic were broken up as combat units at the beginning of the war and were absorbed in the armed forces of the people. The political parties and trade unions of the Popular Front had each raised separate militia columns after the coup d'état. Some of these were based on the Anti-Fascist Workers' and Peasants' Militias, and although these forces were characterized by great enthusiasm, they were

of little use in combat and had little sense of order. In October 1936, the government of the "Frente Popular" decided to establish a regular popular army and ordered the incorporation of the militia battalions in this force. However, by the spring of 1937, its organization in brigades, divisions and corps had only been completed on the Madrid front. On all the other fronts, the Republican forces continued to retain their militia character for a long time and, in most cases, the independence which originated from their different political groupings as well. The strongest branch of the army was the infantry which, however, lacked modern heavy weapons. Although Soviet deliveries of tanks and aircraft had begun at the end of the year, artillery, tanks and aircraft were small in number which was why they could only be used in strength at critical points.

On the evening of the 9th of March, the XIth International Brigade under Lieut. Colonel Hans Kahle took up positions on either side of the national road to the north of Trijueque while the XIIth International Brigade under General Lukács (Máté Zalka, who was killed on the 11th of June at Brunete) dug in to the west of Brihuega on the 10th of March. Already on this and the following day, contact was established with the enemy and fierce fighting broke out, in the course of which all the attacks by the Legionaries at Brihuega were repulsed although, after heavy shelling and the use of flame-throwers, they penetrated far into the Republican lines on both sides of the national road. The

Field artillery of the International Brigades in action. Documentary photo

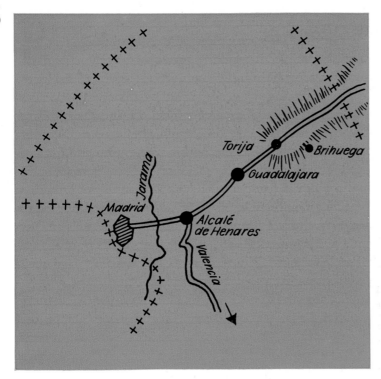

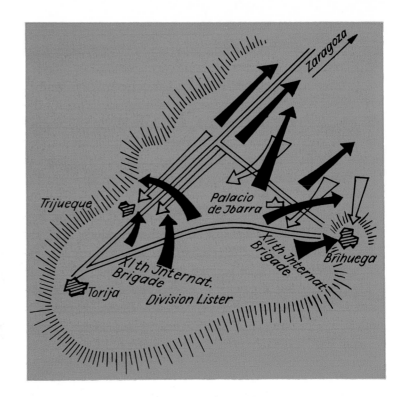

+++   front line in late February/early March

➤   counter-attacks by the Republicans

▷   attacks by the Legionary corps

Legionary troops advanced about four kilometres and occupied Trijueque and were only stopped when they attempted to extend their attacks. During the following night, the first Spanish Republican battalions arrived and formed a division with the brigades which subsequently came and with the two International Brigades, the division being headed by Commandant Enrique Lister. This force manned the section on the plateau and, with the 12th and 14th division on its left and right, formed the IVth Corps under Lieut. Colonel Jurado, who also had an armoured brigade and a cavalry regiment at his disposal.

Fresh attacks by the Legionaries between the 12th and 14th of March were thrown back and, after counter-attacks in which the "Garibaldi" battalion, formed from Italian anti-fascists, played an outstanding part, the Palacio de Ibarra and Trijueque were recaptured. Since the runways for the Legionary aircraft had been turned into mud by heavy rain and these were scarcely able to take part in the

fighting, the far weaker Republican squadrons had favourable conditions for their air attacks on the long enemy columns on the roads. Although the plateau consisted of hard and rocky ground, it was softened up to such an extent by rain and snow that all the vehicles were restricted to paved roads. Weak attempts by the Francoists to break through the front at Jarama and relieve the Legionary Corps did not get very far. Thus the Republican Supreme Command had the unique opportunity to go over to the counter-offensive at Guadalajara and crush the Legionary Corps. The 18th of March, 1937 was set as the date for the beginning of the attack.

At 2 p.m. on that day, the Republican artillery heavily shelled the enemy troops at Brihuega for 40 minutes. An air attack was then launched against the enemy position and communications with the rear, until at 3 p.m. the Republican infantry attacked with powerful armoured support, overwhelming the Legionary troops and forcing them to flee, leaving behind their weapons, vehicles, ammunition and other military equipment. On the following day, the forces stationed along the national road also took up the offensive and, although only a few tanks could be used on the soft terrain, rapidly forced the enemy back towards the Northeast. On the 20th of March, the Lister Division reached kilometre-mark 95 but on the following day it had to halt its attack when thick fog prevented any further advance. At almost the same time, General Roatta was able to replace his beaten and thoroughly demoralized Legionaries by Francoist troops who, on arrival, concentrated on the defence of the positions they held.

Thus the battle of Guadalajara ended with the victory of the Republican Popular Army. Despite their disadvantage in weapons and numbers of troops, they successfully repulsed the repeated attacks launched against Madrid which were now made from the Northeast and, with their counter-offensive, turned the situation into a serious defeat for the enemy. In addition to the several thousand troops killed, wounded or taken prisoner, the Legionary Corps lost most of its equipment, including field-guns, machine-guns, tanks and vehicles, in an almost intact condition.

The victory at Guadalajara (or Brihuega) foiled the intentions of the Francoists to strike the Republic at its most vulnerable point at the beginning of spring 1937 by an of-

Shot-down fighter-plane of the Italian intervention troops. Documentary photo

Parade of soldiers from the International Brigades and the Spanish Popular Army at Torija. Documentary photo

fensive with foreign aid and thus to bring about its downfall. Nevertheless, the war ended in defeat for the Republicans two years later. A single successful defensive battle was not enough to turn the table. While the fascist "Axis" of Berlin-Rome took overt military action with up to 140,000 men on an ever increasing scale, the governments of the Western powers withdrew behind a "policy of nonintervention" and thus left the Spanish Republic to its fate. On the one hand, they feared that the logic of a popular war, in the event of victory, might lead to the establishment of a socialist order for which they had no sympathy and, on the other, they hoped, on the basis of a wrong conclusion, to avoid a "Great War", the signs of which were already appearing on the horizon, by "appeasing" the aggressors.

Things turned out very differently. In March 1939, General Franco entered Madrid, established his long-lived dictatorship and joined the Anti-Comintern Pact. Already on the 1st of September of the same year, Hitlerite Germany started the Second World War with a fake attack on its own radio station at Gleiwitz (Gliwice). The airmen of the "Condor Legion" who in 1937 had "tested" the effect of their bombardments on the women and children of Guernica in the Basque territory were soon to appear over Rotterdam and Eben Emael, London and Coventry.

BATTLE OF BRITAIN / 1940

The Japanese aggressions against China and the invasion of Ethiopia and Albania by Italy between 1931 and 1939 were still "localized", as it was termed in diplomatic language. The intervention of the fascist "Rome–Berlin Axis" in the Spanish Civil War and the invasion by Hitlerite Germany of Austria and Czechoslovakia in 1938–1939 likewise remained unpunished. However, the policy of appeasement, i.e., making concessions to the aggressor within certain limits which were still considered acceptable but imposed the burden of the compromise on others, ended in a miscalculation for the Western democracies—England, France and, indirectly, the USA as well. Far from being satisfied with concessions in Central Europe and the go-ahead for expansion at the expense of the Soviet Union, the masters of "Greater Germany", Japan and Italy, insisting on their military advantages, were aiming at nothing less than a total and absolutely ruthless redistribution of the world. Threatened in their own existence as independent Great Powers, England and France consequently had to enter a war, for which they were ill-prepared and which was to become the Second World War, following the invasion of their ally, Poland, on 1 September 1939.

The course of the war against Poland, Norway, the Netherlands, Belgium and France from the autumn of 1939 to the spring of 1940 demonstrated clearly the exceptional importance of a strategic attack by powerful airforces for rapidly achieving control of the skies, assuming that the state attacked was not sufficiently prepared for this eventuality. At the same time, the close co-ordination between the forces on the ground and in the air offered far-reaching possibilities which were reflected primarily in the mighty strike-capability and increased mobility of armies at war. Nevertheless, the successes of the fascist Luftwaffe did not provide incontrovertible evidence for or against the correctness of the ideas of the Italian general Douhet who—at a time when there was still no threat of war—had suggested that in the event of hostilities one should use very powerful air armadas to gain control of the sky from the enemy and then, by massed bombing raids, devastate the unprotected hinterland, thus causing economic chaos, the demoralization of the population and, finally, the paralysis of the will to resist. In each of the Nazi campaigns, it was always the army which had the last word, no matter how great the support provided by the Luftwaffe.

However, by the summer of 1940, a new situation had emerged which confronted the air-forces of Germany and Great Britain with tasks of a different nature. After the occupation of several countries of Northern and Western Europe and especially after the military collapse of France, Hitler took energetic action to force Great Britain, which as an island had the protection of the sea, to either surrender or come to an "agreement" on the basis of an anti-Soviet programme. Behind all this, there was the decision just about to be taken in June and July by the German leaders to concentrate all their available forces within the not-too-distant future on an attack against the Soviet Union, the main strategic target of the war they had launched. "Great attention to be paid to the East" were the words that General Halder, Chief of the General Staff of the Army, wrote in his military diary on the 30th of June. "England will probably need a demonstration of our military power before she gives way and allows us to attack the East without fear from her quarter."

Instruction No. 17, issued by the Supreme Command of the Wehrmacht (the "OKW") on the 16th of July, "On the preparation of a landing operation against England" stipulated that German command of the air over the British Isles was an essential condition for the "Sealion" operation, which was the code-name for the invasion. An instruction of the 1st of August consequently required the Luftwaffe to eliminate the Royal Air Force (the RAF) by attacking it in the air and its installations on the ground and by destroying the air defences and the aircraft factories. It also stated that port installations and food warehouses should be destroyed, indicating the hope that the British people might be forced to yield without an invasion.

St. Paul's Cathedral in London in the midst of burning streets
after an air raid during the Battle of Britain. Documentary
photo

following double page:
Air-raid observers at British headquarters during an air raid in
the Battle of Britain. Documentary photo

In Western Europe, the 2nd and 3rd Air-Fleets and some units from the 5th Air-Fleet in Norway were available for launching the strategic air-offensive planned. At the beginning of August, 1,015 bombers, 346 dive-bombers, 933 single-seater fighters and 375 tactical aircraft flown by a crew of two were at their disposal. At the same time, the RAF had barely 700 fighter aircraft with which to oppose them. However, this does not represent the whole story. To begin with, the British had about 2,000 anti-aircraft guns and, what was an inestimable advantage, disposed of a network of radio identification stations—the newly developed radar system—which could locate enemy planes at a distance of 130 to 160 kilometres and thus largely eliminate surprise attacks from the air. The tactical and technical characteristics of the types of aircraft also varied quite considerably. The Type Ju 87 dive-bomber (Stuka) had only a low speed and was only lightly armed. The firepower of the He 111 and Ju 88 high-speed bombers was likewise inadequate and they consequently needed a strong escort. The Me 109 fighters, originally designed as interceptors, did not have enough range to accompany bombers to distant objectives. The multi-purpose machines of Type Me 110 intended specifically for this purpose and bombastically described as "destroyers" proved so unsuitable that they themselves needed a fighter escort to protect them against such British planes as the Spitfire and Hurricane. For their part, the Spitfire were faster but, like all the other British aircraft, were inferior to the Me 109 in respect of manoeuvrability and armament.

The Command of the Nazi Luftwaffe boasted that they would be in control of the sky over Southern England within four days and over that of the whole of England within 14 to 28 days. Just how unrealistic this aim was soon became evident when the war in the air increased in intensity on the 12th/13th of August. The British Fighter Command put a stiff resistance and could not be crushed—certainly not within a brief space of time. As it was, the Luftwaffe flew 1,485 missions across the Channel on the 13th of August alone and two days later 1,786 missions. Apart from the days on which there was bad weather, the German airmen flew 600 to 1,000 missions every day, including 250 to 400 with bombs against the airfields, control points and depots of the RAF but not so much against the radar stations, the importance of which was not fully appreciated by the commanders of the Luftwaffe. Already on the 13th of August the Luftwaffe lost 75 aircraft while only 34 machines of Fighter Command were downed. The German fighter squadrons which had hitherto flown independent missions were now ordered to provide close cover for the bombers. However, this reduced their operations against the British fighter pilots who kept strictly to their instructions of going for the bombers first and avoiding dogfights with German fighters. Despite unceasing attacks, the German Luftwaffe was unable to blast the RAF from the skies.

Admittedly, Fighter Command had to survive some very critical days and weeks. The combat readiness of its fighter units dropped and the communications and flight control systems were badly hit. Under the command of Air-Marshal Hugh Dowding, there were four fighter groups, each responsible for the protection of a specific area. 11 Group was faced with the hardest task and its 250 to 300 planes were not enough to throw back all the air attacks. On the other hand, it was not possible to increase the number of planes since there were not enough airfields and the air control system could not handle any more. The squadrons of 10 and 12 Group, however, often failed to find the enemy since their alert times were often too short to allow them to take off in time. Nevertheless, Fighter Command succeeded in making some fundamental improvements in its defensive tactics. From the end of August onwards, the faster Spitfires forced the German escort-planes to leave the bombers, allowing the squadrons equipped with the slower Hurricanes, which had a poorer rate of climb, to deal with the bomber formations. In the time between the 24th of August and the 6th of September, the Luftwaffe lost 378 aircraft and, although Fighter Command's losses were 295 aircraft, the latter lost fewer pilots.

The German Air Command nevertheless reckoned with far higher British losses and consequently decided to carry out major strikes against London. The aim of this was—indicating a total misunderstanding of the British character—to bring terror to the population, cause panic and deliver a death-blow against the English air defences. After the first air-raids on London in the night of the 5th/6th of September, the next phase of the war in the air began on the 7th of September with continuous large-scale raids on the capital. The RAF was indeed caught off balance by the massiveness of this offensive but the change in the principal ob-

"The Battle of Britain". Painting by Paul Nash (1940).
Imperial War Museum, London

jective of the enemy attacks gave it a certain breathing-space in which it was able to reorganize its forces.

Already on the 15th of September, the British air defences destroyed 56 enemy machines whereas the RAF only lost 25. Goering, as the Commander-in-Chief of the Luftwaffe, and those closest to him wanted to continue with new attempts, hoping that it would still prove possible to eliminate the RAF. But it was now clear to the rest of the German leaders that the war in the air against Great Britain could not be won with the aircraft available. On the 17th of September, the landing operation "Sealion" was indefinitely postponed by the OKW and cancelled altogether on the 12th of October. Further preparations and air-raids were intended solely to divert attention from the forces which were beginning to be concentrated for the march against the East.

Nevertheless, the German leaders did not totally abandon the hope of a political compromise with Great Britain and, in order to exert strong pressure, launched night attacks against industrial targets and the big cities. In addition to London, ports and industrial cities were favourite targets and, on the night of the 14th/15th November, Coventry suffered the worst of these raids. It was then that the term "to coventrate" was coined as the designation of senseless and barbaric air-terror against the helpless civilian population.

Although the air attacks were continued on an admittedly lesser scale up to the spring of 1941, it was in August and September 1940 that the Germans lost the battle of Britain. The British economy was not crucially affected. There were many casualties among the civilian population, it is true, and 23,000 people were killed in air-raids between July and December 1940. But the spirit of the nation remained unbroken and the terror of the bombs increased the hatred felt for the Nazis. The RAF lost 915 aircraft but saved most of their pilots whereas the Luftwaffe lost 3,094 planes between the 1st of August and the 2nd of December alone, in the majority of cases together with their experienced crews who, for the time being, could not be replaced.

The victory of the Royal Air Force in the greatest purely aerial battle of history proved to be of the highest strategic value. As Winston Churchill predicted in his realistic speech of "sweat, blood and tears", it formed the basis for surviving the critical period, lasting almost one year, of the war. In atonement for the earlier political mistakes of its statesmen and in sharp contrast to its previous historical experience, it stood alone against a far more powerful enemy block on the Continent until it was joined by the Soviet Union and the United States in 1941.

"View of an underground shelter". Drawing by Henry Moore (1941). Tate Gallery, London

EL ALAMEIN/1942

After the declaration of war by Italy on 10 June 1940, eventful actions were fought along the frontier between Egypt and Libya in which, from the beginning of 1941, fairly small German forces were involved—the "Afrika Corps", as it was called. However, the leaders of the Axis Powers were unable to reach agreement as to further operations in the Mediterranean area. Whereas the Italian headquarters in the spring of 1942 recommended the capture of the British island fortress of Malta, the German Supreme Command refused to provide assistance since the planes and paratroopers needed for this operation could not be made available. Its strategy was clearly concentrated on the theatre of war in the East where—after the severe setbacks of the winter campaign of 1941/42—it wanted to deal a death-blow at the Soviet Union by a second summer offensive. Nevertheless, it was precisely because of this that the German Command wanted to control the North African theatre of war as well so that after the collapse of the USSR it could initiate a pincer movement against the Near and Middle East from here and from the Caucasus. Admittedly, Hitler's headquarters refused the demands of the Commander-in-Chief, General Rommel, of the newly formed German-Italian "Armoured Army Africa" for more armoured and mechanized divisions and more aircraft but allowed him to decide for himself whether he would push forward as far as the Suez Canal in Egypt with the forces which were available or not.

In 1940 and 1941, the British Command had found it very difficult to provide its forces in North Africa with sufficient reinforcements. Several advances on Libya and the fighting that broke out there, particularly around Tobruk, led to severe losses in men and equipment. Despite the aid provided by the United States of America, the extension of the war to Asia and the Pacific precipitated by the Japanese surprise attack on Pearl Harbor in Hawaii on 7 December 1941 rendered the position of the British even more precarious and, on the other hand, naturally provided temporary relief for the German-Italian troops in North Africa. Since

the British navy and air force after the winter of 1941/42 were no longer able to replace their losses and only few convoys bringing supplies survived the attacks on the voyage to Malta, they lost command of the sea-routes between Italy and its colony Libya so that the competent commands of the Axis Powers were able to transport greater quantities of supplies, weapons and fuel for their armies in Africa in the spring of 1942.

On the 26th/27th of May, Rommel opened his offensive against the British Eighth Army under General Ritchie and by the 17th of June had driven it back to Egypt from Cyrenaica. With the aid of powerful armoured, artillery and air units, he was able to capture the fortress of Tobruk, which had been cut off, on the 21st of June. In the meantime, the British Supreme Command used the breathing space which resulted from this to establish a fortified position at El Alamein, about 60 kilometres to the west of Alexandria, the principal feature of which were its numerous minefields. Rommel, who was also fighting against time, decided to attack El Alamein with his battle-weary divisions, against all the rules of military reason, and achieve a breakthrough between the 1st and 3rd of July. As it was, he was obliged to repeat the attacks several times up to the end of the month but it was all in vain. The British defences withstood the variety of attacks and made up for the limited tactical successes achieved by the enemy. In the end, the fronts became finally static under the scorching heat of the Sahara sun.

In the conditions of the North African theatre of war, the two sides could use only numerically small forces but these were equipped with the latest weaponry. The armoured units were the most important forces but had to rely on close co-ordination with the fighters and fighter-bombers of the air force. The motorized artillery with their field-guns, and anti-tank and anti-aircraft guns also played an increasingly important part. The specific climatic conditions of the desert proved extremely severe both for men and machines. The Italian tanks were shown to be capable of operating in the desert but their armour and weapons were not good enough. The Type P III and IV German tanks were equipped with a gun of improved design and proved to be well-suited to desert warfare but needed constant technical maintenance. To begin with, the British had only tanks which were tactically and technically outdated and these made little impression against the German vehicles. It was only at El Alamein that they received newly constructed American tanks, including the excellent "Sherman" type, which were superior to the German models. The tank battles generally began at a range of 2,500 metres, which was very exacting for the tank crews. The support and supply columns played an important role since ammunition, fuel, drinking water, food and other supplies had to be transported across great distances and, to some extent, flown in.

On the 15th of August, General Bernhard Montgomery took over the command of the British Eighth Army. Since, in the meantime, Allied air and naval units had practically regained the control of the sea in the Mediterranean after the German Supreme Command had been obliged to withdraw many of its air squadrons from Sicily and transfer them to the German-Soviet front, Rommel's armoured forces suffered from an increasing shortage of reserves and supplies. This made it easier for Montgomery to take energetic measures to prevent a repetition of the enemy attack on El Alamein. In particular, a technically well-equipped line of defence was built between the Mediterranean coast and the Kattara Depression, itself impassable, 65 kilometres away, the armoured forces were more efficiently organized and more effective co-ordination achieved between the artillery on the ground and the strike forces in the air.

When, in the night of the 31st of August, the German and Italian troops attacked on the south wing so as to encircle the entire British position from here, they came up against minefields which delayed their advance and gave Montgomery time to bring up reserves and prepare his counter-attack. British air-attacks followed without a pause and, on the 2nd of September, Rommel was forced to break off the attack and withdraw to his earlier positions. In addition to losing a large quantity of armoured vehicles and guns, the German-Italian armoured forces also had to abandon irreplaceable stocks of fuel. Their Supreme Command decided to henceforth restrict itself to the defensive and to strengthen its own positions. Rommel himself and also the Italian headquarters endeavoured in vain to procure rein-

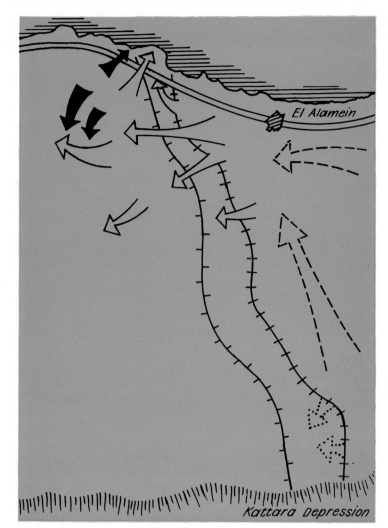

⊢┬⊢	German-Italian main battle line
+++	British main battle line
▶	German-Italian counter-attacks
⟶	directions of British attacks
⇢	British movements after opening of attacks
⋯⋗	British feint attacks

following double page:
German reconnaissance unit passing through a minefield at El Alamein. Documentary photo

The German crew of a captured British tank surrendering to British soldiers. Documentary photo

forcements from the OKW. On account of the severe losses suffered by the Luftwaffe in the East, it proved impossible to allocate additional planes for the protection of the sea-routes as originally promised.

In the meantime, within the framework of strategic planning on a wider scale and aiming for the launching of "Operation Torch", i.e., a massive Anglo-American landing in French North Africa, in November, the Supreme Allied Command for the Mediterranean and the Near East had sent strong reinforcements to the Eighth Army. By mid-October 1942, Montgomery had eleven divisions, including four armoured divisions, and five independent brigades, including two armoured brigades, totalling 150,000 men, c. 1185 tanks, 880 guns and about 850 aircraft. These forces were opposed by the German-Italian Africa Army with some twelve divisions, including four armoured divisions, totalling 96,000 men, about 500 tanks and self-propelled guns, about 600 guns and 360 planes. The British had large stocks of ammunition, fuel and other supplies but hardly anything was getting through to the other side and they only had enough ammunition and fuel for another few actions. The British pilots gained command of the sky and throughout the daylight hours maintained a watch on all the movements of the German and Italian troops.

By the skilful use of decoys, Montgomery managed to convince the enemy aerial reconnaissance that the main attack was going to come in the South. On the basis of this false hypothesis, the enemy command was persuaded to deploy powerful armoured units in this area. In reality, the British commander planned to attack at the road along the coast and to break through the German positions. The British Eighth Army changed over to the offensive on the 23rd of October, following repeated attacks by British aircraft in the days immediately prior to this on enemy positions, strong-points and depots. For the first breakthrough, Montgomery deployed a thousand guns along a narrow section of the front and maintained an artillery barrage for nine hours. Pioneers also cleared ways through the minefields before the infantry and tanks went into action.

Although the Eighth Army was clearly superior in equipment and numbers its troops had repeatedly to be regrouped and attacks to be launched in different directions. Consequently, the British needed several days before they could at last deal the final blow. By flexible tactics and several counter-attacks, Rommel endeavoured to ward off the threat of a breakthrough and finally concentrated his armoured forces, which had been decimated by the constant air-attacks, in the direction of the main British thrust. In the tank battle of the 2nd of November, in which the two sides clashed with tremendous force, the Italian troops lost all their tanks and streamed back to the West. The German armoured units, whose tanks were better able to withstand the British attacks, also lost most of their vehicles.

In the night of the 2nd/3rd of November, Rommel ordered a general retreat, unit by unit. Although the British did not take up the pursuit immediately since they first had to re-form, the withdrawal of the defeated German-Italian armoured force became a precipitate rush in which the Italian infantry divisions were sacrificed by the Germans to cover their own retreat. The British also succeeded in overtaking and destroying the Italian armoured corps lagging behind on the south wing. Rain starting on the 6th and 7th of November allowed the German troops a respite since the British wheeled vehicles became bogged down in the wet sandy soil. As a result, Rommel was able to bring back the rest of his army to Libya but from here had to continue the retreat via Sirte and Tripoli until a temporary halt could be made, at the beginning of 1943, along the "Mareth Line" on the Tunisian border.

The battle of El Alamein ended with a clear defeat for the Axis forces. They lost 59,000 men, 500 tanks and 400 guns while the losses of the British Eighth Army were only 13,500 men and 430 tanks. Although the battle was of pre-eminent importance for the North African theatre of war, it did not mark a crucial turning-point in the course of the Second World War. The forces used on both sides were too small for this end, despite the conquest of Libya by the British, even the politico-military consequences were of a limited nature. Since the German-Italian armoured army was not completely wiped out, and its remnants were still capable of fighting, they took part in the occupation of Tunisia and in the new battles which were fought there. It was only in association with stronger Allied expeditionary troops who marched on Tunis from Algeria that the Eighth Army was able to force the German-Italian army under Col.-General von Arnim to surrender on the 13th of May 1943, thus ending the war on African soil. The soldiers of the Eighth Army subsequently landed on Sicily on the 10th of July on their way to Italy and played a part in the overthrow of Mussolini already on the 25th.

Italian tank in the desert. Documentary photo

STALINGRAD / 1942/43

After the German 6th Army opened the battle on 17 July 1942 with the advance of vanguard units towards the great bend of the Don and crossed the river on the 21st of August, these units reached the north bank of the Volga at Rynok to the north of Stalingrad on the evening of the 23rd. On that and the following days, German aircraft bombed the factories and residential district of the city to weaken its defence and intimidate the population. Yet it was in vain that Hitler's generals, with the arrival of German soldiers at Russia's "holy river", imagined that their "final victory" over the Red Army was within their grasp. Even the attempt by the German 4th Armoured Army to win the bank of the Volga to the south of Stalingrad as well ended in failure some kilometres away from the river on the 29th of August. All the attempts of the aggressors to get into the city from an attack on the move and especially to storm the famous tractor factory in the north proved unsuccessful during these hot August days. These actions demanded a very high price from both sides and were already an indication that the struggle for the possession of the city marked a new phase in the battle of Stalingrad.

None the wiser for the refutation of its "blitzkrieg strategy" in the autumn of 1941 and the eventful course of the winter campaign of 1941/42, the Supreme Command of the Wehrmacht prepared a new plan of operations for 1942. The planners in the Führer's headquarters came to the reluctant conclusion that the balance of power no longer permitted an offensive along the entire front from Murmansk to Rostov and that a limitation in the German operations was necessary. By the concentration of powerful assault forces, including a large number of armoured and mechanized divisions, on Army Group South, it was planned that this would overwhelm the south wing of the Red Army, cross the Don, blockade the lower Volga with the capture of Stalingrad as a strategically important line and finally extend its advance to the Caucasus.

The German leaders were already indulging in fantastic dreams of further attacks via the Caucasus in the direction of the Near and Middle East and also up the Volga towards Moscow. They certainly succeeded in equipping élite units with sufficient numbers of tanks, guns and other weapons plus a considerable quantity of aircraft but there were serious difficulties in finding the number of infantry troops planned. Through the defeats suffered and the extension of the theatres of war to almost the whole of Europe and North Africa as well, the human reserves of Germany had already declined to a considerable extent. To make up for this, Rumania, Hungary and Italy were obliged to provide additional divisions which were to follow as a second wave. Military economic considerations also influenced the choice of the strategic objectives. It was asserted that possession of the rich coalfields in the Donets Basin, the oil-wells of the northern Caucasus and the fertile fields along the Don and Kuban was essential for the high-flown programme of world conquest.

After the successes of the counter-offensive during the winter of 1941/42, the Soviet headquarters examined several possibilities for the continuation of the war in the spring of 1942. Finally, it was decided to achieve a more favourable balance of power by attacks within restricted areas and to start a general offensive along the entire front only in the summer. It assumed, nevertheless, that the Western Allies would undertake at least some military actions to relieve the Red Army. The Soviet leadership was able to base its plans on an increase in war production after the serious setbacks of the previous year and on the numerous units which had been raised in the meantime. With them it was able to restore the combat efficiency of its forces which had been impaired by the losses suffered. In the assessment of the enemy, it was assumed that the special aim of the expected summer offensive would be Moscow and that it was therefore necessary to concentrate strong forces and the best equipment along the central section of the front in particular.

In the meantime, the course of the fighting in May and June in the Crimea and at Kharkov favoured the German

Wehrmacht which was thus able to regain the strategic initiative. On the 28th and 30th of June, it opened its new offensive in echelon formation on the south wing and, despite stubborn resistance, rapidly advanced towards Voronezh and the upper Don and in the direction of Rostov and the lower reaches of the river. The German forces occupied the Donets region and by the 22nd of July had reached the great bend in the Don. The number of prisoners taken was exceptionally small. The Soviet troops and commands were able to largely make up for the lack of a deep defensive line in the strip attacked by the Germans by employing flexible tactics; they maintained their cohesion and they succeeded in limiting or even prevent large-scale enemy breakthrough. Forced to achieve a turning-point in the war with this campaign at any price, the German Supreme Command, which had already reorganized its assault units in Army Groups A and B on the 9th of July, decided to launch a simultaneous offensive towards the Caucasus and in the direction of Stalingrad and the Volga. This meant that the German leadership was dangerously putting everything on a single

—·—·—   front line on July 22, 1942

➤➤   Soviet counter-attacks

⇾   German directions of assault

🚩   army supreme commands

★   Soviet front supreme commands

—·—·—   front-line on November 18, 1942

·········   front-line on December 30, 1942

➤➤   Soviet directions of assault

⇾   failure of German counter-attack

★   Soviet front supreme commands

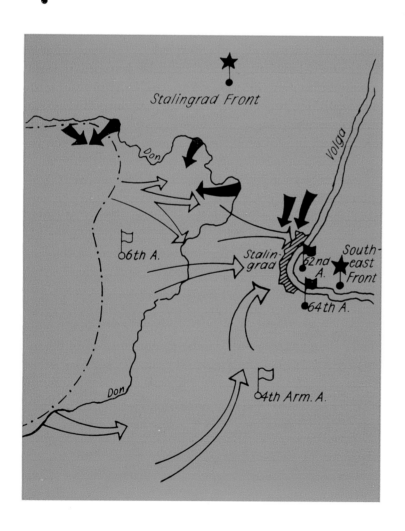

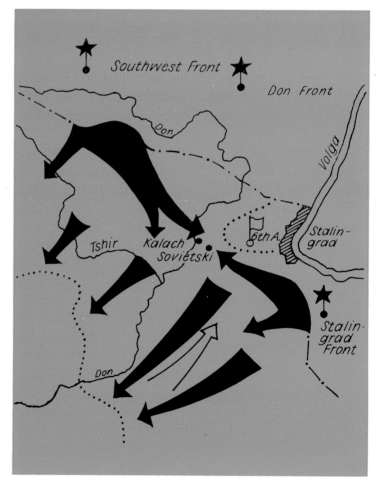

Bitter fighting took place during the battle on the banks of the Volga in the "Red October" tractor plant where tanks continued to be made right to the last. Documentary photo

card, increasing still further the contradiction between its objectives and its possibilities and itself paving the way for a military catastrophe unparalleled in the history of war.

For those commanding the Soviet resistance, Stalin's Order No. 227 of 28 July fully expressed their attitude: "Not one step backwards!" Repeated counter-attacks held up the Germans time and again and forced the enemy to re-organize before every new thrust. In addition, the Army Group A had to give up the 4th Armoured Army for the assault on Stalingrad so that its own advance towards the Caucasus was substantially weakened. However, even with the two assault groups of the 6th Army and the 4th Armoured Army, which were constantly reinforced in the following weeks, it was only in the last ten days of August that Army Group B reached Stalingrad. Yet another concentration, in which all the soldiers available were assembled, down to the last man, had to be carried out before the German troops were able to force their way into the city on the 12th of September. Despite the massive use of tanks, artillery and aircraft, they could not break, in house-to-house fighting, the resistance of the legendary 62nd Army under General Chuikov and the 64th Army under General Shumilov.

In view of the meagre results and the horrifying losses of men and equipment and after Hitler had already boasted at the end of September of the imminent fall of Stalingrad, the German Supreme Command sent specially trained pioneer and armoured units into action in mid-October and these succeeded in capturing the tractor factory and, within the city, in reaching the banks of the Volga. A renewed attempt to finally gain control of the entire city failed on the 11th of November. The successful defensive actions of the Red Army forced the German 6th Army, with the assent of the Army Group Command and the Führer's headquarters, to stop making further attacks. This marked the end of the plan of attack for 1942 since the other thrust towards the Caucasus also failed to achieve any of the objectives set.

The Soviet Command had certainly done everything to strengthen the resistance of its armies on the south wing throughout this period. At the same time, however, significant reserves of men, weapons and units were assembled in anticipation of coming events and were not allowed to be used in the defensive actions. Now that the German offensive had come to a standstill and since there were still powerful enemy forces between the Volga and the Don due to the course of the campaign, the Soviet headquarters decided to use its reserves for a counter-offensive which, from the middle reaches of the Don and from the lower Volga, was to encircle and destroy the German troops at Stalingrad.

Already on the 19th of November, the Southwest Front under General Vatutin and the Don Front under General Rokossovsky broke through the positions of the Rumanian divisions along the middle reaches of the Don. With their mobile vanguard units, they pushed forward to the great bend in the Don and crossed the river in an easterly direction. Other troops carried out irresistible attacks in a westerly direction and reached the Tshir by the end of November. The Stalingrad Front under General Yeremenko pierced the positions on the southern German flank on the 20th of November and reached the Don where it joined up with the northern wedge of the assault forces at Sovietski near Kalach on the 23rd of November. Units from the Stalingrad Front also advanced further to the West as far as the lower Don. This meant that there was a ring around the German 6th Army, parts of the 4th Armoured Army and the Rumanian 4th Army with 22 divisions and several dozen independent units. There was already a distance of 40 to 80 kilometres between them and the other German forces which had been forced to retreat. The encircled troops were concentrated on an area of 1,500 square kilometres.

The German Command, which was surprised by the directions, the forces used and the impetus of the counter-offensive, intended in all seriousness to keep the encircled divisions, now under the command of the 6th Army headed by Col. General von Paulus, at Stalingrad and to defend the area occupied as an advanced position and starting basis for the next campaign. At the same time, an Army Group Don was formed which was rapidly assigned strong armoured and infantry divisions from Western Europe and other sections of the front. Its task was to break the ring encircling the German forces and establish communications between the 6th Army and the rear, without the former being permitted to make a retreat.

In actual fact, the 6th Army did indeed make every effort to reinforce its defences in every direction. Nevertheless, it soon became apparent that the air-lift promised by Hitler and Göring to bring in supply could scarcely meet even the most elementary requirements. While the Soviet Stalingrad Front consolidated the outer ring, the Don Front largely restricted itself in December to shelling the German positions and to preventing any supplies from reaching the isolated troops by air. The German Luftwaffe suffered heavy losses, including 488 aircraft and irreplaceable pilots since only highly experienced air crews were able to execute the landing within the ring. Despite cold and hunger, the soldiers of the 6th Army, deceived by the lies of the Nazi propaganda, continued to fight desperately but their stocks of ammunition were obviously running low. The bitter cold which began to affect this area likewise had a devastating effect on the masses of men and their weapons within the ring.

In the meantime, from the 12th of December, a German assault group launched an attack to the south of the Don in the direction of Stalingrad and, with the help of the new "Tiger" heavy tanks with which the armoured units were equipped for the first time, fought its way to within 40 kilometres of the ring. After the war, the commander-in-chief of the Army Group Don, Field-Marshal von Manstein, irresponsibly asserted that it was only von Paulus's lack of will-power which prevented the 6th Army from being freed at the time.

However, the latter was no longer able to break out of the ring around his troops with his own resources and to join up with von Manstein; the assault-group, for its part, encountered such severe resistance that it was forced to withdraw at the end of December, sustaining heavy losses in the process. This sealed the fate of the 6th Army and its further resistance lost the slight military significance which it might have had up till then, i.e., to await a relief force and in the meantime tie down Soviet units which, while this lasted, could not be used for the continuation of the counter-offensive. Around the outer ring, the Soviet Southwest Front and the Stalingrad Front with their armoured columns had long since been advancing rapidly and by the beginning of 1943 were already threatening the communications with Army Group A in the northern Caucasus and along the Kuban.

On 8 January 1943, the Soviet Supreme Command invited the German commander-in-chief to surrender with honour and, when von Paulus refused this offer, ordered the Don Front to proceed with the destruction of the German forces within the ring. On the 25th of January, a wedge

Soviet field gun in action during the hard-fought defensive actions at the gates of Stalingrad. Documentary photo

was driven between the northern and southern parts, the first hoisting the white flag on the 31st of January and the latter on the 2nd of February. Even before this, many soldiers and officers had been taken prisoner or had stopped fighting of their own accord. Of the 300,000 men, who had originally been encircled, only 90,000, some of whom were seriously wounded or ill, were still left to be taken prisoner. The battle of Stalingrad, which had lasted for six months, was over. The Wehrmacht had suffered its worst defeat ever and had lost the initiative. The two hundred days and nights of the battle, recorded for posterity by Konstantin Simonov, Theodor Plievier and others, became a torch for the oppressed in Hitler's prison of nations, providing them with new strength to resist. The soldiers of the Red Army, however, erected signposts with the inscription "Berlin— 2000 km".

Attack by Soviet rifle squad in the almost totally destroyed city centre of Stalingrad. Documentary photo

KURSK/1943

Through the use of heavy tanks and self-propelled guns, the German Command hoped to achieve an overwhelming success at Kursk. Documentary photo

On the afternoon of 4 July 1943, violent fighting broke out to the northwest of Belgorod when German advance units attacked Soviet flank-protection detachments with the intention of establishing favourable base-positions for a major offensive. A heavy artillery barrage from hundreds of Soviet guns was unexpectedly directed against the German assembly areas to the north and south of the curve in the front at Kursk in the early hours of the 5th of July. This was accompanied by the attacks of tactical aircraft against enemy airfields, causing severe losses to the Germans and forcing them to postpone their attack. Despite this, the German artillery was still strong enough to open fire at day-break on the Soviet sections of the front and their broad defensive areas at the points selected for the breakthrough. This was the start of the battle of Kursk, which may be regarded as one of the greatest of history. About two million men took part in it and fought with almost 30,000 guns, 6,000 tanks and 4,500 aircraft in restricted areas of a few dozen square kilometres in extent.

The bulge in the front at Kursk had come into being in February and March 1943 at the end of the Soviet winter offensive. Between Orel in the North and Kharkov in the South, the front protruded about 150 kilometres to the West, the section around Kursk being 175 kilometres in length. Hitler and his advisers had already decided in March to make use of this bulge for a major attack. Armoured assault forces on both flanks were to break through to Kursk, join up to the east of the city and trap the large Soviet forces occupying the bulge. While these were being eliminated, support was to be given from the shortened line of the front to the German units charged with the recapture of those parts of the Donets Basin which were of great importance for the war effort and had been lost in the meantime. The Nazi leaders and their generals certainly realized that it was now impossible to destroy the Red Army in 1943 with a single blow. Nevertheless, they hoped that the "Citadel" operation, despite its limited objectives, would be a turning-point in the course of the war, allowing them

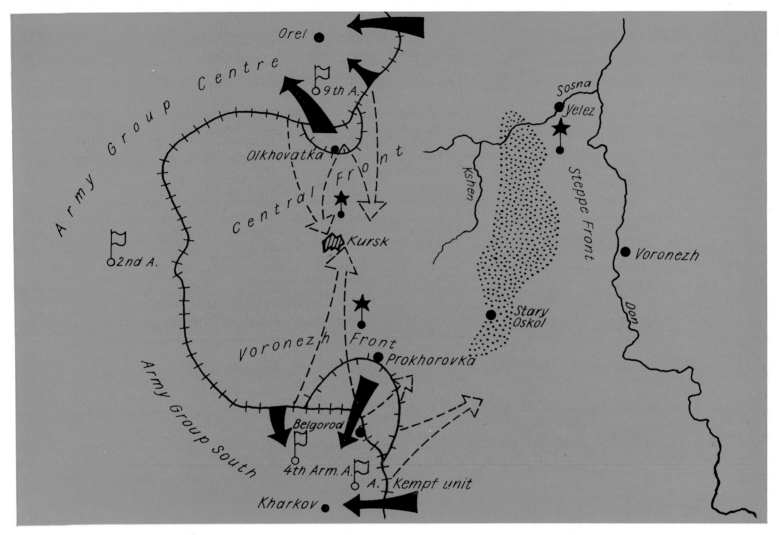

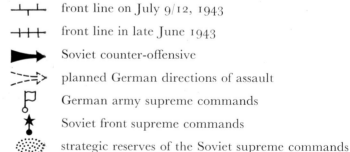

to regain the strategic initiative on the German-Soviet front. All these considerations lacked a solid basis since they underestimated the enemy to a totally unrealistic extent. A meeting of the Soviet commanders with Stalin as the Generalissimo had concluded at about the middle of April that it was the Germans' intention to wipe out the troops of the Voronezh and Central Fronts stationed in the bulge of the front at Kursk. They could choose between the alternative of launching an attack themselves or preparing a defence. The Soviet headquarters decided to remain primarily on the defensive, to absorb the German offensive and only after it had been repulsed to destroy the exhausted enemy troops by a counter-offensive. A major consideration was the assumption that the enemy would try to extend his attack in the direction of Moscow.

front line on July 9/12, 1943

front line in late June 1943

Soviet counter-offensive

planned German directions of assault

German army supreme commands

Soviet front supreme commands

strategic reserves of the Soviet supreme commands

Soviet field artillery changing positions during the battle of
Kursk. Documentary photo

T-34 tanks of a Soviet armoured army with infantry support
attacking during the battle of Kursk. Documentary photo

Beginning in April, the Soviet troops built an unmatched system of defensives within, on both sides of and also behind the bulge in the front at Kursk. Even the tactical zone, which was 15 to 20 kilometres deep, consisted of two lines of defence but at another 20 to 30 kilometres behind this there was a third line of defences which was followed by another two to three lines in the hinterland and even at the Kshen and, 300 kilometres away, at the Don, positions were prepared by way of precaution. The trenches, which were linked with each other, were protected by barbed wire defences and minefields. The defences also included pill-boxes, dug-outs and machine-gun nests. Since the particular forte of the enemy were his armoured units, all efforts were concentrated on anti-tank defence. Tank-traps, anti-tank gun emplacements, obstacles of every kind and gun positions for

direct shelling were constructed in the directions where there was a threat of danger. Then there were the mobile artillery units. The Soviet tank crews were prepared for the struggle with the attacking enemy armour. Most men and weapons were concentrated in the defence zone on the northern flank since the Soviet Command assumed that it would be here that the main German forces would attack.

The large-scale construction of positions and the growing concentrations of Soviet troops at the Kursk section of the front did not escape the notice of the German reconnaissance units. However, it was precisely in this that the Supreme Command of the Wehrmacht saw a unique chance to inflict a fateful strategic defeat on the masses of the Red Army assembled there. In these circumstances, it calculated that it could destroy no less than eight to ten armies at a

single stroke. To be sure, the uncomfortable question was indeed posed as to whether the ratio of the forces involved allowed an attack to be dared at all and even Hitler could not conceal a certain reservation as to this. Confronted with the choice of taking a very great risk or irrevocably permitting the enemy to take the initiative, the German leaders decided to play a dangerous game.

Their expectations were founded on the quality of their officer corps which they regarded as being obviously superior, although the series of catastrophes of the previous winter clearly refuted this, and, in particular, on the penetration capability of the armoured divisions, it being anticipated that the use of these on a massive scale would produce an overwhelming success. The German armoured forces were equipped with medium and heavy tanks of Type P V Panther and Type P VI Tiger plus the Type Ferdinand super-heavy self-propelled guns. Since these vehicles were not delivered on time, the date scheduled for the attack had to be put back several times between the beginning of May and the 5th of July. For the southern armoured wedge, the 4th Armoured Army under Col. General Hoth, supported by the Kempf army unit, was made available by Army Group South while the 9th Army under Col. General Model was provided by Army Group Centre for the northern wedge. On the eve of the battle, these two assault groups together disposed of 900,000 men, 570,000 of whom were actual combat troops, 10,000 guns, mortars and howitzers, 2,700 tanks or self-propelled guns and 2,000 aircraft, organized in Air Fleets 4 and 6. Most of the armoured élite units were included in the assault units of Army Group South, whose commander-in-chief, Field-Marshal von Manstein, had played a leading part in the planning of the operation.

On the other side, the Soviet Central Front under General Rokossovsky and the Voronezh Front under General Vatutin disposed of a total force of 1,337,000 men, about 977,000 of whom were front-line troops, 19,300 guns, mortars and howitzers, 3,300 tanks and self-propelled guns and 2,650 tactical aircraft. This was already a clear indication that the balance of power favoured the Soviet army and there was also the Steppe Front under Col. General Konev with five armies and six independent corps which was assembled further to the rear as a strategic reserve. However, the Soviet armoured forces were mainly equipped with the T-34 tank which was inferior in armour and armament to new German models although the latter were technically not yet so reliable.

The German assault waves which moved forward with air support on the morning of the 5th of July made every effort to achieve a rapid and massive breakthrough in the Soviet defensive zone. The 9th Army with eight infantry divisions and an armoured division attacked to the north of Kursk in a relatively narrow area but did not succeed at any point in making the breach needed for the other armoured divisions to move into action. Already on the following day, Col. General Model was obliged to move three armoured divisions to the front to renew the attack. Very fierce fighting developed at Olkhovatka and although the 9th Army finally committed all its armoured divisions to the front line it was unable to capture the ridges which dominated this section of the front. Its attack lost momentum in the labyrinth of the defensive positions and by the 8th of July it had penetrated to a depth of a bare 12 kilometres at only a single point. Admittedly, Model intended to repeat the attack after re-grouping his already badly shaken forces on the 11th of July but he was never able to implement this since on this very day he was compelled to break off the offensive and even begin with the withdrawal of his divisions from the area where the breakthrough had been achieved since the Soviet troops were attacking on both sides of Orel.

To the south of Kursk, the 4th Armoured Army had attacked with six armoured divisions and three infantry divisions right from the first day. Since the Soviet defences in this section of the front were weaker than in the North, the massed armoured forces under von Manstein and Hoth were able to penetrate the enemy defences in some depth by the 9th of July after fierce fighting and severe losses of men and equipment. After the German troops had re-grouped and fresh armoured units had been brought up, they were able to extend their penetration to 30 to 35 kilometres by the 11th of July. In answer to this and with the agreement of headquarters, a counter-attack was made by the Soviet Voronezh Front under General Vatutin, the 5th Armoured Guards Army and other units from the Steppe Front being brought up at all speed for this purpose. The main armoured forces of the two sides then clashed at Prokhorovka on the 12th of July. A total of 1,200 tanks and self-propelled guns were in action with the roar of their guns while overhead fierce dogfights were fought between hundreds of aircraft.

German medium size tank
knocked out during the battle of Kursk.
Documentary photo

The Soviet tank-crews, equipped only with the T-34 medium tanks, showed that they were capable of destroying German Tigers, Panthers and even Ferdinands by opening fire only at short range and taking the thinner armour of the sides as their target. Although it was scarcely possible for many hours to say which side was attacking and which was on the defensive, the 4th Armoured Army suffered losses on this day which far outstripped all previous ones.

The Kempf army unit had been ordered to provide support for the new thrust by the 4th Armoured Army against Prokhorovka but, with its three armoured and three infantry divisions it was unable to achieve the objectives of the attack by the 12th of July. It was only after the great tank battle, when the German strike capability had already been broken in actual fact, that the gap between the two formations was closed on the 15th of July but by this time the Army Group South had also been obliged to break off its attack.

The 12th of July was the culminating point of the battle. The 4th Armoured Army and the Kempf unit in the South and the 9th Army in the North were still about 130 kilometres apart. In view of the superior Soviet reserves and the deterioration in their own combat efficiency, there was no longer any way of continuing the offensive or of resuming it with fresh troops. The German Command at Kursk had a reserve of only six to eight divisions. Instead of supporting Model and Hoth with these reserves, it had to use them

further to the north and south of Kursk when the Soviet counter-offensive gathered momentum at Orel on the 12th of July and likewise began at Belgorod and along the upper Donets in the following days. After the 15th of July, the exhausted German assault forces evacuated the areas where they had thrust their way into the Russian lines and returned to their initial positions. They were pursued by the Voronezh Front and the Central Front which regrouped on reaching the earlier front line, obtained replacements for their losses which were likewise severe and, either immediately or some time later, took part in the counteroffensive. Orel and Belgorod were finally recaptured on the 5th of August, followed by Kharkov, which had been the scene of stubborn fighting on several occasions since 1941, on the 23rd of the same month.

Instead of paralyzing the capability of the Soviet Army for large-scale offensives for a long time ahead by an offensive battle in the Kursk bulge, which was what the German leaders had expected, the German forces lost, once and for all, every chance of being able to follow an offensive strategy. The Luftwaffe was decimated to such an extent that there was a decline in its combat strength on other fronts as well. In particular, however, Kursk with its mighty tank battles was the grave of the German armoured troops who, up to the end of the war, never again recovered from the losses sustained here.

NORMANDY / 1944

In the early hours of 6 June 1944, an armada of about 6,000 ships and boats, including six battleships and 22 cruisers, under the command of the British admiral Ramsay approached the flat Normandy coast between the peninsula of Cotentin and the estuary of the Seine after a rough crossing. Three divisions of airborne troops had already been landed during the hours of darkness and since midnight aircraft had been continually bombing the centres of the German coastal defences which had previously been identified. The great warships, as floating artillery batteries, opened fire at 5 a.m. and an unprecedented inferno descended on the German positions along the bay of the Seine. At 6.30 a.m. and 7.30 a.m., the first waves of troops landed on the beach despite the surging breakers. The invasion of France by the Western Allies, meticulously prepared and known by the code-name of "Overlord", was under way.

Since 1941, the opening of a Second Front in Western Europe had been the subject of political and military discussions between the Soviet Union and its Anglo-American allies. Certain promises had already been made for 1942 but instead of in France, the only place from where a promising offensive could have been launched against the terrirory of the Reich and also have lessened the pressure on the Red Army, it was in Morocco and Algeria that Allied troops landed in November of that year. In 1943, the Western powers again did not carry out the anticipated invasion of France but preferred Italy where, despite a great advantage in equipment and as a result of an over-cautious approach, the German positions were only slowly forced back to the North. The only success of this—valuable as it was—was the capitulation of Italy and its withdrawal from the fascist war-alliance. It was only on 4 June 1944, exactly two days before "V-day" (Victory Day) in France—long promised and eagerly awaited by the enslaved peoples of the Continent, that the Allies entered Rome which was declared an "open city".

On account of the massive defeats suffered by its troops in 1943 in the battles of Kursk and at the Dnepr, the German Supreme Command was obliged to withdraw a large number of divisions from France and send them to the Eastern Front. This considerably improved the conditions for the landing of powerful Allied forces on the Atlantic and Channel coasts of France. Even in the spring of 1944, an SS armoured corps was transferred to the Eastern European theatre of war although it was not possible to provide front-line reserves for the event of an invasion. The reductions in the German occupation and defence forces on the one hand and the consideration, on the other, that the Soviet Army might defeat the German Wehrmacht and occupy the Reich even without the opening of a Second Front in Western Europe led to the decision by the Governments and Command Staffs of the Western powers to now proceed with the invasion of France with all the forces at their disposal without further delay.

After the Anglo-American command staffs had worked out all the details of the invasion plan at the beginning of 1944 and decided in favour of a landing operation in the bay of the Seine, powerful expeditionary forces were assembled in Great Britain under the command of the American general Dwight Eisenhower or "Ike", as he was nicknamed. These forces comprised 39 divisions and ten brigades, which were at full strength, excellently equipped and well prepared and some of them had already been in action. Whereas the American 3rd Army was under the direct command of Eisenhower, the American 1st, the British 2nd and the Canadian 1st Army formed the 21st Army Group under General Montgomery. About 11,000 tactical aircraft and 2,000 transport planes were provided for their support. The numerical strength of the Allied expeditionary troops totalled 2,276,000 men. In addition, the armed units of the FFI (Forces Françaises de l'Intérieur) with 200,000 men were ready to help in the interior of the country. In the USA, there was a strategic reserve of 40 divisions. Despite this absolute superiority of forces and resources, the planning of "Overlord "allowed for no risks of any kind. For weeks before, the air raids on targets in France had been

stepped up, resulting in the destruction not only of communications and airfields but also of residential areas.

On the other hand, the German forces were very weak indeed. Army Group B, under Field-Marshal Rommel and consisting of the 7th and 15th Armies and an independent general command staff with 33 divisions, four of which were armoured units, was stationed in Northern France, Belgium and the Netherlands. Some of these units were Luftwaffe airfield protection divisions, fortress garrisons and training regiments of low combat efficiency, most of which had no transport facilities and consequently possessed no strategic mobility. As reserves, the commander-in-chief in the West, Field-Marshal von Rundstedt, had only three armoured

US troops landing on the Cotentin peninsula during the battle of Normandy. Documentary photo

divisions, which could only be used after the prior assent of Hitler's headquarters had been received. Admittedly, all the armoured divisions were well-equipped in general. On the eve of the invasion, Air Fleet 3, which was available for tactical support, had 890 aircraft at its disposal but was to be rapidly reinforced if necessary. There were various kinds of fortifications along the coast of Northern France but the "Atlantic Wall", described as impregnable by Goebbels's propaganda, was limited in actual fact to a few concrete fortifications along the Pas-de-Calais and on both sides of

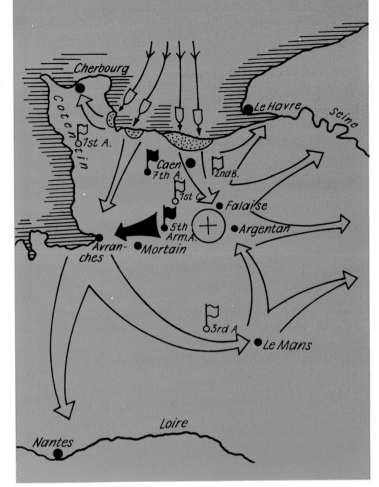

Allied landing manoeuvres

failure of German counter-stroke

Allied directions of attack

army supreme commands

Allied landing zones

encircled German troops

the Seine estuary. The German Supreme Command was undecided as to what measures had to be taken in the event of an invasion since it had been unable to determine with any certainty what section of the coast had been selected by the Allies for their landing. As a result, most of the divisions were scattered along the coast from Brittany to far along the North Sea and only a fairly small force was stationed further inland as an active reserve.

The Allied amphibious operation—the greatest in history—was carried out with technical perfection and, under the protection of naval guns and the absolute superiority in the air and on the sea, several bridgeheads extending for up to ten kilometres in depth were established by the evening of the 6th of June. Only at a single point did the Germans succeed in defending their positions for a fairly long time but this did not endanger the overall success of the Allies. Since the Führer's headquarters and the Supreme Command West had first thought that the landing was intended to divert attention from the "real" invasion, which they expected to come in the area to the north of the Seine, they kept back the majority of their reserves and restricted themselves to issuing illusionary orders to the units already in action to destroy the bridgeheads by the following night. Nevertheless, the Anglo-American troops encountered very great difficulties in landing heavy weapons since the weather deteriorated and the sea broke against the coast with even greater violence.

Admittedly, fairly strong German counter-attacks were made in the following days and for a time the position of the Allies at various points was critical. Nevertheless, as a result of their unrestricted command of the air, they were able to hold up the approach of other enemy forces, including the armoured divisions made available as a reserve. By the 12th of June, the terrain between the bridgeheads had been cleared and a deployment area established which was 80 kilometres broad and 13 to 18 kilometres deep. Despite the raging sea, artificial floating harbours placed before the coast and known as "Mulberrys" permitted the landing of tens of thousands of combat and transport vehicles and large quantities of fuel and ammunition. Thus the Supreme Allied Command had about 16 well-equipped divisions, including three armoured divisions, at its disposal.

On the 12th of June, bitter fighting broke out along the entire front. However, the German divisions thrown into action were unable to form an assault group but had to join the fighting one by one. Already on the march towards the scene of the fighting, decisive losses were inflicted on the armoured divisions by the unceasing attacks of the fighter-bombers so that all further movements had to be carried out at night and this over badly damaged roads and bridges. In addition, due to the strikes against the communications system carried out by the Résistance, the Germans were increasingly hampered by a shortage of fuel and ammunition. On this same day still, the American 1st Army launched attacks in a westerly and then a northerly direction from the deployment area, reaching the large port of Cherbourg on the 22nd of June and encircling it. By the end of the month, the enemy had been driven from both the town and the port and an immediate start made with clearance work so that the whole of the supplies needed could be landed at Cherbourg.

At the same time, the American "First" cleared the peninsula of Cotentin of enemy troops. The British 2nd Army, however, encountered very stiff resistance in the

Part of the Allied invasion fleet with barrage-balloon protection and heavy vehicles already landed on the coast of Normandy. Documentary photo

direction of Caen and until the end of June could only make slow progress. The German units were able to take full advantage of the many hedges crossing the Normandy countryside which enabled them to repeatedly "dig in" and launch surprise counter-attacks, although their numerical disadvantage became more evident with every day that passed. By the 10th of July, Army Group B had lost some 80,780 men and 370 tanks and self-propelled guns. The divisions of Army Group G from Southern France and of the 15th Army from the Channel coast could only be brought to Normandy after innumerable delays on account of the heavy bomb damage caused to the railway system. After the Soviet Union, on the 22nd of June, the third anniversary of the German invasion, had opened a major offensive and practically annihilated the German Army Group Centre within a few days in the Belorussian operation, the OKW needed all the reserves in Germany to hurriedly close the gap thus torn open in the front line as best it could. In these circumstances, it was absolutely impossible to reinforce the German troops in France to any significant extent.

At the beginning of July, the Anglo-American forces launched a frontal attack, too, their primary concern being to extend their deployment area. These actions went on to the 24th of July, widening the base zone to a hundred kilometres in actual fact and increasing its depth to between 30 and 50 kilometres. The balance of power existing since the beginning of July would have allowed the Supreme Allied Command to open a major offensive even with the units landed by then. However, as previously in Africa and Italy, Eisenhower and Montgomery wanted to make 100 per cent sure that there was no possibility of any setback and put safety before everything else. It was only when all 39 divisions were at full strength and equipped with 4,000 tanks and 6,500 tactical aircraft—including several hundred fighter-bombers—that the general attack took place on the 25th of July. Every thrust was prepared by a bomb carpet for which, in individual cases, up to, 2,000 aircraft were used.

The American 3rd Army made excellent progress in the direction of Avranches and Brittany whereas the Canadian 1st and the British 2nd Army only made slight gains in territory to the south of Caen where they were confronted with a comprehensive system of defences which exploited all the natural advantages of the terrain as well. However, their main task was to tie down powerful enemy forces while the Americans developed their strategic breakthrough at Avranches and, since the end of July, their motorized columns drove deep into the practically undefended area up to the Loire. The German Supreme Command attempted to cut them off from their communications with the rear by a tank attack at Mortain. Finally, the Germans sent in a

American "Sherman" tank destroyed by air-attack during the battle of Normandy. Documentary photo

group of five armoured divisions in the night of the 5th/6th of August. But after achieving slight gains in territory on the following day these were shot up by fighter-bombers and halted. Nothing came of the intention either, like all the other attempts up to the 11th of August to break through to Avranches, to use their own fighter-planes to support the tank attack.

In the meantime, the 3rd American Army under General Patton, which had originally been driving towards Brittany, now attacked in a southeasterly direction via Le Mans and then made a sharp turn northwards towards Argentan. Since the Canadians were also making slow progress in the direction of Falaise, it became apparent that the German 7th Army and the former armoured assault group combined in the 5th Armoured Army were becoming encircled. Nevertheless, even though they had sufficiently strong forces, the Allied troops were unable to complete the encirclement so that for several days a narrow bottleneck remained open to the south of Falaise, enabling the German armoured forces, still preserving some sort of order, to escape from the "pocket". On the other hand, the units further to the west practically disintegrated and endeavoured to escape from the encirclement by a disorderly flight through the no-man's-land until the Canadian and American troops finally put an effective end to this on the 19th of August. At the same time, the encircled troops, consisting of what was left from eight infantry and five armoured divisions, found themselves fighting on all sides.

The destruction of powerful German forces at Falaise was the end of the battle of Normandy which had begun on the 6th of June with the landing operation. In the course of these actions, the Anglo-American expeditionary forces eliminated the German Army Group B and initiated the liberation of France from the Nazi yoke. A French armoured division under General Leclerc entered Paris, which had already been liberated by the Résistance with a popular uprising, on the 25th of August, while at the same time the Allied troops who had landed on the Côte d'Azur on the 15th of August moved up the Rhône to join up with those fighting in the North.

Landing of US tanks and trucks during the battle of Normandy. Documentary photo

LEYTE / 1944

In the Pacific, Allied landings had taken place on the northerly Molucca Island of Morotai and on the Palau Iisands in mid-September 1944. From this, the Japanese headquarters in Tokyo correctly concluded that the next enemy strike would be against the Philippines, the loss of which would mean the interruption of the communications by sea between Japan and its sources of raw materials in Southeast Asia, especially the oil of Indonesia. The Command Staffs of the Japanese army and naval forces for the defence of the Philippines consequently prepared a joint operational plan, known as "Sho 1" (victory plan) which specified the use of the entire naval fleet and all available military and naval aircraft.

Admiral Toyoda, the commander of the Combined Fleet, ordered three squadrons to be formed: the "First Assault Formation", forming the centre under Vice-Admiral Kurita in Singapore with most of the battleships and heavy cruisers and a few light cruisers and destroyers; the "Second Assault Formation", comprising the southern forces under Vice-Admiral Shima in Japanese ports with two battleships and only a few cruisers and destroyers; and the "Diversionary Formation", made up of the northern forces under Vice-Admiral Ozawa, likewise in Japanese ports, with aircraft-carriers, reconstructed battleships, cruisers and destroyers.

Ozawa's formation, designated as the "main force" to deceive the enemy, was to be used as a decoy for the major force of the American aircraft-carriers, i.e., the most powerful enemy unit, drawing them away from the area where the invasion was anticipated and diverting their attention. Kurita's formation, on the other hand, was to head the artillery attack on the invasion force and, in particular, inflict heavy losses on the enemy escort-carriers. The second assault formation was to be used as reinforcement, according to the situation. The basic concept of "Sho 1" was to put the enemy fleet of aircraft-carriers out of action.

After internal disagreements about the next stage in "hopping" over the islands of the Pacific, the US Joint Chiefs of Staff had decided in the late summer of 1944 on the recapture of the Philippines and brought the operation originally scheduled for December forward to the end of October. Apart from the importance of the archipelago for the war effort and naval strategy, the main consideration in this decision was also the fact that on the Philippines there was a powerful anti-Japanese resistance movement, the Hukbalahaps, under Louis Taruc, which could support the troops making the landing. The choice fell on the island of Leyte which was within the range of land-based American bomber units and was defended by a single Japanese division. From here, it was possible to continue the offensive across the sea in the northerly and southerly directions. The Gulf of Leyte also offered favourable conditions for the landing.

It was envisaged that the Supreme Commands of the Southwestern Pacific under General MacArthur and of the Central Pacific under Admiral Nimitz should take part in the amphibious operation. MacArthur provided the 7th Fleet under Vice-Admiral Kinkaid with about 740 warships, landing-craft and supply ships for the operation. The 6th Army under Lieut. General Krueger with four divisions was to provide the troops for the first wave of the attack. The 7th Fleet included an escort-carrier group with 18 carriers and 500 planes and a gunnery formation with six battleships, nine cruisers and 51 destroyers. For the protection of the operations led by MacArthur and Kinkaid, Nimitz assigned the 3rd Fleet (previously the 5th) under Admiral Halsey which—in addition to smaller ships—included Task Force 38 under Vice-Admiral Mitscher with four task groups, the main units of which were 16 fast aircraft-carriers and six battleships.

Since the indecisive naval air battle of the Coral Sea in May 1942, in which for the first time naval units fought against each other, although the ships involved never sighted each other, and the highly significant American victory in the battle of Midway in June 1942, there had been a drastic change in favour of the Allies in the balance of power in the Pacific theatre of war. The Japanese had lost the initiative and, after four naval battles for Guadalcanal in the Solomons between August and November 1942, had been forced on to the defensive. With their newly-developed landing-craft for infantry and armoured forces (LCI, LST and LCT), powerful American units on landing-fleets supported by naval forces with aircraft-carriers now "hopped" from island to island, overcoming very fierce resistance from the Japanese garrisons of the islands. In November 1943, they landed on the Gilbert Islands, in February 1944 on Truk in the Caroline Islands, in June on Saipan in the Marianas and in July on Guam and Tinian, drawing closer and closer to the inner ring of the Japanese defences.

The Japanese Supreme Command did not by any means allow the enemy to assume control of the vast expanses of the Pacific Ocean without offering a fight. In the course of several naval air battles, the biggest of which was fought by Vice-Admiral Ozawa against Rear-Admiral Thomas Sprague from 19 to 21 June 1944 in the Philippine Sea to the west of the Marianas for the possession of Saipan, the Japanese lost a large number of their big ships which, with the exception of a few aircraft-carriers, they were unable to replace by new vessels. Most of the big war-

The Japanese super-battleship "Yamato" at full speed. Documentary photo

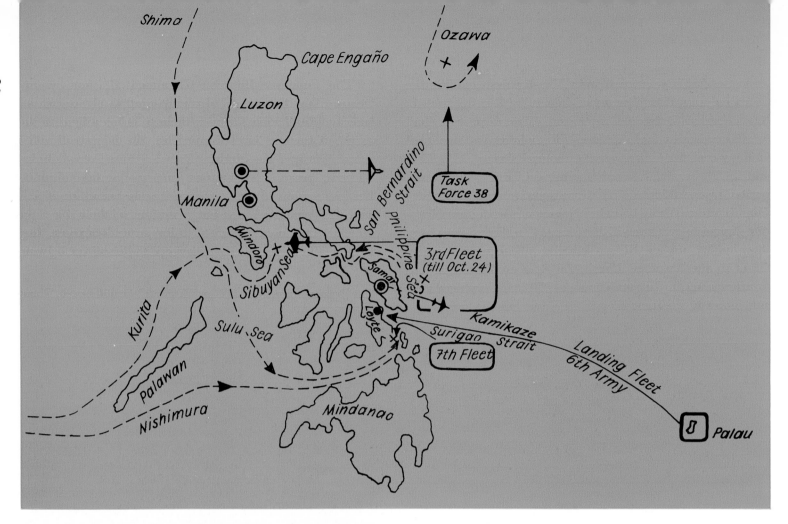

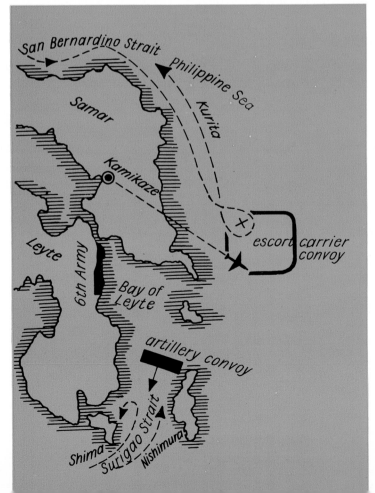

	armed forces of the USA and their Allies
⊙	Japanese armed forces
→	American and Allied manoeuvres
⇢	Japanese manoeuvres
×	sunken Japanese ships

ships still afloat—including the carriers—were anchored in the naval bases in 1944 on account of the shortage of fuel and the lack of air cover on the high seas. As a result, their crews lacked practice in the running of their ships and even the pilots on the carriers had little chance to improve their combat skills. In the United States, on the other hand, more and more warships were launched with every year and entered service as replacements for the vessels lost or were assigned to newly formed squadrons. Even by the end of 1943, these included about 50 aircraft-carriers of all types, for which more than 5,000 flying personnel were specially trained.

Contrary to the official naval doctrines of the pre-war period, the decisive part in naval battles was played not by the battleship with its big guns but by the aircraft-carrier with its carrier-based aircraft. It was the American Admiralty which was quickest to respond to this new situation. It rapidly formed speedy task groups of varying composition but with a nucleus of large or medium carriers supported by the guns of the battleships. These task forces, backed up by supply fleets, remained at sea for long periods at a time, keeping their naval and air crews in constant practice.

Preparing the landing operation on Leyte, the 3rd Fleet with Task Force 38 launched extremely hard-hitting air-attacks on 24 September against the islands in the centre of the Philippines. For the loss of 72 of their own planes, more than several times this number of enemy aircraft were destroyed and it was found that the Japanese air defences there were unexpectedly weak. Between the 10th and the 18th of October, strikes were carried out by 17 American carriers, six battleships, four heavy and ten light cruisers, 58 destroyers and almost 1,100 aircraft against the air bases on Okinawa, Taiwan and Luzon. At Taiwan, the Japanese sent their 2nd Naval Air Fleet and also Army aircraft into action in a counter-attack but only damaged one heavy and one light cruiser. Even this slight success had to be paid for by the loss of 350 aircraft with their irreplaceable pilots. A counter-stroke by carrier-borne machines was unsuccessful. The claim by the Japanese propaganda that 16 American ships, among them 11 aircraft-carriers, had been sunk in the battle of Taiwan only confused their own command personnel.

On the 20th of October, the first divisions of the American 6th Army landed on Leyte under the cover of gun-fire from the battleships of the 7th Fleet. At the bridgehead captured, an immediate start was made with the construction of runways for land-based warplanes. When the news that the invasion fleet was moving towards Leyte was confirmed on the 18th of October, Toyoda gave the go-ahead for "Sho 1" and ordered battle to be joined by the 25th of October at the latest.

Kurita first of all took his squadron to the Bay of Brunei to take on fuel and it was here on the 22nd of October that he divided his forces. The larger part, under his personal command, consisted of five battleships, including the unique "Musashi" and "Yamato"—gigantic vessels displacing 73,000 tons each, ten heavy and two light cruisers and 15 destroyers, and was to proceed along the western coast of Palawan Island to the Sibuyan Sea, move up through the San Bernardino Strait to the Philippine Sea and from there attack the enemy forces in the Bay of Leyte. A smaller force under Vice-Admiral Nishimura with two battleships, one cruiser and four destroyers was to pass through the Sulu Sea to Surigao Strait and then sail on a northerly course to the Bay of Leyte to support Kurita. Since neither force had any carriers, they were to be given air cover by land-based planes from the bases on the Philippines.

Ozawa's diversionary squadron set sail from Japan on a southwesterly course with four aircraft-carriers, two of which were converted battleships, three small cruisers and nine destroyers, plus only about a hundred aircraft. Shima's squadron received orders to provide an escort of three cruisers and seven destroyers for a convoy with reinforcements for the garrison of Leyte.

In the night of the 23rd of October, American submarines located Kurita's forces and attacked on the following morning. They sank two heavy cruisers and damaged another so badly that it had to return to port, escorted by two destroyers. When Kurita arrived in the Sibuyan Sea on the 24th of October, he was attacked by the planes of the 3rd Fleet. With the "Musashi", he lost one of his super-battleships and a heavy cruiser was put out of action. Since the promised air support from bases on land did not materialize to anything like the extent necessary, Kurita turned westwards again. This and other exaggerated reports about allegedly sunken or damaged Japanese ships led Halsey to withdraw Task Force 38 from its position off San Bernardino Strait and, together with it, to set out on the search for a Japanese aircraft-carriers force somewhere in the North. Indeed, in the morning, the American ships had been attacked by Japanese aircraft which had included some carrier-based planes. Most of the aircraft dispatched by Ozawa during the morning hours—about 75 in number —had got lost after attacks against aircraft-carriers. The rest landed on land-bases, from which they took part in the attack on the carriers of the 3rd Fleet.

Nishimura passed through the Sulu Sea almost unnoticed and finally, in the night of the 25th of October, after being detected by the enemy in the meantime, sailed into Surigao Strait. At 11.36 p.m., he was attacked by torpedo-boats but suffered no damage; at 2 a.m., however, a torpedo-attack was made in the darkness of the night by a group of destroyers which sunk one of Nishimura's two battleships, the "Fuso", and two destroyers, another destroyer being left behind in a damaged condition. What was left of the squadron nevertheless continued to sail on in a line-ahead formation until it met its death-blow at the end of Surigao Strait.

On the assumption that San Bernardino Strait was adequately covered by a Task Force 34 specially formed by Halsey for this purpose even after the 3rd Fleet had turned away on a northerly course, Kinkaid had sent the battleships of the 7th Fleet under Admiral Oldendorf to Surigao Strait when he was advised of the approach of a Japanese squadron. Whith his six battleships, four heavy and four light cruisers and 21 destroyers, Oldendorf executed the classical manoeuvre of "crossing the T" as Nishimura sailed into his formation. The last gun-duel in history between battleships then followed. From 3.48 to 4.20 a.m., the Japanese were exposed to very heavy, radar-controlled gunfire, which was returned to only a slight degree, until also the second battleship, the "Yamashiro", was sunk, together with the commander of the squadron. One cruiser and the last destroyer were badly damaged and forced to turn away; these were sunk by aircraft on the following day. With the exception of a damaged destroyer, no losses were sustained by Oldendorf.

Shima's squadron was supposed to support Nishimura but had maintained a distance of about 25 sea-miles between his and the latter's ships. Consequently, it was only at 4.24 a.m. that he made contact with the enemy and by this time everything had already happened. Although Shima immediately put about to try and save his small force, one of his cruisers was damaged and, on the following day, sunk by aircraft.

In the meantime, however, Kurita had again resumed an easterly course and, without attracting much attention, had slipped through San Bernardino Strait with four battleships, six heavy and two light cruisers and ten destroyers. Shortly after sighting the enemy to the east of the island of Samar, he opened fire with his guns at 6.58 a.m. on the group of escort-carriers of the 7th Fleet turning off to the East. The Americans were able to get most of their aircraft into the air. Only six escort-carriers and seven destroyers moved against the Japanese, despite their disadvantage in firepower. Squalls and the smoke-screens laid by the Americans hindered the Japanese gunners in the pursuit-action that followed. Since the Japanese vessels also had to make repeated changes in course to avoid the air and torpedo attacks, their line of battle broke up. When Kurita saw that he had already lost three cruisers and that another cruiser and a destroyer had been forced, by the damage suffered, to break off the action, he doubted whether victory could be won, despite his great superiority and the hits already achieved. Since he wrongly suspected that Halsey's 3rd Fleet was in the vicinity, he ordered his ships at about 9.15 a.m. to break off the action and resume a northwesterly course. Finally, after receiving no news or only discouraging reports from the other formations and since the US landing-fleet, his original objective, had already set sail from the Gulf of Leyte, he decided to proceed in a westerly direction and return to his bases via the San Bernardino Strait.

Neither Kurita nor Sprague had noticed that the first "kamikaze" fliers had taken part in the bitterly fought battle. With "Sho 1", the 1st Naval Air Fleet on the Philippines with its 150 aircraft and the 2nd Naval Air Fleet on Taiwan and in Japan with about 450 planes plus the 4th Army Air Fleet on the Philippines with some 200 aircraft had been given the task of providing active support for the naval forces. Due to the American air-attacks between the 21st and 24th of September and after the 10th of October, this task could no longer be carried out. This was why Admiral Onishi, on the 19th of October, announced his intention of sending Zeros carrying 250-kg (500-lb) bombs which were flown by "death-fliers" against the ships of the enemy.

Kamikaze pilot plunging on the deck of an American battleship. Documentary photo

By the 25th of October, there were four groups with a total of 13 death-pilots and it was these who attacked the escort-carrier group in two waves during the morning. They sank one carrier and damaged another six, three of these seriously. It was only later, when the relative success of the trial action at Leyte had given Japanese headquarters the idea of using thousands of young volunteers to delay defeat by their death-flights, that the term "kamikaze" (divine wind) was coined, recalling the wondrous delivery from the Mongol invasion in 1274 by what was probably a storm at sea.

The American 3rd Fleet and Ozawa's carrier formation found themselves not far away from each other during the night of the 25th of October, Ozawa changing to a northerly course with the idea of drawing the enemy force away from the Philippine Sea. He succeeded in this since Halsey immediately set off in pursuit with the whole of Task Force 38 (one group of which was on the way to its supply ships) at full speed. Halsey still had eleven large and medium carriers, six battleships, two heavy and seven light cruisers and 43 destroyers.

On the 25th of October, Mitscher launched constant air-attacks on Ozawa's ships from 8 a.m. to 5 p.m. from about 130 sea-miles to the east of Cape Engaño, four Japanese carriers and one destroyer being sunk. Ozawa could only get 12 of his planes into the air and consequently had to rely on his anti-aircraft guns. However, only the two converted battleships had an effective air defence and could drive off the enemy planes. In the evening, Ozawa turned back towards Japan with his remaining ships while Halsey hastened to the San Bernardino Strait to the aid of the 7th Fleet but, arriving on the 26th of October, he was too late to catch Kurita.

On the Allied side in the four actions of the far-ranging battle of Leyte there were 216 American and four Australian ships, including 34 aircraft-carriers and escort-carriers, twelve battleships, 24 cruisers, 111 destroyers, 1,280 aircraft and—indirectly—29 submarines with a total of 1,330,000 tons and 140,000 men. They were opposed on the Japanese side by 77 surface vessels with four aircraft-carriers, nine battleships, 19 cruisers, 29 destroyers and 212 aircraft plus 14 submarines, totalling 730,000 tons and 43,000 men. The enormous numerical superiority of the Americans, their better equipment—especially their aircraft—and also their determined leadership enabled them to achieve victory in the greatest of all sea-battles, a victory which afflicted the Japanese navy for the rest of the war. Henceforth, it was obliged to continue the war at sea primarily with light vessels since at Leyte it lost all four of its aircraft-carriers, three battleships, ten cruisers, nine destroyers and one submarine. The losses of the victor, on the other hand, amounted to only one aircraft-carrier, two escort-carriers and two destroyers.

BERLIN/1945

When, at about 3 a.m. on the 16th of April 1945, the whole of the artillery and a large number of tactical aircraft of the 1st Belorussian Front under Marshal Zhukov delivered a crushing blow against the German positions along the Oder to the east of Berlin, the curtain was raised on the final act of the Second World War in Europe.

After an almost unbroken series of defeats and despite stubborn and, finally, desperate resistance, the German Wehrmacht had been forced to abandon, one by one and without fame or honour, the countries which it had invaded between 1938 and 1942. In the autumn of 1944, the Anglo-American armies reached Aachen and, in East Prussia, the Soviet Army set foot on the territory of the German Reich. The war was irresistibly returning to the country which had started it in 1939. In the course of the decisive Vistula-Oder operation and after the liberation of Poland, Soviet forces occupied East Prussia, Pomerania, large areas of Silesia and Lusatia between January and March 1945. They drove the German occupation forces from Slovakia and Hungary and, after several days of fighting, forced the garrison of Vienna to surrender at the beginning of April. The last Soviet winter offensive had ended along the Oder

and the Neisse but several bridgeheads had already been established. At the same time, the Western Allies completed their advance to the Rhine and immediately proceeded with the crossing of the river—first at Remagen and then by the end of March along a broad front. Resistance rapidly declined and British armies forced their way to the Lower Elbe while the Americans advanced as fast as they could towards Thuringia and Bavaria.

Even the political and military leaders of Germany could no longer disregard the fact that there was now no chance whatsoever of avoiding final defeat. Nevertheless, they obstinately insisted on continuing the war, converting Germany itself into a battlefield and mobilizing and sacrificing its remaining strength for this purpose. However, war production had practically come to a standstill and, with the almost complete command of the air by the Allies, the communications system was scarcely functioning any longer. Since the greatest danger threatened them from the East, the Nazi leaders concentrated most of the units still capable of offering resistance in the area between the mouth of the Oder and Lusatia. In particular, since February, an extensive system of defensives had been built in front of Berlin, the backbone of this being provided by the anti-aircraft guns of the Berlin defences. Despite all the evidence to the contrary, the intention was to deliver a crushing blow against the Red Army at the very gates of the "capital of the Reich"—something which the Wehrmacht had been incapable of achieving since Stalingrad. Berlin itself was prepared for the battle and the German Supreme Command was determined to continue the fighting even in the streets of the city with a total disregard for the civilian population, the cultural treasures, the homes and the factories which had survived the air-raids.

To be sure, about a million troops were deployed along the Oder line but these included adolescents and old men

Soviet field artillery in firing position in the Oder basin during the battle of Berlin. Documentary photo

from the German equivalent of the Home Guard, the "Volkssturm". Although they had 10,400 guns, 1,500 tanks and 3,300 aircraft and large quantities of ammunition, fuel reserves were at a low level by this time. They formed the Army Group "Vistula" and, in Southern Lusatia, the left wing of Army Group "Centre". On the day that the Soviet offensive began, Hitler issued yet another hysterical appeal, urging the soldiers and officers to fight mercilessly to the last bullet while he himself was evidently preparing to evade his responsibility and the retribution which he so richly deserved by committing suicide.

The Soviet headquarters had long since planned the operations which were to force Germany into unconditional surrender and to end the war in Europe. It rejected the pro-

posal that the offensive which had begun on the Vistula in January 1945 should be extended to Berlin and, instead, required the thorough preparation of the attack on the German capital since it correctly assumed that powerful concentrations of troops were to be expected here. The individual Soviet armies were assigned the following tasks. The 2nd Belorussian Front was to attack Neustrelitz in Mecklenburg to the north of Schwedt and thus prevent any attempt by the Germans to bring troops still available from the Baltic coast to Berlin. The 1st Belorussian Front was instructed to make a direct frontal attack on Berlin from the bridgehead at Küstrin and, at the same time, to encircle the capital from the north and south with its mobile troops. The 1st Ukrainian Front was given the task of crossing the

Neisse in Lusatia and advancing towards the western suburbs of Berlin. Its right wing was to join up with the left wing of the 1st Belorussian Front in the area to the southwest of Berlin. For the offensive, an unparalleled concentration of units, men and weapons was organized, finally comprising about 2,500,000 men, 41,600 guns of all calibres, 6,250 tanks and self-propelled guns or rocket-launchers and 7,500 aircraft.

Whereas the 1st Ukrainian Front under Marshal Konev was rapidly able to break through the defence zone and into the area on the other side, the 1st Belorussian Army encountered very stiff resistance, the fiercest fighting taking place on the Seelow Heights to the west of the Oderbruch region. It was only on the 18th of April, after capturing

Soviet infantry advancing through the war-torn streets of Berlin. Documentary photo

Disabled heavy guns in an anti-aircraft gun-position after the battle of Berlin. Documentary photo

literally every elevation and village in individual actions, that Zhukov's armoured units were at last able to launch the attack on Berlin speedily. To make up for the delay, Konev diverted two armoured armies to the northwest on the 17th of April. The first Soviet troops reached the edge of Berlin on the 21st of April and established themselves in the suburbs. Three days later, the armoured armies of the 1st Belorussian Front and the 1st Ukrainian Front joined up to the west of Potsdam, thus completing the encirclement of the German capital. The troops of Army Group "Vistula" stationed to the north hurriedly withdrew to the lake district of Mecklenburg and all the attempts by German command staffs to organize counter-attacks from here proved to be a waste of time. Units of the German 9th Army

The ruins of the German Reichstag building in the hands of the victorious Red Army. Documentary photo

and the 4th Armoured Army were cut off to the north of Cottbus and were unable to break through to the West. To the east of Bautzen, Soviet and Polish troops thwarted several attempts by the Army Group "Centre" to influence the fighting in Berlin by launching relief attacks of its own. It was apparent that the German Supreme Command was scarcely in a position any longer to direct its troops who were fighting outside Berlin. Many orders were totally unrealistic and only aggravated still further the chaos existing in the command of the various units.

On the 25th of April, the Soviet 5th Guards Army and the American 1st Army met at Torgau on the Elbe. This event put an end to all the day-dreams of the Nazi leaders as to a possible confrontation between the Soviet Union and the United States. It was this fantasy which had led them to order the 12th Army stationed at Magdeburg to attack in the direction of Potsdam and to restrict the military resistance against the American armies now advancing to the middle reaches of the Elbe to passive actions only. In the bunkers of the Reich Chancellery, the Nazi leaders refused to admit the complete futility of every attempt to bring relief and to spare the inhabitants of the capital the terror of the battle.

The "capital of the Reich" was divided into three defence zones. Whereas the outer zone was formed by the lakes and woods of that area of the Brandenburg Marches which surround Berlin and had already been taken by the Red Army, the second one consisted of the outer districts of the city and the third of the area within the inner ring of the city-railway network. The whole of the city area was also divided into nine defence sections of which the city centre with its massive stone structures was the most heavily fortified. Here, too, the main strength of the defences lay in the anti-aircraft positions with their 12.8-cm guns. As a result of the

course of the previous fighting, about 400,000 men were concentrated in Berlin, including a considerable number of SS units which were capable of any crime at all.

From the 21st of April onwards, four Soviet armies, including an armoured army, fought their way through the second defence zone and reached the suburban railway ring. After the German Supreme Command had rejected Marshal Zhukov's demand to cease the already senseless spilling of blood, the 1st Belorussian Front attacked the city centre according to plan with the street and house-to-house fighting in the heart of the city beginning on the 26th. The Soviet Supreme Command brought up heavy siege guns and were able to deal with the strongest tower shelters. In fighting of untold severity, the Soviet troops inched their way forward and reached the government district on the 30th of April. It was on this day that they hoisted the Red Flag on the building of the Reichstag. But the battle continued.

After Adolf Hitler had committed suicide on that same day, the Minister for Propaganda, Joseph Goebbels, who had been designated by him as the Reich Chancellor, endeavoured in the following night through General Krebs, who had been the German military attaché in Moscow before the war and was able to speak Russian, to negotiate a truce

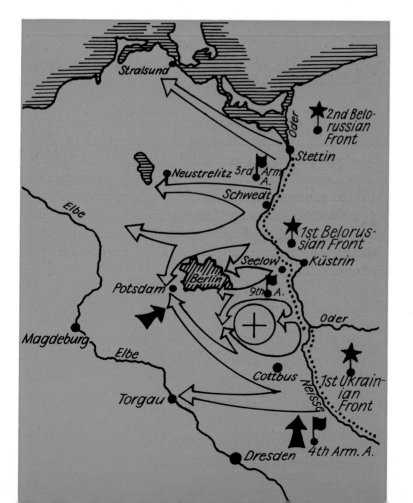

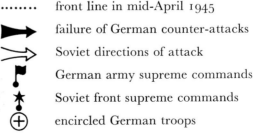

....   front line in mid-April 1945

➤   failure of German counter-attacks

⇾   Soviet directions of attack

⚑   German army supreme commands

★   Soviet front supreme commands

⊕   encircled German troops

with the Soviet Supreme Command to gain time for the formation of a new "Reich Government". However, they rejected the conclusion of an unconditional surrender offered by Zhukov on behalf of Stalin and were thus responsible for the fighting becoming even fiercer in this nightmare situation at "five minutes to twelve". From mid-day onwards, intensive artillery fire was concentrated on the last remnants of the inner defence section and, on the evening of the 1st of May, an attack was launched against the terrain of the Reich Chancellery in the then-time Wilhelmstrasse, forcing the German commander, General Weidling, to surrender at six o'clock on the following morning and to order his soldiers to lay down their arms. Goebbels had taken poison and Martin Bormann had been killed near Lehrte Station in an attempt to get away. The last German troops still fighting in Berlin surrendered at 3 p.m. 70,000 survivors were taken prisoner.

"Victory". Painting by P. Krivohogov (1948). Central Museum of the Soviet Army, Moscow

The end of the Nazi nightmare soon followed. A so-called Reich Government headed by Dönitz in Flensburg no longer had any important military units at its disposal in Germany. The units in Italy, Prague, Copenhagen and Oslo surrendered one after another and, on the 8th of May 1945, Marshal Zhukov as the representative of the Allies accepted the capitulation document of the "Thousand-Year Reich". This marked the end of the darkest chapter in European history.

Epilogue: HIROSHIMA/1945

The overthrow of Nazi Germany meant that Japan, which now stood alone, was in a hopeless political and military position. Since the backbone of its naval fleet had suffered crushing defeats in the two mighty battles of June and October 1944 in the Pacific, Eastern Asiatic waters were totally dominated by the American naval and air forces, supported by the newly reinforced British Eastern Fleet, which were able to attack any objective which was selected. On 7 April 1945, 280 of their aircraft found and sank the "Yamato", the biggest battleship ever built. In preparation for a landing on the principal islands of Japan, almost all of the big Japanese ships still afloat, which had sought refuge in the Japanese inland sea, were destroyed from the air: the new aircraft-carrier "Amagi" and the battleships "Haruna", "Hyuga" and "Ise". In July, for the first time, industrial installations in the vicinity of the coast were hit not only by bombers but also by the guns of the 3rd Fleet of the US Navy. Admittedly, intensified counter-attacks by Japanese "kamikaze" pilots who crashed their planes, loaded with bombs, directly on the American ships caused severe losses. Between April and May alone of 1945 in their eight-week offensive against the US fleet off Okinawa about 2,000 suicide pilots sank 26 ships—although these were fairly small vessels—and damaged another 164. But their influence on the course of the war was a mere nothingness.

Despite this, serious problems still confronted the Americans. In February and March, the occupation of the island of Iwoshima, which was defended by 20,000 Japanese, had taken six weeks and caused about 23,000 casualties. On the larger island of Okinawa, where the 10th Army had landed without difficulty on the 1st of April the garrison of 90,000 men resisted until far into June, killing or wounding almost 50,000 Americans. If this happened at abandoned outposts, what would await the invaders in Japan itself? Was superior technology at sea, on land and in the air really enough to achieve rapid victory already in 1945 against the Japanese Home Army, numbering almost four million men and with another three million reserves on the mainland?

However, the government of the USA was particularly interested in a quick end to the war in the Pacific as well so as to have its hands free for maintaining its interests as a world power in the drafting of the peace conditions in Europe. At the Yalta Conference (in February/March 1945), President Roosevelt had welcomed the agreement of the Soviet Union to take part in the war against Japan two to three months after the ending of the hostilities in Europe but by the summer his successor, Truman, was endeavouring to restrict as much as he could the contribution of the USSR to the defeat of Japan. This was to ensure that America would not have to share its influence on the island state of Japan with its Russian ally after victory had been achieved, a consideration which is also familiar from past coalition wars. In this particular case, however, the situation was complicated by the fact that the two leading Allied powers represented opposing political orders and exercised their influence in their preferred spheres of activity. In all the uncertainties of the post-war atmosphere, they would certainly continue to do this.

Consequently, the dropping of the atomic bomb by the Americans was primarily a politically motivated decision, initially calculated to provide those of the Japanese leaders who were prepared to surrender—and this was also Emperor Hirohito's view—with a psychologically effective shock-argument with which to radically influence the thinking of the military leaders who still wanted to resist and thus to restrict the possible consequences of the declaration of war by the USSR. As long as the American nuclear stocks consisted of two complete bombs and one half-finished one, there could be no strategic importance in dropping bombs on non-military targets. This was why the Supreme Commanders in the two theatres of war, D. Eisenhower and D. MacArthur, expressed reservations to which there was no totally convincing answer.

Albert Einstein had drawn the attention of President Roosevelt to the exceptional significance of the splitting of the uranium atom by Otto Hahn and his associates in 1938.

Mushroom cloud
over Hiroshima.
Documentary photo

Once the absolute suitability of the release of atomic energy for the development of a totally new kind of weapon had been established—especially by the Italian anti-fascist emigrant Enrico Fermi in Chicago in 1941—the American government began in 1942 with the recruitment of 150,000 scientists and technicians for work on the bomb, the project being known by its code-name as the "Manhattan project for the manufacture of a tube alloy". It was believed that Nazis were working along the same lines but in fact Hitler had already abandoned the project (but this was only known later), considering it to be too protracted an undertaking. The passive resistance of anti-fascist German nuclear physicists played a not unimportant part in this.

As a result of the change in the war situation, the American nuclear weapon, which had been envisaged more for use against Germany, was made available for use against Japan. After a successful trial detonation on the Los Alamos test-grounds in the desert of New Mexico on 16 July 1945, the two bombs "Little Boy" and "Fat Man" were sent to Air Force Unit 509 which in June was transferred from Batista Field in Cuba to the heavily guarded northern part of the island of Tinian in the Marianas. The pilots of the special flight under Colonel Paul Tibbets had already been practising for more than a year the dropping of a pumpkin-shaped bomb from B-29 strategic bombers from a height of 9,500 metres by a visual technique although they had not been informed of the purpose of this. They were only told this by their commanding officer immediately before the deadly mission.

On the 24th of July, Truman's order was received from Potsdam: "the first special bomb, as soon as the weather after 3 August 1945 permits bombing with good visibility ... to be dropped on one of the following targets: Hiroshima, Kokura, Nagasaki or Niigata." This meant that the declaration of war by the USSR on Japan expected on the 8th or 9th of August before the expiry of the three-month period had to be anticipated at all events.

At 1.37 a.m. local time on the 6th of August—it was a Monday—the first plane to take off from Tinian was the "Straight Flush", piloted by Major Claude Eatherly. Its task was to report on the weather over Hiroshima, two other machines flying over Nagasaki and Kokura for the same purpose. One hour later, Tibbets took off in the "Enola Gay" with the five-ton "Little Boy" on board.

Eatherly was over Hiroshima at exactly 8 a.m. and found that the weather was satisfactory. He had Master-Sergeant Baldasaro send the following radio message: "Y 2, Q 2, B 2, C 1, cloud at all heights less than one-third, bombing conditions excellent."

The report reached the "Enola Gay" 50 miles from the coast of the island of Shikoku from where it could still reach all three possible targets on schedule. It changed to Course 353, direction north, and appeared over Hiroshima just as the "Straight Flush" disappeared over the horizon. At 8.15 a.m. local time, the first atom bomb dropped from its bomb-bay and from a height of 9,500 metres floated down on a parachute towards the centre of the city which was packed with refugees whose busy working week had just begun. The following entry was made in the logbook of the "Enola Gay": "Bomb away, time 09.15" (Tinian time). After falling for 42 seconds, the bomb was detonated at a height of 570 metres. Five kilograms of cordite set off the chain reaction of two blocks of uranium and the remote-controlled bomb exploded in an "atomic flash" equivalent to the force of 20,000 tons of TNT.

In the centre of the explosion—where the "Park of Peace" lies now—the false star of three times the temperature of the sun extinguished all life in an instant. Stone melted to magma and of the people reduced to ashes in a split second there remained only shadows on scorched stones and walls. The blast wave was followed by a fire-storm which tore through Hiroshima at a speed of about 300 km per hour. Those who escaped from this second zone of destruction with a radius of more than three kilometres were still doomed, however. It is not known exactly how many people died from the effects of the bomb. On 6 August 1945, about 70,000 died and at least the same number were injured, most of these fatally. Tens of thousands died in the months that followed but for years afterwards deaths from radio-active radiation continued to be recorded. On the 6th of August of every year, a new list of names is added to the black shrine under the monument for the victims of the atom bomb. So far, 300,000 deaths have been counted. In addition to this, in the decade after the dropping of the bomb, every sixth child in Hiroshima was still-born or was crippled at birth—without brains, eyes or limbs.

From the viewpoint of the military planning, for which General Leslie Groves was responsible, Hiroshima was a complete success. The vast sum of dollars invested in the project had been well spent and the new weapon had technically proved its effectiveness in practice, on "living test subjects". The crew of the "Enola Gay" returned safe, sound and celebrated to Tinian and President Truman, who was on the way home from the Potsdam Conference, swaggeringly declared on board the cruiser "Augusta" that their mission was "the greatest event in history". The Japanese headquarters sent Lieut. General Seizo Arisu to Hiroshima to obtain a clearer, on-the-spot picture of what had actually happened since there was difficulty in comprehending the event. His report told a horrifying story: "... the city itself no longer exists; it could be said that it has been erased from the face of the Earth." This did not, however, produce any decision from the opposing factions of the political leadership in Tokyo. To force a decision and to convey the—false—impression that the sinister atomic weapon was in series production, the original plan to drop "Fat Man" on the 20th of August was hurriedly changed and the drop was now scheduled already for the 9th—again with the imminent Soviet offensive on land in mind. On account of the poor atmospheric conditions, Major Chuck-Sweeney turned away from Kokura in Northern Kyushu and flew in the direction of Nagasaki, the alternative target. Almost jettisoning the bomb, he detonated it at 11.02 a.m. over the Urakami Valley, an outer suburb in the northwest of the city, and, with a faulty fuel-pump, barely succeeded in reaching Okinawa.

At dawn of the same day, powerful Soviet forces on a broad front crossed the borders of Japanese-occupied Chinese Manchuria (or the satellite "state" Manchoukuo) and of the Japanese colony of Korea. When Premier Suzuki opened the session of the Supreme Council of War in Tokyo at 11 a.m., he based his statement that the continuation of the war had now *finally* become impossible primarily on this event. Indeed, already on the following day, the embassy of neutral Switzerland advised the Allies of the Japanese desire to open negotiations in respect of capitulation and on the 14th of August the government decided to accept the conditions which had been offered to it on the 26th of July at the Potsdam Conference by the USA, the USSR and Great Britain. On the 15th, the Tenno instructed his soldiers to lay down their weapons; he gave up his traditional divine attributes and informed his still unsuspecting

following double page:
"Fire and Water". Section from a painting by Iri and Toshi Maruki. Maruki Museum, Higashi-Matsuyama, Saitama-Ken

subjects of the intention to capitulate. This was then signed on the 2nd of September on board an American battleship and marked the formal end of the Second World War. The unimaginable shock of the 15th of August was felt by the people as the symbolic start of the "democratic reform" which has gone down as the great turning-point in the history of modern Japan.

In this connection, arguments are still going on as to whether or to what extent the atom bomb shortened the war. Two competent American voices may be quoted. Admiral Leahy, Chief of Staff to the President, has this to say: "The use of this barbaric weapon against Hiroshima and Nagasaki did not mean any appreciable support of our struggle against Japan. The Japanese were already defeated and ready to surrender." And Admiral King wrote this in his official report to Congress about the war in the Pacific: "Japan would have capitulated before 31 December 1945 even if the atomic bomb had not been dropped. It is obvious that the effect of the atomic raid was limited to a notably local extent. Outside the two cities directly affected, it came after other demoralizing experiences." There is little to be added to either verdict when it is considered that the daily ration was only 1,500 calories at this time while the number of the bombed-out and homeless amounted to eight million, the unprotected armaments industry had been practically wiped out and fuel supplies exhausted; furthermore, although there were still infantry and artillery weapons for almost half of the military forces in Japan, there was only ammunition for one man in twenty, the number of aircraft left was less than that produced in one month in America and there was no effective anti-aircraft-defence.

Accordingly, the bomb of Hiroshima, which abruptly destroyed so many innocent human lives in such a horrifying manner, had far less to do with the ending of the war than with the beginning of an "atomic diplomacy" which was soon to be exploited as a one-sided demonstration of power in the Cold War which followed not long after. Robert Oppenheimer and other "fathers of the atom bomb", who had regarded their work as a contribution to the fight against fascism, were thrown by the realization of this into a profound conflict of conscience. In view of the initially incomplete state of development of nuclear technology, the reality of the atomic threat did not equal the "deterrent value" propagated and it completely lost its intended function in global strategy when the Soviet Union broke the nuclear monopoly of the USA and, with the "Sputnik", began to attain equality in space and nuclear capability.

Without doubt, the 6th of August 1945 marked a more profound—and striking— turning point than anything else which had happened in the long history of military affairs. Of course, as became apparent only too quickly, it did not at all mean the end of the continuation of politics with "conventional" means and weapons. However, the development and accumulation of a military potential which is theoretically sufficient to wipe out the entire population of the Earth at least ten times over has convinced people of good will of the necessity to prevent and outlaw the use of this weapon for all time. The monument of Hiroshima has thus become the accusing symbol of the movement for peace throughout the world and, at the same time, an expression of the hope that there will never be another Hiroshima.

Appendix

Chronological Table

1206	Election of Temujin as "Genghis Khan" by the Mongol Kurultai
1212	Decisive victory of the Castilians over the Moors at Navas de Tolosa
1214	French victory at Bouvines over an army of German and English knights
1223	Mongols defeat Kumans and Russians at the Kalka
1228–1229	Sixth Crusade by the excommunicated Frederick II of Hohenstaufen
1235	Foundations laid of Mali empire in West Africa by victory of Sunjata at Kirina
1241	Mongol victory at Liegnitz (Legnica) and Móhi on the Sajó
1242	Victory of Alexander Nevsky over the Teutonic Knights on the ice of Lake Peipus
1258	Capture of Baghdad by the Mongols of the Il-khans
1260	Victory of the Mamelukes of Egypt under Baybars over the Mongols of the Il-khans at 'Ayn Jalut
1261	End of the Latin empire at Constantinople and re-establishment of the Byzantine state (from Nicaea)
1266	Charles of Anjou ends Hohenstaufen rule in Lower Italy
1270	Seventh and last "classic" Crusade by Louis VII of France (to Tunis)
1274, 1281	Failure of Mongol attempts to land in Hakata Bay and subjugate Japan
1278	Victory of Rudolf of Hapsburg over Ottokar II of Bohemia in the battle of Marchfeld at Dürrnkrut: beginning of Hapsburg rule in Austria (1282)
1279	Completion of subjugation of China under Mongol rule of Kublai Khan
1282	Expulsion of the French by the popular uprising of the "Sicilian Vespers"
1288	Victory of the citizens of Cologne over their bishop at Worringen
1291	Fall of the last Crusader castle at Acre "Rütli" oath of the three original Swiss cantons—Schwyz, Uri and Nidwalden
1302	French army of knights defeated by a Flemish militia in the "spurs battle" at Kortrijk (Courtrai)
1315	Victory of the Swiss peasants over the knights of Leopold I of Austria at Morgarten
1331	First definite mention of firearms during a siege of Cividale in Friuli
1337	Beginning of the "Hundred Years' War" between England and France (to 1453)
1346	English victory at Crécy, possible mention of Artillery
1347–1352	The "Black Death" strikes Europe
1354	First Turkish settlement in Europe at Gallipoli
1356	Victory of the Black Prince—Edward of England—at Poitiers, capture of the king of France
1358	Peasants' revolt ("Jacquerie") in Northeast France
1368	Overthrow of the Mongol Yüan dynasty in China following a peasants' revolt and the founding of the Ming dynasty
1370	Peace of Stralsund: climax of the political power of the German "Hanseatic League" under the leadership of Lübeck in the Baltic and North Sea area
1371	Serbian princes defeated by the Turks at the Maritza
1379	Defeat of Genoa at Chioggia in the "Forty Years' War" against Venice
1380	Victory of Dimitri Donskoi, Grand Duke of Moscow, against the Tartars on Kulikovo Field
1381	English Peasants' Revolt under Wat Tyler and John Ball
1386	Swiss victory over Duke Leopold III of Austria at Sempach
1389	Serbian defeat in battle of Kosovo Polje against the Turks
1396	Crusader army under King Sigismund of Hungary defeated by Turks under Sultan Bayazid at Nikopol
1397	Union of Kalmar between Denmark, Norway and Sweden under Danish leadership

1399 Grand Duke Witold of Lithuania defeated by Tartars at Vorskla

1402 Defeat of Turks by Timur at Angora and capture of Sultan Bayazid

1410 Teutonic Knights defeated by Polish-Lithuanian army at Grunwald-Tannenberg

1414–1418 Council of Constance, Jan Hus burnt at the stake (1415)

1415 Victory of the English bowmen under Henry V over the French knights at Azincourt
Occupation of Ceuta by the Portuguese: beginning of European expansion overseas

1419–1434 Hussite Wars

1426 Victory of the Hussites at Usti nad Labem (Aussig)

1429 Appearance of Joan of Arc, the "Maid of Orleans", burnt as a witch at Rouen in 1431

1431–1439 French military reform with beginnings of a standing army

1434 Defeat of the Taborites, the radical wing of the Hussites, in the battle of Lipany

1444–1448 Defeat of Crusader armies by Turks at Varna and Kosovo Polje

1451 The French take Bordeaux from the English

1453 Capture of Constantinople by Sultan Mehmed II

1455–1485 "Wars of the Roses" between the Houses of York and Lancaster in England

1459–1479 Conquest of Serbia, Bosnia and Albania by the Turks

1473 Military reform by Charles the Bold of Burgundy: Statutes of Thionville

1476 Charles the Bold defeated by Swiss at Grandson and Murten

1477 Defeat and death of Charles the Bold at Nancy; Burgundian legacy goes to Maximilian of the House of Hapsburg

1478–1577 "Sengoku Period" of a century of feudal civil war in Japan

1480 Russian princes throw off Tartar yoke, disintegration of the Golden Horde

1485 Richard III of England killed at Bosworth, beginning of Tudor period (to 1603)

1492 Fall of Granada marks end of Spanish "Reconquista"
Christopher Columbus discovers America

1494–1559 "Wars of the Renaissance" between France and Spain for domination of Italy

1498 Vasco da Gama pioneers the sea-route from Europe to India

1500 Cabral discovers Brazil

1501 Founding of the new Persian empire of the Safavids under Ismail I

1514 Hungarian Peasants' War under György Dózsa

1513–1515 Switzerland, victorious at Novara against France and unsuccessful at Marignano, withdraws from the struggle for Italy after acquiring Ticino

1516–1517 Sultan Selim I conquers the Egypt of the Mamelukes

1517 Martin Luther nails his theses to the church door of Wittenberg: beginning of the Reformation

1519 Charles of the House of Hapsburg, King of Castile and Aragon, elected as German emperor

1519–1521 Hernán Cortés conquers the empire of the Aztecs in Mexico for Spain

1521 Revolt in Dalarna: Sweden under Gustavus Vasa breaks away from Denmark

1524–1526 Great German Peasants' War

1525 Spaniards under Pescara defeat French army of Francis I at Pavia

1526 Sultan Suleiman defeats Hungarians at Mohács: the Austrian Hapsburgs inherit part of Hungary, Croatia, Bohemia, Moravia and Silesia after the death of the Jagiello king Wladyslaw II on the battlefield
Sultan Babur defeats Sultan of Delhi at Panipat: founding of the "Empire of the Great Moguls" in India

1531 The reformer Zwingli of Zurich killed in the battle of Kappel

1531–1533 Francisco Pizarro conquers the empire of the Incas in Peru for Spain

1541	Victory of the Reformation under Calvin in Geneva
	Turks capture Budapest
1547	Emperor Charles V defeats Protestant German princes at Mühlberg
1553	Duke of Guise successfully defends Metz, acquired in 1552, for France
1555	Religious Peace of Augsburg: *cuiu regio, eius religio.*
	Division of Hapsburg possessions between the Spanish and Austrian branches of the family
1562–1598	Eight French "Huguenot Wars"
1566	Sultan Suleiman the Magnificent dies during siege of the Hungarian fortress of Sziget
	"Iconoclasts" in the Netherlands
1567	Colonization of the Philippines by Spain
1571	Spanish-Venetian victory in sea-battle of Lepanto against the Turks under Don Juan of Austria
1572	Revolutionary war of independence of the Dutch "Geuzen" against Spain
1579	Union of Utrecht of the "Seven Provinces" of the northern Netherlands: declaration of independence, followed by the overthrow of King Philip II in 1581
1581	The Cossack leader Ermak Timofeevich begins the conquest of Siberia
1585–1591	Moroccans capture Timbuktu: destruction of Songhai empire
1587	Execution of Mary Stuart, Queen of Scotland and figure-head of the Catholic Party, by Elizabeth I of England
1588	Destruction of the Spanish Armada sent against England
1592–1598	Indecisive war by Japan under Toyotomi Hideyoshi against Korea
1595–1597	First Dutch expedition to India
1598	Henry IV of France successful in the Peace of Vervins against Spain
1600	Tokugawa Ieyasu defeats Western Forces of the Japanese daimyo at Sekigahara
	Founding of the British East India Company
1603–1868	Rule of the Tokugawa Bakufu (Shogunate) in Japan

1607	Founding of Jamestown in Virginia: beginning of English colonization of North America
1608	Founding of Quebec: beginning of French colonization of Canada
1612	Expulsion of the Poles from Moscow by Minin and Pozharsky
1618–1648	Thirty Years' War
1620	End of Czech independence at the battle of White Mountain
1624–1642	Cardinal Richelieu chief minister of Louis XIII of France
1632	Victory and death of Gustavus II Adolphus of Sweden in the battle of Lützen
1640	Beginning of the English Revolution
	Portugal breaks the personal union into which it was forced by Spain in 1580
1640–1648	The Russian Cossacks reach the coast of the Pacific Ocean
1644	Overthrow of the Ming dynasty, establishment of Manchu rule in China
1645	Cromwell's New Model Army defeats the "Cavaliers" at Naseby
1647–1648	Revolt by Masaniello against Spanish rule in Naples
1648–1653	Anti-absolutist movement of the "Fronde" in France
1649	Execution of Charles I of England
1652	Founding of Capetown by the Dutch
1652–1654, 1664–1667, 1672–1674	Anglo-Dutch trade and colonial wars
1653–1658	Oliver Cromwell Lord Protector of the British "Commonwealth"
1659	With the Peace of the Pyrenees, France takes the place of Spain as the leading power in Europe
1660	Restoration of the Stuart dynasty in England
	Indecisive end of the Baltic Wars waged by Sweden since 1654
1661–1715	Louis XIV absolute monarch of France, climax and exaggeration of absolutism: "L'état, c'est moi!"

1667–1668,
1672–1679, "Wars of Devolution" of Louis XIV
1688–1697

1676 Marshal Turenne killed at Sassbach

1680 Death of Sivaji, the national hero of the Maratha

1683 Second siege of Vienna and defeat of the Turks in the battle of Kahlenberg

1688 "Glorious Revolution" in England: establishment of constitutional monarchy

1689–1725 Peter I, the czar of reform in Russia

1690 Defeat of the Irish and Jacobites at the Boyne

1692 English victory at La Hogue over the French fleet

1697 Treaty of Nerchinsk between Russia nad Manchu China

1699 Peace of Carlowitz between Austria and Turkey gives Hungary to the Hapsburgs

1700–1721 Nordic War

1701–1714 War of the Spanish Succession

1704 Joint victory of Marlborough and Prince Eugene over the French at Blenheim (Höchstädt)
Occupation of Gibraltar by the English

1709 Victory of Peter I over Charles XII of Sweden at Poltava, end of Swedish domination of the Baltic

1710–1740 Disintegration of Mogul empire in India

1713 An "Asiento" gives England a privileged position in the Spanish-American slave trade

1716 Prince Eugene defeats Turks at Peterwardein

1722 Victory of Afghans at Golnabad: end of the Persian Safavid state

1733–1738 War of the Polish Succession

1740–1748 War of the Austrian Succession

1747 Founding of an independent Afghan state under Ahmed Durrani

1756–1763 Seven Years' War

1757 Clive defeats Nawab of Bengal at Plassey: beginning of the conquest of India
Prussian victory at Leuthen

1759 Prussian defeat at Kunersdorf
English defeat French in battle of Quebec

1760 Haidar Ali achieves power in Mysore, Southern India

1763 With the Peace of Paris, France loses Canada and Louisiana

1768–1774 Russo-Turkish War: Czarina Catherine II gains great advantages in Peace of Kuchuk Kainarji

1770 Revolt on Greek islands against Turkish rule

1772 First division of Poland at suggestion of Frederick II of Prussia

1773 Boston "Tea Party" in protest against British colonial rule

1775–1783 Revolutionary War of Independence of the Thirteen American Colonies against England

1776 Declaration of Human Rights drawn up by Thomas Jefferson and Declaration of Independence of the "United States of America"

1777 Surrender of an English colonial army under General Burgoyne to American militia army at Saratoga

1781 Surrender of a second English army to George Washington at Yorktown

1782 French allow democratic revolution to be crushed at Geneva

1784 James Watt patents steam governor for his steam engine

1786–1788 Crushing of a revolutionary movement in the Netherlands against Governor William V of Orange with Prussian help

1787–1792 War by Russia and Austria against Turkey

1788 Beginning of the settlement of Australia as a penal colony

1789 Beginning of the French Revolution

1791 Revolution of Negro slaves on Haiti (later on under Toussaint L'Ouverture)

1792 Beginning of the Revolutionary Wars: cannonade at Valmy, French victory at Jemappes

1793 Introduction of general conscription in France

1794 Victory of Republican army at Fleurus, overthrow of revolutionary Jacobin dictatorship

1796–1797	Successful campaign in Italy of Napoleon Bonaparte
1798–1799	Bonaparte's Egyptian campaign, battle of the Pyramids
1799	Coup d'état of 18 Brumaire: Bonaparte becomes First Consul
1804	Coronation of Napoleon I as emperor
1805	Battles of Trafalgar and Austerlitz
1806	Prussian defeat at Jena-Auerstedt
1808	Beginning of Prussian reforms; popular uprising in Spain
1810	Beginning of War of Independence in Spanish America
1812	Defeat of Napoleon's "Grand Army" in Russia
1813	Tecumseh, commander of an Indian tribal coalition, killed in the battle on the Thames/Ontario Battle of the Nations at Leipzig
1814–1815	Congress of Vienna and the forming of the "Holy Alliance"
1815	Napoleon defeated at Waterloo and exiled to St. Helena
1820–1823	Liberal uprising in Spain under Colonel Riego crushed by France on behalf of Holy Alliance
1821–1830	Greek fight for freedom against Turks
1824	Victory of patriots under Sucre against the Spanish colonial army at Ayacucho
1825	The first railway: Stockton-Darlington Conspiracy of the Dekabrists in Russia
1830	France begins conquest of Algeria July Revolution in France and successful uprising in Belgium against the forced union with Holland
1830–1831	Polish revolt ends in defeat
1839–1856	Era of Turkish reform of the "Tanzimat" (benevolent decrees)
1840–1842	1st "Opium War" by England against China
1841	Collective action by Great Powers force Muhammed Ali to withdraw from Syria to Egypt
1847	Swiss Separatist War
1848–1849	Revolution and counter-revolution in Europe: campaigns in Italy, Germany, Hungary
1849	With the annexation of the Sikh state in the Punjab, England completes its territorial expansion in India
1851–1864	Taiping revolution in China
1853–1856	Turkey, Great Britain, France and Sardinia in Crimean War against Russia
1856–1860	2nd "Opium War" (by England and France) against China
1857–1859	Popular uprising (so-called Sepoy rebellion) in India
1859	War of France and Sardinia against Austria, battle of Solferino
1860–1861	The Risorgimento—the national unification of Italy
1861–1867	French expedition to Mexico
1861–1865	War of Secession in the United States of America
1863	Battle of Gettysburg
1864	Founding of the 1st International Prussians and Austrians wage war against Denmark for Schleswig-Holstein
1864–1870	War by Argentina, Brazil and Uruguay against Paraguay
1866	War between Austria and Prussia, battle of Königgrätz
1867–1868	"Meiji reforms" for the modernization of Japan
1868	English expedition under Napier against Emperor Tevodros of Ethiopia
1869	Opening of the Suez Canal
1870–1898	Samory Touré resists advance of French colonialism in West Africa
1870–1871	Franco-Prussian War, battle of Gravelotte-St. Privat
1871	Paris Commune (18 March–28 May)
1874	British Government purchases shares to become major shareholder in Suez Canal company
1875–1878	Oriental crisis, Russo-Turkish War and Congress of Berlin

1879 Dual Alliance between Germany and Austro-Hungary (becomes Triple Alliance in 1882 when Italy joins it)
War of England against Zulus: defeat at Isandhlwana, victory at Ulundi

1879–1884 "Saltpeter War" fought by Chile against Bolivia and Peru

1881 Beginning of the "Scramble for Africa"; France forces Tunis to become a "protectorate"

1882 Battle of Tell al-Kebir, occupation of Egypt by England

1884–1898 Germany annexes colonies in Africa and Oceania

1884–1885 Congo Conference at Berlin: "Legitimation" in international law of the division of Africa, neutralization of the "Congo state"

1885 The troops of the Mahdi, Mohammed Ahmed, capture Khartoum in the Sudan
Italy occupies the port of Massawa in Eritrea
Great Britain annexes Upper Burma with Mandalay

1889 Founding of the IInd International in Paris

1890 Dismissal of Bismarck as German Chancellor by William II

1893 Union of Vietnam, Cambodia and Laos as the French colony "Indochina"

1893–1894 Franco-Russian alliance

1894–1895 Japan wages a successful war against China; objection by Germany, Russia and France to the peace treaty of Shimonoseki

1895–1898 Revolts against Spanish colonial rule in Cuba and the Philippines

1896 Italians defeated by Ethiopians at Adua

1898 Spanish-American War

1899–1902 Boer War fought by Great Britain in South Africa

1900–1901 Crushing of Ihotwan Rebellion in China by international "punitive expedition" under German command

1902 Anglo-Japanese alliance

1904–1905 Russo-Japanese War, battles of Mukden and Tsushima

1905 Laying down the keel of the battleship "Dreadnought"
First flight by powered aircraft (Wright brothers)

1905/1906 1st Moroccan Crisis

1905–1907 First Russian Revolution

1905–1911 Bourgeois revolution in Persia

1907 Anglo-Russian agreement on spheres of influence in Asia opens way to "Triple Entente"

1908 Young Turk Revolution, "annexation crisis" over Bosnia and Herzegovina

1910 Beginning of democratic revolution in Mexico

1911 2nd Moroccan Crisis ("Agadir crisis"), annexation of Libya by Italy
Beginning of bourgeois revolution in China under Sun Jat-Sen

1912–1913 Balkan Wars

1914–1918 First World War, battles of the Marne, Verdun, Jutland, Cambrai

1917 Russian February Revolution
Russian Socialist October Revolution, establishment of Soviet power by the Bolshevists under V. I. Lenin

1918 Creation of the Red Workers' and Peasants' Army
Peace treaty of Brest-Litovsk, armistice of Compiègne, November Revolution in Germany and Austria

1919 Armed intervention of 14 powers in Soviet Russia, overthrow of Workers' Councils in Munich and Hungary
Peace treaties of Versailles, St. Germain, Neuilly
IIIrd International ("Comintern")

1919–1922 Victory of Red Army over Intervention forces and White Guard troops, battle of Tsaritsyn

1920–1922 Greek-Turkish War ends in victory for Turkish national revolutionaries under Mustafa Kemal (later known as Atatürk)

1921–1926 Rebellion of the Rif Kabyles under Abd-el-Krim against Spain and France, defence of the Rif Republic

1922 Fascists under Mussolini seize power in Italy

1923 Coup d'état by General Primo de Rivera in Spain

1924–1929 Period of "post-war prosperity"

1926 Beginning of the "Northern campaign" of the Kuomintang in China from Canton

1927 Joint front of Kuomintang/Communist Party of China broken by Chiang Kai-shek, leaning towards USA and Chiang Kai-shek's conversion to Christianity

1929–1933 World economic crisis

1931–1932 Japanese invasion of Manchuria, founding of "Manchoukuo" as satellite state (1932)

1931 Proclamation of the Republic in Spain

1932 Election of Franklin D. Roosevelt as President of the USA (re-elected in 1936, 1940, 1944)

1932–1935 Chaco War between Paraguay and Bolivia

1933 End of the Weimar Republic in Germany, beginning of fascist terror regime

1935–1936 Italian invasion of Ethiopia

1936 Election victories of Popular Front in Spain and France

1936–1939 Italian and German intervention in Spanish Civil War which was provoked by a coup d'état led by General Franco: battle of Guadalajara (1937)

1937 Beginning of hostilities between China and Japan after Japanese raid on Marco Polo Bridge near Peking although no formal declaration of war was made

1938 Hitlerite Germany occupies Austria and, covered by the Munich Agreement, moves into Czechoslovakia

1939 Destruction of Czechoslovakia by Germany, invasion of Poland, outbreak of the Second World War

1940 Winter war between USSR and Finland, occupation of Denmark, Norway, Luxemburg, Holland, Belgium and parts of France by Germany; surrender of France, victory of the RAF in the Battle of Britain; Italy enters war and invades Greece

1941 Hitlerite Germany invades Yugoslavia, Greece and the Soviet Union; Japan attacks US fleet at Pearl Harbor, USA enters war

1942 Battles of Midway, Stalingrad, El Alamein

1943 German surrender at Stalingrad and Tunis; overthrow of Mussolini and capitulation of Italy; victory of the Soviet army at the battle of Kursk

1944 Allied landing in Normandy and revolt in Paris; Belorussian operation, destruction of German Army Group "South"; sea-battles in the Philippine Sea (Marianas) and at Leyte

1945 Oder-Vistula operation, Berlin operation; Potsdam Conference; Hiroshima

Bibliography

General Literature

Aron, R.: *On War*. London, 1958.

Clausewitz, C. v.: *On War*. London, 1918.

Curti, P.: *Umfassung und Durchbruch. Kleine Beispiele großer Taten*. Frauenfeld, 1955.

Delbrück, H.: *Geschichte der Kriegskunst im Rahmen der politischen Geschichte*. 7 vols., Berlin, 1920–1937.

Demmin, A.: *Die Kriegswaffen in ihren geschichtlichen Entwicklungen von den ältesten Zeiten bis auf die Gegenwart. Eine Enzyklopädie der Waffenkunde*. Gera, 1891.

Dupuy, R. E.: *The Encyclopedia of Military History from 3500 B.C. to the Present*. London, 1974.

Eckardt, W./O. Morawietz: *Die Handwaffen des brandenburgisch-preußisch-deutschen Heeres 1640–1945*. Hamburg, 1973.

Engels, Fr.: *Ausgewählte militärische Schriften*. 2 vols., Berlin, 1958–1964.

Goody, J.: *Technology, Tradition and the State in Africa*. London, 1971.

Great Military Battles, edited by C. Falls. London, 1964.

Fuchs, Th.: *Geschichte des europäischen Kriegswesens*. 2 vols., Munich, 1972–1974.

Funcken, L. et F.: *Le costume et les armes des soldats de tous les temps*. 2 vols., Paris, Tournai, 1966–1967.

Handbuch für Heer und Flotte. Enzyklopädie der Kriegswissenschaften und verwandter Gebiete, edited by G. v. Alten. Vols. 1–6, 9, Berlin, Leipzig, Vienna, Stuttgart, 1909–1914.

Handbuch der neuzeitlichen Wehrwissenschaften, edited by H. Franke. 3 vols., Berlin, Leipzig, 1936–1938.

Handwörterbuch der gesamten Militärwissenschaften, edited by B. Poten. 9 vols., Bielefeld, Leipzig, 1877–1880.

Henk, L. v.: *Die Kriegsführung zur See in ihren wichtigsten Epochen*. Graz, 1975.

Histoire universelle des armées, edited by J. Boudet. 4 vols., Paris, 1965.

Jomini, A.: *Précis de l'art de guerre*. Paris, 1837.

Klassiker der Kriegskunst, edited by W. Hahlweg. Darmstadt, 1960.

Liddell Hart, B. H.: *Strategy*. New York, 1957.

Lugs, J.: *Handfeuerwaffen. Systematischer Überblick über die Handfeuerwaffen und ihre Geschichte*. 2 vols., Berlin, 1962.

Meynert, H.: *Geschichte des Kriegswesens und der Heeresverfassungen in Europa*. 3 vols., Graz, 1973.

Mitchell, W. A.: *Outlines of the World's Military History*. Washington, 1937.

Montgomery, B. L.: *A History of Warfare*. London, 1968.

Mordal, J.: *25 Jahrhunderte Seekrieg*. Munich, 1963.

Napoleon I.: *Darstellung der Kriege Caesars, Turennes, Friedrichs des Großen*. Berlin, 1938.

Nef, J.: *War and human progress*. Cambridge, 1950.

Nolan, L. E.: *Histoire et tactique de la cavalerie*. Paris, 1954.

Padfield, P.: *Guns at sea*. London, 1973.

Pawlikowski-Cholewa, A. v.: Heeresgeschichte der Völker Afrikas und Amerikas. Berlin, 1943.

Potter, E. B./Ch. W. Nimitz: *Sea Power. A Naval History*. Englewood Cliffs, 1960.

Pratt, F.: *The Battles that changed History*. New York, 1956.

Rasin, J. A.: *Geschichte der Kriegskunst*. 2 vols., Berlin, 1959–1960.

Renn, L./H. Schnitter: *Krieger, Landsknecht und Soldat*. Berlin, (1973).

Richardson, L.: *Statistics of deadly quarrels and arms and insecurity*. London, 1960.

Rüstow, W.: *Geschichte der Infantrie*. 2 vols., Nordhausen, 1862–1864.

Sanderson, M.: *Sea Battles*. London, 1975.

Der Schlachterfolg, mit welchen Mitteln wurde er erstrebt? Studien zur Kriegsgeschichte und Taktik, vol. III, edited by Kriegsgeschichtliche Abteilung I of the Great General Staff, Berlin, 1903.

Schlieffen, A. v.: *Cannae*. Berlin, 1936.

Spaulding, O. L.: *Warfare, a study of military methods from the earliest times*. New York, 1925.

Stegemann, H.: *Der Krieg. Sein Wesen und seine Wandlung*. 2 vols., Stuttgart, Berlin, 1940.

Stenzel, H.: *Seekriegsgeschichte in ihren wichtigsten Abschnitten mit Berücksichtigung der See-Taktik*. 6 vols., Hanover, Leipzig, 1909–1920.

Strokov, A. A.: *History of Military Art* (Russian). Moscow, 1966.

Ukpabi, S. C.: *The Military in Traditional African Societies*. Addis Abeba, 1973.

Urlanis, B. Z.: *Bilanz der Kriege. Die Menschenverluste Europas vom 17. Jahrhundert bis zur Gegenwart*. Berlin, 1965.

Vagts, A.: *A History of Militarism. Civilian and Military*. Greenwich, 1959.

Warner, O.: *Great sea battles*. London, New York, 1963.

Wright, Qu.: *A Study of War*. London, 1965.

Battles of Antiquity

Diesner, H. J.: *Kriege des Altertums. Griechenland und Rom im Kampf um den Mittelmeerraum.* Berlin, 1973.

Diodorus Siculus: *Bibliotheca historica,* with English translation. Loeb Series, 12 vols., 1933–1957.

Droysen, J. G.: *Geschichte des Hellenismus.* Tübingen, 1952.

Galitzin, N. S.: *Allgemeine Kriegsgeschichte des Altertums,* translated by Streccius. 5 vols., Kassel, 1874–1879.

Grundy, G. B.: *The Great Persian war and its preliminaries.* London, 1901.

Herodotus: *History,* English translation by J. E. Powell. Oxford Library of Translations, 2 vols., 1949.

Iuli Frontini Strategematon libri quattuor. Leipzig, 1888.

Köchly, H./W. Rüstow: *Griechische Kriegsschriftssteller.* Osnabrück, 1969.

Kromayer, J./G. Veith: *Antike Schlachtfelder. Bausteine zu einer antiken Kriegsgeschichte.* 4 vols., Berlin, 1907–1931.

Kromayer, J./G. Veith: *Heerwesen und Kriegsführung der Griechen und Römer.* Munich, 1928.

Livy: *History of Rome,* with English translation by E. O. Foster et al. Loeb Series, 1919–1957.

Onosandros: *Strategikos. De imperatoris officio liber.* Leipzig, 1860.

Pritchett, W. K.: *Studies in Ancient Greek Military Practices.* Berkeley, Los Angeles, 1971.

Rodgers, W. L.: *Greek and Roman Naval Warfare.* Annapolis, 1964.

Rüstow, W./H. Köchly: *Geschichte des griechischen Kriegswesens von der ältesten Zeit bis auf Pyrrhos.* Osnabrück, 1973.

Strabo of Amasia: *Geography,* edited by H. L. Jones. Loeb Series, 1917–1932.

From Kadesh to the Catalaunian Plains

Faulkner, R. O.: "The Battle of Kadesh", in: *Mitteilungen des Deutschen Archäologischen Instituts, Abteilung Kairo,* 1958.

Gardiner, A.: *The Kadesh Inscriptions of Rameses II.* London, 1960.

Wolf, W.: *Die Bewaffnung des altägyptischen Heeres.* Leipzig, 1926.

Pritchett, W. K.: "Toward a Restudy of the Battle of Salamis", in: *American Journal of Archaeology,* LXIII, July 1959.

Pritchett, W. K.: "Marathon", in: *University of California Publications in Classical Archaeology,* IV, 2, 1960.

Aeschylus: *Persea,* edited by H. D. Broadhead. Cambridge, 1960.

Hammond, N. G. L.: "The Battle of Salamis", in: *Journal of Hellenic Studies,* LXXVI, 1956.

Xenophon: *Hellenica,* English translation. Loeb Series, 1914–1925.

Isokrates ausgewählte Werke, translated by Th. Flathe. Berlin, n. d.

Arrians Anabasis, English translation by E. Iliff Robson. Loeb Series. 2 vols., 1929–1930.

Curtius Rufus, Q.: *Geschichte Alexanders des Großen,* translated by W. Felsing. Leipzig, 1929.

Justinus, M. J.: *Historiae Philippicae,* English translation by J. S. Watson, 1853.

Fox, R. L.: *Alexander the Great.* London, 1973.

Fuller, J. F. C.: *The Generalship of Alexander the Great.* London, 1958.

Marsden, E. W.: *The Campaign of Gaugamela.* London, 1964.

Ssun-ds: *Traktat über die Kriegskunst.* Berlin, 1957.

Walker, R. L.: *The multi-state system of ancient China.* Hamden, 1953.

Watson, W.: *China before the Han dynasty.* New York, 1961.

Polybius: *The Histories,* English translation by W. R. Paton, 6 vols. London, 1957–1960.

Hoffmann, W.: *Hannibal.* Göttingen, 1962.

Ludovico, D.: *Topografia della battaglia di Canne.* Rome, 1954.

Scullard, H. H.: *Scipio Africanus in the Second Punic War.* Cambridge, 1930.

Walbank, E. W.: *Historical Commentars on Polybius.* Vol. I, London, 1957.

Caesar, G. J.: *De bello civili,* with an English translation. Loeb Classical Library, London, 1914.

Gwatkin, W. E.: "Some Reflections on the Battle of Pharsalus", in: *Transactions of the American Philological Association,* LXXXVII, 1956.

Dio Cassius: *Roman History,* edited by E. Cary, with English translation. Loeb Series, 9 vols., 1929–1930.

Rüstow, W.: *Heerwesen und Kriegsführung C. Julius Cäsars.* Nordhausen, 1862.

Suetonius Tranquillus, G.: *Lives of the Caesars,* English translation by R. Graves, Oxford, 1957.

Tacitus, C.: *Germania, Historiae, Annales,* edited by W. Peterson, with English translation. Loeb Series, 1914–1937.

Josephus Flavius: *History of the Jewish War,* with English translation by H. St. J. Thackeray/R. Marcus. Loeb Series, 1926 ff.

Schürer, E.: *The History of the Jewish People in the Age of Jesus Christ.* Revised edition by G. Vermes/F. Millar, vol. I, Edinburgh, 1973.

Flavius Vegetius: "De re militari", edited by T. R. Philipps, in: *Roots of Strategy (The Military Institutions of the Romans).* London, 1940.

Ammianus Marcellinus: *Römische Geschichte,* Latin and German with a commentary by W. Seyfarth. 4 vols., Berlin, 1968–1971.

Jordanis Gotengeschichte nebst Auszügen aus seiner Römischen Geschichte, translated by W. Martens, Leipzig, 1913.

424   Knights and Mercenaries

Beeler, J.: *Warfare in Feudal Europe 730–1200*. Cornell University Press, 1971.

Frauenholz, E. v.: *Das Heerwesen der germanischen Frühzeit, des Frankenreiches und des ritterlichen Zeitalters*. Munich, 1935.

Frauenholz, E. v.: *Das Heerwesen des Reiches in der Landsknechtszeit*. Munich, 1927.

Oman, Ch.: *Art of War in the Middle Ages*. London, 1924.

Schaufelberger, W.: *Der Alte Schweizer und sein Krieg*. Zurich, 1952.

Sproemberg, H.: *Die feudale Kriegskunst*. Berlin, 1959.

al-Tabari, Jafar Mohammed: *Tarikh al-rusul wa-al mulk*, edited by M. J. de Goeje, 13 vols., 1879–1901.

Verbruggen, J. F.: *De Krijgskunst in West-Europa in de Middeleeuwen (IXᵉ tot begin XIVᵉ eeuw)*. Brussels, 1954.

Nineveh to Saratoga

Arriani tactica et Mauricii ars militaris, edited by J. Scheffer. Osnabrück, 1967.

Christensen, A.: *L'Iran sous les Sassanides*. 2nd ed., Copenhagen, 1944.

Kretschmann, N.: *Die Kämpfe zwischen Heraclius I. und Chosroes II*. 2 vols., Güstrow, 1875–1876.

Runciman, J. C. S.: *Byzantine Civilisation*. London, 1933.

Spuler, B.: *Iran in frühislamischer Zeit*. Wiesbaden, 1952.

Bachrach, B. S.: *Merovingian Military Organization, 481–751*. Minneapolis, 1972.

Fredegar, edited by H. Krusch. *Monumenta Germaniae Historica, Scriptores rer. Meroving.*, vol. II.

Chronicon Moissacense. Monumenta Germaniae Historica, Scriptores, vol. I.

Gesta abbatum Fontanellensium, edited by F. Lohier/J. Laporte. Rouen, Paris, 1936.

Isidor Pacenses. Monumenta Germaniae Historica. Auctores Antiqu., vol. XI.

Lot, F.: *Études sur la bataille de Poitiers*. Brussels, 1948.

Barta, I. and others: *Die Geschichte Ungarns*. Budapest, 1971.

Müller-Mertens, E.: *Das Zeitalter der Ottonen*. Berlin, 1955.

Eberl, B.: *Die Ungarnschlacht auf dem Lechfeld im Jahre 955*. Augsburg, Basle, 1955.

Widukind von Corvey. Monumenta Germaniae Historica, Scriptores rer. Germ. in us. scol., 1935.

Gerhard. Vita des Udalrich von Augsburg. Monumenta Germaniae Historica, Scriptores, vol. IV.

The Bayeux Tapestry: A Comprehensive Survey, edited by F. M. Stenton. London, 1957.

Douglas, D. C.: *William the Conqueror*. London, 1964.

Stenton, F. M.: *Anglo-Saxon England*. London, 1947.

Annales Mediolanenses maiores (Gesta Frederici I Imperatoris in Lombardia). Monumenta Germaniae Historica. Scriptores rer. Germ. in us. scol., 1892.

Annales Romualdi. Monumenta Germaniae Historica, Scriptores, vol. XIX.

Boso: "Vita Alexandri III", in: *Duchesne, Liber pontificalis*. Vol. II, Paris, 1892.

Gottfried von Viterbo. Monumenta Germaniae Historica, Scriptores, vol. XXII.

Hanow, B.: *Die Schlachten von Carcano und Legnano*. Berlin, 1905.

Altrussische Dichtung aus dem 11.–18. Jahrhundert. Leipzig, 1971.

The Text and Versions of John de Plano Carpini and William de Rubruquis, edited by C. R. Beazley. Hakluyt Society, 1903.

Complete Collection of Russian Chronicles (Russian). 2 vols., Moscow, 1962.

Fedorow-Dawydow, G. A.: *Die Goldene Horde und ihre Vorgänger*. Leipzig (1972).

Pelliot, P./L. Hambis: *Histoire des campagnes de Gengis Khan*. Paris, 1951.

Vernadsky, G.: *A History of Russia*. Vol. 3: *The Mongols and Russia*. New Haven, 1953.

Chronology and materials concerning the Mongol Invasions (Japanese), edited by Kawazoe Shoji. Fukuoka, 1971.

Marco Polo: *The Description of the World*. English translation by P. Pelliot. London, 1938.

Aida, Jiro: *Analyse of the Mongol Invasions* (Japanese). Tokyo, 1958.

Ikeuchi Hiroshi: *A new inquiry into the Mongol Invasions* (Japanese). Tokyo, 1931.

Schurmann, H. F.: *Economic Structure of the Yüan dynasty*. Cambridge, 1956.

Chronik des Jakob Twinger von Königshofen, edited by K. Hegel, *Chroniken der deutschen Städte*. Vol. VIII, 1870.

Dierauer: *Züricher Chronik. Quellen zur Schweizer Geschichte*. Vol. 18, Basle, 1900.

Justinger: *Berner Chronik*, edited by G. Studer, Berne, 1870.

Kurz, H.: *Schweizerschlachten*. Berne, 1962.

Detmar: *Lübecker Chronik. Chroniken der deutschen Städte*. Vol. XIX, Göttingen, 1961.

Joannis Dlugosii opera omnia, edited by A. Przezdiecki/I. Polkowski/Z. Pauli. 14 vols., Cracow, 1863–1887.

Magdeburger Schöppenchronik. Chroniken der deutschen Städte. Vol. VII, Göttingen, 1961.

Schilling, Diebold: *Chronik*, edited by R. Durrer/P. Hilber. Lucerne, 1932.

Evans, G.: *Tannenberg, 1410:1914*. Harrisburg, 1971.

Kuczyński, S. M.: *Wielka wojna z Zakonem Krzyżacjiem w latach 1409–1411*. Warsaw, 1966.

Fontes rerum Bohemicarum. Vol. V: *Kronika Vavřinec z Březovce a Bartoška z Drahenic.* Prague, 1893.

Palacký, J.: *Urkundliche Beiträge zur Geschichte des Hussitenkrieges.* Osnabrück, 1966.

Durdik, J.: *Hussitisches Heerwesen.* Berlin, 1961.

Heymann, F. G.: *John Žiška and the Hussite Revolution.* Princeton, 1955.

Macek, J.: *The Hussite Movement in Bohemia.* Prague, 1958.

Commynes, Ph. de: *Mémoires.* 3 vols., edited by J. Calmette/G. Durville, Paris, 1924–1925.

Schilling, D.: *Berner Chronik,* edited by G. Tobler, 2 vols., Berne, 1902.

Frauenholz, E. v.: *Das Heerwesen der Schweizer Eidgenossenschaft.* Munich, 1936.

Hoyer, S.: *Das Militärwesen im deutschen Bauernkrieg 1524 bis 1526.* Berlin, 1975.

Reißner, A.: *Historia der Herren Georg und Kaspar von Frundsberg,* edited by K. Schottenloher, Leipzig, 1913.

Thon, R.: *Die Schlacht bei Pavia.* Berlin, 1907.

Welti, L.: *Mark Sittich und Wolf Dietrich von Ems.* Dornbirn, 1952.

Hayashi, Razan: *The Battle of Sekigahara* (Japanese). Tokyo, 1656.

The Papers of Tokugawa Ieyasu (Japanese). Edited by K. Nakamura. 4 vols., Tokyo, 1954–1957.

Deuticke, K.: *Die Schlacht bei Lützen.* Giessen, 1912.

Frauenholz, E. v.: *Das Söldnertum in der Zeit des Dreißigjährigen Krieges.* Munich, 1939.

Pekar, J.: *Wallenstein 1630–1634. Tragödie einer Verschwörung.* 2 vols., Berlin, 1937.

Gedruckte Relationen über die Schlacht bei Lützen 1632. Halle, 1880.

Roberts, M.: *Gustavus Adolphus. A History of Sweden 1611 to 1632.* 2 vols., London, 1953–1958.

Sveriges Krig. 1611–1632, edited by the Swedish General Staff. 8 vols., Stockholm, 1936–1939.

Wedgwood, C. V.: *The Thirty Years War.* New Haven, 1949.

Forst de Battaglia: *Jan Sobieski, König von Polen.* Vienna, 1946.

Das Kriegsjahr 1683, nach Akten und anderen authentischen Quellen. Edited by Abteilung für Kriegsgeschichte des Kriegs-Archivs. Vienna, 1883.

Stoye, J.: *The Siege of Vienna.* London, 1964.

Woliński, J.: *Jan III Sobieski i Prusy Ksiażece.* Warsaw, 1947.

Braubach, M.: *Prinz Eugen von Savoyen. Eine Biographie.* 4 vols., Munich, 1963 ff.

Churchill, W.: *Marlborough. His Life and Times.* 4 vols., London, 1933–1938.

Feldzüge des Prinzen Eugen von Savoyen. Vol. 6: *Spanischer Successionskrieg. Feldzug 1704,* nach den Feldakten und anderen authentischen Quellen. Edited by Abteilung für Kriegsgeschichte des Kriegs-Archivs. Vienna, 1879.

Israel, R.: *Der Feldzug von 1704 in Süddeutschland.* Berlin, 1913.

Léonard, E.: *L'Armée et ses problèmes au XVIIIe siècle.* Paris, 1958.

Taylor, F.: *The Wars of Marlborough, 1702–1709.* 2 vols., London, 1921.

Haintz, O.: *König Karl XII. von Schweden.* 3 vols., Berlin (West), 1958.

Porfirov, E. I.: *The Battle of Poltava, 28. June 1709* (Russian). Moscow, 1959.

Schustoj, V. E.: *The Nordic War, 1700–1721* (Russian). Moscow, 1970.

Gooch, G. P.: *Frederick the Great. The Ruler—the Writer—the Man.* London, New York, 1947.

Groehler, O.: *Die Kriege Friedrichs II.* Berlin, 1966.

Die Kriege Friedrichs des Großen. Der Siebenjährige Krieg 1756–1763. Edited by Kriegsgeschichtliche Abteilung II of the Great General Staff. Vol. 6, Berlin, 1904.

Mahan, A. T.: *The Influence of Sea Power upon History, 1660–1783.* London, Cambridge, 1890.

Higginbotham, D.: *The War of American Independence. Military Attitudes, Policies and Practice.* New York, 1971.

Nickerson, H.: *The Turning Point of the Revolution.* Boston, 1928.

Trevelyan, G. O.: *The American Revolution.* 6 vols., London, New York, 1899–1914.

From Valmy to Karlshorst

Army Air Forces in World War II, edited by W. F. Craven/L. J. Cate. 7 vols., Chicago, 1948–1958.

Bagrajev, A. D.: *The Art of War in the capitalistic States 1939–1945* (Russian). Moscow, 1960.

Baldwin, H. W.: *Battles lost and won*. New York, Evanston, London, 1966.

Chandler, D.: *The Campaigns of Napoleon*. New York, 1966.

Churchill, W.: *The World Crisis*. 6 vols., London, 1923–1931.

Churchill, W.: *The Second World War*. 7 vols., Boston, 1948–1954.

Deutschland im ersten Weltkrieg, edited by a group of authors under the chairmanship of F. Klein. 3 vols., Berlin, 1968–1969.

Entscheidungsschlachten des zweiten Weltkrieges, edited by H.-A. Jacobsen/J. Rohwer. Frankfurt/Main, 1960.

Esposito, V. I. /J. R. Elting: *A Military History and Atlas of the Napoleonic Wars*. New York, 1964.

Falls, C.: *The Great War*. London, 1959.

Förster, G./H. Helmert/H. Schnitter: *Der zweite Weltkrieg. Militärhistorischer Abriß*. Berlin, 1974.

Fuller, J. F. C.: *The Conduct of War, 1789–1961*, London, 1961.

Fuller, J. F. C.: *The Second World War, 1939–45. A strategical and tactical history*. London, New York, 1949.

Geschichte des Großen Vaterländischen Krieges der Sowjetunion. 6 vols., Berlin, 1962–1968.

Geschichte des zweiten Weltkrieges 1939–1945, edited by S. P. Platanow and others. 2 vols., Berlin, 1961.

Groehler, O.: *Geschichte des Luftkrieges 1910 bis 1970*. Berlin, 1975.

Der große Vaterländische Krieg der Sowjetunion, edited by P. A. Shilin. Berlin, 1975.

Guldiman, W.: *Flieger und Panzer und ihr Einfluß auf den Wandel der modernen Kriegführung*. Frauenfeld, 1946.

Helmert, H./Hj. Usczeck: *Europäische Befreiungskriege 1808 bis 1814/15*. Berlin, 1976.

Helmert, H./Hj. Usczeck: *Preußischdeutsche Kriege von 1864 bis 1871*. Berlin, 1975.

History of the Great War: Military Operations, edited by Great Britain Committee of Imperial Defense. London, 1932.

Horsetzky, A. v.: *Kriegsgeschichtliche Übersicht der wichtigsten Feldzüge seit 1792*. Vienna, 1913.

Der Krieg zur See 1914–1918, edited by Marine-Archiv, 15 vols., Berlin, 1922–1966.

Liddell Hart, B. H.: *Foch, the man of Orleans*. London, 1931.

Liddell Hart, B. H.: *History of the Second World War*. London, 1970.

Military Strategy (Russian), edited by W. D. Sokolowskij, Moscow, 1963.

Nehring, W. K.: *Die Geschichte der deutschen Panzerwaffe, 1916–1945*. Stuttgart, 1974.

Otto, H./K. Schmiedel: *Der erste Weltkrieg*. Berlin, 1977.

Parkes, O.: *British Battleships*. London, 1957.

Quemmevat, J. C.: *Atlas de la Grande Armée. Napoléon et ses campagnes 1803–1815*. Paris, Brussels, 1966.

Quimby, R.: *The Background of Napoleonic Warfare*. New York, 1957.

Richards, D./H. St. George Saunders: *Royal Air Force 1939–1945*. 3 vols., London, 1953–1954.

Rotmistrov, P. A.: *History of Military Art* (Russian). Moscow, 1963.

Die Streitkräfte der UdSSR. Abriß ihrer Entwicklung von 1918 bis 1968. Berlin, 1974.

Terraine, J.: *The Great War, 1914–1918*. London, 1965.

War and Society in Africa, edited by B. A. Ogot. London, 1972.

Warner, O.: *Great Battle Fleets*. London, 1973.

Weigley, R. F.: *The American Way of War: A History of United States Military Strategy and Policy*. New York, 1975.

Der Weltkrieg 1914–1918. Die militärischen Operationen zu Lande, edited by Reichsarchiv a.s.O., 14 vols., Berlin, 1925–1944.

Valmy to Berlin

Goethe, J. W. v.: *Campagne in Frankreich*. Stuttgart, Tübingen, 1829.

Krieg gegen die französische Revolution, nach den Feldakten und anderen authentischen Quellen. Edited by Kriegsgeschichtliche Abteilung des Kriegsarchivs. 2 vols., Vienna, 1905.

Phipps, R. W.: *The Armies of the First French Republic and the Rise of the Marshals of Napoleon*. 5 vols., London, 1926–1939.

Herold, J. C.: *Bonaparte in Egypt*. London, 1962.

Desbrière, E.: *La Campagne maritime de 1805: Trafalgar*. Paris, 1907.

Mahan, H.: *The Influence of Sea Power upon the French Revolution and Empire, 1793–1812*. London, Cambridge, 1892.

Maine, R.: *De la rame à la voile. Lépante-Trafalgar*. Paris, 1977.

Warner, O.: *Nelson's Battles*. New York, 1965.

Beskrovnyj, L. G.: *Russian Art of War during the XIXth Century* (Russian). Moscow, 1974.

Manceron, C.: *Austerlitz*. Paris, 1962.

Aster, H.: *Die Gefechte und Schlachten bei Leipzig im Oktober 1813*. 2 vols., Dresden, 1852–1856

Brett-James, A.: *Europe against Napoleon: The Leipzig Campaign*. London, 1970.

Leipzig 1813. Die Völkerschlacht im nationalen Befreiungskampf des deutschen Volkes. Leipzig, 1953.

Bernard, H.: *La Campagne de 1815*. Paris, 1954.

Brett-James, A.: *The Hundred Days*. London, 1964.

Davies, G.: *Wellington and his Army*. Oxford, 1954.

Academia Nacional de la Historia: Boletin No. 228, Vol. 57, Caracas, 1974.

Arosema Garland, G.: *El Monumento a la gloria de Ayacucho*. Lima, 1974.

Friede, J.: *La Batalla de Ayacucho, 9 de diciembre 1824*. Bogotá, 1974.

Der Krieg in Italien 1859, nach den Feldakten und anderen authentischen Quellen. Edited by Generalstabsbüro für Kriegsgeschichte. 3 vols., Vienna, 1872–1876.

Moltke, H. v.: *Der italienische Feldzug des Jahres 1859*, edited by Historische Abteilung of the General Staff. Berlin, 1860

Pieri, P.: *Storia militare del risorgimento: Guerre e insurrezioni*. Milan, 1962.

Austin, V.: *Der amerikanische Bürgerkrieg in Augenzeugenberichten*. Düsseldorf, 1966.

Coddington, E.: *The Gettysburg Campaign*. New York, 1968.

Commager, H. S.: *The Blue and the Grey. The Story of the Civil War as told by Participants*. 2 vols., Indiana, 1950.

Haskell, F. A.: *The Battle of Gettysburg*. Boston, 1958.

Craig, G. A.: *The Battle of Königgrätz. Prussia's victory over Austria 1866*. Philadelphia, New York, 1964.

Der Feldzug von 1866 in Deutschland, edited by Kriegsgeschichtliche Abteilung of the Great General Staff. Berlin, 1867.

Österreichs Kämpfe im Jahre 1866, nach den Feldakten, edited by Generalstabsbüro für Kriegsgeschichte. 4 vols., Vienna, 1868.

Bonnal, H.: *La Manoeuvre de Saint-Privat. 18 juillet–18 août 1870*. 3 vols., Paris, 1904–1912.

Der deutsch-französische Krieg 1870/71, edited by Kriegsgeschichtliche Abteilung of the Great General Staff. Part 1, vols. 1 and 2, Berlin, 1874.

La Guerre de 1870–1871, published by "Revue d'histoire", revised by Section historique of the Generel Staff of the Army. 10 series, Paris, 1907–1911.

Der 18. August 1870. Studien zur Kriegsgeschichte und Taktik. Vol. V, edited by Kriegsgeschichtliche Abteilung I of the Great General Staff. Berlin, 1906.

Battaglia, R.: *La prima guerra di Africa*. Rome, 1957.

Berkeley, G. F. H.: *The Campaign of Adowa and the Rise of Menelik*. London, 1953.

Guébré Selassié: *Chronique du règne de Menelik II, roi des rois d'Éthiopie*, translated by Tesfa Selassié, edited by M. de Coppet. 2 vols., Paris, 1930–1932, Amharic editions, Addis Abeba, 1959, 1966–1967.

Marcus, H.: *The life and times of Menelik II: Ethiopia 1844–1913*. Oxford, 1975.

Erfahrungen außereuropäischer Kriege neuester Zeit. Aus dem russisch-japanischen Kriege 1904 bis 1905. Kriegsgeschichtliche Einzelschriften. Number 48–49, edited by Kriegsgeschichtliche Abteilung I of the General Staff. Berlin, 1912–1913.

Kuropatkin, A. N.: *The Russian army and the Japanese war*. London, 1909.

Der russisch-japanische Krieg. Vol. IV, 1st Part. *Der Schlacht von Mukden unmittelbar vorausgehende Ereignisse und die Schlacht selbst bis einschließlich 6. März*. Official presentation of the Russian General Staff. Berlin, 1911.

The Russo-Japanese War. Reports from British Officers issued by the War Office. London, 1908.

Les armées françaises dans la Grande Guerre. Vol. I, Parts 1–2, Paris, 1922–1925.

Contamine, H.: *La victoire de la Marne*. Paris, 1970.

Galaktionov, H.: *The Battle of the Marne* (Russian). Moscow, 1938.

Ritter, G.: *The Schlieffen Plan: Critique of a Myth*. London, 1958.

Tyng, S. T.: *The campaign of the Marne, 1914*. London, 1934.

Blond, G.: *Verdun*. Paris, 1961.

Falkenhayn, E. v.: *Die Oberste Heeresleitung 1914–1916 in ihren wichtigsten Entschließungen*. Berlin, 1920.

Horne, A.: *The Price of Glory. Verdun, 1916*. New York, 1962.

Bennet, G.: *Naval Battles of the First World War*. London, 1968.

Jellicoe, J. R. J.: *The Grand Fleet, 1914–16*. London, 1919.

Macintyre, D.: *Jutland*. London, 1958.

Scheer, R.: *Deutschlands Hochseeflotte im Weltkrieg*. Berlin, 1920.

Eimannsberger, L. v.: *Der Kampfwagenkrieg*. Munich, Berlin, 1938.

Fuller, J. F. C.: *Memoirs of an unconventional soldier*. London, 1936.

Ullmann, R. H.: *Anglo-Soviet Relations, 1917–1921. Britain and the Russian Civil War. November 1918–February 1920*. New Jersey, 1968.

Schmid, A. P.: *Churchills privater Krieg. Intervention und Konterrevolution im russischen Bürgerkrieg, November 1918 bis März 1920*. Zurich, 1974.

Schmiedel, K./H. Schnitter: *Bürgerkrieg und Intervention 1918 bis 1922*. Berlin, 1973.

Bayac, J. D.: *Les brigades internationales*. Paris, 1968.

Broué, P./E. Témine: *The revolution and the civil war in Spain*. Cambridge, 1972.

Lister, E.: *Nuestra Guerra*. Paris, 1966.

Renn, L.: *Der spanische Krieg*. Berlin, 1955.

Longo, L.: *Le brigade internazionali in Spagna*. Rome, 1956.

Bishop, E.: *The Battle of Britain*. London, 1960.

McKee, A.: *Strike from the sky; the story of the Battle of Britain*. London, 1961.

Weber, T.: *Die Luftschlacht um England*. Wiesbaden, 1956.

Carrer, M.: *El Alamein*. New York, 1962.

Haupt, W./J. K. W. Bingham: *Der Afrika-Feldzug 1941–1943*. Borheim/ H, 1968.

Montgomery, B. L.: *El Alamein to the River Sangro*. London, 1948.

Craig, W. E.: *Enemy at the gates. The battle for Stalingrad*. New York, 1973.

428

Kehrig, M.: *Stalingrad. Analyse und Dokumentation einer Schlacht.* Stuttgart, 1974.

The Battle of Stalingrad (Russian), edited by A. M. Borodin, Wolgograd, 1969.

Klink, E.: *Das Gesetz des Handelns. Die Operation "Zitadelle" 1943.* Stuttgart, 1963.

Koltunov, G. A./B. G. Solovev: *The Battle of Kursk* (Russian). Moscow, 1970.

Manstein, E. v.: *Lost victories.* London, 1958.

Markin, I. I.: *Die Kursker Schlacht.* Berlin, 1960.

McKee, A.: *Last round against Rommel, battle of the Normandy bridgehead.* New York, 1966.

Morison, S. E.: *The Invasions of France and Germany, 1944 to 1945.* Boston, 1975.

Turner, J. F.: *Invasion 44. The First Full Story of D-Day in Normandy.* New York, 1959.

Krueger, W.: *From down under to Nippon. The story of the Sixth Army in World War II.* New York, 1953.

Morison, S. E.: *Leyte, June 1944—January 1945. History of United States Naval Operations in World War II.* Vol. 12, Boston, 1958.

Polmar, N.: *Aircraft Carriers.* New York, 1969.

Woodward, C. W.: The Battle of Leyte-Gulf. New York, 1947.

1945. Das Jahr der endgültigen Niederlage der faschistischen Wehrmacht, edited by G. Förster/R. Lakowski, Berlin, 1975.

Rosanow, G.: *Das Ende des Dritten Reiches.* Berlin, 1965.

The Memoirs of Marshal Zhukov, translated from the Russian. London, 1971.

Epilogue: Hiroshima

Feis, H.: *Japan Subdued. The Atomic Bomb and the End of the War in the Pacific.* Princeton, 1961.

Groves, L. R.: *Now it can be told.* New York, 1962.

Hiroshima in Memoriam and Today, edited by Takayama. Hiroshima, 1974.

Russel, B.: *Common sense and nuclear war.* London, 1959.

Stulz, P.: *Schlaglicht Atom.* Berlin, 1973.

Sources of Illustrations

We express our thanks to all those persons and institutions who kindly supplied the originals of the illustrations on the following pages:

ADN Zentralbild, Berlin: 320; Alinari, Florence: 72/73; Franz Ansprenger, Berlin (West): 314; Archäologisches Institut der Karl-Marx-Universität, Leipzig: 37, 42, 47; Archiv für Kunst und Geschichte, Berlin (West): 39, 65, 78, 79, 81, 101, 134, 200, 258, 313; Armeemuseum der DDR, Dresden: 124, 125, 179, 266, 309, 311, 333, 353, 387; Bibliotheek der Rijksuniversiteit Leiden: 138; Bibliothèque Nationale, Paris: 35, 133, 201, 202, 283; Bildarchiv Foto Marburg: 109; Bilderdienst Süddeutscher Verlag, Munich: 374; Blenheim Palace, Oxford: 196, 198; Board of Chamberlains, Imperial Household Agency, Tokyo: 152/153; British Museum, London: 15; Christa Christen, Leipzig: 26, 29, 129, 208; Collection Karger-Decker, Berlin: 203; Deutsche Fotothek, Dresden: 166, 167; Deutsches Archäologisches Institut, Rome: 20/21, 23, 64, 74, 84/85, 87, 90, 116/117; Fotoatelier Urwyler, Zurich: 172/173; Reiner Funck, Markkleeberg: 185, 273,; Giraudon, Paris: 222, 265, 293; Heeresgeschichtliches Museum, Vienna: 193, 199, 291, 302, 304, 305; Herzog-Anton-Ulrich-Museum, Brunswick: 187; Hirmer Fotoarchiv, Munich: 24, 52/53, 112; Imperial War Museum, London: 363; Kadokawa Publishing House, Tokyo: 408, 409; Kestner-Museum, Hanover: 104/105; Keystone Pressedienst GmbH, Hamburg: 388, 389; Koehler & Amelang, Leipzig: 148, 149; Kyodo News Agency, Tokyo: 404/405; Lane Studio, Gettysburg: 297; Militärverlag der DDR, Berlin: 354, 355, 357, 380, 383, 402; Murhardsche Bibliothek der Stadt Kassel und Landesbibliothek: 158, 159,; Musée d'Art et d'Histoire, Geneva: 174; Musée de Versailles: 256, 268; National Archives, Washington: 298, 299; National Maritime Museum, London: 220/221, 261, 263 top, 263 bottom; Novosti, Moscow; 350, 381; Gerhard Reinhold, Mölkau: 237; Scala, Florence: 33, 38, 92/93, 176, 177; Ivan Shagin, Moscow/Fotokino-Verlag, Leipzig: 247, 398, 399; Arkady Schaichet, Moscow/Fotokino-Verlag, Leipzig: 375; Fred Schindler, Leipzig: 43, 99; Wolfgang G. Schröter, Markkleeberg: 31, 56, 62; Georgi Selma, Moscow/Fotokino-Verlag, Leipzig: 376, 377; Service de documentation photographique de la Réunion des musées nationaux, Paris: 252/253, 257; Shueisha Publishing House, Tokyo; 182, 183; Staatliche Museen zu Berlin: 10/11, 18/19; Staats- und Stadtbibliothek, Augsburg: 139; Asmus Steuerlein, Dresden: 120, 124, 171, 209, 271, 275, 307, 309; Tapisserie de Bayeux: 140/141, 142; TAP Service, Archaeological Receipts Fund, Athens: 67; Tate Gallery, London: 362; Viktor Tjomin, Moscow/Fotokino-Verlag, Leipzig: 400; Ullstein GmbH Bilderdienst, Berlin (West): 216, 217, 238, 245, 324, 325, 330, 336, 337, 339, 344, 345, 359, 360/361, 368/369, 370, 371, 385, 395; Verlagsarchiv: 58, 123; Victoria and Albert Museum, London: 277 top, 280/281; Zentralbild/TASS, Berlin: 347

Illustrations preceding the three main chapters:

I. Battle of the Greeks and the Persians. Detail from the south frieze of the temple to Athena Nike on the Acropolis, c. 420 B.C. Staatliche Museen zu Berlin.

II. "Knightly Combat", from the *Jungfrauenspiegel*, end of 12th century, Kestner Museum, Hanover.

III. Break in the battle of the Marne in 1914. Documentary photo.

Index of Persons and Place Names

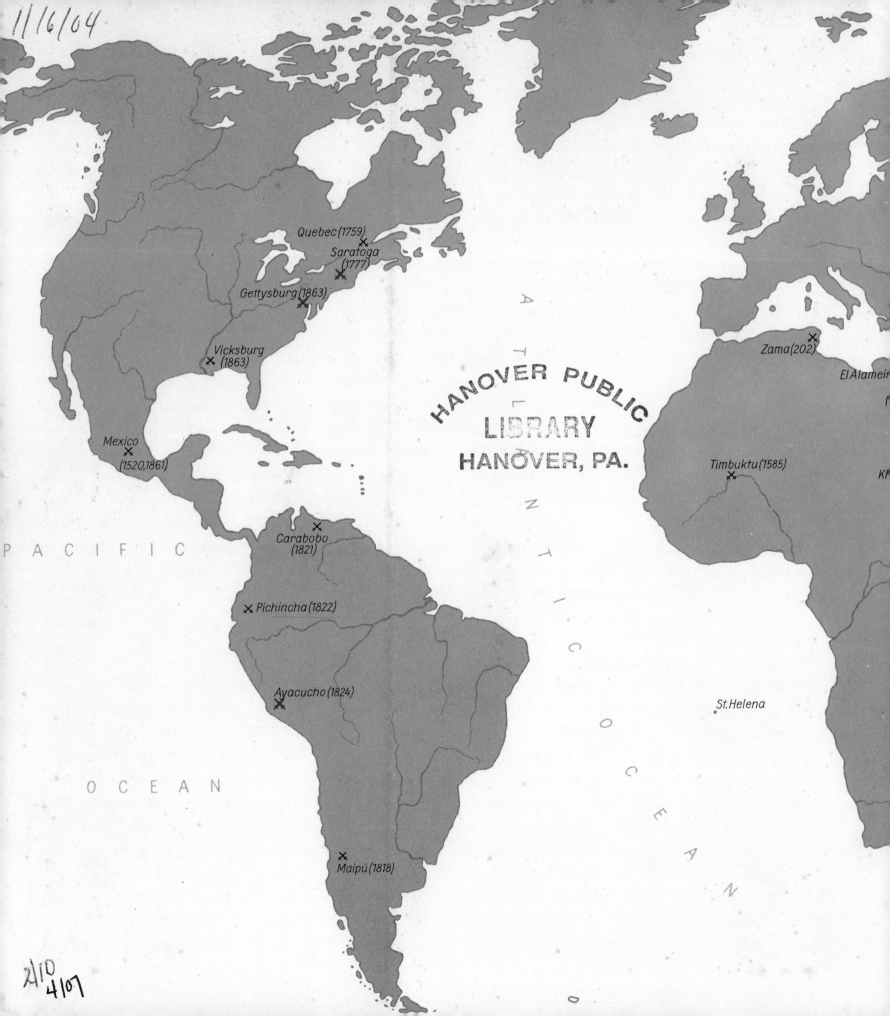

11/16/04

Quebec (1759)

Saratoga
(1777)

Gettysburg (1863)

Vicksburg
(1863)

Zama (202)

El Alamein

Mexico
(1520, 1861)

Timbuktu (1585)

KI

Carabobo
(1821)

Pichincha (1822)

PACIFIC

Ayacucho (1824)

St. Helena

OCEAN

Maipú (1818)

ATLANTIC OCEAN

210
4107